The Englishwoman's Diary

The Englishwoman's Diary

Edited by
Harriet Blodgett

FOURTH ESTATE · *London*

First published in Great Britain in 1992 by
Fourth Estate Limited
289 Westbourne Grove
London W11 2QA
First published in the United States in 1991 by
The University Press of Virginia

The copyright notices can be found on pages xii–xiv of the
Acknowledgements.

A catalogue record for this book is available from the
British Library.

ISBN 1–85702–012–X

Printed in Great Britain by Cambridge University Press

For Bill and in memory of Goldie

What sort of diary should I like mine to be?
Something loose knit, & yet not slovenly, so elastic
that it will embrace anything, solemn, slight
or beautiful that comes into my mind.
I should like it to resemble some deep old desk,
or capacious hold-all, in which one flings a mass of
odds & ends without looking them through. . . .
The main requisite . . . is not to play the part of censor,
but to write as the mood comes of anything whatever.

Virginia Woolf, *Diary*, 20 April 1919

Contents

❦

Acknowledgments

I am grateful to Ms. Brigitte Schaeffer of Davis, California, and to Professor Michael Fuller of California State University, Stanislaus, for help translating French and Italian passages in the diaries; I hope I have not superadded any inaccuracies to their suggestions. I am grateful, too, to Ms. Laura Boyer, reference librarian at Stanislaus, for her unstinting and knowledgeable help with securing permissions; likewise to Carol Rossi of the University Press of Virginia for her labors to bring the endless business of securing permissions to an end. I am grateful to the Marilyn Yalom Research Fund of the Institute for Research on Women and Gender at Stanford University for a generous grant to help pay for those expensive permissions, once secured.

But I am grateful most to my husband, Bill, as much for his faith in me as for his patient proofreading and always good advice.

Selections by Lady Cynthia Asquith reprinted by permission from *Lady Cynthia Asquith: Diaries; 1915–1918*, edited by E. M. Horsley (London: Hutchinson, 1968).

Selections by Fanny Boscawen reprinted by permission of Peters, Fraser, & Dunlop from *Admiral's Wife: Being the Life and Letters of the Hon. Mrs. Edward Boscawen from 1719 to 1761*, by Cecil Aspinall-Oglander (London: Longmans, Green, 1940).

The extracts from *Chronicle of Friendship* by Vera Brittain, her *Diary of the Thirties, 1932–1939*, are included with the kind permission of Paul Berry, her literary executor, and Alan Bishop, the Editor, and Victor Gollancz Ltd.

Selections from *The Diary of Lady Anne Clifford* Copyright Victoria Sackville-West, reproduced by permission of Curtis Brown Ltd, London.

Selections by Hannah Cullwick reprinted by permission from *The Diaries of Hannah Cullwick, Victorian Maidservant*, edited by Liz Stanley (London: Virago, 1984).

Selections by Florence Farmborough reprinted by permission from *Nurse at the Russian Front: A Diary, 1914–1918* (London: Constable, 1974).

Selections from *Mrs. Elizabeth Freke, Her Diary: 1671 to 1714*, edited by Mary Carbery (Cork: Guy, 1913), reprinted by permission of Lord Peter Carbery on behalf of the estate of Mary Carbery.

Selections by Mary Hardy reprinted by permission of the Norfolk Record Society from *Mary Hardy's Diary*, edited by B. Gozens-Hardy, Norfolk Record Society Publications, 37 (Norfolk: Norfolk Record Society, 1968).

Selections by Lady Margaret Hoby reprinted by permission from *Diary of Lady Margaret Hoby*, edited by Dorothy M. Meads (London: Routledge, 1930).

Selections by Loran Hurnscot reprinted by permission from *A Prison, a Paradise*, by Loran Hurnscot. Copyright © 1958 by Victor Gollancz Ltd. Copyright renewed © 1986 by Kathleen Raine.

Reprinted by permission of Viking Penguin, a division of Penguin Books USA Inc. and by Victor Gollancz, Ltd.

Selections by Ivy Jacquier reprinted by permission from *The Diary of Ivy Jacquier: 1907–1926* (London: Victor Gollancz, Ltd., 1960).

Selections by Nella Last from *Nella Last's War: A Mother's Diary, 1939–45*, edited by Richard Broad and Suzie Fleming (London: Sphere Books, 1983). Reprinted by permission of Falling Wall Press.

Selections by Emily Pepys reprinted by permission from *The Journal of Emily Pepys*, edited by Gillian Avery (London: Prospect Books, 1984).

Selections by Elizabeth Raper reprinted by permission from *The Receipt-Book of Elizabeth Raper*, edited by Bartle Grant (London: Nonesuch Press, 1924).

Selections by Frances Stevenson reprinted by permission from *Lloyd George: A Diary by Frances Stevenson*, edited by A. J. P. Taylor (London: Century Hutchinson, 1971).

Selections by Hester Thrale from *Thraliana: The Diary of Mrs. Hester Lynch Thrale*, vol. 1, edited by Katherine C. Balderston, 2d ed. (Oxford: Oxford University Press, 1961). Reprinted by permission of Oxford University Press.

Selections by Beatrice Webb reprinted by permission of Virago Press Ltd., from *The Diary of Beatrice Webb*, vol. 1 (London, 1982). Also reprinted by permission of the publishers from *The Diary of Beatrice Webb*, edited by Norman and Jeanne MacKenzie, Cambridge, Mass.: Harvard University Press, Copyright Editorial Matter and Arrangement © 1983, 1984 by Norman and Jeanne MacKenzie. The Diary of Beatrice Webb, The Passfield Papers © 1983, 1984 by the London School of Economics and Political Science.

Selections by Ellen Weeton from *Miss Weeton: Journal of a Governess 1807–1825*, vol. 2, edited by Edward Hall (Oxford: Oxford University Press, 1939). Reprinted by permission of Oxford University Press.

Excerpts from *The Diary of Virginia Woolf, Volume II: 1920–1924,* edited by Anne Olivier Bell, assisted by Andrew McNeillie, copyright © 1978 by Quentin Bell and Angelica Garnett, reprinted by permission of Harcourt Brace Jovanovich, Inc., The Hogarth Press, and the Estate of Virginia Woolf.

Selections by Myrtle Wright from *Norwegian Diary, 1940–45* (London: Friends Peace and International Relations Committee, 1974). Reprinted by permission of Patrick F. Radley, Executor for Myrtle Wright.

The Englishwoman's Diary

Introduction

❧

"Next to being a mother, I'd have loved to write books," confesses the diary entry for 8 October 1939 written by Nella Last (1890–1966),[1] a devoted parent and housewife who fulfilled her desire for words by keeping a spirited daily record. Like letters, their diaries have been Englishwomen's most common sort of writing for centuries, expressing a resilient creative impulse that through serial writing could find outlet in a sanctioned form. For a reader, in turn, Englishwomen's diaries are invitations to participate imaginatively in female lives as they are in process, through literature with a compelling power to engage the mind and heart. Their diaries, moreover, are also central documents in the recovery of female history. Without distortion by an intermediary they reveal what women take to be true about themselves, their world, and its representability. To all that has been hypothesized and predicated about women by men, they add what women can say and intimate about themselves. The thirty diarists in this anthology, whose writings come from the late-sixteenth to the mid-twentieth century and many of whom are not famous women, offer a glimpse of that rich diary lore that finally has begun to be valued and studied.

There is no one diary style; diaries are as diverse in phrasing and contents as those who compose them differ in temperament and circumstances. Each diarist speaks with a unique voice; each reading is an act of discovering the unpredictable. To give a sense of that truth, the first section of this anthology provides a look into varied lives and perceptions at different times in history: the diarists range in age from ten-year-old Emily Pepys (1833–37) to seventy-year-old Elizabeth Freke (1641–1714); they span the social classes from laboring domestics such as Hannah Cullwick (1833–1909) to aristocrats such as Mary, Countess Cowper (1685–1724); and they speak on different themes, from their daily lives to their ambitions to their conflicts to their fears. The rest of the book, however, is arranged thematically to present diverse experiences and conceptions of topics frequent in women's diaries—friends and lovers, marriage and motherhood—or, as in the case of diaries written during wartime, topics significant to a particular period. Here are included, for example, the fluctuations of close female friendships experienced by Virginia Woolf (1882–1941) and by Vera Brittain (1893–1970) with very different outcomes, and the ultimately contrasting courting ordeals of Elizabeth Raper (d. 1778) and of Clarissa Trant (1800–1844), plus the love affairs of other diarists. Here too are diarists whose marriages and motherhood were grievous to them, such as Ellen Weeton (1776–1845) and Lady Cynthia Asquith (1887–1960), and those for whom their sanctified roles were a source of delight, such as Fanny Boscawen (1719–1805) and Elizabeth Gaskell (1810–65). The wartime diaries encompass both world wars, from Sarah Macnaughtan's (d. 1916) achievement in setting up soup kitchens in Belgium during the First World War, for instance, to Myrtle Wright's (1903–) courageous participation in the Norwegian underground during the second one.

Even if there is no one diary style, it bears mentioning that, amidst all the diversity, readers will recognize certain recurrent female attitudes and experiences. After all, the patriarchal preconditions of the diarists' writing, their lives in a male-dominant culture, remained much the same over the centuries. Even though the diary's essential property as a form is its more-or-less dailiness, so that a diarist cannot know how her book will proceed in the future, the diarist always brings to her writing all her feminine adaptations from the past. Consequently, women's diaries show certain commonalities, the impress, as it were, of female conditioning. Well-known characteristics of traditional female existence—such as reticence, for example, self-devaluation, and desire to serve others, on the one hand, and conflicts over female roles and with male power, on the other—almost inevitably find expression in women's diaries, whether in words or through silences.

Meanwhile, of course, women's diaries do change over the course of history, for only gradually did the English diary by women (or by men) become the personally expressive form and "capacious hold-all" (to use Virginia Woolf's good phrase)[2] we think of it as today. The history of the English diary is a progression towards ever greater expressiveness and inclusion that began in the sixteenth century when the diary form emerged because the keepers of factual daily records started adding brief personal comments to their business and professional entries.[3] It is well known that by the sixteenth century the male travel diary existed in England, and, more important, the regular-entry record kept as a duty, such as the military-campaign annual or ship's log or embassy or work record. The handful of such men's writings that have survived shows increasing personalization after mid century. Less well known is that women too were keeping diaries. Indeed, not only were women keeping diaries from the infancy of the diary form but also the earliest extant English diary proper is that of a woman, Lady Margaret Dakins Hoby (1571–1633), the first diarist included in this anthology. Even before Hoby, Lady Grace Sherrington Mildmay (1522–1620) apparently kept a diary from which years later (between 1570 and 1617) she compiled for her daughter a retrospect along with religious meditations; unfortunately her original records have not survived.

We may thank the circumscribed conditions of female lives, not usually construed as a blessing, for the early appearance of women's diaries. Having no careers, commands, or embassies to write of, women noted the minutiae of domestic affairs, creating the sort of record that by the eighteenth century would mature into the diary as we customarily think of it: simply stated, the serial record of personal memorabilia that gives us a sense of the diarist too. But we must also credit religious faith for encouraging diary keeping. The late-sixteenth and the seventeenth centuries brought the formulaic diary of conscience (religious soul-searching in forms prescribed by devotional manuals) kept by male and female Covenanters, as it would later be by Quakers and Methodists. Hoby began her diary as such a Puritan record, to catch out her derelictions of duty, only to have her religious fervor give way before more mundane concerns as her diary progressed. The diary of conscience was the ancestor of the secular diary preoccupied with the inner life that was to emerge in less religious times, but as yet the inner life apart from religion was not a concern, much less a diary focus. Witness, for example, these laconic civil war–period entries for 1644 / 45 by a diarist not included in the anthology, Lady Isabella Twysden (1605–57), whose husband was imprisoned by the Parliament at the time:

> the 8 febri, I came to peckham great with child, and ride all the waye a hors back, and I thank god had no hurt.
> the 6 of march 1644 between one and 2 in the morning I was brought a bed of a boye, the 7 he was chrissened and named charles, the gossops [sponsors] were my bro: Tho and Fra: Twysden and my la: astlye [Lady Astley], Jamme stode for hir. he was borne at peckham being thursday.[4]

She rode on a pillion behind a manservant, and never regained her strength after her son's birth. We can only imagine what the ordeals of the trip—or the birth—were like for her; what fears and longings may have surged within her are not matters for her diary to know.

Although not only devotional diaries were being written in the seventeenth century, as Hoby and Twysden show, personal diaries were not yet the norm. By now the businesslike regular-entry record had evolved (as one of its developments) into the public diary, a form focused not on the diarist but on public events and persons of interest to the diarist. During the next century, Elizabeth Percy (1716–76), Duchess of Northumberland, a lady of the bedchamber to Queen Charlotte, began essentially such a diary, with the representative aim, as she wrote on 2 November 1769, "throughout these Anecdotes to scatter here & there forms, customs, rules &c of the Court to show their variations at different periods & likewise the manners of the Times."[5] No excerpts from entirely public diaries, however, are included in the anthology. Like travel diaries, which never ceased to be written, public diaries would continue to be written throughout the centuries, often by women such as Mary, Countess Cowper, who served at court or moved in court circles. Cowper's diary, which has been included in the anthology, was intended as a public diary but soon escaped such confines. As Cowper's practice suggests, whatever the lure of others' behaviors and the fascination of gossip, during the seventeenth century the more personal diary consisting of brief entries of one's own memorabilia and family records—germ of the diary proper—also became an established form.

In seventeenth-century diaries, as Twysden evidences, activities predominate. Yet feelings begin to claim space too. The anthology includes an excerpt from Lady Anne Clifford (1590–1676), one of the more expansive of the seventeenth-century personal diarists. Unlike Hoby, who never admits her sorrow that her husband is a bully and that she is childless, Clifford does not hesitate to note, however laconically, her frequent melancholy because she and her spendthrift husband are at odds over her claims to her property. Had she written a hundred and fifty years later, she might even have included some of the anguish she felt when her husband cavalierly invited his mistress and her spouse to the family home, Knole, for a visit. As it is, Clifford holds her feelings at arm's length and in a side note on 24 August 1619 says only of their visit, "This coming hither of Lady *Peniston's* was much talked of abroad and my Lord was condemned for it."[6]

By the eighteenth century, the diary was flourishing as an eclectic form. Along with personal memorabilia, it took in the accounts and anecdotes of the famous characteristic of public diaries, and, more important, the subjective self-realizations of religious diaries. Romantic self-dramatizing of feelings might even be added during the second half of the century, replacing the dispassion that had been characteristic of seventeenth-century secular diaries. After the 1740s, novels of sensibility such as Samuel Richardson's *Clarissa Harlowe* (1747–48) encouraged some passionate explorations of consciousness. But most diaries remained largely factual records, with little subjective probing. A more popular eighteenth-century innovation was the keeping of letter diaries, daily entries to be sent to a recipient with the writer keeping a copy to serve as a diary. Entries from two letter diaries are included in the anthology: from Frances Boscawen's unflagging correspondence with her adored husband, Admiral Boscawen, in the eighteenth century and from Emily Augusta King's (dates unknown) lengthy letters to her family in the nineteenth, when she accompanied her husband on his tour of duty as an administrator in India. It also became a regular practice during the eighteenth century to keep bound pocket diaries that assigned a space for each day in which to record appointments or visits or other daily doings. Such bound pocket diaries are necessarily more laconic and selective (in any century) than self-devised books. Some diarists were ambitious enough to keep two diaries, expanding their brief pocket jottings between covers that offered them less restricted space. Diarist Nancy Woodforde (1757–1830), part of whose longer effort is included in the anthology, fortunately did so for 1792, when her female friends were important to her, and probably kept expanded diaries for other years as well, though they have not survived.

Because the diary by the eighteenth century had become a highly respectable form that women were encouraged to keep, during the nineteenth century not only did advice manuals tell them how to keep diaries; women's diaries even began to be published, beginning with Fanny Burney's (Frances D'Arblay, 1752–1840) in 1842. Spurious diaries purporting to authenticity were a popular form of reading by now, and diarists had become much more self-conscious about the literary qualities of their writing. Eventually they even became a bit receptive to foreign influences. Near the end of the century and afterwards, some women studied the effusive confessional *Journal of a Young Artist* of the Russian-born French diarist Marie Bashkirtseff (1860–84), published posthumously in 1887, in hopes (or despair) of imitating her candor, much the way others would take the six-volume *Diary,* published 1966–76, of French-born Anaïs Nin (1903–77) as an inspiration a century later. But although by the early twentieth century the conventions of the confessional French *journal intime,* the serious exploration of the psyche, especially of its responsiveness to stimuli, had been imported, they gained no widespread acceptance, probably because the practice of indulging in protracted subjectivity was so at odds with English female training in self-abnegation and modesty. Nonetheless, the diary of part-French Ivy Jacquier (b. 1890), an artist whose response to becoming a mother is included in the anthology, reflects the French mode with its emphasis on interior life rather than outside events.

The scarcity of intimate journals by Englishwomen points up a salient characteristic of their diary writing—it is best not to hope for too many revelations from these women's diaries. Even if nowadays the resurgent women's movement has encouraged women to keep a kind of intimate journal as a tool of consciousness-raising or heightened feminist awareness and of self-therapy, such diaries are scarce. Despite the progress of the English diary in subjectivity and communicativeness over the centuries, the tradition of female English diary writing has been characterized rather by reticence and circumspection than by revelation and confrontation with the deepest feelings. Virginia Woolf's ideal diarist may not censor her capacious hold-all, but Virginia Woolf herself does. What she has said of diarist Elizabeth, Lady Holland (1770–1845), she might have said of most other diarists before the recent past too: "it was not the purpose of her diary to follow her feelings closely, or indeed to record them at all, except to sum them up now and then in a businesslike way, as though she made a note in shorthand for future use."[7] Twentieth-century diarists are more open than their forebears, though some eighteenth-century ones can be quite frank, but women's diaries on the whole—at least the published survivors—are not the repositories of their most intimate thoughts and feelings or of any potentially damaging remarks. Diarists protect themselves from possible reading by others (or if letter diarists, unflattering presentation to them) and from damaging discoveries by their own selves.

Although diaristic reticence is not a gender-specific trait, having been observed in male diaries too, the reasons why women are more prone to objective narrative are not far to seek. They lie in the taboos of social censorship and rigid indoctrination in presenting a good image. They lie in acculturation, which has historically not taught women to accept or even understand their feelings but to concentrate on obliging the feelings of others. They lie in the burden of a "man made language" (in feminist Dale Spender's term)[8] encoded by the dominant male group to suit its own perceptions, not those

of subordinated, and therefore muted, females. And yet for all that
women do not say in their diaries, their diaries are very important to
them. Thus even if they do not necessarily make their diaries full
confidantes, women have shown themselves to be avid diarists, willing
to sustain the labor of their own writings, often over a long lifetime,
and curious to read the diaries of other women. The discoveries of
Mass Observation offer interesting proof. Mass Observation, founded
in 1937 by sociologists Tom Harrisson, Charles Madge, and Humphrey Jennings to conduct an intensive investigation into the lives
of ordinary Britons, employed as one of its methods a system of ob-
servational record keeping by volunteers (amateurs, and known as
Observers) who were instructed to keep detailed diaries of their daily
activities. Mass Observation reached the peak of its volunteer activities between 1939 and 1945, when a large body of wartime diaries was
accumulated that has since been deposited at the University of Sussex.
Significantly, those coordinating the study discovered that women
not only outnumbered men in the national panel of Observers by the
latter half of the war, but more revealing, sent in longer, more regular, and more detailed contributions.[9] Nella Last's loquacious diary,
story of a woman's growth in independence and included in the anthology, was kept as a Mass Observation record.

      Why do Englishwomen—why do women—so like to keep
diaries? For some, it is the needed outlet for a creative urge, as Nella
Last discovered while keeping her book. Other diarists claim that
they are recording their days as an emotional resource or for self-
correction or as an aid to memory to recall time past. Some expressly
keep their diary books for the sake of their children or because it is
a family tradition or because their parents or teachers introduced them
to the habit. But beyond all such conscious motivation and justification lies another impulse. All diarists pursue an interest in self, even
those who keep public diaries, which may not focus on the writer
herself, but still record only her choices of subjects. Diaries support
and reinforce the sense of being an important entity, someone whose
perceptions matter. A woman's diary thus subliminally provides some
escape from the sense that her life is lived only through and for others
and that her existence is justified only through providing a reference

point for men. Therefore, even if the diary form is not a female form of writing and performs a comparable service for men, still the diary has been especially meaningful to female being in patriarchal society. Beatrice Webb (1858–1943), whose marriage was an egalitarian working partnership, makes a pertinent comment in her diary in discovering that "In writing I am parasitic on Sidney; I never write, except in this diary, in my own style, always in a hybrid of his and mine. But I *must* speak my own words and sentences" (8 December 1913).[10] A diary is the place to be one's own self—and untouched by critical controversies over the reality of such an entity, a diarist does feel that she is an individual self. Or in the more eloquent terms of diarist Katherine Mansfield (1888–1923), perhaps "the rage for confession, autobiography . . . is explained by our persistent yet mysterious belief in a self which is continuous and permanent; which, untouched by all we acquire and all we shed, pushes a green spear through the dead leaves and through the mould" ([April 1920]).[11]

Diarists vary in how they approach the task of recording the days of this self. Many endeavor to write up each day's events without much, if any, delay. They can be ingenious in finding time to do so, as witness an eighteenth-century diarist, Mary Hamilton (1756–1816), who remarks on how "Betty generally is an houre & sometimes longer, & so my hairdressing is never lost time, I most commonly also take part of that time to scribble in my Diary" (24 July 1784).[12] When the faithful daily reporters miss a day or more, they are likely to include abject apologies and careful explanations for their lapses; implicitly they take their record keeping as a major commitment. Yet many other diarists fulfill the commitment just by keeping daily notes that they write up only as time allows—often, like Hester Thrale (1741–1821), making entries but once for each week in their diaries. The longer the lapse between event and entry, the more the temptation to hindsight, but diarists characteristically refuse it, intent on retaining their immediate perceptions instead. A remarkable feature of a diary not included here, that was written up only annually from notes by Margaret Fountaine (1862–1940), is her refusal to allow later wisdom to color even her story of a courtship that almost deceived her into a bigamous marriage.[13] Likewise, even though women diarists show themselves to be frequent later rereaders of their own texts, they typically prefer, as diarist Loran Hurnscot (Gay Stuart Taylor, d. 1970) illustrates, to use marginalia or notes for updating or otherwise amending their records rather than altering their original claims.

The diarist's urge, however, is not the autobiographer's: where the autobiographer aims to reconstruct in a coherent self-valorizing work the self that once she was (or thinks she was), the diarist ordinarily seeks to retain a self in process as she currently sees it, unconcerned about whether the parts all fit or focus in one direction. Consistency and avoidance of repetition belong rather to the more shapely form of autobiography than to the diary, whose virtues lie in its casualness and candor of the moment and whose repetitions are valuable for what they inadvertently reveal of obsessions and preoccupations. This is not to say that diarists simply set down whatever occurs to them. They are selective, and they are protective: diaries, it bears repeating, are a form of self-presentation, and diarists, however unconsciously, take care not to picture for themselves a self they cannot tolerate, not to mention their fears of other possible readers. Thus, for example, Anne Clifford virtuously declares it "my chief help to pass away the time at work" (12 November 1616),[14] referring to her stitching, when in fact she relieves her boredom during her husband's frequent absences more often by gambling at Glecko (and losing) than by embroidering, judging by the number of entries for each. But besides being selective and careful of their images, diarists ordinarily do not follow any master plan.

Yet the results clearly are not chaotic. Instead of an accumulation of discrete days, a diary is a coherent entity. It consists of interwoven themes and sequences, large blocks of which may constitute the working out of an action from its inception through its stages of growth to its ending—though the pace is likely to be leisurely and digressive and regrettably sometimes the ending and crucial details are left only to inference. (The excerpts from Vera Brittain's diary, with their undescribed but destructive letter, nicely illustrate the problem of missing details.) Nonetheless, if the reader is called upon to recognize the shapes within what life is shaping on the diarist's page, the reader, as the following excerpts attest, is also given the essential wherewithal to do so, for the diarist provides not only the contours but details enough to summon the lights and shadows within them.

Indeed, much of the special pleasure of reading diaries may lie in the inspiration they give us to reconstruct the world of their origination: to assemble bit by bit the imagined scenes and movement, the voices and gestures and facial expressions, and to live vicariously through another sensibility even while looking on at it. If such is a pleasure that first-person fiction too can give, with diaries there is the added—and captivating—sense that this is an actual life in process, subject to all the vagaries of chance; it cannot and will not be tidied up, aesthetically or otherwise, at the novelist's choice. The innocent-looking detail—diarist Mary Hardy's remarking a boil on her son's neck, for example, or Cynthia Asquith's her son's willfulness—may later prove portentous through no plan of the diarist's (and in these two instances proves ominous). Surprise and suspense are inherent in diaries—like the unexplained happenings and interwoven themes—not as aesthetic devices but as a function of life; even autobiography, therefore, cannot duplicate the peculiar quality of "reality" that diaries afford. A diary is not in any absolute sense a "true" record; it is a subjective interpretation of life. But less manipulable by the writer than are the novel or autobiography, whatever posturing the diarists may engage in, the diary has the unique ability to reenact the story of how life goes. We recognize it—and believe it. It can make diary reading an addictive pleasure.

It remains only to be said that the excerpts in this anthology, all by women born or settled in England, have been taken from published diaries, the editing of which has largely been retained. The notes are my own, though I am sometimes indebted to the original editors of the diaries for information. The diaries have been selected for their variety and their ability to represent types of diaries as well as for the inherent interest of their contents. The arrangement used for dating the diary entries in some instances duplicates a diarist's (or perhaps her editor's) format; in others, modifies it. That is, assuming a diarist gave such information or it can be deduced, the entries for most diarists have been uniformly identified by day (in the form chosen by the diarist, whether ordinal or cardinal number), month (unabbreviated), and year (whenever a new year in the diary begins). If a diarist preceded or followed day and year with the name of the day, the name has been retained, in her preferred order. However, even though some diarists also included the locale of their writing, locale is not given. The formats used by the earliest diarists, Margaret Hoby and Anne Clifford, have been duplicated as a matter of historical interest, with any emendations bracketed; at the request of the original publishers, the formats of Ivy Jacquier and Vera Brittain have likewise been duplicated.

Limitations of space precluded listing additional diaries in the bibliographies, except for those earlier referred to in the notes. But readers whose appetites for more diaries have been whetted by the excerpts can increase their future reading choices exponentially by consulting the list of bibliographies of published Englishwomen's diaries included at the back of the book.[15] Not only is diary literature extensive; fortunately, it is also becoming increasingly accessible. Women's diary keeping has created a literature that commands admiration and respect—even invites gratitude—for stimulating imaginative participation in so many different lives and teaching the subjectively perceived truths of female history vividly, eloquently, memorably. It deserves to be, as it has begun to be, better known.

Notes

1   *Nella Last's War: A Mother's Diary, 1939–45,* ed. Richard Broad and Suzie Fleming (London: Sphere Books, 1983), p. 19.

2   *The Diary of Virginia Woolf,* vol. 1, ed. Anne Olivier Bell (New York: Harcourt Brace Jovanovich, 1977), p. 266 (entry for 20 April 1919).

3   For a more detailed history of the English diary, especially the female diary, see chapter 1 of Harriet Blodgett, *Centuries of Female Days: Englishwomen's Private Diaries* (New Brunswick, N.J.: Rutgers University Press, 1988; Gloucester: Alan Sutton, 1989).

4   "The Diary of Isabella, Wife of Sir Roger Twysden, Baronet of Royden Hall, East Peckham, 1645–1651," ed. F. W. Bennitt, *Archaeologia Cantiana* 51 (1939): 117.

5   Elizabeth, Duchess of Northumberland, *The Diaries of a Duchess,* ed. James Greig (New York: Doran, 1927), p. 95.

6   *The Diary of the Lady Anne Clifford,* ed. Victoria Sackville-West (London: William Heinemann, 1924), p. 103.

7   "Elizabeth Lady Holland," in *Books and Portraits: Some Further Selections from the Literary and Biographical Writings of Virginia Woolf,* ed. Mary Lyon (New York: Harcourt Brace Jovanovich, 1977), p. 189.

8   Dale Spender, *Man Made Language* (London: Routledge and Kegan Paul, 1980).

9   Angus Calder and Dorothy Sheridan, eds., *Speak for Yourself: A Mass-Observation Anthology, 1937–49* (London: Jonathan Cape, 1984), p. 151.

10   *Beatrice Webb's Diaries,* ed. Margaret I. Cole, 2 vols. (London: Longmans, Green, 1952–56), 1:16.

11   *Journal of Katherine Mansfield,* ed. J. Middleton Murry (London: Constable, 1954), p. 205.

12   *Mary Hamilton: Afterwards Mrs. John Dickenson: At Court and at Home,* ed. Elizabeth and Florence Anson (London: John Murray, 1925), p. 229.

13   See Margaret Fountaine, *Love among the Butterflies: The Travels and Adventures of a Victorian Lady,* ed. W. F. Cater (Boston: Little, Brown, 1980).

14   *The Diary of the Lady Anne Clifford,* p. 42.

15   An additional useful recent resource is Cynthia Huff's *British Women's Diaries: A Descriptive Bibliography of Selected Nineteenth-Century Women's Manuscript Diaries* (New York: AMS Press, 1985).

I

Diverse Daily Lives from the Past

_____

Lady Margaret Hoby

(1571–1633)

MARGARET DAKINS HOBY was the only daughter of Thomasine
Guy (or Gye) Dakins and her husband Arthur of Linton and Hackness
in Yorkshire, a large landowner of importance in the district. Following contemporary custom for girls of Hoby's station, at maturity
she was taken into the household of Catherine, Countess of Hunting-
don, wife of the third earl and a strict Puritan, to be trained for marriage. At eighteen she was married to another protégé of the household: Walter Devereux, second son of the earl of Essex. Either from
her mother or the countess (or both) Hoby learned to read, write, and
play the alpherion (a stringed musical instrument) and, like other
women of the landed gentry, to do simple doctoring and supervise
not only a household but an estate. After Devereux died in 1591,
because she was an heiress in need of protection, she was quickly
married again to Thomas Sidney, brother of Sir Philip Sidney. When
Thomas too died, in 1596 she took as her final husband, again probably not by her own choice, Thomas Posthumous Hoby, second
son of Sir Thomas Hoby, the translator of Castiglione's *Courtier*.
Thereafter they lived at Hackness except for occasional trips to London. Their marriage was childless and, though Margaret never com-
plains, possibly not a happy one (or so neighborhood gossip claimed).
A devout Puritan, she apparently began her diary in 1599 as a religious exercise to catch out her sins, but as these excerpts from 1599–
1605 indicate,★ her recorded religious fervor abates noticeably as
the diary continues, especially during its last two years; she reports
instead her busy days as a landed gentlewoman. Hers is the earliest
extant English diary of daily life. Unfortunately, its opening pages are
partly missing and the diary, whose entries have become considerably
shorter, finally breaks off abruptly in midpage in 1605. Possibly Hoby
repudiated a record become more worldly than devotional.

From Margaret Hoby's Diary

Friday [*17 August 1599*]   After priuat prairs I went about the house
and read of the bible and wrought tell dinner time: and, after dinner,
it pleased [the Lord], for a Iust punishment to corricte my sinnes,
to send me febelnis of stomak and paine of my head, that kept me
vpon my bed tell 5: a clock: at which time I arose, haveinge release of
my sickness, according to the wonted kindnes of the Lord, who,
after he had Let me se how I had offended, that so I might take better
heed to my body and soule hereafter, with a gentle corriction let me
feele he was reconsiled To me: at which time I went to priuat praier,
and praises, examenation, and so to work tell supper time: which
done I hard the Lector[1] and, after I had walked an Hower with Mr
Hoby, I wente to bed[.]

Saterday 18   After I was readie I praied priuatly, and, because I was
weak and had paine in my head, I wret litle but wound yearne and
walked tell dinner time: after which I went about the house, and did
walke abroad, workinge litle all that day because of my weaknes, least
I should be disabled to keepe the Lordes day as I desired and am
bound: before supper, I praied and examened my selfe, not so perte-
culerly as I ought to have don, which I beseech the Lord to pardon for
his christs sack, and giue me grace here after to be more carefull:
then I walked tell supper time: after supper I taked wth. Mr Rhodes[2]
of the lordes praier, and, after lector, I medetated a little of that I
had hard, and so [manuscript torn] went to bed[.]

•   •   •   •   •

Munday 10 [*September 1599*]   After priuat praers I went about the
house, an then eate my breakfast: then I walked to the church with
Mr Hoby: after that I wrougt a litle, and neclected my custom of
praier, for which, as for many other sinnes, it pleased the Lord to
punishe me with an Inward assalte: But I know the Lord hath pardoned it because he is true of his promise, and, if I had not taken this
Course of examenation, I think I had for gotten itt: After dimer I

walked with Mr Hoby and, after he was gone, I went to gett tithe
aples: after I Came home, I praied wth. Mr Rhodes, and, after that,
priuatly by my selfe, and tooke examenation of my selfe: and so, after
I had walked a whill, I went to supper, after that to the Lector, and
so to bed[.]

．　．　．　．　．

Friday 14 [September 1599]　After order taken for the house, and priuat
praers, I writt notes into my testement and then brak my fast: after,
I wrought, and kept Mr Hoby compenie tell allmost diner time: then
I praied and, after dimer, I walked awhill and went to church Wth.
Mr Hoby, and when I Cam home wrought tell 6:, then I examened
my selfe and praied, and walked tell supper time: then I hard the
Lector, and after wrought a whill, and so went to bed: Lord, for
Christs sack, pardone my drousenes which, with a neclegent mind,
caused me to ommitt that medetation of that I had hard, which I
ought to haue had.

．　．　．　．　．

Tewsday the :9 day [October 1599]　After priuat praers I did eate my
breakfast with Mr Hoby: then I walked abroad, and tooke a lector:
after, I Came in and praied, and then went to diner: then I went about
and deliuered corne: then I Came into my Chamber, & wret notes
in my testement, and after receiued Rentes,[3] and walked awhile: and
then examened my selfe and praied: after, I walked a while, and read
of Babington,[4] and then went to supper and, sonne after, went to bed,
Mr Hoby Cominge home late[.]

Wensday the :10: day　After priuat praers I went about and did eate my
breakfast: then I wret some notes in my bible, then went to diner:
after, I walked, and presarued some sweet meat: then I wret notes
againe in my bible, then I walked, and then came in and examened
my selfe and praid: then I went to supper, and, after, paied seruantes
wages, and so went to bed[.]

．　．　．　．　．

The 5 day of the week :25: [25 January 1600]　After I was readie I went
about and was busie tell all most :11: a cloke: then I praied, read of

the bible, dined, and after kepte Companie with a kinsman of mine that Came to se me: after that I bused my selfe in the House and in my Closett tell all most :6:, and then I went to priuat praier and examenation: then I went to supper, after to publect praers, then to priuat, and lastly to bed:

The 6: day of the week the 26: After priuat praers I went about the house and then I reed of the bible tell dinner time: after diner I dresed vp my Clositte and read and, to refreshe my selfe beinge dull, I plaied and sunge to the Alpherion: after, I tooke order for supper and the next day, and then, after I had Conferred a whill with Mr Hoby I went to priuat examenation and praier[.]

. . . . .

Janur The 3 day of the week 30: 1599: [*30 January 1600*] After I had praied priuatly I dressed apoore boies legge that Came to me, and then brake my fast wth. Mr Hoby: after, I dressed the hand of one of our seruants that was verie sore Cutt, and after I wrett in my testement notes Vpon James: then I went about the doinge of some thinges in the house, paiynge of billes, and, after I had talked with Mr Hoby, I went to examenation and praier, after supper, then to the lector: after that I dressed one of the mens handes that was hurt, lastly praied, and so to bed:

. . . . .

The 6 day of the weke 2: [*2 February 1600*] After I had praied I dressed the sores that Cam to me: after, I dined and talked with som of my neighbours the afternone tell about 3 a Cloke: then I rede of the arball [herbal?], went a bout the house, and returned to priuate praers: after, to supper, then to publeck praier, and lastly to priuat[.]

. . . . .

The 3 day of the weeke 26: [*27 February 1600*] After priuat praier I did eate, then I dressed my patients, reed, talked with a neighbour, praied, and then dined: after, I was busie weyinge of wooll tell all most night and then, after talke with Mr Hoby and order for supper, I went to priuat exercises in my Closet: then after I supped and, after that, praied and so went to bed[.]

· · · · ·

The :5: day of the weke:28: [*29 February 1600*]   After priuat praers I did
eate, went about diuerse thinges in the house with some paine of
the toothach: after diner I talked a whill with an neighboure, but, beinge in great paine, was forced to vse diuerse medesons that did litle
profett, for, all the next day and all the week after, I to goe out [*sic*] of
my chamber, nor the lordes day after, which was the 9 of March I
durst not goe to the Church, which was much greffe vnto me, beinge
by that means depriued of the word and Sacrementes: and, though I
know the Lord is powerfull And hath promised to keep his Children
without the meanes, when he doth not afford them vnto them, yet,
when he depriueth them of the ordenarie Instrumentes wherby he
hath promised to Conuaye his graces vnto His people for their sinnes,
there is great Cause of sorowe and greffe. . . .

· · · · ·

The 4 day the 13: [*13 March 1600*]   I was this day so ill with Could as I
kept my Chamber, and had some of my neighbours, with whom I
took occasion to speak of diuers nedfull dutes to be knowne: as of
parence Chousinge [marriage partners] for their children, of the
charge of godfathers, and of the first instetuting of them: after they
were gone frome me I praied, went to supper, and then hard the
lector: after, I talked with Mr Rhodes touchinge his match and so
went to bed, takinge order for sundrie thinges to be don the next
morninge[.]

· · · · ·

The :18: [*July 1600*]   After priuatt praers I went about the house and
deliuered some directions to Iurden:[5] after, I talked with my Cosine
Isons and about his goinge to yorke, and then I went to diner: after, I
was busie p[r]ouidinge some thinge to be carried to Yorke: afte, I
wrought and, lastly, I went to priuat examenation and praier: after, I
went to supper, then I walked abroad: after, I Came in to publeck
praers and, after, to priuat, wher I please the lord to touch my hart
with such sorow, for some offence Cometted, that I hope the lord, for
his sonne sake, hath pardoned it accordinge to his promise, which is

ever Iust: after, I reed apaper that wrought a farther humiliation in me, I thanke god[.]

19: of July 1600: After priuat praier I wrett an answer to a demand Mr Hoby had giuen me ouer night:[6] after, I went about and then wrett in my sarmon book: after that, I praied and then I dined: the after none I wrought tell all most 5 a clok, and then I went about the house: after, I returned vnto my Clossitt and altered that a litle which before I had wretten, and then I examened myselfe and praied: after, I went to supper, then to publeck praers and, lastly, after priuat, I went to bed[.]

The 20 day the lordes day After I had praied I reed of the Testement and did eate: after, I walked and did medetate of that I had reed: after, I went to the church, and, after the sarmon, I praied: then I dined: after, I talked with my neighbours of that we had hard, and Reed some thinge to them: after, I praied and went to the church againe: after, I talked with my Cosine Isons, and, when it was 5 a Clok, I went to priuat examenation and praier: after, I walked dawne and then went to supper: after, I hard the bubleck [public] Exercise and then prainge, and, giuinge Mr Hoby that that I had wretten, I went to bed:

. . . . .

The :11: day [11 November 1600][7] After priuat praier I went about and reed of the bible: after, I helped my mother to washe some fine linan, my Maide france beinge not able: after, I strung som pearles, and then went to Cast vp som accountes that Concerned my beinge at Malton: and so, sonne after, tooke order for supper, and then went to priuat examenation and praier: after, to supper & then to bed[.]

The :12: day After I was readie I was busie to make some readie for Sir Edward Hoby, Mr Docter perkins, and Docter lister,[8] that came to vs to dinner: and so, hauinge praied, I went to Dinner: after, I was busie about some linan, and at night I praied and so went to supper: then I went to Read a whill and, when I had praied, I went to bed[.]

The :13: day After praiers I went to diner: after, I went to a standinge to se the quene Come to London, were I Reed a serome[9]: after, I Came home: beinge not well, I went to supper and so to bed[.]

. . . . .

The :30: day [*December 1600*]   After priuat praiers I kept all this day
with Mr Hoby, who was very farr out of temper with a lousnes,
fearinge auguy[10]: at night I went to priuat praier and readinge: we were
visited by Mrs Thornborowe, who dined with vs, and, in the after
none, wth. Mr Smith and Mr Dene[.]

. . . . .

The :5: day of May 1601:   After praers I went to the church, wher I
hard a sarmon: after, I Came home and hard Mr Rhodes read: after
diner I went abroad, and when I was come home I dresed some sores:
after, I hard Mr Rhodes read, and wrought with in a while: after, I
went to see a calfe at Munckmans, which had :2: great heades, 4 eares,
and had to ether head a throte pipe besides: the heades had longe
heares like brissels about the mouths, such as n'other Cowe hath: the
hinder legges had no parting from the rumpe, but grewe backward,
and were no longer but from the first Ioynte: also, the backe bone
was parted about the midest bicke, and a rowne howle was in the
midest into the bodie of the Calfe: but one would haue thought that
to haue comed of some strocke it might gett in the Cowes bely: after
this I Came in to priuat medetation and praicr [.]

The :6: day   After I had praied, buesed my selfe about dyinge some
cloth: and, after I had dined, I went to the dales wher I was, all the
after none, seeing som work: and, after I Came home, I kept Mr
ward Companie tell praier time [.]

. . . . .

The Lordes euen :17: [*October 1601*]   After priuatt prairs I walked
abroad: then I was busie wt. i [with] my Maides: after, I praied and
dined, and then went about the house: and at night paied the saruantes
their wages, and workmens bills[.]

The Lordes day :18:   After briuatt prairs I went the church [*sic*], and,
after the sarmon and dimer, I reed to the wiues and talked of the
sarmon: then I want to the afternone sarmon, and after I walked
abroad wt. [with] my Mother: and when I Came home I went to
priuat praier, hauinge receiued a Letter from Mr Hoby[.]

. . . . .

The :4: day [2 February 1601][11]   I was sent for to Trutsdall [Troutsdale]
to the trauill [travail, labor] of my Cossine Isons wiffe, who that
Morninge was brought to bed of a daughter: the same day, at night, I
hard of a fish that was taken vp att Yarmoth, 53 foott Long and 23
broade[.]

The Lordes day :7:   I was a wittnes for my Cossine Edward Isons
Child[.]

. . . . .

The :27: day [March 1603]   the sam day my Cossine Gates brought his
daughter Iane, beinge of the age of 13 yeares auld, to me, who, as
he saied, he freely gaue me[.]

Aprill :1603: the 4 day   Came Letteres from the Kinge[12] that euerie
Counsiller and other offecer should Continew in their places vntill his
further pleasur were knowne, bearing the date the 30 of March[.]

Aprill :11:   This day Mr Hoby and my selfe tooke our Iornie from
Hacknes, and that night lay at Linton, where I entertained my Cossine
Dakins wiues wiues daughter to serue me: the day followinge we all
went to Yorke[.]

. . . . .

The 28: day: [April 1603]   Was our Late gracious Quene buried at
wesminster, in that sort as became so great a prince[.]

. . . . .

The :5: day [October 1603]   Mr Hoby, my Mother, and my selfe, went
to the dalls this day: we had in our Gardens a second sommer, for
Hartechokes bare twisse, whitt Rosses, Read Rosses: and we, hauing
sett a musk Rose the winter before, it bare flowers now. I thinke
the Like hath seldom binn seene: it is a great frute yeare all ouer[.]

The :6: day   After praier I buesied my selfe wt. presaruing, and other
thinges wch. was to be done in the House: in the morninge my
Mother went to Newton[.]

The :7: day   This day I fasted untill Euening, eatinge nor drinkinge
anythinge, begging of the Lord that blissinge wch. yet I want[13]: the
Lord Heare me for his Christs sack, amen[.]

. . . . .

The :5 6 et 7 [April 1604]   day verie stormie and snowie wether.

Easter day :8:   A great snowe and did snowe allmost all the day[.]

The :9: day   All the morninge till none, sleet and extreme Could:

The :15: day which was the Lordes day   This morninge Came Mr Hoby Home from London, I praise god, very well, and in a good time for diuerse respectes for vs both.

. . . . .

Aprill 1605 [1 April]   The first day Mr Rhodes preachd in the Morninge: Mr Hunter, his father in Law, and he, after the Sarmon, took possision of Vnderill his house to Mr Hobys Vse and mine: at Night I thought to writt my daies Journee [journal] as before, becaus, in the readinge over some of my former spent time, I funde some profitt might be made of that Course from which, thorow two much neccligence, I had a Longe time dissisted: but they are vnworthye of godes benefittes and especiall fauours that Can finde no time to make a thankful recorde of them[.]

The 2: day: This day after priuatt prairs, I went about vntil dinner time: and in the afternone Came Mrs Bell wt. hir daughter, good wiffe Langdall, and hir sister warde: after, I walked about a litle, and then went to priuatt praier[.]

. . . . .

The 5 day[14]   This day I entertained Elzabeth Darfeld: all the day I was busie in the Garden, and after I went to priuatt praier & readinge.

The :6: day   This day I bestowed to much time in the Garden, and thereby was worse able to performe sperituall dutes[.]

The Lordes day :7:   This morninge, after priuatt preperation, I went to Church: & so likewise in the afternone: and after the exercises I went to readinge and priuatt praier[.]

. . . . .

The :13:   from the 9 to the 13, I praise god, I had my health, and was buseed in my garden the most of the day[.]

. . . . .

The :7: day [May 1605]   This after none we all went abroad to take the Aire and to fishe: and after I Came Home I went to priuatt praier.

. . . . .

The 29 day   This daye I continewed in health and Comfort, I praise god.

Notes

❧

*These selections are taken from *Diary of Lady Margaret Hoby,* ed. Dorothy M. Meads (London: Routledge and Sons, 1930). Hoby's exact dating is followed, with bracketed corrections and expansions where necessary for accuracy and clarity. Hoby's dates were sometimes wrong, and she did not begin a new year on 1 January.

1 Hoby uses the word *lector* to mean a passage to be read or perused or the act of doing so, or, as here, a reading of it aloud by another.

2 Richard Rhodes appears to have been Margaret Hoby's private chaplain, although there is no direct evidence that he resided in the household.

3 Hoby served as steward of the estate.

4 Gervaise Babington (1550–1610) was the author of many Puritan theological treatises and sermons.

5 One of the menservants.

6 This "demand," like the "paper" of the preceding day, may have been a request that she sign over her lands to her husband before her death; if so, it was a request granted only the year before she died.

7 Hoby was visiting in London at the time of these November entries.

8 Respectively, her brother-in-law; a theologian and writer; and probably the brother of her physician in York.

9 A sermon. Hoby apparently carried about with her a book of sermons and read from it while waiting to see Queen Elizabeth.

10 That is, he had an attack of diarrhea and feared that ague or shivering fits would follow.

11 This day's entry includes also the marginal notation "this day I had a fatherly warninge of god."

12 James I.

13 Perhaps a child.

14 The marginal notation reads "I must giue her 8s. at Mar:".

Elizabeth Freke

(1641–1714)

ELIZABETH FREKE was the daughter of Raufe and Cecily Cul-
peper Freke of Hannington in Wiltshire. She was probably educated
on the family estate by her parents and a maternal aunt who helped
teach her and her two sisters fine needlework and stitchery and the
preparation of pharmacopoeia. In the latter Freke became so firm
a believer that her diary preserves 440 home remedies, like the enthu-
suastic recipe for laudanum included here. After being engaged for
six or seven years to her second cousin Percy Freke (d. 1707) of
Country Cork despite her father's objections to her choice, she married Percy on 14 November 1671. From that day until within seven
weeks before her death in 1714, she kept a diary whose emphases are
embodied in the subtitle she gave it: "Some Few Remembrances of
My Misfortuns Which Have Atended Me In My Unhappy Life Since
I Were Married." Besides objecting that Percy perpetually cheats
her of her money and goods (he managed to squander a considerable
part of her marriage portion) and regularly deserts her, Elizabeth
liberally vents her spleen over lying neighbors, thieving servants, insulting acquaintances, and ungrateful relatives, not excepting her only
surviving child, Ralfe, born in 1675. The following selections (1712–
13)* from her diary while in her seventies show that age did not
mellow her outlook. By her husband's wish, she often lived in Ireland
during her marriage, though sometimes in England with her father.
But with his help, Percy purchased the estate of West Bilney in Norfolk and there she ended her days, finally with a home of her own
if often in litigation with her tenants and neighbors. When Freke finally took possession of Bilney Hall in 1698 upon its former owner's
death, she undertook minute inventories of her household possessions
for her diary, which thus reflects not only her grievances but the
satisfactions she could take in things if not always in people.

From Elizabeth Freke's Diary

First January 1712   Jannuary the First and My unhappy Birthday I
have by God's Permission, providence and Goodness to mee fully Accomplished the seventieth or three score & Ten yeare of my Age, for
Which I doe most humbly thank him, and Begg whatt Longer Time
he gives mee of Life may by me Elizabeth Frek [be] spentt In thank-
fullness and to my God's Glory and In his service; affter [I] have Laine
above five yeares In the Tortter of A Tissick [phthisic; pulmonary
consumption] and the severall distempers which dayly A Tend Itt, not
able the Least to help my selfe butt assisted by Two of my servants
and noe frind Neer me butt all Cheats. And by his permission as
I have begun this New year I doe most humbly beg of my God frome
the Bended knees of my hartt A More Moderate health then I have
had this six yeare past [since] My deer Husband Left me, being June
the 2d. 1706 (My son's Birth day 1675)[.]

.   .   .   .   .

19 January   Satterday, I had A third Letter from my sister Austen to
send her daughter Away, she Wanted her, tho she had her Eldest then
Wth her, And neer Forty yeares of Age, And this is the sister that
has hadd all the Industry of my Life.

I writt her Word I would doe Itt by Candlemas Iff possible, as she
before dereicted.

.   .   .   .   .

11 February   Monday Morn and the 11 of Febuary my Cosin Betty
Austen Leftt mee and Billney and wentt to London Whither I bore her
Charges and I there Gave her by my Cosin John Frek Fiffty pounds
to Lay outt In plate to Remember me by. My deer sister Austen sentt
for her three Times before I sentt her, tho' she had Another Daughter
With her & I A Lone & Never more will I be Troubled wth Friends
pd by my Kinsman John Frek.

14 February   Febuary 14: thursday, I were Taken With A violentt plurisy In my Left side for Which In the Night I were by Mr. Smith
Blouded, Who made the orrifice soe Wide thatt I Lost Above three-
score ounces before Itt Could be stoped att the Age of Above seventy

years. Which tho' Itt gave me some ease, yett I Lay very Weake Ever since with A Most Violentt Cough as to be unculpable of Any Business, expectting my Last sumons, & Noe Frind Neer mee. (From) want of rest & so much Bleeding, I am allmost Totally deprived of my eye sight, an Insuportable Griefe to me. E. Frek.[1]

·   ·   ·   ·   ·

14 March   I had a second Letter from my Daughter [in law] outt of Ireland thatt she designed me A visitt Wth her Two eldest sons this sumer & to Give A Name to the Child she now goes with And to signe my sons Commission.

I answered Itt For the First she was Wellcome to me and for her Children the Care was too greatt to entrust me with. Iff she would stay to Take Care of them they are Wellcome. And for the Child she now goes with, Iff she approve Itt I named Itt Arthur, my Husbands Fathers Name, And for my sons Commission I were too old to Take Jorneys to London, Nor would I be Troubled with them [the commissioners] downe to me, Nor sell my Land to Confirme my Cosin John Freks Follyes with Kelly, by giveing Away My Right Wch he Maintained.

17 March   Thomas Pallmer, my Tennantt, dyed of the small Pox, A hundred pound In my debt and Fiffty more than he was Worth, wch I am in greatt Hazard of Loosing or I must undoe the poore Widow Who Lost her Husband & her two eldest sons of this Fattal Distemper. A Quiett Man He was And He Lefft three Children behind him.

·   ·   ·   ·   ·

3 Aprill   Thursday the 3d of Aprill, three Rogues of Baylyes Came to Arest Mr Langly, and Missing of him, violently Forced Away my Coachman, and Carryed him to Norwich Jayle Withoutt soe much as permitting him to speak to me or give me an Accountt of Any of my things under his Care, Which was Neer Twenty pound Loss to E. F[reke].

4 Aprill   I sentt Mr Langly of Winch Word Whatt these Rogues of Baylyes said att my house (thatt tho they Missed him now they would soon have him A Live or Dead), And I Invited him to shellter himselfe In my House[.]

6 April   And I writt A Letter In his behalfe the sixth & sentt Itt open to him to His Mother (on his desire) E.F.

A boutt the second of Aprill I had Another Letter outt of Ireland from my Cosin John Frek In London to Come up and signe my sons Com Mission, [I] thatt have Hardly bin Cross my Chamber this Twelve Monthes withoutt the Asistance of Two to help mee, with my Astma And Very shortt breath Wth A Fixtt plurisy In my Left sid. And In shortt I Refused Coming up or permitting the Commissioners to Come downe to mee. E. Frek.

7 or 8 April   I answered this my Cosin John Freks Letter And thatt I did thankfully except his Release of my Trust, Assureing him I would Never Trust him wth my Grand children thatt had wronged me And my dr Husband of soe many thousand pounds as he had done by my Letter of Aturney to him, tho he had bin gratifyed by me In six years, six hundred pounds Att Least Tis True. Eliza Freke.

And I Concluded my Letter—from such friends Good Lord deliver Eliz: Freke.

• • • • •

20 Aprill   Easter Day & the Twentyeth of Aprill being sunday, I invited my new Tennantt, his Wife and His Two Children to diner; and the first Time I ever saw her; she was full of Care, aboutt her Lying In, Butt I bid her Leave those things to God, For I saw Death In her Face; that Nightt she Rid home to Winch, And dyed the Nextt Day, being Easter Monday.

21 Aprill   Monday, Mr. Langly wrott to me to Christen his Daughter.[2] Which I Refused them; the sunday affter they Came to me both to desire Itt of Mee butt I excused Itt, my Wantt of health besids my Resolution fixt Against Itt Att my Age to under Take whatt I could not performe.

• • • • •

11 May   Sunday Morneing, by the Carelesness of my Two Maids, Mary Ram & Mary Chapman, I Lost all my Clothes & all my Houshold Linnen, stole from me one Sunday Morne by Leaveing them outt a Satterday Night, to Whitten, unknown to me. Att Least six weeks washing was Stole All by sun Rise, for Which I offered Twenty pound to Mary Ram to Recruitt them, I having butt A boutt three days before Turned outt of my house Diana Davy and Goode Kneeve for stealing of my fences & cutting of my wood Whch I proved Against them att the Justice sitting.

15 May   With aboundance of Ill Language the 15 they broughtt A warrantt from Justice pell Against mee on wch at the Justice sitting I wrott to the Bench my Complaintt A Gainst Goode Kneeve & Diana Davy, who ordered them both A Good Whiping And what further I pleased, which I saw done to them both outt of my window Att the Carts Taile 27 of May, satterday, Till the Bloud spun, for examples sake. And Iff Further complaintt to be sent to Bridwell.

24 May   24 of May My own Maid Mary Chapman Complained of her Head And Back which I then Told her would prove to bee the small Pox. Three days she Lay very Ill & on Tuesday the 3 of June they Appeared.

Wensday I Removed her outt of my own house In to A Little House In the parrish & Tooke her A nurse Att a Crowne A week for Neer three weeks besids Meatt & drink, Doctters, Cordialls, Apothycaryes, wher she Lay past all Recovery Neer A Fortnightt as Mr Smith and All that heard of her Condition said Itt was Impossible for her Recovery, besids I am sure forty shillings would not pay for her Cordials she had outt of my Closett besids Another Nurse for A bove A week to Tend her, Goode Maw. Blind she was the second day & soe she Lay till a boutt the 26, And affter Neer A Monthes Care & Charge of Mary Chapman, (& the Loss of all my Clothes) & Above Five pounds in Mony I trusted them with as Iff my Neer Relations up she Gott And Run Away, Thursday the 30: of June, After she had spoyled me A Fether Bed, Two Boulsters, 2 Blanketts Two pillows And A coverlid & a paire of sheets & I pd Mr Hogan her apothicarys bill & Two and thirty shillings for Close for her & her Husband Roger Chapman wch I were on my word bound for And pt her Coming downe. Away she Run to Norwich Jaile to her husband & never soe much as said God Buy. And all this I did In pitty to her As A stranger & her faithful promise of paymentt.

27 May   A Note of whatt Cordiall waters I putt into the severall
Cubards In my Closett for my own use: May 27: 1712: Eliza: Frek:
> In the Greatt Cupbord Is of Quartt Bottles.
> 1 Three quartt bottle of hott surfett Watter i705
> 5 Quarts of Pallfry Watter i708: i702
> 4 quarts of Cordiall Watter double stilled—i708
> 2 Quart Scurvigrass Double stilled—i684
> 6 Quarts of duable still Cor: With Cinamon—i705
> 3 Quarts of Angellicoe Watter—First—i705
> 9 Quarts of Lemon Water & Brandy—i705
> 5 Quarts of Rosemary Water Wth Licor:—i708
> 2 Quarts of Tinture of Lavender—i709
> 5 Quarts of Ague Watter First—i705
> i quartt of hungary Watter La: N:—i709

. . . . .

20 September   To make Lodinum. The Lady Powells Receitt sentt me
by my dr sister Austen In my distress, of wch she has Taken of Itt
neer Two years her selfe:—Sep: 20: sent 1712: For the Collicke—&c
   Take Two ounces of the Best opium; And one ounce of fine saffron;
Cutt the opium very thinn and small; And pull the saffron Into small
peices; then Infuse them In A quarte of the best sack In A Deep
Earthen Pott Covered with a Blader pricked full of Pin Holles: And—
then sett Itt In A kettle, or skillitt of Boyleing Watter, Till the Quanti-
tye In the Pott bee halfe Wasted. Lett Itt Infuse still keeping the vessell
Conveniently Filld up as Itt Wasts—and when Itt is Done enough
(Which will be A Great While First) Iff you please dr Madam To
straine Itt and Squeeze Itt hard outt, and keep Itt Close stopt for yr
use:—
   The dereictions follow, how to vse this Ladynum.

MRS. AUSTEN'S LETTER.

I have sentt my Deer sister the Receitt of the Ladynum as I make
Itt puntially, And I have Taken Itt once A day for Almost A
yeare and Halfe: And I begin with Itt att Twenty drops Att A
Time: butt by vseing of Itt: Itt must be Increased Soe thatt now I
Take Five and Twenty Drops In A day In A spoon full of Wyne

or Beere or Coffy: And In any violentt fitt of the Colicke you
must Double the proportion off Drops for Itt To Master the
Humour; (which I hope my deer sister Itt will doe) Both In your
Head & Back: My Lady Powell Who Gave me this Receitt says
she had bin Dead many years since butt for Itt shee Haveing
Tryed all the Conciderable phisitions In London and by them
Brought to A skellitton In Weakness and To noe Effectt. shee has
since Taken for severall Years Fifty Drops A day; And by soe
Doeing keeps her selfe In A Moderate degree of Ease: And my
Daughter Judith when shee takes Itt has offten the Benifitt of
putting her Into a sleep For six or Eightt howers together tho In
the Collick: And tho Itt has nott thatt Godd Effectt on me Yett
Itt Composes my Rest the better In the nightt. And To give
me thatt Effectt I Take Itt A boutt Two or three A Clock In the
After Noone And I have A Neighbour by me Tells me she Takes
Itt Twice A day thirty Drops att A Time.—All these Informa-
tions I Give my deerst sister thatt you may see Itt is A safe thinge
And Nott be Affraid of Itt. Otherwise then to have Itt Carefully
Droptt, Whatt Ever Is Taken—It sometimes Flyes to the Head, as
perhaps you may Find, And to the Frightning of you Butt for
all thatt I wrightt Itt my deer sister Wth Pleasure Hopeing Itt
may doe you Good. and then Itt is butt A small penance To
purchas To ourselves A Little Ease Whilst We Live In this World:
God send you A suden and Joyfull meetting of your Deer Familly outt of IreLand Is the Dayly prayer of &c

Judith Austen.

· · · · ·

15 March 1713   Being Midlentt sunday, Mr Smith of Winch preached
att Billney, and aftterwards gave the sacramentt there, Where I doe
most Humbly thank God I weare A Most Miserable unworthy par-
taker of Itt with my Few Neighbours & my daughter In Law, my son
goeing outt of the Church, Where I had not bin In allmost Two years
nor my son with me Above this seven years before, My Greatt &
Good God Forgive him this & all his other mistaks to Elizabeth Frek.

'Twas with the greatest of Diffyculty & the help of Fowre servants
I Compassed to my Church, and [in] Misery I sate ther (and nott
Lessened to see my son sett Frowning on me ther for an howr for I
know nott whatt—except Itt were his feare of my Coming A Live

home Againe). This his Cruell usuage of me gave me A greatt Trouble tho' I were att the sacramentt, Where I had not bin—nor In Any Church—In Two years before by my Miserble Tissicke. And affter diner when Before Mr. smith I asked him Iff hee had nott Latly Received Mercyes enough from God, First from his deliverance by the severall Tempest by sea Last Michellmas day when soe many ships were Lost, and himselfe, his Wife & three sons were all preserved by God's providence, and since thatt his youngest son, John Redman, Lay sick heer with me (and att my Charge) all most A Month given over of the small pox, besids severall others Mercyes Received His Answer to me was I Talked to him as Iff he were butt eighteen years of Age When att this very Time hee owes mee Above Three Thousand pounds In Redy money I Can Lay him up for.

And since sunday, Which is now Fowre days, my son Has gone by my Chamber doore and Never Called on me to see how I did Butt Twice (an I soe very Ill); my Greatt & good God forgive hime and support unhappy mee his Wretched Mother, Elizabeth Freke. The like was his eldest son percy freke dereicted to do, Who for Above A week pased my Chamber Neer Twenty Times A day, Never once Call'd In to see mee His grandmother; 'Tis butt as my deer Husband before me has bin Treated by them both and there eldest son In the yeare 1705 In London. E. Freke.

• • • • •

26–29 Aprill   Sunday the 26 of Aprill I Left my house att West Billney & went for London with my son and his Wife and his three sons and his Fowre Men and my Coachman and Maid, affter they had bin all with me above Fowr Monthes heer with ther disorderly servantts; & I Came to my deerst sister Lady Nortons house Wensday the 29the Aprill In my Coach wth my two Coach horses and Five persons In my Coach beside Lunber, and beyond my expectation well concidering I had hardly moved from my Chair in 17 Monthes before.

The day I Left my house my daughter Came Rudely In to my Chamber and Told me I Owed her husband Fifty pounds and Twenty pounds (when he now owes me Above Five 5000 11 thousand [*sic*] pound) and they had of me heer above three hundred pound of Mr Rolfe & my selfe, And by the Tenants discharges. In Which Time ther youngest son lay too month dyeing of the small Pox, Who infectted Fowre of my servants, of Which one of Them dyed. I will nott say more then from such another Time Good Lord deliver mee, & make thankfull to God Eliz. Frek.

5 May   Tuesday, the 5 of May, was the peace proclaimed by the Order of the Queene & persuantt to the Actt of Parliamtt;[3] butt such A peace I never heard of In my Liffe. The Greatt God send us A good end of soe odd a Beginning.

14 May   My son & daughter being both desirous of more Quality, I did aboutt the Midle of May Purchas by my Cosin John Frek the patentts of A Barronett from the Queen, for Which I paid and for the Ingroseing of Itt and the quiet test[4] above Five Hundred pounds, and gave my Cosin John Frek for his trouble Forty Guinyes, and this my deer sister Norton giveing my son and Daughterrs Rude Family the Freedome of her house. I staid In London Nine weeks, and on my own Charge kept there disorderly familly, and I paid for Coach hire Five pounds–16 shillings, tho' I had A Coach of my own In London; and for Meatt and drink for him & his Family to ther own apoynt-mentt, and gave my daughtyer Fiffty pounds for her own spending; & I paid Mr. Cross eight ginyes for drawing his picture, and severall other things; and yett all deserved noe thanks, tho' for Nine weeks I kept open house for all Comers & goers to them both & all their Acquaintance.

24 June   Wensday, And Midsomerday the 24 of June, being very Ill by A voylentt fitt of the Colick, I Attempted my goeing outt of [Lon-don] In hopes of A Little quiett (haveing had none In six months before) and Being Quitt Tired outt, and my son apprehending my death Neer, Came in the Coach downe with mee, tho' I begg'd the Contrary of him; and by God's Great mercy to mee I Came home in my own Coach In five days,

being Sunday, Late att Nightt, the 28 of June, very Ill. Heer my deer son (Now Sr. Ralph Freke) staid with me Till the six of Septembr, being

Sunday Morning; in Which Time his Groome & his honestest ser-vantt of the Fowre stole A Maire he valued att Twenty Guinyes and

Aboutt Twenty pound in Gold and sillver he Run Away with, and Left him severall bills to pay In Linn hee had Trusted the Mony with him to Cary and Pay Itt.

My son Sr. Ralph Frek proclaimed the peace, & had Itt with prayers In the Church, And with Cakes, Wyne and A Barrell of Ale and A great burne fire In the Common of Aboutt Two or 3 Load of Wood besids &c.

6 September   Sunday the sixth of September My son (& his bosome frind Gin) Leftt me and begun his Jorney for London By Way of Northamton, Wher Gin had perswaded him he might buy a sett of good Coach-Horses as he did A little before att Norwich, both Which Jorneys were Lost; however the Morning hee Left me he brought me a bill of Above A hundred pounds & Ten pound In his Debtt Which 100 11[pounds] I paid my son as by accountt outt of Whatt I Left to Bury mee. E. Frek.

Notes

*

*These selections are taken from *Mrs. Elizabeth Freke, Her Diary: 1671 to 1714*, ed. Mary Carbery (Cork: Guy and Co., 1913). Freke's old-style dating has been preserved.

1   Freke often signed her entries.

2   That is, to act as sponsor.

3   Queen Anne and the Peace of Utrecht, ending the War of the Spanish Succession.

4   The "quietus est": a legal term signifying that the transaction has been completed. The term *quietus* (quit) was used by auditors in discharges and acquittances given to accountants, which often concluded with *abinde recessit quietus* ("hath gone quit thereof"), known as a "quietus est."

Mary, Countess Cowper

(1685–1724)

MARY CLAVERING, later Countess Cowper, was the daughter
of John Clavering, Esquire, of Chopwell, Durham. In 1706 she married William, Lord Cowper, who had recently become lord keeper
of the Great Seal and soon afterwards would become lord chancellor
to King George I. The marriage was kept secret for six months perhaps because of her birth, although her husband claimed to have chosen her for her modest origins and good understanding, rather than
for passion. Well educated and studious, besides being talented at
the harpsichord, not only did she regularly translate her husband's
writings into French so that they would be intelligible to the Hanove-
rian king; she also collected a large library of books, many of them
on abstruse subjects and many annotated by her. The marriage apparently was happy; she prided herself on being a devoted wife and had
the reputation of being an excellent mother as well, besides being
something of a beauty. She was also presumably quite ambitious and
kept up a diligent correspondence with Princess Caroline of Anspach
(later Queen Caroline as wife of George II) in the expectation that
when Caroline came to England, there would be a special place for
her in Caroline's service. When in 1714 her efforts bore fruit and
she was named a lady of the bedchamber to Caroline, since become
Princess of Wales, Cowper began the diary of her observations of
court life from which the following excerpts (1714–16) are taken.* It
reveals that she did not suffer fools gladly or condone cruel or immo-
ral behavior. Only two portions of her diary are extant: from 1714–
16 and from part of 1720. When Lord Cowper resigned his office
in 1722 after being accused (falsely) of conspiring against the crown in
a Jacobite plot, his wife protectively destroyed much of her diary
and correspondence. Thus she was never to carry out the ambition
she announced at the outset, someday to rewrite her diary in more
polished form.

From Mary Cowper's Diary

1714   The perpetual Lies that One hears have determined me, in spite of my Want of Leisure, to write down all the Events that are worth remembering whilst I am at *Court;* and although I find it will be impossible for me to do this daily, yet I hope I shall be able to have an Hour or two once a Week: and I intend this only for my own Use, it being a rough Draft only, which, if *God* bless me with Health and Leisure, I intend hereafter to revise and digest into a better Method.

I believe it will be necessary, in the first Place, to recollect what passed in order to my coming into the *Court:* and to give a better Light in that Matter, I must tell that for four Years past I had kept a constant Correspondence with the *Princess* now my Mistres;[1] I had received many, and those the kindest, Letters from her. Upon the Death of the *Queen,* after she had done me the Honour to answer my Letter of Congratulation,[2] I wrote another Letter to offer her my Service, and to express the perfect Resignation I had to whatever she would think fit to do, were it to choose or refuse me. This Letter she answered, telling me she was entirely at the *Prince's* Disposal, and so could give me no Promise; but that she did not doubt the *Prince's* Willingness to express his Friendship to me upon all Occasions. By the whole Letter I took it for granted that she had so many Importunities upon that Subject, that she could not take me into her Service, and therefore I resolved not to add to the Number of her Tormentors, and never mentioned the Thing any more. I was the more confirmed in my Opinion, when I saw myself treated with such Marks of Distinction, and at the same Time two new Ladies made, and I had heard Nothing; but I knew that the Necessity of Affairs often forces Princes to do many Things against their Inclinations, and I daily received so many distinguishing Marks of the *Princess's* Favour that I had great Reason to be satisfied. Things stood in this Manner till the Coronation,[3] which was *October* 20, 1714.

I went thither with Lady *Bristol,* who had still a greater Mind to be a Lady of the Bedchamber than I had; she told me I was to be one, but durst not then tell me she had heard it from the *Princess* herself. When we came from the *Hall* into the *Abbey* (for we saw every Part of

the Ceremony), the Peeresses' Places were so full, that we and several
other Ladies went to the Bishops' Benches at the Side of the Altar.
I sat next the Pulpit Stairs on the back Bench, and several Ladies coming by me to go nearer the Altar, at last my Lady *Northampton* came
pulling my Lady *Nottingham*[4] by the Hand, which Last took my Place
from me, and I was forced to mount the Pulpit Stairs. I thought this
rude, but did not suppose there had been any Design in it, though we
had both been talked of for being Governess to the young Princesses,[5]
and she, I believe, had really solicited for it, and apprehended I had
done so too, notwithstanding I had never thought of it. However, her
Ill-breeding got me the best Place in the *Abbey,* for I saw all the Ceremony, which few besides did, and I own I never was so affected with
Joy in all my Life; it brought Tears into my Eyes, and I hope I shall
never forget the Blessing of seeing our holy Religion thus preserved,
as well as our Liberties and Properties.

My Lady *Nottingham,* when the Litany was to be sung, broke from
behind the Rest of the Company, where she was placed, and kneeled
down before them all (though none of the Rest did), facing the *King,*
and repeating the Litany. Everybody stared at her, and I could read
in their Countenances that they thought she overdid her High Church
Part. But to return to my Place. The Lords that were over against
me, seeing me thus mounted, said to my Lord, that they hoped I
would preach; to which he answered that he believed I had Zeal
enough for it, but that he did not know that I could preach; to which
my Lord *Nottingham* answered, 'No, my Lord? Indeed you must
pardon me. She can, and has preached for these last four Years such
Doctrines as, had she been prosecuted in any Court for them, you
yourself could not defend her.' This he said with such an Air, that my
Lord spoke of it to me. That, joined to what my Lady *Nottingham*
had done that Day, and some other little Passages that had happened,
opened my Eyes, and showed me how that Family maligned me,
and helped to persuade me that it was impossible the *Princess* could
think of me.

At the Coronation, my Lord *Bolingbroke* for the first Time saw the
King. He had attempted it before without Success. The *King,* seeing a
Face he did not know, asked his Name, when he did him Homage;

and he (Lord *B.*) hearing it as he went down the Steps from the
Throne, turned round and bowed three Times down to the very
Ground. The Ladies, not walking in the Procession, had no gold
Medals.

One may easily conclude this was not a Day of real Joy to the Jacobites. However, they were all there, looking as cheerful as they
could, but very peevish with Everybody that spoke to them. My Lady
Dorchester stood underneath me; and when the *Archbishop* went round
the Throne, demanding the Consent of the People, she turned about
to me, and said, 'Does the old Fool think that Anybody here will
say no to his Question, when there are so many drawn Swords?'
However, there was no Remedy but Patience, and so Everybody was
pleased, or pretended to be so.

Sunday, 24 October   I went to the Chapel in the Morning, and when it
was done, to the Drawing-room; and the *Princess* seeing me, called
to me, and said, 'Did Lady *Essex Robartes* deliver my Message to you?'
To which I answered that I had not seen her since her Royal Highness
had spoke to her last Night at the Opera. 'Then,' said she, 'I will
tell you myself that you have made a Conquest;' and seeing me blush,
she laughed, and said, 'I am resolved to shame you, or rather to
do you Honour. 'T is Mr. *Bernstorff,*[6] who never was in love in his
Life before; and 't is so considerable a Conquest, that you ought to
be proud of it; and I, to please him, have ordered him to make
you a Compliment from me.' And with that she went out of the
Room.

When I came to the Bottom of the Stairs, I found Mr. *Bernstorff's*
Man, who desired me to name an Hour for him to come to me. I
named Four; and Mr. *Bernstorff* came punctually, to tell me that he had
Orders from the *Princess* to offer me to be *une Dame du Palais.*[7] I was
very glad to hear this, and told him that I wished it mightily, but that
I had never made any Application for it after the Letter I have already
mentioned, because I would not add to the Number of the *Princess's*
Persecutors; upon which he made me a thousand Compliments, both
from the *Princess,* the *Prince,* and himself, and ordered me to go the
next Day to kiss the *Princess's* Hand. I gave him at the same Time

a Treatise on the State of Parties, which I had transcribed and trans-
lated for my Lord, in French and English, to give the *King*.

25 October   In the Morning, by Eleven, I waited upon the *Princess*. I
found the Duchess of *St. Albans* in the outward Room upon the same
Errand. She went in first and kissed the *Princess's* Hand, and I followed. The *Princess*, when I had done it, took me up and embraced
me three or four Times, and said the kindest Things to me—far
beyond the Value of any Riches. There were present the Duchesses of
St. Albans and *Bolton*, Mrs. *Clayton*, Mrs. *Howard*, the Governess,
and two or three of the foreign Ladies. The *Prince* also saluted the
Duchess of *St. Albans* and me upon our being declared; and we both
waited that Night in the Drawingroom.

·   ·   ·   ·   ·

17 December   This Morning I sent early to Baron *Bernstorff*, to desire
to see him. He had requested me to give him Notice if Mrs. *Oglethorpe*
was recommended to my Mistress, and withal to give him Notice of
another Piece of Intelligence, which was, that Mrs. *Kirk* (Widow of
that Mr. *Kirk* who killed *Conway Seymour*) was recommended by the
Duchess of *St. Albans* for a Bedchamber Woman. I told him what
both those Ladies were; that Mrs. *Kirk* had managed all the Intrigue
between Lady *Mary Vere* and the Duke of *Ormond*, took care of the
Child, was Manager of all the Intrigues of the *Oxford* Family, had an
ill Reputation as to herself, and had been the Duke of *Somerset's* Mistress. *Bernstorff* took down their Names, and promised to speak about
them.

I could have told him a good deal more of this last Lady, if it had
been fit for me to do so; but I never opened my Mouth in relation to
what I know of her upon my Account in my whole Life, and therefore
it won't be amiss to set down here, by way of Memorandum, what
she formerly did towards making me unhappy. But I thank *God* I
have escaped that Snare.

My Lord being a Widower when the late *Queen* gave him the Seals,
it was no Wonder the young Women laid out all their Snares to catch
him. None took so much Pains as Lady *Harriet Vere*, whose Poverty
and ruined Reputation made it impossible for her to run any Risk

in the Pursuit, let it end as it would. She had made several Advances
to my Lord, by Mrs. *Morley*, her Kinswoman, and finding Nothing
came of it, they immediately concluded my Lord must be pre-engaged
to Somebody else; so they set a Spy upon him, and found that he
had country Lodging at *Hammersmith*, where he lay constantly, and
upon Enquiry they found I was the Cause of this Coldness to Lady *H*.
Upon this, they settled a Correspondence under a feigned Name
with him; and in those Letters (which were always sent by a Fellow
dressed up in Woman's Clothes, who could never be overtaken) they
pretended to be some great Person, that threatened him, if he married
me, to hinder the Passing of his Title. The first of these Letters came
the Day before I was married. However, it did not hinder our Marriage, though my Lord thought it advisable to keep it a Secret; and so
he removed the next Day to *London*. His Correspondents, seeing
they had made him leave the Place, thought it would be no hard Matter to break the Match; and from that Time to the Beginning of *January*, which was almost four Months, my Lord had a Letter every Day,
some of whole Sheets of Paper, filled with Lies about me; to say I
was a mean Wretch; that I was Coquette, and should be more so; that
my playing so well was, and would be, a Temptation to bring all
the Rakes in Town about me; that it had been so thus far in my Life;
and that I was treated so familiarly by the rakish Part of Town, that
one Night, at a Play, my Lord *Wharton* had said to my Lord *Dorchester*,
'Now that the Opera is done, let's go and hear *Molly Clavering* play
it over again' (which was all a plain Lie, for I never did play in any
public Company, and only at Home when Anybody that visited my
Aunt *Wood*, with whom I lived, asked me; and for those two Lords, I
had never been in a Room with either of them in my whole Life).
These are only Specimens of what Lies they invented to hurt me. At
last, when they thought they had routed me, by the ill Impressions
they had falsely given of me, upon a Day when my Lord was at the
House of Lords, one Mr. *Mason*, of the *House of Commons*, came to him,
and told him that Mrs. *Weedon* (a Client of my Brother's, that had a
foul Cause in the *Court of Delegates*) desired to speak with him. My
Lord at first refused; but at length she teased him so much that he
consented to see her; and by her Appointment, and saying she had a

very fine Lady to recommend to him (which gave him a Thought
he should find out his Correspondent), he waited upon her at Mrs.
Kirk's, which was the Place appointed. He had some little Jealousy
before he went that the fine Lady was Lady *Harriet Vere,* for she and
Mrs. *Kirk* had always been in a Hackney Coach every Sunday for
at least a Month, to ogle him and pass and repass his Coach when he
went and came from the Chapel. He found he was right; for there
she was, set out in all her Airs, with her Elbow upon a Table that had
two wax Candles on it, and holding her Head, which she said ached.
There she displayed herself, and so did her two Artificers, and not
a Word said of the Cause. This Interview brought on several others,
and those Visits to my Lord from Mrs. *K.* and Mrs. *W.,* to try to
make this Match. They told him that the *Queen* had promised Lady
H. 100,000 *l.* when she married. He said upon that Score he durst not
presume to marry her, for he had not an Estate to make a Settlement
answerable to so great a Fortune; and at last they pressed him so
much, that he owned he was engaged to me, and that it would be
barbarous to ruin an innocent young Woman, who had no Fault but
receiving his Visits so long. They could not agree with him that it
was barbarous, for it was only serving me in my own Kind, for I was
contracted to Mr. *Floyd,* whom I had left for him. My Lord said
they were mistaken in that Affair (which he knew full well). However,
this did not discourage them; and once, when he seemed to yield, he
brought Mrs. *Kirk* to confess the Pains they had been at to bring
this about, and she mentioned particularly the Letters, which were
contrived and written at her House, and copied afterwards by Lady
H. V. herself. As soon as my Lord had got this Confession, he wrote to
Lady *H.,* in answer to a Love-letter from her (for she pretended to
be terribly in love with him), to excuse himself, and say that he resolved to marry me, for now he was assured that he had met with a
wife whose Conduct was unblemished, for that the greatest Enemy I
had in the World had been writing every Day an Invective against
me, which was duly sent to him; and that now all the Letters were
laid out before him he did not find Anything I was accused of, but of
playing the best upon the Harpsichord of any Woman in *England,*
which was so far from being a Fault, that it was an Argument to him

that I had been used to employ many of my Hours alone, and not
in the Company of Rakes, as they would suggest. But they thought
that there was Hope, since they did not believe we were actually married, and my Lord could never get quit of their Importunity till he
owned our Marriage to them, though it was before he owned it publicly; and even after that, both Mrs. *K* and Lady *H.V.* wrote
frequently to him. This I had not inserted, but as a Justification for
my endeavouring to hinder her coming into the *Princess's* Bedchamber.

· · · · ·

10 February 1716 I went to *Court* in the Afternoon. The *Princess* heard
a Cause that kept her an Hour. It was a Dispute between the Ladies
of the Bedchamber and the Lord Chamberlain and Vice-Chamberlain,
in which I believe the Ladies were in the Wrong. It was about the
two Officers above mentioned coming into the Bedchamber, which
has been a Right always pretended to by them, and always contested
by the Ladies.

11 February My poor *Spencer*[8] pretty well, for which I heartily thank
God. This Morning, before I went out, I bought a Parcell of small
Rubies and Emeralds of *Mizan*. Two Letters from Mademoiselle
Schutz. 'T is very troublesome to be writing thus at every Turn.
I wish she had as much Occupation as I have. I dined at Mrs. *Clay-
ton's* with my Lord and Lady *Halifax*, Lady *Dorchester*, and Lady *W.
Pawlet*. . . .

· · · · ·

13 February Stayed at Home with my Lord, who is very ill. I was to
dine at Baron *Bernstorff's*, but excused myself. The Ladies that were
there came here in the Afternoon. Mademoiselle *Schutz* is a very
unreasonable Body, and would take no Hints that I wished to be
alone, but took a Pleasure in staying, because I was uneasy at it.

14 February The News was confirmed Yesterday. The *Pretender*[9] is
gone. My Lord is so ill that he has a Mind to quit Office. I have made
a Resolution never to press him more to keep his Place. I had a Letter
from Mademoiselle *Schutz*, to offer to come to stay with me all Day.
I thank her for Nothing. I had too much of her Impertinence last
Night.

15 February My Lord mighty ill, and still had a Mind to quit Office.
I told him that I would never oppose Anything he had a Mind to
do; and after arguing calmly upon the Matter, I offered him, if it
would be any Pleasure done him, to retire with him into the Country,
and quit too, and, what was more, never to repine at doing so, though
it was the greatest Sacrifice that could be made him. I believe he will
accept.

16 February Mademoiselle *Schutz* came. She had been in the City to
get a Suit of gold Ribbons. She had a Mind to have me give her them,
but I can't help turning my deaf Ear to such unreasonable People.
She had a Mind also to have some of my Jewels; which is pretty im-
pertinent, when I am to be at the Birthday myself. Madame *Gouvernet*
offered me an emerald Necklace; which I accepted rather because it
was offered me, and I was afraid of disobliging her, than to make
myself fine (for I don't care one Farthing for setting myself out, and I
hope always to make it my Study rather to adorn my mind than set
off a vile Body of Dust and Ashes). Being thus provided of a Necklace, and Mademoiselle *Schutz* hearing of it, she desired to borrow
my fine Pearl Necklace, which being of so great Value, I thought
I had as good put it into my Hair; and so I told her I should be glad to
accommodate her, but that all the Jewels I had I should use, and that
I had so few, that I was often forced to borrow upon those Occasions
myself. My Lord still ill. I am out of my Wits to see him suffer,
which I declare is ten Times worse than Death to me, and would
rather live with him all my Life on Bread and Cheese, up three Pair of
Stairs, than be all this World can make me and at the same Time see
him suffer.

My Lord still ill. In my Perplexity, I told Mrs. *Woodford* my Griefs,
and bid her ask Mr. *Woodford's* advice; which she says he gave very
kindly, and proposed that I should let him hint to old Mr. *Craggs* that
my Lord *Cowper's* Office was too hard for him; and proposed that
old Mr. *Craggs* having in the Days that the Ministry were cold to my
Lord *Cowper* offered to Mr. *Woodford* that if my Lord was weary he
might be Privy Seal; and that being now designed for Lord Chief
Justice *Parker,* who would certainly come into my Lord *Cowper's*
Place, he[10] might have the Privy Seal; and that the Reversion of Sir

John Shaw's Place should be added for two Lives. Sir *David Hamilton* had a Letter from my Lord *Cornwath*, who is his second Cousin, desiring to speak to him. He has had Leave, and is gone To-night.

17 February   Mrs. *Woodford* came to see me, not having rested well after I had told her the Night before my Lord was better, and did not talk so much of quitting. His Illness, I really believe, proceeded from the Fall he had.

The Duchess of *Marlborough* came in the Evening. I saw her, though I was very ill. She says the Duchess of *Roxburgh* is the greatest Enemy that either my Lord or I have. The Duchess of *Roxburgh* is certainly an ill Woman. She does not care what she says of Anybody to wreak her Malice or Revenge.

18 February   My Lord better, to my great Joy. No Talk of quitting To-day, though I fairly laid it in his Way. This Morning Mademoiselle *Schutz* came to see me. She's always begging Something or other, and would have borrowed my Diamonds to put in her Hair, and at the same Time said, 'I make no Scruple in borrowing them from you, because you are best in your State of Nature, and always worse when you are dressed out, your Jewels not becoming you.' Commend me to the Assurance of these Foreigners!

· · · · ·

23 February 1716   . . . I carried the Gag which was brought from *Preston* by Mr. *Carter* to *Court*, by order of the *Princess*. A great Number of them were found at the House of one *Shuttleworth*, a Papist, afterwards hanged. He was famous for saying he hoped in a little Time to see *Preston* Streets running as fast with heretic Blood as they do with Water when it has rained twelve Hours. The Gags are really frightful. They go down the Throat a great Way, with a Bend, and under that there is an iron Spike that runs into the Tongue if it is stirred, and the Ends have Screws that screw into the Cheeks. We sat up till past Two, to do a pleasing Office, which was to reprieve four of the Lords in the *Tower*, though the Earl of *Nithsdale*[11] had made his Escape; but it was not then known, and so he was reprieved with the Rest.

· · · · ·

4 April Countess of *Buckenburgh* said in a Visit, that the English Women did not look like women of Quality, but made themselves look as pitifully and sneakingly as they could; that they hold their Heads down, and look always in a Fright, whereas those that are Foreigners hold up their Heads and hold out their Breasts, and make themselves look as great and stately as they can, and more nobly and more like Quality than the others. To which Lady *Deloraine* replied, 'We show our Quality by our Birth and Titles, Madam, and not by sticking out our Bosoms.' The Countess of *Buckenburgh* speaks English pretty well, but sometimes makes comical Mistakes; the other Night she wanted to know what they call the Man of a Goat (meaning a He-goat), and the Man of a Sheep that is mentioned in the *Psalms.*

· · · · ·

The 28th October the *Court* left *Hampton Court.* The Ladies came with the *Prince* and *Princess* by Water in a Barge. The Day was wonderfully fine, and Nothing in the World could be pleasanter than the Passage, nor give One a better Idea of the Riches and Happinesss of this Kingdom. The *Sunday* se'nnight following, being the 4th of *November,* the *Princess* fell into Labour, upon which the Council was called. There was a German Midwife (whose Countenance prognosticated ill, she being the very Picture of the French Resident), and Sir *David Hamilton* waited as Physician. The English Ladies all pressed to have the *Princess* laid by Sir *David Hamilton,* but she would not hear of it. The Council, as well as the Family, sat up all Night, but there were no Signs of Delivery. On *Tuesday* the *Princess* had a shivering Fit, which held her a good While, and violently. Everybody but the *Princess* and the Germans were now in a great Fright, which caused the Council to send down for the Countess of *Buckenburgh,* to desire her to let the *Prince* know that they were there to beseech him to have the *Princess* laid by Sir *D. Hamilton;* which he was angry at, and when I came on *Wednesday* Morning I was in Amaze to see the Hurly-burly there was about this Affair. The Midwife had refused to touch the *Princess* unless she and the *Prince* would stand by her against the English 'Frows,' who, she said, were high Dames, and had threatened to hang her if the *Princess* miscarried. This put the *Prince* into such a Passion, that he swore he would fling out of Window whoever had said so, or pretended to meddle. The Duchesses of *St. Albans* and *Bolton* happened to come into the Room, and were saluted with these Expressions. Everybody's Tone was now changed, and Nothing was talked of but the *Princess's* good Labour and Safety. Nay, Lord *Townshend,* to show his Readiness to comply, met the Midwife in the outward Room, and ran and shook and squeezed her by the Hand, and made kind Faces at her: for she understood no Language but German. This I think the Tip-top of all Policy and making One's Court.

The poor *Princess* continued in a languishing Condition till *Friday* night, when she was delivered of a dead Prince.

Notes

*These selections are from *Diary of Mary, Countess Cowper, Lady of the Bedchamber to the Princess of Wales,* ed. C. S. Cowper (London: John Murray, 1864).

1 Caroline of Anspach.

2 Upon the Death of Queen Anne; *she* refers to Princess Caroline.

3 The coronation was that of George I of Hanover, an unhappy day for the Jacobites, supporters of the House of Stuart.

4 Anne, the daughter of Viscount Hatton and the wife of Daniel, second earl of Nottingham.

5 Anne, afterwards princess of Orange, and the Princesses Amelia and Caroline.

6 The king's German minister and one of his principal favorites.

7 A lady of the court.

8 Her second son, afterwards dean of Durham and author, among other works, of *A Dissertation of the Distinct Powers of Reason and Revelation.*

9 James Edward Stuart, known as the Old Pretender, whom The Jacobites wanted to restore to the throne, and who had fomented an unsuccessful rebellion in Scotland.

10 Presumably Mr. Woodford.

11 A Jacobite, taken prisoner at Preston, who escaped to France.

Lady Charlotte Bury

(1775–1861)

LADY CHARLOTTE BURY was the younger daughter of John, fifth duke of Argyll, and Elizabeth Gunning, duchess of Hamilton, and for awhile lady-in-waiting to Charlotte of Mecklenberg, fiancée of the future King George III; in 1810 she became lady-in-waiting to the infamous Caroline, Princess of Wales, who was to be publicly accused of adultery. Bury's beauty was greatly admired at the court of George III, and as a duke's daughter she moved in the highest society. However, in 1796 she married a handsome but impoverished kinsman, John Campbell, who left her widowed at thirty-four with nine children to rear. To enhance her income, she turned to writing, and, after a successful novel in 1812, published thirteen more books, mainly novels, from the 1820s to the 1840s. In 1818 she married the Reverend Edward John Bury, who took it upon himself in 1838 to publish her diary of mainly court scandal and gossip, kept from 1810 to 1820; to preserve her anonymity, he altered the diary to refer to her in the third person. Historically interesting for what it reveals of court and society life, her diary has additional interest for its unintentional revelations of female attitudes. In the brief, but telling, 1819 selection included here from a later restoration of Bury's original diary,* the diarist who writes of her decline is but forty-four years old.

From Charlotte Bury's Diary

17th June 1819   A long lapse in my Diary; but it matters little, for I
have had nothing to record of interest during the last few months. I
find myself now once more immersed in the gaieties of a London
season, in which I had thought I never should again participate. But
my young orphan niece, a girl of great beauty, and not less amiable
than beautiful, and very dear to me, is the object which induces me to
seek such scenes. At first a few of my old acquaintances were amazed
when they discerned my altered and aged face in the gay crowds.
But now their wonder is at an end, and I pass unobserved, like the
rest of the old and the *passées* that nightly haunt the scenes of mirth in
the metropolis. There is no accounting for the fact; yet I must confess
the old stagers, who have without intermission gone on living in
constant dissipation, look less aged than those who have been absent
for some years, on their return to the world. Not one of my contemporaries appears to be half as old as I am; yet many of them have
suffered sad and strange vicissitudes, and lost many friends, even like
myself; nevertheless their countenances do not betray so much anguish as mine does. There is Lady St. Leger, and Mrs. Hillsborough,
and a hundred other ladies past forty, by I will not say how many
years, who look as if they might be my daughters; their well-rouged
cheeks are so smooth—their curls so raven—and their teeth so white.
I will not look worse than they. I have a great mind to begin again
wearing rouge, and get a new "front," and grow young. Yet I shrink
from assuming youth now it is gone. I cannot buy a young heart,
and fling away the old worn-out wearied one that beats feebly within
my aged breast, and is such a faithful warder over the memory of
the bright days of my real youth. Ah, no! fictitious youth is a clumsy
piece of acting. I will not play the part. My pretty Sophy's partners
will not admire her the less because her chaperon looks old:—so be it
then.

   Last night we went to Lady [____]'s concert, and heard some fine
finished singing; but there was nothing of pathos or of sentiment
in the difficult and scientific pieces which were performed. The music,
however, was good enough for all the attention that was paid to it

by the company, who only meet (with few exceptions) to see and be seen, talk and be talked to, and care little in fact for the merits of the music they nominally assemble to listen to. The company was a great mixture of trumpery and finery, like a lady maid's rubbish-box. I saw there Lady C[____]t, who looks all sweetness, though the world says it is only look. Lovely she is without doubt; yet hers was a loveliness which never transported the beholder. Why is this so? The defect must lie within.

Mrs. R[____]y was there also. She is much the same that she was twenty or thirty years ago, only less fire in her eyes. Voilà ce que c'est d'être *une belle laide* et avoir de l'esprit![1] The mind does not deteriorate with time, but the reverse; and it sheds a grace over decaying or faded beauty, that leaves much less to regret. General Alava was there; the only man I should have liked to have been acquainted with; but he was engaged in conversation with Lady S. W[____].

Poor Mrs. G. L[____]e, how she has changed! Her fair freshness gone, and all the ripeness of her youth prematurely withered! Still there is something fine in her full rich lip; and it is some praise to be beaten down with sorrow. I fear she has had her share.

We remained at Lady [____]'s till two in the morning. I was pleased with the music, and amused with my own reflections, more than with any particular circumstance or person I saw—yet wearied with the heat, and happy in the thought that my happiness does not rest in such scenes.

Notes

❧

*These selections are from *The Diary of a Lady-in-Waiting,* ed. A. Frances Steuart, 2 vols. (London and New York: John Lane, 1908); all selections here come from vol. 2.

1   See what it is to be quite homely and yet have spirit.

Emily Shore

(1819–39)

EMILY SHORE was the daughter of an unbeneficed Anglican clergyman, the Reverend Thomas Shore, M.A. of Wadham College,
Oxford, whose religious doubts precluded his advancement in the
church. Therefore he supported himself and his family by taking
in pupils to prepare them for the university. Educated by her parents,
Emily, who capably tutored her four younger siblings in turn, was
a precocious child and an indefatigable scholar. She was especially
interested in history, art, and natural history, of which she was a close
and patient observer who made talented drawings and precise de-
scriptions. But she also wrote stories, poems, and plays. An intellec-
tually ambitious girl who set herself demanding goals despite illness,
she persisted in her studies until she died of tuberculosis at nineteen
on the sland of Madeira, to which she had been removed for her
health. Earlier, her parents had discouraged a relationship with an ad-
mirer because of her illness. From eleven and a half years old until a
fortnight before her death, the articulate Shore kept regular diaries
(1831–39); for the last four years even two separate diaries simulta-
neously: one to record brief accounts of daily family life, another for
more extended reflections. The earlier diaries, for which she composed an index, are given largely to observations of nature. The later
and extended diaries endeavor to be more introspective. But Shore
knew that fear of a reader inhibited her, "had grown into a sort of
unconscious habit, instinctively limiting the extent of my confidence
in ink and paper, so that the *secret chamber of the heart* . . . does not find
in my pen a key to unlock it" (6 July 1838).★ Thus, although she
knew for years that her tuberculosis was advancing, she could not use
her diary to unburden the full weight of her regrets or apprehensions;
she writes instead of the studies that were her solace, as in these
selections from 1837–38.

From Emily Shore's Diary

18 September 1837, Monday   In looking back on the beginning of my illness, I feel sure that one of the principal causes of it was overworking my mind with too hard study, which is no uncommon cause of consumption. For many months before I was actually ill, I tasked my intellectual powers to the utmost. My mind never relaxed, never unbent; even in those hours meant for relaxation, I was still engaged in acquiring knowledge and storing my memory. While dressing, I learnt by heart chapters of the Bible, and repeated them when I walked out, and when I lay in bed; I read Gibbon when I curled my hair at night; at meals my mind was still bent on its improvement, and turned to arithmetic, history, and geography. This system I pursued voluntarily with the most unwearied assiduity, disregarding the increasing delicacy of my health, and the symptoms that it was giving way.

26 September   I am going to turn author. I am writing some articles for the *Penny Magazine,* which I shall first send to Arthur[1] for his inspection. I shall explain to him, with mamma's high approval, and consult him about it, my plan of publishing a book entitled "Extracts from a Naturalist's Journal." I want to know if the market for such works is overstocked.

. . . . . .

1 October, Sunday   . . . My cough is gradually returning with the approach of winter, more than it did last year. My short breath and palpitations of the heart on moving or lying down are very annoying; my heart beats so loud at night that it is like the ticking of a clock. I am subject, too, to pains in the chest and side; and altogether I am very weak and out of health. I feel as if I should never recover the strength of body and unwearied vigour and activity of mind I once possessed. God's will be done, it is meant for the best, though so early in life, when I have but just quitted childhood; it is a painful prospect, and a severe trial both in endurance and anticipation.

2 October, Monday   I am installed housekeeper; mamma has given the whole of the household accounts into my keeping. I am glad of it;

it will greatly assist mamma, and will be of much service to me. I am highly pleased at the idea of making myself of use in some way, now that I cannot do it by teaching my brothers and sisters.

5 October, Thursday   I began regularly to-day the plan of study I intend to pursue for some time. The books I am reading are, "Sketches of Venetian History," "India," in the "Modern Traveller," and the "History of the United States" in Lardner's Cabinet Cyclopaedia. In the morning, I am up but a short time before breakfast, and am employed in my room in reading the Bible till prayer-time. After breakfast, while my own room is being put to rights, I sit in the drawing-room, employed with the "United States." I first draw out (from the book) a short chronological abridgment of my preceding day's lesson; then I read a fresh portion, of course with maps. Then I go and sit in mamma's room, painting one or two maps, by way of relaxing my mind sufficiently. Then I go to my own room, and study chronology. This I do by means of my tables of comparative chronology; I carefully read through a portion of one, and then learn by heart all the dates I think it necessary to remember. This occupies me for some time. Then I take up the Venetian History, doing the same as with that of the United States. I then take up the "India." As yet I have not got further than the geography, natural history, etc., so I do not yet abridge it. In these readings of history, I make great use both of my chronological tables and of the Society maps, which I take in. All this occupies me till about two or three o'clock; till tea at eight, I am employed in taking exercise, in desultory reading, in lying down, and in accidental occupations. After tea I read, in the "Biographie Universelle," the life or lives of one or more distinguished individuals mentioned in my English studies of the day, which both keeps up my knowledge of French, and impresses the history more strongly on my memory.

In addition to this, I learn by heart, or rather keep up what I have already learnt, from the New Testament. This I do while I am curling my hair in the morning.

I do not know whether I shall be strong enough to pursue this system of study very long, particularly as my health seems getting worse. Mamma is afraid of my overworking my mind again; still I cannot bear the idea of living, even in sickness, without systematically acquiring knowledge. So I shall devote myself at present to making myself mistress of history, chronology, and geography; the study of languages, mathematics, arithmetic, and the sciences of mechanics, etc., I must leave until I am quite restored to health.

· · · · ·

25 October, Wednesday It is a great satisfaction to me to find myself daily making a very visible progress in my present studies. I have just finished the first volumes of the Venetian and American histories, abridging each as I go on. With neither of these histories have I been previously acquainted, so that the reading of both adds greatly to my stock of knowledge. I am particularly pleased at the insight the former gives me into the different and complex annals of the great families and principalities of Northern Italy, such as the Carrara of Padua, the della Scala of Verona, and the Visconti of Milan, of whom I before knew little but the name. Really there is hardly any pleasure equal to that of acquiring knowledge. And yet, at the same time, evey step we make in the path of learning opens to us so vast a number of endless vistas and newer tracks (just as in our forest rambles), that it quite discourages one. It is hopeless to think of exhausting all the stores of knowledge. In chronology, too, I am making great progress. I really think my memory is improving, which at my age is more than I could expect.

· · · · ·

7 November, Tuesday . . . I have finished learning from my four charts of general history down to the present time; they are complete in themselves, and begin with ancient history. The first chart contains the histories of the Jews, Greece, Rome, Egypt, and Syria, in comparative columns, to the Christian era; the second, the Roman emperors, those of the East and West, Persia, the caliphs, and I dare say that I shall add to it continually, besides beginning another set of charts.

8 November, Wednesday Finding myself stronger, I am resolved to begin again the study of languages. I rather think I shall study Greek one week and Latin another. I began to-day with Greek, and spent about half an hour on it, which is the utmost I shall give to either that or Latin at present. My intention is to resume Herodotus, of which I have already read three books, pursue it regularly through and, besides, read alternately a speech of Demosthenes and a Greek play. As my time is now so much more occupied, I only read the Indian History every other day.

• • • • •

14 November, Tuesday . . . This reading of lives is very laborious, and always leaves me thoroughly fatigued. Papa and mamma are both afraid that I am overtasking my brain again. But what shall I do? It is so delightful to be at all able to study again, and I have so much lost time to make up for, that I really cannot restrain myself. Sometimes I am quite disheartened at the huge mountain of knowledge which I have to climb, and feel myself like an ant at the foot of the Andes. Still it is encouraging to see what can be done by exertion and industry, and I am gratified to find myself making a very visible progress every day. I now generally spend the last half-hour or twenty minutes be-fore tea in reading Shakespeare, being then so tired with my matter-of-fact studies as to require some relaxation in the way of works of imagination. I am at present engaged with the "Tempest."

15 November, Wednesday I have begun to teach geography to Mackworth[2] regularly on the following plan:—I give him the name of some town, as Jerusalem; he is to examine the maps, and find out every town of note on the same degree of latitude; the next day he is to tell me them, and give an account of their situation, and everything he can find in books about their history, natural productions, etc. This is, I think, a useful and entertaining way of learning geography.

17 November, Friday . . . I usually repeat a chapter from the Bible by heart while I am dressing in the morning, and a chart of genealogy (from about seventy to a hundred dates) while undressing at night.

• • • • •

15 December, Friday Well, it is of no use to go on always struggling with weakness and incapability of exertion, I cannot hold out for ever; and now I begin to feel thoroughly ill. I am afraid I must relax.

16 December, Saturday   I have now concluded my batch of writings
for the *Penny Magazine,* and I find it no small relief to be rid for the
present of the cares of authorship! I do not think I could have gone on
with it much longer, in my present state of health, especially as I am
now suffering from pain in the side. How ridiculous that, at the age of
seventeen, I should have anything to do with the cares of authorship!
It makes me laugh. The articles I have just finished are, "Account
of the Willow-wren," "A Tame Squirrel," and "Anecdotes of Dogs."

. . . . .

25 December, Monday, Christmas Day   And am I really eighteen years
old? Am I no longer a child, and are so many of the years allotted
to me for intellectual and spiritual improvement already past? How
quickly they have flown! How appalling is the progress of time, and
the approach of eternity! To me, that eternity is perhaps not far distant; let me improve life to the utmost while it is yet mine, and if my
span on earth must indeed be short, may it yet be long enough to
fit me for an endless existence in the presence of my God.

. . . . .

5 January 1838, Friday   . . . Of all these [papers] by far the most interesting to me was the number for the last month of the *Penny Magazine,* which I have been longing to see, for I knew it was to contain my
articles. I seized it, but before I had opened it, papa, also in great
glee, took it into his own hands, and looked into it while I poured out
the tea. My brothers and sisters, too, and even Tilla,[3] were all watching anxiously, and I believe all were delighted to see in the title-page
the words, "Account of a Young Cuckoo," and "The Golden-Crested
Wren." My feelings were very odd at this moment; I can hardly explain them. So I am actually in print, have actually begun my career as
an authoress! I say career, for I fully hope to follow it up. And I have
begun it, too, at the age of seventeen, for though I am now eighteen,
my birthday had not taken place when these little articles were published. It seems to me very odd. Three articles of mine are now in
print—those which I have mentioned, and two anecdotes, and I shall
soon see some more. At night, when I went into Tilla's room, she
very coolly said, "Emily, if you ever become a very clever woman,

and distinguish yourself, I shall certainly write your life, and this night shall enter into it!" "Oh, Tilla!" I said, shouting with laughter, "what a ludicrous idea! That's taking it for granted that I am to die first!" "But I may write your life while you are alive, may I not? I am determined to do it."

27 January, Saturday . . . So that on the whole I think I have crammed a good deal of fresh information into my pate to-day, and it is very encouraging for me to know that without any trouble I shall retain nearly all of it. Nevertheless, as often happens with me, in the middle of my reading, the conviction of the utter hopelessness of ever learn-ing a millionth part of all I ought to learn, and of the littleness of what I have already learnt, suddenly darted into my mind so forcibly, that it cast a gloom over me, and, in a melancholy and desponding fit, I felt for a time inclined to give up altogether the gigantic task of acquiring knowledge, and I seriously debated whether I should not do so. But the thought that by cultivating my mind I might render my-self some day useful to others finally decided the question; otherwise, had only my own gratification been concerned, I doubt whether I might not have come to a different determination. And this is no new story with me; my despondency at times is almost overpowering.

· · · · ·

9 April, Monday . . . I have been for some days so busy with the needle that I have not had much time to devote to study. However, I have managed to read in the *Cyclopaedia* to-day the lives of the great Elector of Brandenburg and all the Kings of Prussia to the present one; to look over again the history of Este; and to continue the life of Napoleon. Being very much fatigued with my walk, I was obliged to lie down, and while on my bed I read, or rather skimmed, the reigns of Louis XIII., XIV., and XV. in Eyre Evan Crowe's "History of France," for the sake of getting a good general view of those times. I also continued exercising myself in dates, and learning new ones.

· · · · ·

6 July, Friday The eleventh volume of my journal, begun, like the two last, at Bartley Lodge, our lovely home in the Forest, but where it will end I know not.

I always consider this a memorable day to me, being the anniversary
of that on which, two years ago, I went to Hastings with the faint
hope of its benefiting my health, at a time when I felt dying. Yet it has
pleased Heaven to prolong my life up to the present time, as so far
to restore my health that with care it may not be materially shortened.
Even this, indeed, I sometimes doubt in my secret soul; for though I
am not steadily going back, yet I do not go forward in the progress to
strength.

My cough, however, is materially better to-day. I even joined the
rest of the party for half an hour in drinking tea at seven o'clock at
Beechwood, in the garden too, which we found very pleasant. . . .

· · · · ·

14 July, Saturday   Here is a query, which I shall be able to answer
decidedly at the end of this volume, most likely before. What is indi-
cated by all these symptoms—this constant shortness of breath, this
most harassing hard cough, this perpetual expectoration, now tinged
with blood, this quick pulse, this painfully craving appetite, which
a very little satisfies even to disgust, these restless, feverish nights,
continual palpitations of the heart, and deep, circumscribed flushes? Is
it consumption really come at last, after so many threatenings? I am
not taken by surprise, for I have had it steadily, almost daily, in view
for two years, and have always known that my lungs were delicate.
I feel no uneasiness on the subject, even if my ideas (I cannot call
them fears) prove right. It must be my business to prepare for another
world; may God give me grace to do so![4]

Notes

❧

Journal of Emily Shore [ed. not identified] (London: Kegan Paul, Trench, and Trübner, 1898), p. 263. All selections here come from this edition.

1 The diary does not identify Arthur further.

2 Her brother.

3 Matilda, who is visiting with the Shores, perhaps a cousin.

4 Shore died a year later, in July 1839.

Elizabeth George

(Nineteenth century)

LITTLE IS KNOWN about Elizabeth George, except that she was the daughter of a farmer at Stowe, a tenant of the duke of Buckingham in the mid-nineteenth century, and had two married sisters living nearby. Her mother died in George's infancy, and her father in 1844. During the diary period she was serving as her bachelor uncle's housekeeper. Seemingly she was past the marriageable age for her times and had no aspirations to leave home. Her published diary covers mainly two occasions on which she entertained guests of the duke, first the luncheon in 1840 excerpted here and then a coming-of-age celebration for the marquis of Chandos in 1847 that was even more taxing on local hospitality. The diary appears to have been written up retrospectively, though probably soon after the events. Characteristically—for she is not accustomed to praising herself, except perhaps for domestic skills—George deprecates her engaging diary as "written in a careless piecemeal sort of way at odd times, and I know it is very badly composed and full of mistakes." But she composed her two accounts because her family feeling was strong, she was evidently proud of sustaining the family honor by serving the duke, and she wanted, as she says rather wistfully, to leave an account for "the young people amongst our kindred who may come after us. . . . I know I should have been highly delighted had I ever found a book of this sort. . . . I have never even had the happiness of seeing a letter of my dear Mother's—I should have consider'd one quite a treasure (1847).★ Hardworking and selfless, George extended unstinting hospitality, even on short notice, and without caring about participating in any festivities. Though her uncle is referred to as "the Duke of Buckingham's 'good old Tenant' at Stowe," the reference perhaps applies even better to her.

From Elizabeth George's Diary

30 January 1840   Memorable as the day on which we had the honour
to entertain two Royal Personages, together with his grace the Duke
of Buckingham and Chandos, several other noblemen and a large
party of untitled gentlemen all 30 people.

The Duke of Buckingham had for some years made a practice of
coming to luncheon with my uncle several times during each shooting
season—in fact our house appeared to be quite a favourite rendezvous
with his Grace and not without good cause—I will venture to say.
In the first place our family had been Tenants of the same farm in
regular succession from father to son, for 240 years, ever since the
land had been purchased by Sir Thomas Temple and the present Duke
has told us, that he finds from old title deeds, our farm and some
other lands adjoining, belonged to a John George, before it became
the property of the Temples of Stowe. It is therefore very probable
that the farm had been *occupied* by our fore fathers long before they
ceased to be the owners.

Notwithstanding this, my Uncle never presumed the least on the
influence such a position might be expected to give him over his
Landlord. He was always the most upright and straight-forward of
Tenants with an independent spirit that would have scorn'd to seek for
favour in any underhand way, altho' he had for 20 years suffered
grievously from Game depredation[1] (to such an extent that we did not
get the seed again on the ploughed land, and had never had compensation for the loss) yet he had (altho' a plain Farmer) such a nice sense
of what was handsome and honourable, that he would never make
the least complaint or ask for any redress when the Duke came to see
us—he said it would be taking an unfair advantage as the Duke could
not very well refuse when seated at our table and being gratuitously
entertained with all the Gentlemen of his party. It was not therefore
surprising that he should say he 'never felt so comfortable or so much
at home as when sitting with Uncle his "good Old Tenant"'—I think
myself Uncle carried his delicacy rather too far some times, he certainly did a great injustice to himself, and it served to encourage the

Duke in his unfair and wasteful preservation of Game. However let that pass—no matter how great cause we might have to complain, his Grace was always so exceedingly kind and affable in his behaviour and of so noble and distinguish'd a presence that he possessed a sort of fascination that made most people forget everything at the time, except the pleasure of being in his company.

For my own part, I always felt quite at my ease when conversing with him and was pleased to afford him the best accommodation in my power. Our house being large and generally pretty well provisioned made it less trouble to us, though it would have been to some others and his Grace used to laugh and say, he liked to bring a large party, because Uncle was an old 'Batchelor so he would have no pity upon him and would give him a good benefit'.

He had been here twice before during the present winter—and we heard that it was expected the Queen's Uncle and cousin (the Duke of Cambridge and Prince George) would come to stay a few days at Stowe before the shooting season was over. On the evening that the firing of cannon and the bells announced the arrival of the Royal Visitors I said to Uncle, 'Suppose the Duke should bring them here to lunch some day when they are out shooting'—my supposition was held to be a great improbability—for Uncle said, "O he wont think of coming here when they are with him'. So I felt in a manner free from anxiety on that point and was thankful to be so, for I had taken a cold, which caused severe inflammation of my chest and lungs, insomuch that I could not even *whisper* a single word, and my doctor enjoined perfect quiet, desiring that I would keep in bed a few days.

We had been compelled to dismiss our Dairymaid, and her successor only arrived two days before, the other girl was comparatively a stranger, coming the last Michaelmas, and did not know where to find any things that were not in common use.

I knew the Duke had pass'd through the village accompanied by his Royal Visitors and a large party and I understood they were shooting on our farm, but felt little concern about their movements thinking I should have nothing to do in it—therefore I was sadly startled and almost shudder'd in my bed after hearing a thundering rap at the front door—the Girl answered it, and I recognised the head keeper's voice and distinctly heard him say 'the Duke desires his compliments to Mr George and if quite agreeable will come and take Lunch with him' and I was to say, 'the party would be 30 in number'. This message was repeated to Uncle and the answer he returned was 'Tell his Grace I shall be pleased to accommodate himself and friends in the best way I can'.

In a few minutes both the maids rush'd upstairs to tell me, not thinking that I had overheard the message—I took my slate and chalk being obliged to write every word I had to say. They held up their hands exclaiming "Whatever shall we do'. Ill as I felt I saw that I must get up, tho' I knew what additional suffering it would cause me, and it was impossible I could dress and write directions to them at one and the same time. So I desired they would go light fires in the Parlour and sitting room—also get a good fire made in the kitchen and plenty of boiling water. I knew, rump of beef had been boiled for dinner, there was also part of a roast spare rib and some raised pork pies—mince pie etc., but the beef was of course neither hot nor cold then—so I ordered it to be set out at the cellar window on the snow, and I knew what we had ready cooked in the house was not sufficient to set out a table for 30 persons. I told the Girls to ask Uncle to come up to me; when he came he seemed inclined to take the matter very easily and begged I would not hurry or flurry myself. I said 'Uncle it is no use preparation must be made directly, there is but little time before us, they will be here in less than 2 hours'.

There are two couples of Fowls put up to feed—they must be killed directly and prepar'd for roasting, we shall also require a large dish of frizzled ham—gravy and egg sauce and plenty of hot mesh'd potatoes—he said it could *not* be done. I said, it must be done it would never do to accede to the Duke's proposal and not prepare what was sufficient (all this I had to write) and I wrote 'now pray dont ask more questions than you can help, but please do as I ask you without questioning me, for I shall never get thro' it if I have to hinder all the time to write'. I said, 'have the fowls killed, put them into a pan and tell the Girl to cover them with boiling water and let them lie a few minutes; the feathers will then strip off quickly—there is not time to pluck them, then if she draws them and gets a good fire, I will be with her to make gravy and sauce if I am able to stand'—and I asked him to have the pony saddled and get a large flag basket ready while I wrote a hasty note to each of my two sisters who lived near, requesting them to send all the butter they could spare, also any ready cooked meat—adding 'I will repay you in kind next week.' The boy was to go to Anne at Brick Kiln farm first, then on to Mrs Bennett at New Inn.

When I got downstairs, so many things had to look'd out, and so much to do, I really hardly knew however I should get all done, had I been only tolerably well and able to speak, I should not have minded it a bit, but it was so distressing to me for I could not move my arms without paining my chest and there was nothing I could quite leave to the Girls, not even to get the mesh'd potatoes done, and I had to be present and help set the tables as well as to help cook. Our dining table when set out full length in the large parlour, would not, I knew, seat more than 20 or 22 comfortably—so I set out the centre table in the sitting room for eight—taking care to have a large cheerful fire in each—there was also a large fire in the front kitchen, as well as in the back where we work'd.

I had 3 wash stands with plenty of napkins in the front kitchen, also a lot of Uncle's stockings airing before the fire—in case any wet footed Gentleman should require a change of dry, and had a sofa set along before that fire and my couch in front of the sitting room fire.

When the rooms were ready I felt so ill and exhausted that I should have been glad to creep any where to lie down, but that could not be, I had got the sauce to make and to see to the fowls and the boiled ham and before it was quite ready the whole company came flocking in, glad to get out of the snow—it was half an hour before the appointed time.

The Duke was as usual very kind—Uncle had told him I could not speak, but he little thought how ill I was—he said 'I will see that every one well cleans his shoes'—and set the example himself, the royal Duke and the prince also following his example, very energetically scraping and brushing their boots before they came in. I was introduced to them by the Duke, who very considerately spoke for me for the Duke of Cambridge like his father George the Third is remarkable for asking a multitude of unnecessary frivolous questions. He was thoroughly soaked about the feet, and took his place on the couch in front of the fire ordering his own tall Game Keeper might be sent in to act as Valet—so, in stalked a gigantic keeper and kneeling down on the hearthrug he drew off his royal Master's wet boots and stockings and exchang'd them for others that he had got ready in his pocket.

The Duke meantime turning his head round to stare at me, when I was obliged to go in for some thing that I wanted, I should have drawn back when I saw how the two were occupied, but he said 'O come in, never mind an old gentleman like me. What is your name and how long have you kept your Uncle's house?'—I could not speak to answer, so made a curtsey and escaped out of the room as speedily as I could.

All the others had washed their hands and gone into the large parlour. I soon found some of them would be willing[2] to come back into the sitting room to take their lunch at the table I had set there.

It was impossible all could sit at the same table as the Duke and other grandees, but they were determined to remain in the same room so three or four Captains and the Mayor of Buckingham drew a side table in front of the large sofa and wedged themselves in to it some way without any table cloth, merely asking the Girl who waited to fetch them some knives and forks with the cruets out of the other room. Our Duke insisted that Uncle would take the head of the table, which he would rather not have done, but his Grace said 'Nobody shall sit at the head of your table but yourself' and 'you must carve for his Royal Highness who will sit at your right hand'.

Accordingly, they were placed so, the Duke of Cambridge on one side, and Prince George on the other, then the Duke of Buckingham, Lord De L'isle and Dudley, Lords Holland and Hotham, Sir Wm. Clayton, George Simon Harcourt, M.P. for Bucks and others of less

note, Colonel Hall, Captains Johnson, Neville, Carrington and
Dewes.

I thought when I looked round the room, how immeasurably inferior all the rest were to the Duke of Buckingham, in person and
deportment—as for the Duke of Cambridge so far as manners went I
should have considered he was a vulgar old man even had he been a
Farmer—his son, Prince George[,] was much more decorous, and
evidently felt greatly annoyed by the vicious and frivolous discourse
of his Papa—The young Prince has a fine, tall lithe figure and not bad
features, but a blotchy, bad complexion.

I only went into the room now and then, the poor girl who waited,
said, directly I disappeared, the Duke of Cambridge talk'd to her in
such a way that she would have left them to wait upon themselves had
it not been for 'Master' and the Duke of Buckingham. She said she
hardly knew how to be thankful enough to Uncle when he spoke up
so fearlessly to vindicate her character. She said, the Queen's Uncle
must had led a loose, bad life himself or he would not have been
so suspicious of other people.

His Royal Highness did not indulge in that kind of language when I
was present, but I thought what I heard him say, was very frivolous
and ridiculous, among other speeches (he talked incessantly) he said to
Uncle—'I say do you know that you are kin to me'. What answer
could Uncle give to such a question, he simply said 'No'. His Royal
Highness ask'd if he was not the 'Son of Farmer George'. Uncle said
"yes'—'Well then,' replied the Duke, 'I am also the son of "Farmer
George" so we must be kin I think'. He had seen our draining machine
standing in the Dairy Ground—wanted to know if that was the ruin
of a favourite old tree and if Uncle had not put the frame and chain
round it to preserve it, and then, casting his eyes up suddenly to the
ceiling he said 'What is up over here? bedrooms I suppose, how many
bedrooms have you etc, etc' and many more questions equally trifling. His Royal Highness certainly was very affable, showed no hau-
teur, but one naturally expects some kind of dignity in a Prince of
the Royal blood, and I had always understood the Duke of Cambridge
to be the best of George the 3rd's numerous sons. After partaking

very heartily of our lunch, the company had wine and departed. When the Duke of Buckingham observed that His Royal Highness did not let Uncle fill his glass again after the 3rd time he said 'O my G—d, I cant drink any more I am as full now as ever I can stick'. Which I thought we should have considered rather a vulgar reply had the speaker been an old Farmer, instead of being H.R.H. the Duke of Cambridge.

Candles had been lighted two hours and it was nearly 7 o'clock before our Guests departed. The Duke of Buckingham asked if the Shooting Omnibus had arrived to convey them up to Stowe, he found it was waiting in the yard—several Gentlemen preferred walking, the Prince for one.

I heard a few days later that the Duchess was very much displeased because the Duke did not come home earlier, all the Gentlemen having of course to dress, which delayed the dinner half an hour.

The head Cook was also aggrieved, having exerted his abilities to set on a first rate Banquet.

All the Shooters had already spoiled their appetites and could not do justice to what was placed before them.

The Duke found fault with his cooks—saying—he found things much more to his taste at Farm houses particularly vegetables. His Grace forgot to make allowance for the difference there must be between a keen, and cloyed appetite—and perhaps did not know how a dinner was deteriorated in quality by remaining half an hour beyond the time specified.

Everybody seemed to think we had been highly honour'd; yet I much doubt whether any of our neighbours would have willingly incurred the trouble.

I *know* I was not able to get up for a week afterwards.

When Uncle went to Buckingham on Saturday, the first persons he met were Messrs Hearn and Smith the Lawyers, who jokingly enquired whether he would condescend to shake hands with them after having entertained a Royal Duke and a Prince.

Notes

❧

*"The Journal of Elizabeth George, 1840–47. Kept at the farmhouse of the Duke of Buckingham's 'good old Tenant' at Stowe," *Cornhill*, no. 180 (Summer 1974): 311. All other selections here come from pp. 283–89 of this edition.

1   That is, from having his crops destroyed by the game that the duke kept for the sake of the hunt.

2   Has George (or her *Cornhill* editor?) perhaps omitted the word *not?* The next paragraph shows the guests *un*willing to dine in the sitting room.

Emily Pepys

(1833–77)

EMILY PEPYS (pronounced "Peppis") was the youngest daughter of
Henry Pepys, then bishop of Worcester, and of Maria Sullivan Pepys.
The bishop's official seat was Hartlebury Castle near Kidderminster,
but because the bishop attended the House of Lords the family maintained a London home as well. From the diary Pepys kept for seven
months (July 1844–January 1845), begun when she was ten years
old and covering a return to Hartlebury, come the following engaging
excerpts for 1844. Pepys had two older brothers and a sister, of all of
whom she was clearly fond; two other siblings had died in infancy
and two more sisters, next in age to Pepys, had died of scarlet fever
probably not long before the diary opens. She was taught at home by
her mother and then, though her diary shows she anticipated the
change with distaste, by a governess. In 1854, in a youthful wish come
true, she was to marry a clergyman, the Reverend William Henry
Lyttelton, thirteen years her senior and soon to take over the Lyttleton
family living at Hagley in Worcestershire, where she would spend all
her married life. She died childless. Life in the Pepys household as
presented by precocious Emily was most agreeable, with frequent
visits from and to cousins and family friends, dances that she delighted
in, and local outings and activities. Although significantly for her
times she was allowed to read imaginative books and sometimes reports herself enjoying them, she was evidently not a bookish child,
preferring outdoor games instead. Of her speculations on her neighbors, her enthusiasm for preadolescent crushes, and her estimates
of sermons, she writes with great candor. Her diary is inscribed
"Journal belonging to Miss Emily Pepys who began to write it July
4th 1844 aged 10 her first Journal,"* as if many more such books were
intended. But if the articulate Pepys kept up her record, unfortunately
no other pages have survived.

From Emily Pepys's Diary

Sunday, 7th July 1844   Went to Church in the morning and had a very dull sermon which I do not think I learnt much from, as I am afraid I did not pay much attention.

·   ·   ·   ·   ·

Monday, 15th July   A beautiful day. In the afternoon Mama and I went to the school, which I always like very much. I think in that way I shall be quite fit to be Teddy's wife, as he is going to be clergyman.[1] I long to go to Mrs. Clark's to give her my baby clothes. At Botleys they gave me a book called "Influence"[2] to read, and I think it did me a great deal of good, the "Ellen" there was so like me, and I only hope I shall improve as she did. Since I read that I have felt much happier, and have prayed to God much oftener than I used. Last night at Desert Papa and Mama told me to go to bed at 9 instead of half past which I am sorry to say I did not do as I ought to have done. Instead of saying "Hey me" and gone when I was told, I began speaking crossly, and said that Mama told me I need not go till half past in the summer, but I hope another time I shall be a better girl. In reading "Influence" I had a good lesson how nothing can be done without praying to God to help you, so I have prayed that I might do what I was told without being cross. Mama told me yesterday that Alfred Tyler would not come here certainly and most likely Gwinnet would not, therefore I thought of course, [*gap*] and Teddy would come or at least some of them, but when I asked Mama, she said that she was not very anxious to see them, whether she had guessed about Teddy and me I do not know, but I hope he will come at all events.

Thursday, 18th July   I am happy to say Mama has written to Aunt Harriet to ask her to bring her two girls and to leave the *three* boys in charge of their tutor, which though of course I am very sorry Teddy does not come yet it is something to have Cay and Louy. Aunt Harriet has not answered the letter yet, so we do not even know whether they will come but I hope they will. Mama also wrote to Mrs. Stuart Sullivan to ask her and Harriet and Katey to come here for a few days which of course I shall like very much, though Herbert[3] does say that they are two romping bouncing girls. I am very fond indeed of

Harriet from the little I saw of her in London. Being so nearly my age and so exactly like me in every way, I certainly think we shall be great friends: I hope she will love me! I think Katey will get rather in the way, but I shall see when the time comes. Perhaps Herbert may take a fancy to her and get in love with her, but then I am afraid he will get in my way, though I ought not to think so. Their answer is not come yet, and I dare say never will come, as we do not know exactly where they are. If the Railroad is made from Worcester to Cardiff how jolly we shall go to Cottrell. Teddy has not written to me for a very long time, but I have written to him very often.

Friday, 19th July   A very showery day, and a little thunder. The Bishop of Durham and Mrs. Maltby, Mr. and Mrs. Sandford came here yesterday to stay till Monday. I like the Bishop very much and all the rest tolerably; the Bishop is very deaf with one ear, which is rather disagreeable. Today we went out in the morning but being caught by a shower of rain we were obliged to come in and then I did not go out again as I was obliged to come in to my horrid music which I think is a great bore sometimes. This afternoon we went to Stourport to see about a boat which Papa is going to let us have; the man showed us one which Papa said was too long and narrow, and I think myself it was not a very safe one. He says it must be 20 ft. long and 5 ft. broad, but the man said he would be about a month making that, and as we want it by the time the Tylers come here, that would not exactly do, so I think the best way will be, either to write a note to the man at Bristol and ask him to send us one as we know the size, or else to ask Gwinnet to go down to Bristol and get us one, but I hope we shall get one soon anyhow. Last night Louisa[4] and Herbert played at Chess, I read "Martin Chuzzlewit" and the others talked. After tea I went to bed, and even offered myself, which I thought at the time was very good, but was no more than I ought to have done. Tonight Herbert and I had a conversation about being shy. I think Mama says that being shy is merely being afraid of what people think of you. Tonight we had a dinner party, Mr. and Mrs. Ingram dined here, and Mr. and Mrs. Claughton dined and sleep one night. At Desert I sat next to Mrs. Claughton which I liked very much, as I like her very

much; we talked and even laughed a great deal, and it was altogether
very pleasant. After Desert we were idle part of the time and then
for something to do we went to the round table to look at some medals and to say "yes, that is very *Bewe-we-we-weteful*" which was not
very amusing, even so dull that Herbert went to bed. A little time
after that Mama at the request of Mrs. Claughton, played the Polka.
A little time after that Henry[5] and Louisa at the request of the same
person, began to Polk, and then I was very sorry that Herbert had
gone to bed as I had nobody to Polk with. Mrs. Claughton and Mama
sang a Duet and then Mrs. Claughton sent me all the way to the
Pink room to get her singing book, which I was very glad of, as I like
obliging anybody I like. After that Mrs. Sandford sent me all the way
to the Blue Room, or rather to the end of the Gallery, to get her Music
Book, but when I had got there Mr. Sandford came running out,
and said he thought he could get it quicker than me, "a great insult to
such legs as mine". About 11 went to bed.

Saturday, 20th July   Was up and dressed at 8 and instead of doing
lessons went out with Louisa and Mrs. Sandford and was very tired.
When I came in to my great delight I found Mama had had a letter
from Mrs. Stuart Sullivan to say she would have great pleasure in
coming here with Harriet and Katey on Saturday next to stay till
Wednesday. After breakfast we went out and Mrs. Claughton insulted
me (as she generally does once every time she comes) by saying,
when I offered her my hand down the steep steps, "Much good you
would do me if I was to lean on your hand" which I did not like at all.
After luncheon Mama and the company went out in the carriage—
Henry and Herbert went out riding—and Louisa and I went to the
park to read. I read the "White Lady" a *ghost story,* then we talked
about the delightful time to come when the Stuart Sullivans come and
then the Tylers and the Disbrowes, then we came home. We had another dinner party tonight, Mr. and Mrs. Talbot, Mr. Hastings and
Captain Winnington. At Desert I took my glass to Papa and asked for
a little wine, and while I was there Mr. Talbot said to me "Young
Ladies generally ask their partners how they are". At first I did not
know what he meant, as I did not remember having danced with him

at Mrs. Peel's. It was very awkward for me as I could not go up and put my hand between him and Mrs. Maltby to shake hands with him. After Desert we were sitting together and all of a sudden he came up to me and said "Have you made any conquests in London". I looked at Louisa and Herbert, not knowing the least what he meant till at last he said "Did you win anybody's heart in London". I blushed deeply and faintly said "no" for I thought of Villiers Lister, though that did not amount to "winning his heart" I believe. Mrs. Talbot looked very *glum* as if she was a wee bit jealous, though I am sure she need not fear, for I do not care for Mr. Talbot, on the contrary I think he takes great liberties, and sometimes is very tiresome to me. Louisa and I played our Duet, and the first thing Mama said this morning was "How execrably bad you played your Duet last night" but *I* did not think so. We went to bed about half past ten.

Sunday, 21st July Up and dressed by quarter past 8 this morning to breakfast, as Mama, Papa and the company went to Worcester to see the Judges go to the Cathedral. We went to Church, and had a sermon from Mr. Baker, which was rather too old for us, so I did not pay much attention, and the Church was dreadfully hot. The Text was from 17th John Gospel 8th verse, it was a charity sermon for the Christian Knowledge Society. Mama gave us each half a crown apiece to put in. In the afternoon we had a dull sleepy sermon from Mr. Niven—thought of Teddy and Harriet S. Sullivan all the time. Mama came home about 6 dreadfully tired. Judge Tindal, Marshall Tindal and Marshall Erskine dined here today. Marshall Erskine took Louisa into dinner and I thought seemed rather "tender towards her", but perhaps it was only a small piece of flirting. He seemed a nice young man, and I don't think I should object to having him for my brother-in-law. It was a very warm evening and we went out for a little while.

· · · · ·

Tuesday, 23rd July Another very hot day and now I am nearly roasted.

Wednesday, 24th July Herbert and I have proposed to make another harmonicon [harmonica] as now we have only three instruments and four to play. I am going to make one for Louisa. We have great fun now in the morning when we go out in having small concerts out of doors. This morning we sat down in the boat and played. This afternoon I have not been quite so good as I ought to have been, as when Mama told me to do my work I did not do it at first as it was so dreadfully hot, but after a long time I did 6 stitches. When Mr. Sandford was here, he said he would get us some bows and arrows in London and we expected them last night but they did not come. At present we propose shooting by the side of the avenue which will be a very nice place I think. I hope soon we shall be good *Archers and Archeresses*. I think at least our bows and arrows will come tomorrow. This evening we went out, but it was very damp and foggy, and altogether I did not like it at all and I almost thought something was going to happen.

Thursday, 25th July   I had the oddest dream last night that I ever dreamt; even the remembrance of it is very extraordinary. There was a very nice pretty young *lady,* who I (a girl) was going *to be married to!* (the very idea!). I loved her and even now love her very much. It was quite a settled thing and we were to be married very soon. All of a sudden I thought of Teddy and asked Mama several times if I might be let off and after a little time I woke. I remember it all perfectly. A very foggy morning but Henry said it would be fine, but I do not think it has. It feels very *thundery*. This afternoon we began making our Harmonicons. I did not succeed very well, and got rather out of patience. Sent one piece to the Carpenter to plane, as that is the only thing we cannot master. Went out for about half an hour. It rained hard, this evening, so we did not go out.

· · · · ·

Saturday, 3rd August   A very wet day, so we none of us went to Worcester except Papa, so I was not able to get anything for Harriet. Today everybody is cross to me except dear Mama and Papa who never are. Henry is unbearing. It is all I can do to restrain my temper, which I am afraid does break out rather oftener than it ought to do. Sometimes I cannot help crying. Our bows and arrows came last night though now it is so wet that we cannot shoot. I think Mr. Sandford must have forgot them till Papa wrote. We began shooting yesterday and liked it very much. I shoot at present about 40 yds. I should think. Sometimes I shot very bad and sometimes pretty well but never hit the target. Louisa hit it twice, once in the red and once in the outer white but then she shot much longer than we did as she shot before breakfast and after dinner. Of course Henry shot the best as he is used to it at Cambridge but he did not hit the bull's eye once. I was not so much laughed at by Henry as I expected but he seemed to think my shooting a horrid bore. As I only shoot about half way I have my turn after the others have all done, which I do not like so much. I have hit the target twice but just as I expected Henry said there was not near so much merit in my hitting it as I only stood half way.

Wednesday, 7th August   This being Mama's birthday we had a holiday and were out shooting all morning. Louisa did not hit the target at all for some time but at last she hit the *bull's eye* which I shall for the future call the *gold* as that is the proper name. Have got a cold in my head. I was determined to be the first to wish dearest Mama "Many happy returns of the day" on her birthday, so of course was glad of an excuse which was, that I was to go in at about 7 and ask if I might go out. At the same time I wished her the "happy returns". I wanted to give her her present at breakfast time as we always do, but Louisa, Henry and Herbert all said that we had better not, as the Stuarts were in the house. Our present was a box-wood case for letters answered and unanswered—Papa's was [a] handsome velvet workbox ornamented with gold. Altogether she seemed to like her presents very much. . . .

· · · · ·

Friday, 9th August   This is my birthday, I am eleven years old today. Henry[,] Louisa and Herbert gave me the prettiest little penholder I ever saw. It was white spotted with something bright—a little ring of Turquoises round the bottom—a little silver hand to hold the pen, with a ruby on its finger. Mama gave me a nice little Harmonicon, it was not quite such a nice one as the first one I had, which is now spoilt, but it has very good tones. Of course we had a holiday.

Saturday, 10th August   Today the Stuarts went away, and also Miss Millish and Miss Smith did, who I believe I forgot to say came on Thursday. It was tonight too that we heard of poor dear Mrs. Wood's death: she was quite delirious poor thing, but was sensible before she died. She asked to see her baby and the doctor said she should see it the next morning. "I do not think I shall see anybody tomorrow morning" was her answer, meaning she would be dead, but she did not die till 11 o'clock the next morning. She was a dear creature, and though she was so much older than me I was as fond of her as anybody; she was about twenty I think, and had just had her first child, who is, I believe, at present quite well, though it did go and see its poor mother before she died. I am afraid she must have caught from the doctor, who was attending her in her confinement. It is indeed a sad thing for the poor parents, but all we can say is "God's will be done". He alone can support us in the hours of trial. I believe poor Mr. Ingram was heard to utter a piercing shriek when the news of her death was brought to him. Since we have been here that family has had nothing but misfortunes, a son first, then a son-in-law, then a nephew and lastly poor Mrs. Wood who they doted upon. . . .

Sunday, 11th August   Not a very fine day. Went to Church both morning and afternoon. Had a beautiful sermon in the morning from Mr. Baker, who seemed to preach it upon Mrs. Wood's death, as it was upon that subject. It was the first sermon I ever heard that I was sorry when it was over, but I really was in this, for I felt that probably as soon as I was out of the church I should forget it. I do not think I ever heard a more affecting sermon. In the afternoon it rained as we went and we came back. Had a dull sleepy sermon from Mr. Niven, not to be compared to Mr. Baker's.

· · · · ·

Tuesday, 13th August   Today poor Gwinnet went away at half past five, so that we were obliged to wish him Goodbye over night. Of course we felt lonely without him, and I do not think we shall see him again for a long time. In the afternoon, Papa[,] Tiny[,] Louisa and I went out walking. The conversation turned upon what profession her brothers were to be in. I am very sorry she said dear Teddy wanted to go out to India, which I should not like at all, as I should like to be a clergyman's wife. When we were at Cottrell he said he was to be a clergyman, and when I go back I must try and persuade so to be. We polked again this evening.

Wednesday, 21st August   Today there was a grand cricket match at Waresley against the Stourport Club, we all went to see it, but I am sorry to say the Stourport beat, by a hundred. Herbert Peel plays very well, and was very much applauded. I am rather laughed at about Herbert Peel, as Robert happened to say that when I was at Waresley I never danced with anyone else, which was quite false, so now they all laugh at me about it; my love for Teddy has rather gone down. Tomorrow being Mr. Peel's birthday, we are to go to Waresley and have a nice little dance, which will be very nice. I believe the little Bakers are to be there, which I am very glad of, as they will make some nice partners for me.

Thursday, 22nd August   Today Mr. Peel is 46 years old I believe. We had capital fun at the ball, if so it may be called, at Mr. Peel's. We went about 9 o'clock, the Bakers came in just afterwards, and I suppose we began dancing about half past 9. We danced Quadrilles, Waltzes, 5 or 6 Polkas, 2 or 3 Lancers, Boulanger, Mazurka. I did not dance the Mazurka as I do not know it, but it seemed to be very easy. I do not much like being so much flattered when I dance, there is always "This is my favourite partner", "This little girl dances it the best", "You always know everything perfectly", "How very prettily you dance it" going on. I like a little of it but not so much. Robert always makes me dance with those horrid Mr. Leas, who certainly do smell most dreadfully of snuff and tobacco. I danced first a quadrille with young Percival, a very stupid long legged dull man. (I have just remembered that it was another dance I danced with Percival, and this I danced with Frederic Baker.) The second dance was a Polka, which I did not dance as Mama does not like us to dance it with gentlemen except brothers and cousins, though I do not see more harm in that than in a Galop. The next was the Lancers, which I believe I danced with Percival and of course all the others but Mr. Niven

and I made a horrid mess of it. The next was a Waltz which of course
I did not dance as I do not know how. The next was another Quadrille
which I danced with John Lea, who I cannot bear, and is very vulgar
and stupid and short. The next was another Polka which I danced
with Herbert, and Mrs. Peel said as we went by "I never saw anything
so pretty". The next was a Galop, which I did not dance, and Herbert
and Miss Dudley Percival, and I believe they were rather laughed
at. The next was another Quadrille, which I danced again with that
horrid Percival, as Robert always comes up and says "Emily, will you
dance with young Percival". The Talbots came in just after that, and
she danced the Polka with Henry, this Polka I did not dance and Mrs.
Talbot danced it very bad, and thought she danced it very well. The
next was the Mazurka, which of course I did not dance, as I do not
know. Robert was bothering every body to dance, but very few people
could. The next was a Boulanger, which I danced with Mr. Talbot,
who could not dance it a bit, and kept pulling me round as he did not
know what to do. After that supper came and I was afraid Mr. Talbot
would take me in to supper, so I said "Let us go to Mama" and as
soon as we got there, he said "I am afraid my partner wants to get rid
of me". Then we went into supper, and I walked in with Louisa,
and got next to Mr. Talbot! There was one amusing anecdote, viz:
The servant came up and said "Your plate please sir". Mr. Talbot was
talking so I just took his plate and gave it to the servant. He turned
round and said "Thankyou ma'am", and afterwards I found out he had
not finished. It was a capital joke at the time! There were a great
many toasts and speeches. After supper we had another Polka, which
I danced first with Jane then with Herbert, then with Louisa. Minnie
polked with Miss Baker, she asked if she danced it well, as she wanted
her to dance gentleman [sic], so Miss Baker puts on a very gracious
smile and says "They tell me so"! Another Waltz, which I did not
dance. Another Quadrille which I danced with Mr. Niven, he made
me another compliment and said "This is my favourite partner".
Another Polka which I don't remember, the Lancers which I danced
with Mr. Pakington, who was the nicest partner I had. Miss Peel
was my viz-a-viz, which I liked very much. I did not dance with Her-

bert Peel once, and only once with Frederick Baker. They all three talked together, and never spoke once. Altogether I enjoyed it very much and of course was very sorry to come away.

· · · · · ·

Saturday, 24th August   . . . I believe the school here is soon to put out of Chancery, and then I hope Aunt Harriet will let Teddy and Hubby come there, as they can always come down here on a half-holiday, which I think would be very delightful. I am sorry to say I forgot to send my love to any of them when Aunt Harriet went away, so I am afraid Teddy will forget me. Whenever there is any chance of seeing him again, my love always comes back again, so now there is a chance of his coming to the school I long to see him again. The only time I ever really lost my heart was to Villiers Lister, a very handsome boy about 11 years old, with long curls, but though I have ever since, and I daresay shall for ever like him very much, yet the actual love only lasted 1 night. I remember I told him he should see me at the riding-school when Louisa went, but Louisa did not go, so I did not, and he did not see me. I do not know whether he cared or not I am sure. I believe his real love is a certain Amelia Berkeley who I met at the same dance. I[t] was at Mrs. Drummond, the mother of our friend Mary, that I met them. There are two or three generations of Listers, that is to say from a different wife, but this Villiers is a son of Lady Theresa Lister, and has a very nice little sister, about 9 years old, her name is Theresa, but she is called Toddles. As this is all a long description about a boy and his relations I shall now pass on to

Sunday, 25th August   A tolerably fine day. . . .

Monday 26th August   Today we were up and began lessons regularly which I do not much like. At present I do French exercises for ¾ hour, Maps 1 hour, Music 1¼, read French and English ¾ hour, write French Copy ½ hour. I liked doing Maps very much; they are traced out, and one only has to put the names in and paint it. I have made this description in case I get married and have children it may be useful to them. I remember Mama often tells us of what she used to do, she said there were hardly any children's books then and she aston-ished me the other day by saying she had never read the "Child's Own

Book"! I was looking in Mama's trunk for something the other day
and the first thing I saw was, at the top of a great many Journal books
or something of that sort a piece of paper on which was written "If I
die, let these be burnt", and something else which I did not see! I
am sure I should like to see them very much, and I do not see why
they should be burnt. This morning we resumed our Archery, but I
did not get in once. Henry got rather exasperated because he did
not shoot very well. . . .

Tuesday, 27th August   This afternoon Papa, Mama and I went to Nor-
chard (the name of a little hamlet where a certain Mrs. Clark lives)
to give Mrs. Clark her baby clothes; her present baby is too old I
should think, but it will do for the next one, if she has another. We
have been meaning to go for a long time, but something has always
prevented us till today. I do so like going among poor people if they
are clean and do not cry as some do, but this Mrs. Clark is as clean
and nice as anyone can be; it is a very small poky little cottage with
two rooms, and she pays 5£ year, she has 6 children at home and
1 out. I should very much like to buy something more for the poor
people, but as I have not got a halfpenny at present it is impossible;
there is not much chance of getting anything either for if I say to
Mama "I have not got a halfpenny" she says "No worse than me", as
she spent all hers in London; I do not think I shall get much next
year as I do not expect to have much from my allowance this year, but
I should like to do something more about the poor people. I must
persuade Teddy to be a clergyman, if he ever means to be my husband, for I have quite set my heart upon being a clergyman's wife or
the wife of an independent gentleman; the last I should not in the least
object to, as I could do just as much good among the poor people.
We were talking today of Papa's being made Archbishop of Canterbury, that is the only thing I should like if he left here, except Win-
chester, and I do not think I should object to that, though I do not
suppose my opinion would be asked. I should not like to go to London at all, and Canterbury is what I should like best. Papa says he
would not refuse London if offered to him. I wish I had a little money
now, as I am full of the poor people. I think if I do not see Teddy
soon I shall give him up, as there is no use loving a boy one is never

to see. It would seem by this as if I did not love him much, but really I think if I was to see him again my love would all return, as it is not near gone yet. In fact I still like him very much indeed, and if he comes to the school here I shall love him as much as ever again, if he still cares for me; he has not written to me for a long time. I expect and hope Jane will write soon, as I do not think I can well write to her till she has written to me. Mama had a letter from Aunt Harriet this morning, she crossed safely and all are well.

Notes

~

The Journal of Emily Pepys, ed. Gillian Avery (London: Prospect Books, 1984), p. 27. All selections here come from this edition.

1   Her eleven-year-old cousin, who did eventually go into the church. Other young relatives mentioned subsequently are Alfred, Gwinnet, Cay, Louy, Harriet, Katey, and Tiny.

2   Published in 1822 by A Lady (Charlotte Anley), *Influence* is the tale of a girl lured by the joys of high society into forsaking her Methodistical Welsh heritage; she eventually repents, declines, and dies.

3   Her brother (b. 1830).

4   Her sister (b. 1827).

5   Her brother (b. 1824).

Hannah Cullwick

(1833–1909)

HANNAH CULLWICK was born in Shifnal, Shropshire, daughter of
a saddler and a housemaid and, after two years of charity school, at
eight years old began full-time work for pay. For most of her life she
was a lower servant: maid of all work, nurserymaid, housemaid,
char, housekeeper; also once a cook and once a pot girl in a Shifnal
pub. In 1854 she met Derek Munby, a well-educated man-about-town
subsidized by a wealthy father; he was also a barrister, poet, teacher
at Working Man's College, and photographer of working girls, who
fascinated him, especially if grimy. In 1856 she moved to London
to be closer to Munby. During the eighteen years that they maintained
a secret courtship, at his insistence she wrote seventeen diaries (1854–
73) to inform him about her daily drudgery; the excerpts here are
from 1863–73.* In time her diary became an emotional resource for
her as well. Munby also made more unusual demands. For years,
she not only washed his feet but wore a padlock and chain around her
neck to which only he had the key; in their early relationship she
coated herself in black lead for him. Their relationship appears not to
have been sexual in the genital sense before marriage and perhaps
even after it. After Cullwick married Munby in 1873—reluctantly, for
she wanted neither to wed nor to be a "lady"—she lived in the basement kitchen of Munby's chambers in the Temple for four years and
served as his domestic servant, though periodically obliged to dress up
as wife and entertain a few of his close friends; she also began to attend evening classes at the Working Women's College. Because of
growing friction, however, the couple separated, and she returned to
domestic service in Shropshire, until in 1888 she moved to a cottage
that Munby rented for her and where he often visited her. Their
unusual marriage (kept secret from his family) lasted for thirty-six
years. However, the year of Cullwick's marriage was also the last year
of her diary.

From Hannah Cullwick's Diary

Wednesday 14 October 1863[1]   Clean'd 3 pair o' boots & lit the fires.
Swept the steps & shook the mats. Got our breakfast & wash'd up
after. Clean'd the knives & made the fire up & got dinner. Clean'd
away after & got ready to go to Massa.[2] Reach'd him 'fore 5 & we had
a nice evening together. I told M. I was sorry about that Sunday[3] &
he talk'd about it a little & then I was good again, & so Massa told me
to black my face like it was that night I clean'd after the coalmen. So
I did, & got the dinner & clean'd the boots & wash'd up the things
& Massa's feet with it black, & M. seem'd pleas'd wi' it so but said my
hands wasn't looking so thick & red as they did the Sunday when he
read them verses to me. They was rhymes in the country talk & some
o' the words I know'd how to speak better than Massa even. While I
made the cigars I sat 'tween his knees & heard Massa read some verses
he'd made up for me. They was very nice & all just as I should o'
said if I could o' made 'em, for they was wrote as if I was saying it, &
I'd to kiss Massa at all the best parts—about going up the chimney
& that. When the cigars was done I put coals on & had a little petting,
for I'd wash'd the black of my face in the water I wash'd the feet in,
& at ½ past 9 Massa walk'd wi' me up the lane & saw me get in an
omnibus. I got home by ½ past ten & to bed.

Friday 16 October   Got up & open'd the shutters. Got our breakfast
over & wash'd up. Made the fire up & got dinner. Clean'd away &
begun to scrub the tins & covers—Master Charley said I look'd like a
milkmaid only blacker. Sarah took the boys to Bromley & Mary
went out so Fred & me was alone.[4] I worked till eight o'clock & then
had supper. Clean'd away & then to bed at ten o'clock. I'd a capital
chance to go up the chimney, so I lock'd up & waited till ½ past till
the grate was cool enough & then I took the carpets up & got the
tub o' water ready to wash me in. Moved the fender & swept ashes
up. Stripp'd myself quite naked & put a pair of old boots on & tied an
old duster over my hair & then I got up into the chimney with a
brush. There was a lot o'soot & it was soft & warm. Before I swept I
pull'd the duster over my eyes & mouth, & I sat on the beam that
goes across the middle & cross'd my legs along it & I was quite safe &
comfortable & out o' sight. I swept lots o' soot down & it come all

over me & I sat there for ten minutes or more, & when I'd swept all round & as far as I could reach I come down, & I lay on the hearth in the soot a minute or two thinking, & I wish'd rather that Massa could see me. I black'd my face over & then got the looking glass & look'd at myself & I was certainly a fright & hideous all over, at least I should o' seem'd so to anybody but Massa. I set on & wash'd myself after, & I'd hard work to get the black off & was obliged to leave my shoulders for Massa to finish. I got the tub emptied & to bed before twelve.

· · · · ·

Tuesday 1 December   Clean'd 2 pairs o' boots & lit the fires. Swept & dusted the room & the hall. Shook the mats & clean'd the steps. Wash'd myself & got the breakfast up. Had my own & then the bell rang & I got the orders & clean'd the things off & wash'd 'em up. I clean'd the knives & fill'd the scuttles, made the kitchen fire up & got the dinner ready. Had our'n in the kitchen, clean'd away after & scrubb'd the tables. Clean'd the hearth on my knees. I got a letter saying how poorly my Aunt Small had bin & how badly off, so I was much troubl'd & I give Miss Very[5] the letter to read after breakfast was over, & the Missis came down at the time & ask'd me if I was in trouble. So I told her as short as I could & she says, 'I'll give you a sovereign at once, & I'd ask some others if I was you.' I made a curtsy & thank'd her & said I would, & give a lb [pound] myself, & I *did* ask Mr Lane the G. Grocer when he come in ('cause I've heard he's rich), but he said he couldn't afford to give anything, so 'fore tea I went & got an order & sent the 2 lbs & wrote a letter to Aunt. After tea I wash'd up in the scullery. Got supper over & then I wash'd my cap & made it up again. Mr Saunderson was here & was late & it was 12 when I went to bed.

Wednesday 9 December   Clean'd 3 pairs o' boots & lit the fires. Swept & dusted the room. Got the breakfast up. Had mine & clean'd away after. Carried coals upstairs & made the kitchen fire up. Wash'd the breakfast things & clean'd the knives. Wash'd up in the scullery & got the dinner. Clean'd away and & clean'd the kitchen hearth. Wash'd

the dishes up & myself & as the family was going out to supper I
thought I would go round to some of the gentry & ask 'em to give
me something for aunt as Massa said it'd be right, & I've had it on my
mind so as I shouldn't 'a' bin satisfied not to o' gone. So I put my
best bonnet on & my green shawl & frock & went first to Captain
Dutton's. He wasn't in but the housekeeper said she would ask him for
me & send it over to me tomorrow if he give anything. I thank'd her
& then call'd at 25 where I used to live & ask'd the servant if she
thought the lady would speak to me & she said *NO*.

I then call'd at 22 & the servant was very civil & ask'd me in, tho
she said that Mr Weir was at dinner. So I thank'd [her] & said I'd wait
in the hall till he'd done if she thought it best, but she presently call'd
me in. Mr Weir stood up & I curtsied low to him. 'Well, young
woman,' he said '& what do you want, & where do you live?' I said, 'I
live at Mrs. Fosters, sir, & I've come to ask you if you would be so
good as help me with my subscription for my aunt in Shropshire, as
Mrs. Foster had give me a sovereign & told me to ask others as well.'
'Oh,' he said, 'I know nothing o' the people in Shropshire, anyone
might as well come from Scotland & say that, besides he says I always
know plenty o' cases at home—the churches & hospitals & places &
there's my servant Martha that got married to a conductor, she deserves help, & I said to Groom only last night that my next gift must
be to her.' I said, 'Yes, sir, I dare say you do know plenty o' things
to give to, & the public things [are] sure to get help but,' I said, 'my
aunt doesn't know I'm *begging* for her.' And I felt it was right (and the
tears come then) but I shan't like to go anywhere else nor hardly.
'Oh,' he said, 'it's quite right of you to ask, but *how* do I know you
come from Mrs Foster's & how is it your aunt wants help?' So I said 'I
think your servant has seen me over the way & knows me by sight,'
& then I told him how my uncle & aunt had been little farmers & was
bankrupt & paid 17s [shillings] in the lb [pound]. He said they did
get well then, & then I said ever since they've bin trying to get on at
something or other but have been unlucky & now the misfortune
& hard work had bin too much for my aunt & she'd been ill & wanted
wine to strengthen her.

The old gentleman then took his purse out & emptied a lot o' gold out & says, 'Well, I'll give you ½ a sovereign then & I hope it'll bene-fit them a little.' I said, 'I'm very much obliged to you, sir, I'm sure, & it's very kind of you to o' seen me'—I curtsied again & he rang the bell, & when the servant came he laugh'd & says, 'Groom, do you know this young woman?' She said, 'Yes, sir, she lives over the way'— & he said, 'All right, but you know I didn't want to make the police come in the morning and say I'd been encouraging an imposter— let her out.' I turned & smil'd at him for I could see that he was a really kind man tho' he seem'd harsh. I back'd out o' the room he was in & then follow'd the servant to the door. I could tell by her manner that he wasn't unkind. She was very civil & told [me] to be careful o' the steps. I thank'd her & come out into the dirty road again.

I can't tell how I felt hardly. I walk'd up & down & pass'd the houses 3 or 4 times & then I cross'd the road just by 14 Carlton Villas. I knew General Williams lived there & I'd seen the lady once about a place for Ann Stuart, so I got courage & rung the bell. The cook open'd the door, & I ask'd if Mrs Williams was at dinner & she said no, & then I said, would she ask her to please speak to Mrs Foster's servant, & she said, wait here & the housemaid'll be out soon. So I stood on the mat & the housemaid came & I ask'd her to tell Mrs Williams that a servant from Mrs Foster's of 22 would be glad to see her a minute. So Mrs W. came out dress'd up and with gloves on. She star'd at me terribly when I curtsied & said what I wanted & where I came from, & she look'd so cross & said *I* don't know Mrs Foster, & couldn't think of giving to people I know nothing of. I said, 'I am sorry for troubling you, ma'am, & I'm sure I would not ask if it wasn't for a good cause,' but she said no. So I open'd the door & said, 'Thank you, ma'am, for seeing me,' but she never spoke—I doubt she would be angry with the cook for letting me in.

Well I got in the road again rather out o' heart & walk'd up & down again, & then I thought I'll just to Mr Pike's at 25, & when I got there Mr P. had just rung the bell & was putting the key in & open'd the gate so I said, 'Would you speak to me in the hall, sir, please.' He said, '*What*!' & I said it again, & he look'd fiercely at me &

shouted, '*No, certainly* no,' and slamm'd the door in my face. So that was enough & I came in and cried a little, not wi' anger, nor yet vex'd but I'd learnt som'ut of life I shan't soon forget, & I think I could die freely rather than be beholden to the world for charity for myself.

· · · · · ·

Sunday 1 January 1871 This is the beginning of another year, & I am still general servant like, to Mrs Henderson at 20 Gloucester Crescent. This month on the 16th I shall o' bin in her service 2 years & a ½, & if I live till the 26th o' May when I shall be 38 years old, I shall o' bin in service 30 years & have known Massa 17 years. Now there's such a little boy kept here I've a deal more to do of jobs that's hard, like digging coals & carrying 'em up & the boxes, & high windows & the fanlight over the door to clean & anything as wants strength or height I am sent for or call'd up to do it. All the cabs that's wanted I get, & if the young ladies want fetching or taking anywhere I've to walk with them & carry their cloaks or parcels. I clean all the copper scuttles & dig the coals[,] clean the tins & help to clean the silver & do the washing up if I'm wanted, & carry things up as far as the door for dinner. I clean 4 grates & do the fires & clean the irons, sweep & clean 3 rooms & my attic, the hall & front steps & the flags & area railings & all that in the street. I clean the water closet & privy out & the back yard & the area, the back stairs & the passage, the larder, pantry & boy's room & the kitchen & scullery, all the cupboards downstairs & them in the storeroom. And at the house cleaning I do the walls down from the top to the bottom o' the house & clean all the high paint, & dust the pictures. I get all the meals down stairs & lay the cloth & wait on the boy & the housemaid as much as they want & if it's my work, like changing their plates & washing their knife & fork & that.

Missis never goes away—hardly for a day throughout the year, so as there's no change & no good chance for thorough cleaning. I'm getting more used to the family now so I don't mind them seeing me clean upstairs as much as I used to, but I do like the family to be away for house-cleaning, 'cause one can have so much more time at it & do it more thoroughly & be as black at it as one likes without fear o' being seen by the ladies. 'Cause I know they don't like to see a servant look dirty, however black the job is one has to do.

I've two days & two nights' holiday since last October twelve months, & bin to no theatres or Crystal Palace or anything except to Exeter Hall once wi' the young ladies & heard the ragged school children sing. And I've read nothing but a book call'd *Adam Bede*,[6] excepting my Bible. I've bin to church every chance I've had when Massa's bin away or when I've not gone to him of a Sunday. It's rather unpleasant to ask leave so I seldom get out of a weekday. I go with notes or parcels, & fetch my beer or for any errands. Yet I get very little outing all together. The most fresh air is washing the front door steps & flags in the street and out at the back door washing the yard. Still, I'm quite content & like service—especially if I could get to Massa more & without having to ask. But that I canna so am obliged to make the best of the time I do have & do as much in it as I can for him. . . .

· · · · · ·

Wednesday 28 June   . . . Now Elizabeth's[7] gone I have to carry the trays up to the doors for the lad, 'cause he's too young to be trusted with 'em either heavy or light, for fear of his slipping the glasses or tea things off. I'm not allow'd to go in for Miss M. says to me, 'Bring them up, to the door outside, but mind you're not seen.' I know she meant I am not fit to be seen by ladies, & I told Massa about it when he was sitting on my lap o' Sunday.

Then M kiss'd me & said, 'Oh dear, you're not fit to be seen by ladies as a *servant*, & however shall us two be seen together then?' I said, 'Ah, *indeed*, but there is one thing, Massa, I don't *want* anyone to see us.' I *like* the life I lead—working here & just going to M. when I can of a Sunday, & a chance time to clean of a weekday when I can get leave now & then, oftener of course if I could—better even I think than a married life. For I never feel as if I *could* make my mind up to that—it's too much like being a *woman*. Still I do think it's bad that the *world* shd so interfere & mar one's happiness if it chances to *know* of love 'twixt two different stations like we are. However it always *was* the way o' the world, & will be I reckon til it's levell'd, when the new earth is made. So let it be, only I don't wish the world to see *me* anything else nor a servant, but M.'s love I *couldn't* do without.

. . . . .

Saturday 23 November   Got a letter from Massa to go & see him at the Temple[8] by 3 o'clock. I was glad, but I felt weak rather. I was just going to wash his feet when someone came upstairs. I escaped wi' the basin & my things into the back room & hid myself. And it was a *lady* & gentleman, great friends of M.'s & they talk'd ever so long, that M. made excuse that he was staying away, & so they went. M. was annoy'd a bit at having to hide me but, as I told him that didn't matter a bit to me, for many a time I've bin crouch'd in the cupboard, & hid in the back room & no one dream'd of a soul being there. I wash'd M.'s feet, & then it was time for him to go to dinner, & I got back at 7 & had my tea. Before the visitors came M. show'd me a licence he'd bought—a *marriage* licence—for him & me, & he said, 'Doesn't this show how much I love you, & what do you say to it?' I told him I had *nothing* to say about it, but I hoped he would never be sorry for it, nor *I.* Tho' I seem'd so cool & said so little I really *meant* what I said. I car'd very *very* little for the licence or being married either. Indeed I've a certain dislike to either, they seem to have so little to do with our *love* & our union. *They* are things what every common sweet-hearts use whether they love really or not. And ours has bin for so long a *faithful, trustful* & pure love, without any outward bond, that I seem to *hate* the word marriage in *that* sense. And yet of course I respect it as a *duty,* which ought to be done on Massa's part. Not as a *reward* to me for I want *no* reward, but as a simple duty he owes to himself, 'cause I canna be with him nor serve him as a servant nor be a helpmeet for him as I ought without it, 'cause of my *name.*

. . . . .

Tuesday 26 November   Strange, this is the date of my birthday. It was tolerably fine this morning & I started at 11. The sun broke out in Hatton Garden & I took that for good luck & come along with a better heart, carrying my bundle, & a bag with all my working things in. And I thought, 'O *come,* this sun looks *better,* & I *do* hope this is my last move, for I am tired o' going to fresh places.' So about 20 minutes

past 11 this morning I enter'd Massa's service, as his own real servant
& maid of all work, & come to live in his kitchen, after eighteen
years o' loving and serving him in other folk's kitchens. Mrs. Newton[9]
was here & I ask'd her if she pleas'd to give me keys. She let me in,
& was very pleasant & talk'd to me some time. She said Mr Munby
was a good payer, & she seem'd to like him, only said he was very
fidgety & old maidish. I knew that, but I was glad she spoke well of
him, & I said, 'If he is particular, & from what little I've seen of him I
think he *is,* he wants one servant to himself, for there's plenty to do,
it's not likely a person coming in for an hour or so can do all,' &
she said, 'No.'

Mrs Newton left me, & I took my cloak & things off, & put my
striped apron & bonnet on. Lighted a fire in the kitchen. Swept the
floor after I moved all the lumber out, belonging to Mr Rees,[10] &
I wash'd the bedroom floor first. Then I went out for my beer, & got
my dinner in the kitchen after I clean'd the floor all over on my knees.
Massa said he shd like to see me scrubbing outside when he come at
½ past 4 or so and I plann'd it. I'd clean'd the area, & the rough hole
out under the window, & the grating with my hands, & was washing
the flags when M. came. I'd [had] to get in & out the window for
the water till my frock & skirts was draggled & I was looking a regular
drudge.

M. came to the entry corner & spoke quite unexpected, for I'd
forgotten about him coming & it was nearly dark—'Is that you Hannah?' 'Yes, Massa, it is,' I said, but quite low. It seems he didn't hear
me say it, & then he said, 'What time did you come?' I felt confused &
said, 'This afternoon,' still low, & I crept in at the window. Then M.
came down to the kitchen & spoke again. I didn't say 'sir' of course,
'cause I'd no idea any one was above likely to be listening. Then M.
went upstairs & rang the bell, & I thought, Well that is showing off
certainly, & I went upstairs with my temper up to its highest, & M.
began to question me about not saying *'sir'* to him, as the lad was
on the stairs. I felt so *angry* 'cause I thought if M. knew the boy was
on the stairs he oughtn't to o'come down, not only for the humiliation
the first day, but because I didn't even know Mr Rees kept a lad as
clerk. I was really in a passion & I said a great deal I didn't *mean,* & I

declar'd that if M. tantalised me in that way again I would leave him whether we was married or not, for I didn't care a straw for that. Of course I meant that for the moment, for I felt I couldn't stand to be treated as such a 'nothing' & with no consideration after having [unreadable] so much all these years, & coming at last to be only as a servant to everyone's eyes except his. And being really & truly a servant to him & willing to endure all things for his sake, whether it was life or death, so long as I was near him. So that my passion was only the effect of love, & I thought M. knew me so well that he'd soon forget & forgive that.

Wednesday 27 November   I slept middlingly well for I didn't know half how I'd vex'd M. till I got a letter from him at eight this morning— telling me to go back to Mrs Smith's,[11] for he felt it'd never do for me to be here in disguise. And so my trouble commenced again, & yet I wasn't sorry I'd spoke my mind. For if M. had gone on, speaking to me crossly or sharp as he used to Mrs Mitchell, I know I shd go out o' my mind, & a very bad end would come to him as well as to me, for I canna bear it, altho' I'm humble, & wish to be only like a *servant*. But for *him* I've sacrificed so much & *done* so much for, & loved so unselfishly & disinterestedly, that I will *not* be mock'd nor deceived. And so this letter shows he's in earnest, & wants me to leave him again, & I will not, unless it's for always. Massa shall never see me again if he sends me away now, but of course I *will* go if he persists in it. He came at 3 o'clock this afternoon, & talk'd to me. [He] took the keys from me at dinner time (for he dined here) & put 'em in his pocket, but he gave me them afore he went away for his class work at the College just before eight.

·   ·   ·   ·   ·

Saturday 30 August 1873   11 o'clock a.m. I am just return'd home after ten days' tour in France with my darling Massa & husband. We started from Boulogne at two o'clock this morning after lying in our berths nearly an hour. I kept well *to* Boulogne, & it was my first sea voyage too, except crossing the Solent for the Isle o' Wight with M. this year, & *this* journey was *rough*. But I kept well a long time, *going up & down* with the waves in imagination & not opening my eyes, but I could hear all going on, & that my husband was very bad. I ask'd after him several times from the steward & sent messages. At last I was a little bit ill, & the man didn't know till I told him. He said, 'Oh, ma'am, that was through me talking to you I doubt. However, I mustn't say anything about it.' I said, 'No, don't, I shall be all the better off.'

And I went to sleep, for when I woke I was so pleas'd to see it was daylight & I felt better, & my first thought was to go & see Massa. So I jump'd out o' the berth & run along the floor tottering a little, & I found M. still sick & hoarse with retching. I wiped his face, & said I thought we were in harbour. He call'd me his child, & said how ill he'd bin & told me to go & lie down again, & so I was glad to do, for I felt sleepy & knock'd up. But soon after the man said we must land, & I got up again & fasten'd my clothes & pick'd my things up to go ashore. Massa came for me & when we landed it was a fine calm morning, the sun just rising & all so quiet & still. So different to the night [we] came to & started from Folkstone.

This ten days has been quite new to me of course, crossing from Folkstone to Boulogne & from Boulogne to Rouen. There we saw the ancient buildings & statue of Gean D'arc [sic] and the beautiful churches. And at the Hotel d'Alvion where we stopp'd was a most amusing little maid, bowing & scraping in the most lively attitude, & most civil to Monsieur & Madame. When I left she help'd me on with my cloak & as well as I could [I] said, 'Nous reveney,' & then, 'How funny that you & I cannot understand one another,' me meaning both being servants. But she only laugh'd & said, 'Oui, Madame.' We had a long sail from Rouen to Honfleur in the boat, but a very pleasant one, along the river Seine. Most days we have had long journeys, by rail & road or water & seen a great deal in the time, & only stayed one night in a place except at Caen, & that was over the Sunday.

And everywhere I was treated most respectfully, just as if I was a real lady. And Massa says I behaved nicely & look'd like a lady too. He bought me a felt hat & plume of cock's feathers to wear, & a veil, & a new brooch to pin my shawl with, & a new waterproof cloak. But I generally wore my blue skirt and jacket over my grey frock, with frill round my neck, & white cuffs, & grey kid gloves, & carrying my striped sun shade. All so different to anything I had got used to, but one day in the train I got almost ill-temper'd at being so muffled up, & felt I'd much liefer feel my hands free as they used to be. But M. made me put the gloves on again, & I thought it was hard to be forced to wear gloves—even harder than it was to leave 'em off altogether before I was married, as I did for over 16 year I think. When I started I wore my old black bonnet to Folkstone & changed it there, & the same back again, & put my plaid shawl over my skirt so I wasn't noticed coming into the Temple nor going out.

Two young girls came over in the boat with me—one English, & the other French as couldn't speak a word of English, so when M. left me at Charing Cross I went to see after them. The English girl had lost her box & didn't know the name o' the place it was put in at, so I told the man & went with her to the office & they promised to tele-graph for it & to send it on to her home. There was no one to meet the French girl, & she didn't know where to go to, but was to 'restey ici' she said till her brother came. I spoke to a porter for her, & he spoke French, & was kind & civil, & promised to take care of her. I left her in the waiting room & shook hands with her & come on here after getting a cup o' coffee at the station.

And here I am again, very glad to get back. I've doff'd all my best clothes & put my own on again—my dirty cotton frock & apron & my cap—taken the top dust off the things & lighted the fire, fetch'd in some bread & butter & got my dinner. Then I rested till M. came in, & we unpack'd our bags & things & then pack'd the large port-manteau for M. to start home with. He was gone by ½ past 5 after wishing me a hearty goodbye & hoping I should not be dull. I said I shouldn't & didn't mean to be, but I think it's not possible to be any other, quite alone in this very quiet place, & not a soul to speak to confidentially. For I'm obliged to look at my words lest I shd say any-thing to Mrs. Newton or anyone to betray myself. Monday if all's well I'm going after the workman & tonight I go to bed soon to have a long rest, for I feel upset & very tired & sleepy.

· · · · ·

Friday 12 September   This morning I nail'd the fringe on the wood (I took it off to wash it) & hung up the red curtains. Wash'd 2 pair o' the

long white curtains & left 'em drying. Went up & black'd the parlour
grate & fender & laid the fire. Got my dinner early & the rest o' the
day I was dusting the books out o' the two ranges of shelves each side
o' the fireplace. It was a dusty job & jumping up & down & reaching
so high tired me worse than scrubbing does. I got my tea, & happen'd
to go upstairs for something when, lo & *behold,* I pick'd up a telegram
for 'Hannah Culick' & so I was sure by that (the way my name was
spelt) it was from Massa. But I was rather afraid of its meaning till I
read it. 'Coming tonight, Friday, ten to 11—to see black work tomorrow—sleep downstairs—French dress.' I understood it all, that he
wish'd to sleep downstairs & be with me in the kitchen, just to say
so & that I was to be clean'd & in my French servant's dress tonight &
he would see me dirty tomorrow. I was very much pleas'd as well as
surprised you may be sure, & I took off the tired feeling I had.

First while it was light I finish'd M.'s room upstairs in case he would
rather go up, & put sheets to air, & then I went out for errands without washing me. Come in & clean'd the kitchen round on my hands &
knees & made a good fire. Trimm'd the lamp & put the tea things
ready, & then I wash'd me. Put my French cap & frock on, clean collar
& apron & white stockings, & my new French shoes. I hadn't long
to wait before Massa came down to the kitchen, looking so well &
jolly, & he clasp'd his drudge & kissed her *for ever* so long, & she was
a pleas'd to see him tho' she said not much. By eleven or so I got
the toast & clean'd away, but we had so much to talk about that it was
nearly one o'clock afore we had prayers & nearly two before M.
came to bed. And then M. dwelt so long on seeing me work next day
& being thoroughly black.

· · · · ·

Sunday 14 September   Altho' Massa has bin & gone away again so
sudden I've not felt dull today, nor last night either. Mr Rees (the
gentleman on the ground floor) coming while M. was saying goodbye, & Massa of course not wanting to be seen especially in the
kitchen it started both of us. M. was off to get dinner before going to
King's Cross, & I up Fetter Lane in the rain to get my errands in.
So when I come back to my tea in the kitchen I was at home again, &
all was again as afore M. came, only I felt *happier.* How could I help

it, after having such a proof of his love—to come from impulse 2
hundred miles just to see me after I had written to him what I didn't
think was anything especially nice. But *he* liked it, & in the afternoon
couldn't help starting from Wigan, to me, instead of going to his
other home—all for *love*. And I was as much pleas'd as I was surprised
when I got the telegram soon after six to say he would be here from
ten to 11. I'd begun to feel very tired, but all that was gone, & I made
haste & made his bedroom quite ready & air'd things. Went out
afore I wash'd me for things for his tea, & then I clean'd the kitchen
round on my hands & knees & made a nice bright fire & tea things
laid & all for my dear lord & master. And it seem'd so much nicer &
more homely & cosey somehow, getting the *kitchen* ready for *him*.

Should I have felt *such* pleasure for a common working man? I *might*
if I had found a working man as could love as purely & be as Massa
is (I mean in everything but his learning) & honour him as much, but
that's a difficulty I doubt, the finding such a one. And so when I
was young & *did* meet with Massa (whose face I'd seen in the fire) I
made my mind up that it was best & safest to be a slave to a *gentleman,*
nor wife & equal to any vulgar man, still with the wish & determination to be independent by working in service and without the slightest
hope o' been rais'd in rank either in place or by being married. And
so at last after all these nearly twenty years, by God's help & Massa's
true heart & fervent love to me (more than ever I could dare to hope
for from anyone but him, & I always trusted Massa). I am as I am. A
servant still, & a very low one, in the eyes o' the world. I can work
at ease. I can go out & come in when I please, & I can look as degraded
as ever I like without caring how much I'm despised in the Temple,
or in Fetter Lane or in the streets.

And with all that I have the inward comfort o' knowing that I am
loved & honoured & admired & that I am united in heart & soul as
well as married at church to the truest, best, & handsomest man in my
eyes that ever was born. No man I ever see, or ever saw, is so lovely.
And M. is pleas'd with me & after all this there can be no doubt of
our being made for each other. And so may God bless together, & give
us both wisdom to live happily always, & health & strength to do
the work afore us, & grace that we may never forget who is the giver

of all our comforts, & to praise Him more & more. But Massa would not sleep in his own room, but downstairs in the kitchen bedroom with me & we talk'd till two o'clock. And in the morning he noticed how rough my knees are. They feel like a nutmeg grater, so different to his, & M. was so pleas'd to feel 'em 'cause he said, it was such a true sign of being a servant. . . .

Notes

*These selections are taken from *The Diaries of Hannah Cullwick, Victorian Maidservant*, ed. Liz Stanley (London: Virago, 1984).

1 Cullwick was a general servant at Kilburn during 1863 with a family named Foster.

2 Her term for Munby.

3 On Sunday she had been moody because she felt he was being remote, whereupon he became cross about her moodiness; later they agreed that she had been "naughty."

4 Sarah is the Fosters' nursemaid; Mary, their housemaid; and Fred, Sarah's nephew, who occasionally helped out during busy times.

5 Mrs. Foster's younger sister.

6 George Eliot's novel, published in 1859.

7 A former servant.

8 His rooms at the Inns of Court, the Inner and Middle Temple, which are on the site of the onetime headquarters of the Knights Templar.

9 A servant at the Temple.

10 A subtenant of Munby's.

11 Cullwick's friend, at whose home she had been staying, having left service.

Emily Augusta King

(Nineteenth century)

EMILY AUGUSTA KING (Mrs. Robert Moss King) was the wife of an English administrator in India who published her diary of five years abroad—"some of the happiest years in our lives" (28 April 1882)—in the hope that "it may interest those who have a sister or daughter whose married life is cast, as mine was, in India."* During the diary period (1877–82), her husband had been assigned to a station in Meerut in northern India as collector for a large district; later he undertook a judgeship. Her first experience of India, seven years earlier, also lasted for five years while her husband held a position at Oudh. After a two-year leave, the Kings returned to India in November 1877, boarding their children with relatives in England. Their son Carlie (Carleton) was born in July 1878, but is first mentioned in the diary only when he is a month old. King's dispassionate, if not unbiased, record is a letter diary written for her family circle and sent home every few weeks to recount her experiences and observations on Indian culture: she admires the Indians while betraying the condescension of her class, despite her liberal attitudes. King records her days of maintaining a household, camping in the hills to escape the hot weather, performing some charitable works, and traveling about to see the country. On matters that arouse strong feelings in her, such as cures for female infanticide, she asserts her opinions at length, but of her personal inner life she says little. In 1896 King also published *Italian Highways,* which may have been an account of further travels. Apparently well read and evidently talented, she illustrated her Indian text with thirty-two skilled paintings and drawings, most signed "AK," probably because she preferred to be called Augusta rather than Emily. But as she is not the focus of her diary, such personal information can only be conjectural. The selections here are limited to 1878–79.

From the Diary of Emily Augusta King

1 February 1878 . . . It is said that a good deal of mischief is being done by the fashionable visitors who now flock to India in the cold season, are delighted and flattered by all the novelty of native hospitality, courtesy and often servility, and to whom the English officials are of course in no way either novel or interesting, and who then return home and spread the idea that the English in India require snubbing and the trusty natives exalting. It may be so, but these passing visitors are not in a position to be good judges. A visitor can only see things very superficially, he is wholly irresponsible, and he finds it pleasant to pose as a kind of champion, and be lavishly gracious to the natives and studiously cold to his fellow-countrymen. If his life were cast, as theirs is, among these same natives, he would find this enthusiasm and novelty wear off. He would find that a gulf was fixed between him and men who, however long their acquaintance, would never admit him into their home life, would consider their wives and daughters insulted if he so much as alluded to them, would sooner die than eat at his table, and who in their inmost heart would not sorrow if every Christian were driven into the sea.

While Robert was having a Turkish bath at Delhi, I drove about the bazaar and chose some brasswork and a few other specimens of native work, but at the bearer's earnest request I only *selected* certain things, and have to-day sent him in to make his own bargains for them. He is a wonderful man at a bargain, and it distresses him to see me offer more for a thing than he considers it worth. I am really quite ashamed sometimes to confess to him what I have given for a thing, and as he keeps all the money I can never get off without confession. I doubt his driving a bargain to-day with the brass-worker; the man professes to ask *prix fixe,* but the bearer scouts the idea, and feels his credit involved in getting the things for less than the man asked me.

Once, in Meerut, I wanted some calico, and Mrs. D—— told me it ought only to cost twelve rupees the piece. Armed with this information, I sent for a cloth merchant, who showed me the quality required, but swore with many oaths that its price was thirteen and a half, and nowhere could it be bought for less. I assured him it had been bought for twelve. Nothing would shake him, and as neither of us would give in, the bargain fell through and he gathered up his bundles and departed. The bearer was present, and even he was shaken as to the value of the calico. However, he took his stand on this, that *if* Mrs. D—— had bought it for twelve rupees it was ridiculous to suppose that he, Chaudri Rám, should not be able to get it for less. So out he sallied, and finally brought me in triumph the identical quality for which he had paid eleven and a half. Robert's opinion is that, rather than allow that he could not beat Mrs. D—— at a bargain, he would have paid the half-rupee out of his own pocket!

He is somewhat distressed at the charges made by the Khansáma, who certainly does write down a surprising amount of eggs and other things supposed to be consumed by Robert and me, but, being an excellent servant in other ways, I rather wink at his accounts. Sometimes I own I have to wink hard, and cannot always refrain from a smile; but if ever I venture mildly to say that the number of eggs is really astonishing, I have them all, so to speak, thrown at my head, and have to listen to a voluble account of how many went to the soup, and the rissoles, and the salad, and the pudding, and the anchovy toast, till I am quite suppressed, and ready to declare that we could not possibly have dined with an egg less. Being, however, a woman, and convinced against my will, it is not surprising that I should be of the same opinion still.

· · · · ·

7 March　Yesterday our cow was taken ill; she refused to eat, and a great swelling came in her throat. The servants, full of faith, sent for the village medicine-man, who combines the characters of a holy man and a worker of magic. Thinking there is safety in numbers, our zealous bearer indeed summoned three of these wise men, who duly came and practised as follows. The first doctor gathered a twig of the Neem-tree (a wych-elm would perhaps answer in England), and with profound gravity stroked her throat with it for some time, muttering charms and incantations the while. The second heated an iron red-hot, and with it made a magic mark on the ground where her footprint was; he also asked for a needle, and with it pierced her ear.

The third made a ball of coarse sugar and caused a dog to lick it all over, after which the cow was made to swallow it. Proper prayers and charms having been muttered over her, the wise men's work was over, and from that time the cow began to eat and is now getting well,—so scoff not at the means adopted. Are there not stranger things in heaven and earth than are dreamt of in our philosophy?

·   ·   ·   ·   ·

17 August   The baby a month old, and as big as a native child three times his age. We have a dhaie, a native wet-nurse, for him, but were afraid we should have to part with her, as her husband is a most violent-tempered man, and after she had been a week with us came vowing she should not stop and that he would hang himself unless she returned home. Considering that she had come with his full consent, this conduct on his part was very 'contumacious and indecent,' as Mrs. Proudie[1] would express it. However, we at once looked out for another dhaie, and when he found that we had taken him at his word, he repented him, and thought of the rupees he was throwing away; and this so worked on him that he came to tender his abject submission, and agreed to sign a paper in which he promised not to interfere with his wife as long as we require her services.

She is a regular villager, of bucolic intelligence, but improving. She has lately begun to notice the various strange ornaments and furniture, and even ask simple questions. I pointed out a large print of Herring's three horses' heads, and asked her what animals they were. She studied them attentively for some time, and then said, 'Perhaps they were camels.' You must remember that never in her life had she seen a picture, which is a state of mind we are hardly able to realize. Most of the servants in hanging a picture would hang it upside down, so little can they see any meaning in it. I suppose it is chiefly a matter of education. I wonder if a dog could be taught to recognize a portrait? . . .

·   ·   ·   ·   ·

25 January 1879   The last few days we have had the District Superintendent of Police marching with us, who has had to inspect sundry villages near here suspected of practising female infanticide, and put

therefore under special police surveillance. They have to pay themselves for the special police force, and have to report all births, and
show all dead bodies of children to some police or medical authority.
Their lives are in every way made a burden to them until such time
as they shall see the error of their ways and consent to bring up more
girls than they can provide for.

The Superintendent has been at this work now for years, and says
he is perfectly certain that the practical result of our legislation is
that now an equal number of boy babies are destroyed in order to balance the proportion of male and female deaths.

You cannot force parents to rear a child. You may prevent their
killing it by an overdose of opium, because that can be detected and
punished. But you cannot punish them when a child simply will
not thrive, and after a few painful months dies 'a natural death.'

This, therefore, is another result of our efforts, that the children die
a death of suffering instead of a quick and unconscious one. As to
the children themselves, there can be small doubt that it is better for
them to die as soon as born, than to live, to grow up and struggle,
and finally die of starvation or lead a life of wickedness—and one or
the other lies before these girls as long as the country is over-
populated. As to the moral guilt of the parents, it cannot be great.
Till we made the law against infanticide, it was perhaps *nil*, for sin
surely includes and signifies *consciousness of sin*, and of that they had
none. It was the immemorial custom of their people and they could
not bring up more than a certain number of girls in decency.

It might perhaps be well to make England clean in this respect
before interfering with these people; and when such things as baby-
farms are no longer known in Christian England, and no such things
as foundling hospitals needed, then to begin to remodel Indian customs with a more encouraging result to point to as our aim than
the England of the present day affords.

If a cup is full it is a truism to say that more cannot be poured in
without some being spilt. And yet this is a problem—substituting
countries and population—which all our legislators are bent upon
solving. To what end? is the unavoidable question. Is it truly thought
better to rear 100,000,000 to poverty, famine, and vice, than to rear

50,000,000 who can live and find work and food? This seems to be the question, and the modern tendency is decidedly to say, 'Rear your 100,000,000,' and to add, 'and the Lord will provide'—knowing practically that the Lord, having made certain fixed laws as to food and population as well as to cups and water, will not interfere in the working out of these laws—not even to favour the most humane legislation.

· · · · ·

7 May I have been busy this morning weighing out ounces of tea to be sewn up in bags, and dyeing six dozen eggs scarlet, blue, yellow, purple, and green. For this evening we have a tea-party for all the waifs and strays we can collect, and expect nearly sixty children— some half-castes, and nearly all pie-balds of varying proportions. They belong to no regiment, and are nobody's business in particular, so they never get a treat of any kind.

The Scotch minister is my chief aide-de-camp, and is most kind and useful. When he came to talk over the arrangements he said, 'It is not to be denominational, I suppose?' 'Certainly not,' quoth I. 'You even include'—he added doubtfully—'the Roman Catholics?' I assured him poverty was to be the only passport, irrespective of creed. So we shall have what may be called 'a Christian mixture'—for I believe they will all be Christians of one kind or another; queer ones some.

We are grieved to hear that the Hussars buried four more of their men yesterday who had died of cholera. Should another case occur, the whole regiment is to go into camp tomorrow. It is the only hope; but at this time of the year, with the thermometer at 114 in the shade, the cure is nearly as bad as the evil.

8 May Our treat yesterday was a great success, and if eating may be taken as a gauge of enjoyment, the children enjoyed themselves thoroughly. The Easter eggs were a great pleasure, one little boy beginning to cry for fear all the scarlet ones should be gone before his turn came.

We had provided a merry-go-round and some first-rate jugglers. They performed the famous mango trick, which is always inexplicable, especially when performed as here on the bare ground, and with spectators in front and on all sides of the jugglers. Then they put one of their people into a trance, and during the trance put a skewer through her tongue, and finally with great deliberation cut a piece off and handed it round for us to see. It certainly was flesh, and had we not known that we were there for the sole object of being imposed upon, we should have sworn that it was a piece of her tongue, and that we had seen it cut off, and could still see her tongue hanging out and with the end gone.

How very little we can trust the evidence of our own senses! and therefore how little it weighs with us when we hear a person say, 'But I *saw* it!' Yes, we reply; not for a moment do we doubt your honesty in saying that you saw it, but if we had seen it *ourselves* we should still not believe it, or rather believe that our senses had been cheated in the outrageous way we know they may be cheated.

The woman could not have had her tongue cut off and then healed; but if she had not, then we have no right ever to place the evidence of our eyes alone beyond contradiction.

When all was over, and it was quite dark, the minister made a little speech on behalf of the children. He was saying how much they had enjoyed the treat—'And whom have we to thank for all this?' One little boy promptly said 'The Lord;' but his remark falling flat the others saw his mistake, and chorussed "Mr. and Mrs. King,' and cheered very heartily.

I paid rather heavily for venturing out earlier than I do on other days; for though I kept in complete shade, yet the air at 5.30 is like that of a furnace, and I got a smart touch of sunstroke. At the time I only felt my head queer, but at night such pain came on and such violent and prolonged sickness, that we quite thought I was in for cholera.

Warm wraps and mustard plaisters, however, with iced cloths on my head, presently took effect, and to-day I am nearly right again.

• • • • •

25 June . . . There is one characteristic of an Indian hot season, good or bad, according as you think. Time simply flies, and before you are well into a month you are out of it again.

It is owing to the absolute monotony. There is nothing to look back upon, and nothing to look forward to. One lives more absolutely in the present than at any other time of one's life. Sufficient unto the day is the evil thereof, and the heat and the fatigue; but as the next day will be like unto it, and the next, and the next, there is no particular desire to get it over, only to make it as little wearying as may be.

So one eats one's breakfast leisurely, dawdles over one's bath— the pleasantest time of all—then reads, works, writes, without ever looking out of doors, or even thinking of looking out of doors, till the dusk shows it is time to venture forth, and the servant announces that the carriage is round. Then a drive up and down the Mall—the only watered road, therefore the *only* road—home to a quiet dinner, and lo! the evening and the morning proclaim that another day is gone.

Notes

ᕕ

*_The Diary of a Civilian's Wife in India, 1877–1882_, 2 vols. (London: Bentley and Son, 1884), 2:268, 1:vii. All selections here come from volume 1 of this edition, which King published as Mrs. King.

1   Character in Anthony Trollope's _Barchester Towers_.

Beatrice Webb

(1858–1943)

BEATRICE (née Martha Beatrice) WEBB was the daughter of
Richard Potter, a wealthy railway promoter, and his wife, Lawrencina
Heyworth Potter, who allowed their nine daughters to read and discuss widely, encouraging the development of their minds. After her
mother died in 1882, Beatrice ran her father's household and supervised her younger sister, Rosie. Although Webb seemed headed for a
conventionally successful marriage, being well-to-do, intelligent,
beautiful, and eager to be "feminine," these 1882–84 excerpts* show
that she also repudiated the standard contemporary role for women,
yearning for independence and a public success that marriage would
preclude. Nonetheless, the obsessive passion she conceived for the
politician Joseph Chamberlain, after rejecting him as a suitor, tormented her through the 1880s. She found her mission and some peace
of mind in doing social work in London's East End and, almost reconciled to spinsterhood, had settled on a career as a social scientist
when she married Sidney Webb in 1892, not for passion but with the
understanding that their alliance would be a working partnership to
enhance their usefulness to society. So it proved. Within the next
seven years, they jointly published a history of trade unionism and
two other books on industrial problems, became the dominant figures
in the Fabian Society as well as experts on educational and municipal
reform, and founded the London School of Economics. In 1913,
they would also help found *The New Statesman*. Their collaboration
continued after the war, when they remained significant figures in
political and social thought. But although the partnership succeeded,
Beatrice treasured the diary (1873–1943) she kept until eleven days
before her death, because it allowed her to express herself independently of Sidney. It also and evidently ministered to a conflicted personality in need of a confidante.

From Beatrice Webb's Diary

24 July 1832 . . . Altogether the last week has been spent unworthily.[1] Father and Rosy neglected, no work done, every day a restless ambition grows, an ambition for a life with some result, vulgarly apparent to myself and others, and yet the necessary self-denial, even sufficient to accomplish well the duty nearest me, is not there. If a weakly mortal is to do anything in the world besides eat the bread thereof, there must be determined subordination of the whole nature to the one aim, no trifling with time which is passing, with strength which is only too limited. My short intimacy with Mr. Main[2] has at least given me an example in determined self-control; of a delicate constitution conquering ill-health and succeeding in the world's struggle. . . .

3 August What I should like to do this autumn would be to get on with arithmetic, if possible going in for a little mild mathematics and geometry, and to take up chemistry so as to have some sound practical knowledge of the elements of one science.

13 August Alfred [Cripps] and I had a long discussion over Mr Spencer's[3] résumé of his philosophy, resulting in my taking it up to bed and spending a couple of hours over it, eventually rushing downstairs and plunging in to *First Principles,* a plunge producing such agreeable sensations that I have since continued the practice every morning before breakfast.

So far I seem to be able to work my brain with greater ease than hitherto, and so long as I do not neglect the duties nearest to me, I think I may indulge in dreams of attainment, perhaps never realized or even approached, but still as an incentive to self-culture. Now I have within me a definite ambition, perhaps a foolish and vain one. Still, it has taken possession of me and filled a vacancy with—wind? Anyhow, I know more decidedly than ever what materials and what tools I want—the mastery of some sympathetic philosophy to bind together isolated groups of ideas and experiences, experiences of human nature by careful observation and experiment, and certain necessary tools such as a fair knowledge of numbers and their relation, and some power of correct expression. I feel sadly the lack of a good groundwork. I am simply ridiculously stupid with arithmetic—a sort of paralysis taking place in my brain when I look at numbers.

My diary, which began as a register of good intention, shall continue such. I do honestly and earnestly pray that no foolish vanity will lead me away from the *thorough* accomplishment of my real duties. It is so difficult with my very limited energy not to devote it to pleasant occupation, especially when that occupation advances self. One good thing about my present study is that it naturally inclines me to sympathy, to an interest in persons as the only means of collecting material. . . .

· · · · ·

4 November   Two or three weeks passed in the mental contortions consequent on attempting mathematics, without possessing mathematical faculty. I naturally refuse to believe that it is the highest faculty of the brain, though perhaps a necessary tool in the application of the highest faculties to the most important subjects. Anyhow, without it one cannot get even a glimpse of the land of science. . . . I confess my attention has been mostly confined to getting over so much ground daily. The geometrical side is the most pleasing—it is always easier to prove the existence of something which you *see* exists. Numbers are to me only half-believed-in facts which my unimaginative mind persists in deeming fictions. . . .

How subjective women are. Does it belong to their education or their nature? Certainly if psychology is to be advanced by self-analysis, women will be the great psychologists of the future. A perfectly frank account of the inner workings of our brain would be interesting, a quantitative as well as a qualitative analysis of motive and thought. As it is there is much that goes on within one, which one, as a prudent mistress winks at and overlooks. To dwell on it even with disapproval might give it an ugly significance. It is not wise to stop the ruffianly-looking vagrant, and inquire from him whence he comes and whither he goeth. If thoughts and actions really run in the line of least resistance, we should be careful of enlarging with self-consciousness the channels in the wrong direction. . . .

25 November   Making but small progress with mathematics and doing nothing else. Anyhow it is a healthful life—forcing one to own inferiority to the average man's mind, and a splendid corrective for the daydreams of last summer. Altogether the winter months with the short and often dreary days do not lend themselves to exaltation like the long sunlit hours of the summer months. . . .

What a blessing I can write in this little book without fearing that anyone will ever read and ridicule the nonsense and half-sense I scribble. That has been the attraction of a 'diary-book' to me—one can talk one's little things out to a highly appreciative audience, dumb but not deaf. And sometimes this is a necessary safety-valve to save one from that most painful operation, watching one's most cherished chicks hatched by unwearied perseverance coolly trodden underfoot. Now my honest desire is to appear commonplace and sensible, so that none of my dear kind family will think it necessary to remark to themselves or to me that I am otherwise than ordinary; to be on the right side of ordinary is the perfection of prudence in a young woman, and will save her from much heartburning and mortification of spirit. . . .

· · · · ·

14 February 1883   Tomorrow we take possession of our house in London. I go with a sincere intention of devoting myself to Society and the family, but that familiar 'daemon' of desire for self-improvement threatens to overcome intention. Perhaps vanity will step in and help 'good' intention.

22 February   One word before leaving. . . . A conflict has been going on within me. Shall I give myself up to Society, and make it my aim to succeed therein, or shall I only do so as far as duty calls me, keeping my private life much as it has been for the last nine months? On the whole the balance is in favour of Society. It is going with the stream, and pleasing my people; it is doing a thing thoroughly that I must do partially; it is taking opportunities instead of making them; it is risking less and walking on a well-beaten track in pleasant company.

. . . and lastly, and perhaps this is the reason which weighs most with me, there is less presumption in the choice.

Therefore, I solemnly dedicate my energies for the next five months to the cultivation of the social instincts, trusting that the good daemon within me will keep me from all vulgarity of mind, insincerity and falseness. I would like to go amongst men and women with a determination to know them, to humbly observe and consider their characteristics, always remembering how much there is in the most inferior individual which is outside and beyond one's understanding. Every fresh intimacy strengthens the conviction of one's own powerlessness to comprehend fully any other nature, even when one watches it with love. And without sympathy there is an impassable barrier to the real knowledge of the inner workings which guides the outer actions of human beings. Sympathy, or rather *accepted* sympathy, is the only instrument for the dissection of character. . . .

•   •   •   •   •

1 March   Huge party at the Speaker's [House of Commons]—one or two of such would last one a life-time. Find it so difficult to be the 'universally pleasant'. Can't think what to say. Prefer on the whole the crowd in Oxford Street, certainly the feminine part of it. 'Ladies' are so expressionless. Should fancy mental superiority of men greatest in our class. Could it be otherwise with the daily life of ladies in society? What is there in the life which is so attractive? How can intelligent women wish to marry into the set where this is the social regime?

•   •   •   •   •

24 March   Reading Herbert Spencer's *Psychology* diligently every morning. Those quiet three hours of study are the happiest ones in the day. Only one trouble continually arises—the stimulus a congenial study gives to my ambition, which is continually mortified by a gleam of self-knowledge. Meeting with the most ordinarily clever person forces me to appreciate my own inferiority. And yet, fool that I am, I can't help feeling that could I only devote myself to one subject, I could do something. However, I suppose that the most commonplace of persons every now and again catches sight of possibilities in his nature which from lack of other qualities are doomed to remain undeveloped. . . . What distresses me about my own little work is the

small amount of material I have to work upon, the trivial subjective-
ness of my thought. That is what I am painfully conscious of when I
meet really clever men. My work, if it can be dignified by that name,
is so amateurish and yet I don't know that I have a right to pretend
to anything better and more businesslike. All my duties lie in the
practical direction; why should I, wretched little frog, try and puff
myself into a professional? If I could rid myself of that mischievous
desire to achieve, I could defend the few hours I devote to study by the
truly satisfactory effect it has on my physical nature. It does keep me
in health, whether through its direct influence on my circulation or
through the indirect effect of a certain self-satisfaction it induces.
Dissipation doesn't suit me, morally or physically, and I don't see why
I shouldn't be true to my own nature and resist it.

• • • • •

24 April . . . Now my life is divided sharply into the thoughtful
part and the active part, completely unconnected one with the other.
They are in fact an attempt to realize the different and almost conflict-
ing ideals necessitating a compromise as to energy and time which
has to be perpetually readjusted. My only hope is that the one ideal is
hidden from the world, the truth being that in my heart of hearts
I'm ashamed of it and yet it is actually the dominant internal power.
Fortunately for me all external forces support the other motive, so
perhaps the balance is a pretty just one. But it is a curious experience
moving about among men and women, talking much, as you are
obliged to do, and never mentioning those thoughts and problems
which are your *real life* and which absorb, in their pursuit and solution, all the earnestness of your nature. This doubleness of motive,
still more the disemblance towards the world you live in, extending
even to your own family, must bring with it a feeling of unreality;
worse, a loss of energy in the sudden transitions from the one life to
the other. Happily one thing is clear to me. This state of doubtfulness
will not be of long duration, and the work that is done during that
state will not be useless to me in whichever vocation my nature and
my circumstances eventually force me into. I shall surely some day
have the veil withdrawn and be allowed to gaze unblinded on the
narrow limits of my own possibilities.

• • • • •

5 November   Three weeks thoroughly enjoyed at The Argoed,[4] and some good work done. Solitude too has matured my plans for the future. *If* I remain free (which alas is a big if) I see pretty clearly where the work is which I *would* do. Whether I have sufficient faculty remains to be seen. Proof of incapacity will not be wanting if I am strong enough to see it. At present, in this phase of my work, my duties as an ordinary woman are not interfered with by the pursuit of my private ends. I doubt whether they would ever need be, if one chose to remain unmarried. It is almost necessary to the health of a woman, physical and mental, to have definite home duties to fulfil: details of practical management and, above all things, someone dependent on her love and tender care. So long as Father lives and his home is the centre for young lives, I have mission enough as a *woman*. If to this *most* important work I could join another work and work that would satisfy the restless ambition of my nature, then possibly I might remain content to know only through sympathy those feelings which absorb the energies of most women. A time would come when I should stand alone; destitute of those close intimacies, which become ever more precious as animal spirits and intellectual energies fail. If I could not honestly say, 'the work was good', I should bitterly regret the absence of human ties, the neglect and disease of those powers for good which belong to all women alike. Still, one must have courage, faith in oneself, trusting to the sincerity of one's nature to tell one when it is misplaced. All I can pray for is vigour, freedom from petty self-congratulation, vain castles which hide from view the clear horizon. . . .

•   •   •   •   •

7 December   I began my account but a practical problem has intervened[5] and I must keep all my strength of mind to deal with it. One thing I will *not* do. I will not give way to a feeling, however, strong, which is not sanctioned by my better self. I will not desert a life in which there are manifold opportunities for good for a life in which my nature is at war with itself.

27 December   Rather a miserable dinner-party. Old philosopher[6] very low, feeling his pulse and looking suspiciously at every morsel of food, speaking grudgingly every word. . . .

Yesterday better. 'It would never have done for me to marry,' he said. 'I could not have stood the monotony of married life and then I should have been too fastidious. I must have had a rational woman with great sympathy and considerable sense of humour.' 'Rather difficult to find,' I observed. 'Rational women are generally odiously dull and self-centred.' 'That is a very erroneous generalization; George Eliot was highly rational and yet intensely sympathetic, but there the weak point (which appeared a very important one to me) was physique.' 'I could not have married a woman who had not great physical attraction,' added the withered old philosopher, stretching his bony limbs out and leaving that patent theory-making machine on the side of the armchair, his upper lip appearing preternaturally long and his eye preternaturally small.

Father, what between past remembrances and future prospects, was excited and really unhappy, though he did his best to appear genial and happy. Slight feeling of jar in the whole party, and consciousness of wide difference of opinion on a possibly *coming* question. When host and hostess are not at peace with themselves and the world there is not much chance of real geniality. However, my tortured state cannot long endure. The 'to be or not to be' will soon be settled.

New Year's Eve   Rosebud and I alone.

It is indeed an Eve for me. Two distinct ways open to me, one of which, it seems inevitable, that I must take. Herbert Spencer's last words: 'It is not only foolish but absolutely wrong of you not to publish your Bacup[7] experiences. At the present time, a protest, formed on actual observation of the working man in his normal state against the pernicious tendency of political activity, would be invaluable. I shall arrange with Knowles about publishing an article from you.' And while the old philosopher is discussing with the editor of the *Nineteenth Century* the desirability of encouraging a beloved disciple to come into the literary arena, the same beloved disciple is entertaining with no *untender* feeling the arch-enemy, the very embodiment of the 'pernicious tendency'.

And this horrible dilemma which appears to threaten me (principle versus feeling) renders all my thought egotistical. My own immediate fate stares me in the face wherever I turn. I seem to be moving onward amidst a company of phantoms, some pushing others restraining; but both parties equally ghostly in their powers, equally immaterial in their influence on the result. I, too, seem to be as in a dream, acting a part with my own family as audience, a part which *makes itself* as I go on, the final scene of which lies not within that healthy region of free-willing foresight. And as the time approaches I *dare* not *think,* but trust that the energy stored up in days of thought*lessness* will suffice for the last struggle; or that perchance some current arising within the 'whirlpool' will drift me outward. This truly is my last hope; if I do hope for continued independence of mind and body.

12 January 1884 Another small episode of my life over. After six weeks of feverish indecision, the day [of Chamberlain's arrival] comes. House full of young people and the three last days passed in dancing and games: I feel all the while as if I were dancing in a dream towards some precipice. Saturday 5th remainder of the ball party chatting round the afternoon tea table, the great man's son and daughter amongst them. The door opens—'Mr Chamberlain', general uprising. I advance from amongst them, and in my nervousness almost press six pounds just received into his hand. General feeling of discomfort; no one quite understanding the reason of Mr Chamberlain's advent. There exists evidently no cordiality between him and his host, for Father in a few minutes returns to play patience with an absent and distressed look, utterly disgusted at the *supposed* intentions of his visitor.

At dinner, after some shyness, we plunged into essentials and he began to delicately hint his requirements. That evening and the next morning till lunch we are on 'susceptible terms'. A dispute over state education breaks the charm. 'It is a question of authority with women; if you believe in Herbert Spencer you won't believe in me.' This opens the battle. By a silent arrangement we find ourselves in the garden. 'It pains me to hear any of my views controverted', and with this preface he begins with stern exactitude to lay down the articles of his political creed. I remain modestly silent; but noticing my silence he remarks that he requires 'intelligent sympathy' from women. 'Servility, Mr Chamberlain,' think I, not sympathy, but intelligent servility: what many women give men, but the difficulty lies in changing one's master, in jumping from one *tone* of thought to the exact opposite—

with intelligence. And then I advanced as boldly as I dare my feeble
objections to his general proposition, feeling that in this case I owe it
to the man to show myself and be absolutely sincere. He refutes my
objections by re-asserting his convictions passionately, his expression
becoming every minute more gloomy and determined. He tells me
the history of his political career, how his creed grew up on a basis of
experience and sympathy, how his desire to benefit 'the many' had
become gradually a passion absorbing within itself his whole
nature. . . .

And so we wandered up and down the different paths of the Standish garden, the mist which had hid the chasm between us gradually
clearing off. Not a suspicion of feeling did he show towards me. He
was simply determined to assert his convictions. If I remained silent he
watched my expression narrowly, I felt his curious scrutinizing eyes
noting each movement as if he were anxious to ascertain whether
I yielded to his absolute supremacy. If I objected to or ventured to
qualify his theories or his statements, he smashed objection and quali-
fication by an absolute denial, and continued his assertion. He remarked as we came in that he felt as if he had been making a speech. I
felt utterly exhausted, we hardly spoke to each other the rest of the
day. The next morning, when the Playnes had left, he suggested some
more 'exercise'. I *think* both of us felt that all was over between us,
so that we talked more *pleasantly,* but even then he insisted on bringing
me back from trivialities to a discussion as to the intellectual subordination of women. 'I have only one domestic trouble: my sister and
daughter are bitten with the women's rights mania. I don't allow any
action on the subject.' 'You don't allow division of opinion in your
household, Mr Chamberlain?' 'I can't help people *thinking* differently
from me.' 'But you don't allow expression of the difference?' 'No.'
And that little word ended our intercourse.

Now that the pain and indecision are over, I can't help regretting
that absorption in the peculiar nature of our relationship left me so
little capable of taking the opportunities he gave me of knowing him.
The political creed is the whole man; the outcome of his peculiar
physical and mental temperament played upon by the experiences of
his life. He is neither a reasoner nor an observer in the scientific
sense. . . .

By nature he is an enthusiast and a despot. A deep sympathy with the misery and incompleteness of most men's lives, and an earnest desire to right this, transforms political action into a religious crusade; but running alongside this genuine enthusiasm is a passionate desire to *crush* opposition to *his will,* a longing to put his foot on the necks of others, though he would persuade himself that he represents the right and his adversaries the wrong. . . .

And now that it is all over, I have a stunned feeling as I gradually wake up to the old surroundings. . . . Plenty of practical work immediately in front of me, which will absorb my small bit of energy for the next six weeks. Then a return to the old work. Only everyday actual observation of men and things takes the place of accumulating facts from books and boudoir trains of thought. Undoubtedly the Bacup trip is the right direction. To profit by that kind of observation I *must* gain more knowledge of legal and commercial matters, understand the theory of government before I can appreciate the deficiencies in the practice. The time is now come for some defined object towards which all my energies must be bent. . . .

.   .   .   .   .

22 April   Settled at last![8] I was thankful to read the other day in Bacon that it was advisable to keep some record of your motives and aims, that on the whole it helped forward consistency. Looking back through my diary I find that I have had a decided motive for work the last two years, over and above the practical aim of fulfilling my domestic duties and making the best of my position. This aim has been based on the belief that I have faculty for literary work. *Now,* I think this has been a delusion. Still I don't see how I could do better than keep up my own individual interests. There is so much spare time in my life, it must be filled somehow. If I were, in a fit of discouragement, to throw up everything (for if I gave up my aim it would mean this with me, I couldn't do purposeless work) I should become miserably restless, probably give way to some strong feeling and find my own nature too much for me. My nature is like a strong wilful ship; unless I keep it occupied it gives me endless trouble. If I once begin to humour it, give way to it and allow it to amuse itself in its own sweet fashion, it becomes unbearable and a curse to its owner. And lately I have allowed it free play, and must have a struggle with it, before I can again have peace. Can I begin this struggle bravely and instantly? What is the use of drifting, unless indeed I half desire to be where the current of my own feeling will bring me? And there is the trouble. My own mind is not made up. I have been meditating over the question for five months,[9] have done little else but think about it; now I am no nearer solving it. Practically I have resisted, have refused to take the line of subordination and absolute dependence which would have brought things to a crisis. Possibly my refusal to consent to the conditions will have cured all desire on the other side. Then, though mortified, I shall be relieved. I shall have been only decently truthful and honest and can abide by the consequences. But if the question be put in another form?

Let me look facts clearly in the face and take counsel with myself. Ambition and superstition began the feeling. A desire to play a part in the world, and a belief that as the wife of a great man I should play a bigger part than as a spinster or as an ordinary married woman. Let me analyse the part I should play. He has taken his line for better or for worse in politics; he has an overpowering ambition, he will not hesitate much as to the means of gaining his ends. He has told me distinctly that he will not bear his opinion being 'controverted' or his action criticized. He desires a woman who is personally attractive to him, who will sympathize and encourage him, be a continual rest to him, giving him the uncompromising admiration which the world withholds. His temperament and his character are intensely attractive to me. I feel I could relieve the gloom, could understand the mixed motive and the difficulties of a nature in which genuine enthusiasm and personal ambition are so curiously interwoven. The outward circumstances of the life of a politican's wife would be distasteful to me or, rather, they would be supremely demoralizing, unless they were accepted as a means to an end in which I myself believed. And here is really the kernel of the question. Do I believe in the drift of his political views and do I believe that the means employed are *honest*? If I do not believe that this line of political action is right, if I do not believe that the end is pursued without deviating from the first moral principles, and were yet to sign both aims and means with my signature, I should be selling my soul and should deserve misery. It is no use saying that my signature is of no importance. Certainly not to the world; but all important to me. The first duty of the individual is to live truly and honestly according to the nature which has been given to him. Once married, I should of course subordinate my views to my husband's, should, as regards his own profession, accept implicitly his views of right and wrong. But I cannot shirk the responsibility of using my judgment before I acknowledge his authority.

Social questions are the vital questions of today. They take the place of religion. I do not pretend to solve them. Their solution seems largely a matter of temperament. Still, the most insignificant mind has a certain bias, has an intellectual as well as a moral conscience. If we wilfully deny the laws of our special mental constitution, we must suffer the penalty of a diseased and twisted nature; we must leave this life conscious of faithlessness to the faith which is in us. And even if I put on one side the question of the right or wrong in the aims pursued in political action, as one on which I could form no opinion, and might therefore safely accept that of another person, there still remains the question of means. I *can* and *must* judge as to the honesty and straightforwardness of these. It requires no special knowledge, no great reasoning power to understand a lie: information withheld and falsified, false accusations advanced, passions appealed to, to attain other ends than those proposed. A higher standard of motive is asked for in social action more than in any other.

The social reformer *prefers* to be an uncompromising altruist. He solemnly declares that he is working for the public weal. His whole authority, derived from public opinion, arises from the faith of the people in his honesty of purpose and fine strength of understanding. If he uses his mind to manipulate facts, to twist them so that they shall serve his own personal interests, if the craving for power is greater than the desire for truth, he is a traitor to the society to which he professes loyal service. Interested as I am in the welfare of human-ity (however incompetent I am to help it forward), I could not help judging each separate action according to the laws of my own mind, and if I could not express the judgement, had to sit silently and ac-quiesce in wrong-doing, not only acquiesce but help it forward with my devotion and sympathy, where could I turn to for peace, that

peace which passeth all understanding, the peace of a satisfied conscience, the deep content arising from the consciousness that, however
minute our intellectual and moral qualities may be, we are striving
honestly to develop them and use them for the good of our fellow
creatures? I should *not* influence him. He has shown me that distinctly.
He has been straightforward all through, has told me distinctly his
requirements. When I have been absolutely honest with him he has
turned away. That is not what he wants and *I know it*. It is only when
I have simulated *la femme complaisante,* turned the conversation from
principles to personalities that he has desired me. He has pointed
out to me plainly the hardships in the life of the wife of a man absorbed in public life, has not wished me to be influenced by any
glamour that may surround it, has said in so many words 'only devotion to my aims would justify you in accepting it'. And I have not
only no devotion to these aims, but have to twist my reasoning in
order to *tolerate them.*

And now, what is the straightest course? It is not to cut the knot by
refusing all further intercourse. I know how strong the temptations
are which would entice me into it. Great personal attraction and the
immediate gratification of a woman's instinctive longing for love and
support and for settled and defined occupation. And beyond this,
the desire for the personal prestige and the importance I should acquire
by becoming his wife. And if he no longer wishes for it what is the
use of playing further with my own nature? Looking back on the
whole affair, I confess to myself that my action and thought have been
wanting in dignity and nicety of feeling. I have *chattered* about feelings
which should be kept within the holy of holies. The only excuse
has been the extraordinary nature of the man and his method and the
interest which public position lends to his personality. But now I
can make a fresh start; force my thoughts from their dwelling-place
of the last five months, and devote myself vigorously to my duties
and to the nature and true development of my own nature.
Amen. . . .

The remaining months of the Season then I shall devote myself
body and soul to my home duties, to settling Father and Rosy in their
new life, making this house a centre to the family and of real sociabil-

ity. I shall look about me for some permanent work, some sphere
of practical usefulness. . . .

9 May I shall not write again in this book. It is the close of a period
with me. I began it with my old ambition strong upon me; working
my little faculties to their utmost, in the full belief that some day I
should have somewhat to tell the world. This strange conceit was fos-
tered by the retirement of a woman's life, living and striving by herself, shielded from all tests as to the real worth of her work. Midway
in this period, another path seemed opened to me, another highway to
prominence. That also is closed. I remain weakened and discouraged,
my old ambition fallen irretrievably. I prayed for light and I *have it.*
I see clearly that my intellectual faculty is only mirage, that I have no
special mission. . . .

Strength too fails me now. I look hopelessly through the books on
my table and neither understand nor care to understand what I read.
My imagination has fastened upon one form of feeling. The woman's
nature has been stirred to the depths; I have loved and lost; but possibly by my own wilful mishandling, possibly also for my own happiness; but still lost. Let me look that fact bravely in the face and learn
by it. I may not again trifle with my nature: and yet—I would not be
without the experience of the last months. It has broadened the basis
of sympathy, as all true experience does, even if it be the experience
of our own gains, of our own craving for the devotion of another
being. One must *feel with (mitgefuhl)* in order to understand, and to
feel with, one must have felt before. One person stands out bound up
with the last sounds of a departing day. Mary Booth's[10] gentle and
loving contempt for any *special* work outside the ordinary sphere of a
woman's life; her high standard of excellence which should discourage
any vain attempt to leave the beaten track of a woman's duty. And I
having revelled in feeling, having yielded up my soul, believing that it
was desired, found satisfaction in this. She made me ready to
renounce my old aims and acknowledge the sway of the new feeling.
Those three days at Southsea seemed designed to increase the sensi-
tiveness to the blow. And when it came, when I realized by the tone
and expression that all was over, my whole nature gave way before it.
Both ideals had fallen. Life alone, life together, remaining only the

seemingly daily round of commonplace duties. And the blankness and weariness within my soul brought strikingly into relief by the luxury and enviableness of my surroundings. The whole seems a nightmare.

There is glitter all around me and darkness within, the darkness of blind desire yearning for the light of love. All sympathy is shut from me. I stand alone with my own nature now too strong for me. I clutch desperately at *my duty* to those around me, that last hope for the soul despairing of its own happiness. . . . Still there rises up before me, the misty forms of three maidens: Humility, Tenderness, Discretion, and they beckon me with loving pity to follow them. Amen.

Notes

～

★The selections here are taken from *The Diary of Beatrice Webb,* ed. Norman and Jeanne MacKenzie, 4 vols. (Cambridge, Mass.: Harvard University Press, 1982–85), and are all drawn from volume 1: *1873–1892, "Glitter Around and Darkness Within."*

1   Webb was on holiday in Switzerland with her father and Rosy.

2   John Frederick Main, who taught at the South Kensington School of Science and was a fellow guest at the hotel, was suffering from tuberculosis.

3   The philosopher and social scientist Herbert Spencer (1820–1903), who was a family friend.

4   An extended Jacobean farmhouse in the Wye Valley, acquired by the Potters as a holiday retreat.

5   She had met the Radical politician Joseph Chamberlain at a dinner party in June and recently invited him and two of his children to visit the Potters at the family home, Standish, at the New Year; she had reason to anticipate his marriage proposal.

6   Herbert Spencer, who disliked Chamberlain, as did Webb's father.

7   Webb had tested her powers of social observation by a long visit to Bacup in Lancashire, where her maternal great-grandfather had been a millowner. There she became deeply interested in both cooperative and state socialism as correctives to individualistic profiteering.

8   Webb's father had given up the home at Standish and moved his London home to York House, a fashionable house in Kensington Palace Gardens.

9   Webb had continued to see Chamberlain and even gradually discovered in herself a passionate attraction to him, which she was to confess to him in 1887.

10   Webb's first cousin and close friend, whose father had a home at Southsea where Webb had visited.

II

Of Friends and Lovers

_____

Nancy Woodforde

(1757–1830)

N A N C Y (née Anna Maria) W O O D F O R D E was one of the five children of Heighes Woodforde, a Somerset attorney, and his wife, Anne Dorville. At eighteen, in October 1779, she went to live at Weston Longeville Parsonage in Norfolk with her genial uncle, James Woodforde, rector of Weston, and to remain for twenty-four years as his housekeeper. She did no domestic work, except for making jams and preserves, but she oversaw the servants and was well pleased with her housekeeping role, though she also sought her uncle's help in studying Latin and history. James was a convivial soul who often entertained his neighbors and was invited in turn to enjoy their hospitality, and Nancy was welcomed into their company. As her diary excrpts for 1792 evidence, a circle of women friends was very important in her life. Woodforde was stout—her concerned uncle at first attempted to convince her to eat less—and chronically lame; for her lameness she regularly took long walks in the garden, often tramping two or three miles, whatever the weather. Her fond uncle occasionally found her saucy and pert; a neighbor reported her as merry and jolly. She was passionately fond of two of her brothers, William and Samuel, but at odds with a mother who, she complained, refused her children a fair share of their father's estate after he died in 1789. In 1803, after the death of her uncle, who had left her half his estate, she went to London to live with her brother Samuel but in 1805 arranged to live with relatives at Castle Cary. Bath being near Cary, she was able to resume her friendship with the Mrs. Custance of the excerpts here, whose remove to Bath had so depleted her circle of agreeable friends. Only Woodforde's laconic memo-book diaries are extant for other years, but for 1792 this expanded diary has also survived, and luckily Uncle James, famous for his *Diary of a Country Parson,* included in it a record of his adored niece too.★

From Nancy Woodforde's Diary

Sunday, 1 January 1792   O Lord I pray thee to preserve me and all my Friends from sickness and all the Misfortunes of this Life and restore my amiable Friend Mrs. Custance who I am very sorry to say now lays dangerously ill after her lying in:[1] we should be very unhappy to loose so good a Neighbour. May God Almighty grant that I may continue to walk as well as I can now, and that I may enjoy as good a state of health through out this Year as I do at present. Walked a Mile this Morning, a mild pleasant Day.

Monday, 2 January   Uncle and self took a ride to Witchingham. Saw Mrs. Jeans[2] who appeared pleased to see us and was very chatty and civil, bought of Mrs. Jeans a Muslin Handkerchief for which I paid her 4 shillings which I thought a bargain. On our return home our Horse fell down on all fours but got up again in a Moment and thank God we did not meet with the least hurt. Mr. Jeans was out a hunting. Mrs. Custance very ill indeed which grieves us greatly.

Tuesday, 3 January   Sent a long letter to Mrs. Bodham by our Servant Betty Dade who went home to see her friends. Three of Mrs. Custances Sons made us a Morning Visit, I was very sorry to hear by them that my amiable Neighbour Mrs. Custance was extremely ill and that she has not turn'd in her Bed for several Nights. Uncle return'd home with them and Named their Sister Charlotte.[3] Mr. C. very uneasy about Mrs. Custance. Uncle came home to Dinner.

•   •   •   •   •

Wednesday, February 15   This morning my good friend Mrs. Custance sent her Coach for me to make her a Morning Visit, which I did and was happy to find her in good spirits notwithstanding the Dear Soul was not able to move in her Bed nor have not for these seven Weeks, and its greatly feared that she will not be able to sit up in her Bed these two Months to come. Her complaint is strain across her Loins which happened when she was brought to Bed. Last Friday was the first Day of her seeing Company. She was very glad to see me and I keep up my Spirits as well as I could tho' it was with difficulty that I

refrain'd from tears at seeing my good friend in such a Melancholy
situation. She said that she should be glad to see me at all times and I
promised to call on her as often as possible. I staid with her an hour
and a quarter and returned home in the Coach. Uncle went out a
coursing and brought home a Hare. A very damp Day. Won at Cards
6d [pence].

Thursday, 16 February A very Cold Day with Snow. Mr. Du Quesne
call'd in his way to Mr. Jeans where he was going to dine and which
we should have done also had not we been prevented by the Weather.
Mr. Du Quesne would have taken me with him had he known of
our being invited to meet him at Witchingham, therefore I was not
dress'd when he call'd and of course could not go. Mrs. Custance sent
me The Devil upon two Sticks in England Publish in 1791 to read,
which is a very clever entertaining thing indeed and gives you an idea
of many wonderful characters in the present age.

· · · · ·

Wednesday, 29 February Another charming pleasant Day. Mrs. Custance sent us the Life of Baron Frederic Trenck containing his adventures, his cruel and excessive sufferings during ten years imprisonment
at the Fortress of Magdeburg by command of the late King of Prussia, also Anecdotes, Historical, political and Personal—translated
from the German by Thomas Holcroft, second edition 1791. This
afternoon one Mr. Burdon and his Wife call'd with Muslins, Chintz
Patches for Gowns, Cambricks &c. I bought a Worked Muslin Apron
for which paid eleven and sixpence also a Muslin for which I gave
six and ninepence and for half a yd of Muslin three shillings and
threepence. They left with me a very handsome Chintz Gown which
I lik'd very well and which they are to call again for in May if I do
not chuse to keep it. I am to give two Guineas and half for it as that
they declared is the lowest price I shall buy it as it is a very handsome
good Gown.

Thursday, March 1 Finished reading the first Vol of Baron Trenck,
the account of his suffering filled my mined with sorry and pity for
him. Walk'd two Miles to Day. Play'd at Cards with Uncle.

Friday, 2 March   Walked up to Weston H——e to see Mrs. Custance.
Was caught in the Rain going up and was very warm and much Fatigued owing to the Rain when I got there. Heard that Mrs. Branthwaite was with Mrs. Custance, therefore I went into the Housekeepers
Room to rest myself and had a great deal of Conversation with Mrs.
Tooke who I found a very clever sensible Woman. Mrs. Layton came a
few minutes after I was there. I would not let Mrs. Custance know
that I was there till after the above Ladies were gone, as I did not like
to make my appearance while they were there. As soon as they were
gone Mrs. Custance was informed that I was there and she sent word
to me that I must stay and dine there and she would send me home
in the Evening. I accepted her invitation but did not see her till an
Hour after the Ladies were gone as she had been fatigued with the
above Ladies Company.

I was desired to walk up into her Room about half an hour before
Dinner and found Mrs. Custance better and very glad to see me. I
was very happy to hear that Mrs. Custance had turned in her Bed on
Wednesday for the first time since her illness and that she had turn'd
two or three times since, but with great pain. She offered me a beautiful Rose which Mrs. Branthwaite brought her out of their hothouse
but I would not take it on any account. Mr. Custance was in the Room
when I went to see Mrs. Custance and was glad to see me. Betty
walked with me and she carried my New Gown and Apron which I
shewed to Mrs. Custance, both of which she admired very much
indeed as did Mr. Custance likewise. I also carried up my Carlton
House Magazine for Mrs. Custance as I thought it might entertain her
for a short time, as any little thing is amusing to a Person in confinement.

I din'd with Mr. Custance and we had a deal of Conversation about
Books and other things so that I spent my time very agreeably. I
went up to Mrs. C. Room after Dinner and sat and chatted with her
near an Hour. Heard that the Duke of York had lately lost seventeen
thousand Pounds at gaming and that the Duchess was not so happy as
could be wished. It was a very wet evening there, Mrs. Custance
sent me home in her Coach, Betty came with me in it also—I got
home to tea. Brought home the second Vol: of Baron Trenck and

Mrs. Custance lent me the first Vol: of Hogarth illustrated by John
Ireland. Sent a Letter to Br. Sam. Play'd at Cards with my Uncle
in the Evening.

· · · · ·

Monday, 19 March   Took a walk up to Weston H——e to see Mrs
Custance. Do not think that she looks so well as when I saw her last,
tho' she says that she is getting a little better, but she does not think
that she shall be able to get upon her feet these three Months. I am
quite grieved to see her in such a Melancholy situation. Soon after I
was there came Mrs Branthwaite who is a very fashionable and agreeable Woman, she was dressed in a Riding Dress and a Black Beaver
Hat with a small thread lace Morning Cap under it. She very politely
offered to bring me Home, which favour I could not refuse to accept
as it was done in so kind a manner. She said she should be happy
to do it at any time when ever she sho'ld meet me at Weston House.

· · · · ·

Saturday, 24 March   Betty and I set off on a Walk to Weston but was
prevented from proceeding on my Journey by Rain, which was a
great disappointment to me as I wish'd very much to have spent an
Hour or two with poor Mrs Custance in her Melancholy situation.
Mrs England sent me a nice Pot of Honey for which my Uncle gave
James Atterton a Shilling. Had my Carlton House Magazine which
should have come at the beginning of this Month. Rcd. of John Priest
the following ingredients for a Diet Drink. Senna 2 oz—8d. Sassafras
2 oz 2d. Guiacum 6d. Jalap 1 oz 4d. Saffron 4 oz one Shilling. Rhu-
barb one Shilling. Maiden Hair 3d. Sweet Fennel seed 1 oz 2d. Anni-
seeds 1 oz 1d. Creme Tartar ½ oz 1d. For the above paid four Shillings.

· · · · ·

Thursday, 29 March   Mr Custance sent his Carriage for us. Dined
there with Lady Bacon and Mrs Press Custance. After Dinner Lady
B. and self went up stairs and sat with Mrs Custance, who was glad to
see me, and I was happy to see her on her Couch for the first time.
She look very well but she still remains very helpless, which I fear will
be the case a long time. Lady Bacon told me how miserable she had
been about her Sister. Her Ladyship was dress in a Dark Chintz Gown

and a Muslin Petticoat, a very smart Bonnet. I have made myself one very like it.

•　•　•　•　•

Tuesday, 8 May　Cold Winday Weather. Mrs Custance sent her Carriage for me this Morning. I went and spent two or three Hours with her. Was press'd much by Mr and Mrs Custance to stay to Dinner but did not chose it on account of dyning alone with Mr Custance which is not so pleasant for a single Woman, but promised to spend the day the next time I walked up.

•　•　•　•　•

Friday, 18 May　Went to Reepham with Uncle to the Visitation. I din'd with Mrs Priest and her Daughters and the Miss Priests and myself went to Church. Heard Mr Jewel Preach. A very disagreeably Windy and stormey Morning but was desirous of going as I was engaged. Got there much better than I expectd, Call'd on Mr Lamb, saw Mrs Wymer and Miss Varlo there. Bought of Mrs. Batcheler 2 yds and a Quarter of Muslin for which I paid 14 6. Mr Jeans, Uncle and self and three Miss Sandles drank Tea at Mr Priest. Supp'd and sleept at Witchingham which I wished on account of Miss Lloyds being there. Mrs. Jeanss Brother was there, he is a poor Proud dull Soul and has but *very* little to say for himself. Play'd at Cards and lost Sixpence. Miss Lloyd and I talk'd till two o'Clock in the Morning. I find that she does not like the Jeans and I don't wonder at it for they treat all people in too cheap a manner and their Pride affectation and management in their House is worse than ever.

Saturday, 19 May　After Breakfast Miss Lloyd and self walk'd sometime in Mr. Jeans's Garden, Mrs. Jeans being up stairs with her Child. We had a great deal of Conversation together. Play'd at Cards in the Evening, neither lost or winn'd.

•　•　•　•　•

29 May　Uncle[,] self and Mr Du Quesne din'd at Weston House with Mrs. Green and Mrs. Loobe. I went with Mr. Du Quesne, Uncle walked. Found Mrs. Custance very findly [*sic*]. I went in my Blue Gown for the first time. Mrs. Custance liked it extremely well.

30 May   Bells ringing all Day on account of Mrs. Custances coming down Stairs for the first time since Christmas. . . . Finished working my double Handkerchief.

Friday, 1 June   Uncle and self walk'd up to Weston House to Congratulate Mrs. Custance on her first coming down Stairs. She was very glad to see us and pressed us to stay to Dinner, which I did but Uncle return'd Home and came again in the Afternoon to Tea. I saw Mrs. Custance walk down Stairs to Day. She, Mr. Custance and myself din'd together, this being the first time of her dining below Stairs since Christmas. After Dinner she walked up Stairs with her Stick much better than we expected she could. Uncle and self walk'd home after Tea, Mr. Custance went part of the way with us. Warm Day.

. . . . . .

Wednesday, 20 June   Uncle and self took a ride to Mattishall and dine'd with Mr. & Mrs. Bodham, where we were very genteelly treated and pressed very much to sleep there as it was very likely to be a wet Evening it having Rain'd almost the whole Day. Call'd on Mr. Du Quesne on our way to Mattishall, thought he looked poorly. Mrs. Bodham lent me a Tucker and Ruff⁴ all in one by which I intend to make myself one like it. We returned home safe and without much rain at half after 8 o'Clock. The Road very dirty and like Winter. Cold Evening.

Thursday, 21 June   Very busy all Day making a Tucker like Mrs. Bodhams which I accomplished. This Morning Uncle received a Letter by Mr Custances Servant from Miss Pounset in London saying that she does not give up the hopes of seeing us at Cole this Summer. She does not mention a word of my Br. I am surprised they have not seen each other.

Friday, 22 June   Wrote a Note to Mrs. Bodham with the Tucker and sent it to Miss Browne who is to give it to Mrs. Bodham. The three young Custance's and Mr. Bacon call'd this Afternoon and brought us the News paper and an invitation to dine with them on Tuesday next when their Sister Charlotte is to be Christned.

Sunday, 24 June   Went to Church this Morning. After Service went and spoke to Mrs. Custance and Lady Bacon as I thought Mrs. Custance was not so well able to come to me as she used to do. Staid and chatted with them some little time, being prevented from going out of Church by Rain.

Tuesday, 26 June   Uncle and self dined at Weston House with Lady Bacon and Press Custance, Miss Charlotte being Christend this Morning. Mr. Du Quesne call'd on his way to Reepham. Lady Bacon lent me a Tucker to take the Pattern of it. Uncle had a Letter from Miss Pounsett.

. . . . .

Friday, 29 June   Mrs. Custance and Lady Bacon made us a Morning Visit, this is the first time of seeing Mrs. C. in our House since before Christmas. Lady Bacon brought me a Pattern to worke my Muslin Petticoat by it from Lady Ca Hobart who has worked one like it. I drew of the Pattern and return'd it to Lady B this Evening. Shall not work at my Coat till the Winter. I told them the way to make Tuckers out of their old fashion Double Ruffles with which they seem'd much pleased and said they would see about making some.

. . . . .

Monday, August 6   Mrs. Custance called on me this Morning and took me with her to make Mrs. Townshend a visit. Saw Mrs. Townshend, Mr. T. not at home. Mr. & Mrs. Jeans call'd whilest I was out. They staid about half an Hour with my Uncle. I was not in the least sorry at [not] being at Home as Mrs. Jeans is a very bad Neighbour having not call'd on us but once before these two years. Very hot Day.

Tuesday, 7 August   Mrs. Custance her two Daughters and her Son John drank Tea with us. She brought a Cloak for me to make a Handk. out of part of it for her like my new one, which I offered to do for her. I shewed her my new Bonnet with which she was so much pleased that she beg me to send to my Milliner for one exactly like it only it was to be all White. I wrote a Note to Miss Browne for one whilest Mrs. C. was here and her Servant is to carry it to morrow.

Wednesday, 8 August   Work'd very hard all this Day on Mrs. Custances Handkerchief.

Thursday, 9 August   Very hot Day. Worked all Day very hard indeed on Mrs. C. Handk. which I have almost finished and hope I shall be able to send it Home on Saturday Evening.

·   ·   ·   ·   ·

Saturday, 1 September   Wrote a Note to Mrs. Custance to desire the favor of hers and Mr. Custances Company to meet the Townshends which she said in a Note they would do. Mr. Custance call'd on us just after I received the Note. He came to inform us that they were going to leave Weston and live at Bath, where he had taken a House. We were greatly surprised and extremely sorry to hear such disagreeable news which occasions me to shed tears of sorrow at the thoughts of loosing such good Neighbours.

Sunday, September 2   We were very low Spirited all this Day on account of loosing our only Neighbours. Mr. & Mrs. Townshend, Mrs. Cornwallis, two Miss Townshends, Mr. & Mrs. Custance and Mr. Du Quesne drank Tea with us this Afternoon. I told Mrs. Custance how sorry I was at hearing that she was going to leave Weston. She said that she was sorry on my account and Mr. S. that we were the only people they left with regret. Mrs. Custance said that she would write to me and tell me every thing she could to entertain me. Uncle shewed the company my Brothers Pictures[5] which they greatly admired. Mrs. Custance brought us a brace of Partridges. They all left us at half after Eight.

Mrs. T. was dress'd in a worked Muslin Jacket a dark Green Sash and a Hat trimm'd with dark Green Ribbon in two Cockades before. The Miss Townshend were also in Jackets and hats trimm'd in the same manner with two sorts of Ribbon, Straw Colour and Brown. Mrs. Custance in work Muslin Gown and petticoat, Broad Coloured Sash and a Hat trimm'd with a Handkerchief. I was dress' in my Blue Gown and Straw Colour'd and Purple Bonnet. Mrs. Custance admired my dress and told me that I never look so well in anything as I did in Blue.

· · · · ·

Saturday, October 6   A very Dull Day. Mrs. Custance sent her love to me with a Present of a fine Pheasant and a Bottle of Pickled Mushrooms and a Bottle of preserved Gooseberrys. This is the last time we shall hear from them before they arrive at Bath. We never shall have such good Neighbours again in Norfolk, their going away is the greatest loss I could meet with here.

Sunday, October 7   Uncle and self took a walk in the Garden this Morning and saw Mr. Custances Carriage pass by for the last time *which made me very low indeed.* God only knows when we shall see them again. Went to Church this Afternoon. Heard that Mr. Custance was very low at leaving Weston. Read a Sermon to Uncle in the Evening. Very dry and dusty walking.

· · · · ·

Wednesday, 31 October   This Evening Uncle rec'd a Note from Jeans desiring to know if he would accommodate Mrs. Jeans, her two Children and Nurse for two or three Days as he was obliged to go up to Town about his Tyth business and Mrs. Jeans did not like to stay at home during his absence. It was not very pleasing to us to take them on account of the Children but on such an occasion my Uncle could not refuse them, therefore he answered the Note saying he should always be glad to oblige Mr. & Mrs. Jeans, and if she could partake of part of my Bed we should be glad to see them, and desired that they would come to Breakfast to Morrow Morning as Mr. Priest Carriage was coming here for Mr. Priest, who was to come from Mr. Du Quesnes to Breakfast with us on his way home. They thought of going to Mr. Du Quesnes if we could not [have] taken them in.

Thursday, 1 November   Mr. & Mrs. Jeans, her two Children and Nurse came to Breakfast with us. Mr. Jeans came on Horseback and Mrs. Jeans, Children and Nurse came in Mr. Priests Carriage with Miss Mary Priest who Breakfasted with us also as did her Father likewise; after Breakfast Mr. Jeans set off for London and Mr. Priest return'd home with his Daughter. Mrs. Jeans and self sleept together and her eldest Daughter in my room also on a Mattress, which I did not much admire as she disturbed me early in the Morning. The young Child was also dressed in my Room in the Morning which was not very pleasing to me not being used to the noise of Children, however was obliged to make the best of it.

Friday, 2 November Mrs. Jeans Breakfasted, din'd, supped and slept here as did her Children and Nurse, cann't say that their Company is very agreeable Mrs. Jeans being a very dull Companion and the Children troublesome. Mrs. Jeans is a good Mother but she makes too much fuss with her Children. Her Ideas are much too high for her line of Life, she talks of nothing but Drawing Rooms, Lawns and Servants, I wish she was fonder of Needlework. Mr. Du Quesne came unexpectedly to Dinner and brought us a nice piece of Cod Fish. . . .

Saturday, November 3 Mrs. Jeans received a Letter from Mr. Jeans informing her that he was going to Hampshire to see his Friends. I suppose that was a plan concerted before they came here. I don't hear a word when he intends returning. No Letters from our Friends.

Sunday, 4 November Fine dry Day, but could not go to Church on account of Mrs. Jeans being with us. She dress'd herself in a White Gown and Coat for the first time since she has been here, having appeared in nothing but a shabby coloured Gown ever since she had been before. She should not treat people quite so cheap, however, I was even with her in that respect for did not dress in anything smart during her stay with us.

Monday, 5 November Received a Note of invitation from Mrs. Bodham to spend a few Days with them at South Green this week. Returned an answer saying that I could not wait on them on account of having Mrs. Jeans and her Children here and did not know when they would leave us, therefore could not fix any time for going, but said I thought it would not be in my Power till the Spring of the Year as we must now begin to expect bad Weather for travelling in an open Carriage. A charming pleasant Day. Am sorry to say that I have not now one agreeable Female friend in Norfolk. The loss of Mrs. Custance I greatly lament, indeed she was a charming Neighbour.

Mrs. Bodham never calls and Mrs. Jeans is a mear nothing at all and I am determined not to call often on them, therefore shall spend my time as happy as I can and give up the thought of any Society, thank God I have very good spirits and can always amuse myself with reading, working and walking which is my chief delight. Pray God continue to bless me with good health and I hope I shall be thankful, as that is the greatest blessing we can enjoy in this Life.

Tuesday, November 6   Lent Mrs. Jeans a Pattern of a Handkerchief and taught her the way to work it. We are quite unsettled with Mrs. Jeans and her Children and I am disturbed by them every Morning and sometimes in the Night. Mrs. Jeans is one of the dullest Women I was ever in Company with—she does not seem fond of working, reading or any amusement and I would much rather be alone than have such a Companion.

Wednesday, November 7   Mrs. Jeans and Children Breakfasted, din'd supped and Slept with us. Made myself a Morning Cap like Mrs. Jeans's.

· · · · ·

Saturday, November 10   Mr. Jeans returned from London to Witchingham, he sent for his Wife and Children in the Afternoon. Can't say that we were sorry at their leaving us.

Friday, November 16   Wrote a long Letter to my Friend Mrs. Custance at Bath whose absence from Weston I daily lament, she being my only Female neighbour in Norfolk worth thinking of. Uncle wrote to my Cousin Jane Pounsett informing her that he intended making them a visit next Summer.

· · · · ·

Friday, November 30   Went out with Mr. Peachman a coursing with our Dogs and brought home a fine young Hare. No Person has call'd on us since the 16th. I have spent the latter end of this Month in walking, reading the History of England and making Shirts for Uncle.

Notes

☙

*Nancy's diary is included in *Woodforde Papers and Diaries,* ed. Dorothy Heighes Woodforde (London: Peter Davies, 1932), pp. 35–85, the source for all the selections here. For Uncle James's extensive diary, see James Woodforde, *The Diary of a Country Parson,* ed. John Beresford, 5 vols. (Oxford and New York: Oxford University Press, 1981).

1   Squire John Custance and his wife were prosperous neighbors whose fifth child had been born on Christmas Day.

2   Wife of the rector of Witchingham, Norfolk.

3   The newborn child.

4   A tucker is a piece of lace worn at the neck, as is a ruff, which consists of linen or other fabric starched in folds.

5   Her brother Samuel was an artist.

Virginia Woolf

(1882–1941)

VIRGINIA (née Adeline Virginia) WOOLF was the third child of Leslie Stephen, distinguished man of letters and editor of the *Dictionary of National Biography,* and his second wife, Julia Jackson Duckworth. Following contemporary upper middle-class custom, Woolf was educated at home by her parents and tutors, but had the benefit of her father's ample library and learned guests. In a life plagued by mental instability and loss, her happy childhood ended abruptly in 1895 when her mother died suddenly, occasioning a serious mental breakdown; others followed the deaths of her stepsister Stella in 1897 and her father in 1904. Upon her recovery, Woolf moved with her siblings to a home in the Bloomsbury district, where they gathered about them a circle of compatible friends. Woolf now began her literary career, writing reviews for papers such as the *Times Literary Supplement,* during a period of great happiness that ended when brother Thoby died in 1906 and sister Vanessa married in 1907. In 1912 Virginia herself married Leonard Woolf but again suffered a serious breakdown. Nonetheless, the marriage proved a durable and happy one, in which, besides their successful careers as writers, the Woolfs operated Hogarth Press. Virginia published her first novel, *The Voyage Out,* in 1915, and her stature grew with each book she wrote thereafter, especially the novels *Mrs. Dalloway* (1925) and *To the Lighthouse* (1927). But she remained insecure, and her published diary (1915–41)*—one of the great diaries of all times—reveals that she regularly relied on Leonard's approval to validate her work. During the years covered by the diary excerpts, 1920–24, the insecurity she always felt over her reputation is reflected in her ambivalent attitude to writer Katherine Mansfield: friend yet rival at modernism. In 1941, despondent over the war and fearing the onset of another breakdown, Virginia drowned herself in the River Ouse.

From Virginia Woolf's Diary

Wednesday, 26 May 1920   . . . This morning Katherine writes a stiff &
formal note thanking me for my kind post card, & saying she will
be delighted to see me though 'grown *very* dull.' What does this
mean—*she* hurt with *me?* Anyhow I go on Friday to find out, unless
stopped as is always possible. I praised her story warmly; sincerely
too.[1]

Monday, 31 May   . . . I had my interview with K. M. on Friday. A
steady discomposing formality & coldness at first. Enquiries about
house & so on. No pleasure or excitement at seeing me. It struck me
that she is of the cat kind: alien, composed, always solitary & observant. And then we talked about solitude, & I found her expressing
my feelings, as I never heard them expressed. Whereupon we fell into
step, & as usual, talked as easily as though 8 months were minutes—
till Murry[2] came in with a pair of blue & pink Dresden candle pieces:
"How *very* nice," she said. "But do fetch the candles." "Virginia,
how *awful* what am I to say? He has spent £5 on them" she said, as he
left the room. I see that they're often hostile. For one thing—Murry's
writing. "Did you like C. & A.?" No, I didn't. "Neither did I. But I
thought D. of an I.[3] too dreadful—wrong—Its very very difficult,
often . . ." Then Murry came back. We chatted as usual. Aldous was
our butt. Aldous has brought out Leda:[4] will the public canonise
him too? But Murry going at length, K. & I once more got upon
literature. Question of her stories. This last one, Man without a T., is
her first in the new manner. She says she's mastered something—is
beginning to do what she wants. Prelude[5] a coloured post card. Her
reviews mere scribbling without a serious thought in them. And
Sullivan's praise in the A[*thenaeum*]. detestable to her. A queer effect
she produces of someone apart, entirely self-centred; altogether con-
centrated upon her 'art': almost fierce to me about it, I pretending
I couldn't write. "What else is there to do? We have got to do it.
Life—" then how she tells herself stories at night about all the lives in
a town. "Its a spring night. I go down to the docks—I hear the travel-
lers say—" acting it in her usual way, & improvising. Then asked
me to write stories for the A. "But I don't know that I can write sto-

I said honestly enough, thinking that in her view, after her review of me, anyhow, those were her secret sentiments. Whereupon she turned on me, & said no one else could write stories except me—Kew [Gardens] the right 'gesture'; a turning point—Well but Night & Day? I said, though I hadn't meant to speak of it.

'An amazing achievement' she said. Why, we've not had such a thing since I don't know when—,

But I thought you didn't like it?[6]

Then she said she could pass an examination in it. Would I come and talk about it—lunch—so I'm going to lunch; but what does her reviewing mean then?—or is she emotional with me? Anyhow, once more as keenly as ever I feel a common certain understanding between us—a queer sense of being 'like'—not only about literature—& I think it's independent of gratified vanity. I can talk straight out to her.

Saturday, 5 June   . . . Murry sent a balance sheet of his accounts: came at Christmas with plum pudding & curd cheese; 'Now I'm here, its all right'. Then she went to him for assurance; didn't get it; & will never look for that particular quality again. I see what she means, vaguely. She is nervous about her book coming out;[7] fearing lest she hasn't done enough. What she feels exactly for fame & criticism, I don't know; but then in our perhaps too exalted talk, this is not very exactly told. Anyhow, I enjoyed myself; & this fragmentary intermittent intercourse of mine seems more fundamental than many better established ones. . . .

• • • • •

Wednesday, 25 August   For the third time this summer, though no other summer, I went to London Monday, paid 5/–for a plate of ham, & said good bye to Katherine. I had my euphemism at parting; about coming again before she goes; but it is useless to extend these farewell visits. They have something crowded & unnaturally calm too about them, & after all, visits can't do away with the fact that she goes for two years, is ill, & heaven knows when we shall meet again. These partings make one pinch oneself as if to make sure of feeling. Do I feel this as much as I ought? Am I heartless? Will she mind my going either? And then, after noting my own callousness, of a sudden comes

the blankness of not having her to talk to. So on my side the feeling
is genuine. A woman caring as I care for writing is rare enough I
suppose to give me the queerest sense of echo coming back to me
from her mind the second after I've spoken. Then, too, there's something in what she says of our being the only women, at this moment
(I must modestly limit this to in our circle) with gift enough to make
talk of writing interesting. How much I dictate to other people! How
often too I'm silent, judging it useless to speak. I said how my own
character seemed to cut out a shape like a shadow in front of me. This
she understood (I give it as an example of her understanding) & proved
it by telling me that she thought this bad: one ought to merge into
things. Her senses are amazingly acute—a long description she gave
of hosing plants—putting the hose over the high trees, then over
the shrubs, then over the mignonette. And Murry said slowly, "You've
got it wrong, Katherine. Youth wasn't like that. At least I'm sure
mine wasn't." Murry playing tennis all day; an oddly detached couple.
She wants to live in an Italian town & have tea with the doctor. It
suddenly strikes me as I write that I should like to ask her what certainty she has of her work's merit.—But we propose to write to each
other—She will send me her diary. Shall we? Will she? If I were left
to myself I should; being the simpler, the more direct of the two.
I can't follow people who don't do the obvious things in these ways.
I've recanted about her book; I shall review it; but whether she really
wanted me to, God knows. Strange how little we know our friends.

So I missed my train; & what I wanted most in the world was to
catch it & travel back with L[eonard]. . . .

· · · · ·

Sunday, 12 December   Nearing the end of the year. Everything muffled
in snow & crisp with frost; streets knobbed & slippery; hands grimy
as cold for some reason always makes them. Here we sit over the fire,
expecting Roger—whose book is out; as everyone's book is out—
Katherine's, Murry's, Eliot's.[8] None have I read so far. I was happy to
hear K. abused the other night. Now why? Partly some obscure
feeling that she advertises herself; or Murry does it for her; & then
how bad the Athenaeum stories are; yet in my heart I must think her
good since I'm glad to hear her abused. . . .

Sunday, 19 December   This I see will be the last page of the year, since I go to Janet tomorrow for the night; dine in London at a festival party on Tuesday night; & leave for Rodmell on Wednesday. I shan't take this book with me, though if I'm in the mood I might scribble a page to bring back. I ought to say how happy I am, since one of these pages said how unhappy I was. I can't see any reason in it. My only guess is that it has something to do with working steadily; writing things out of my head; & never having a compartment empty. That doesn't mean that I dont stuff the corners with idle moments. I gaze at the fire. I make phrases—well, thats all well known. I can't help suspecting that both Mr & Mrs Woolf slowly increase in fame. That helps to fill compartments. No doubt I like getting letters from publishers: even to be asked to preside over Mr Beresford[9] slightly kindles me. Next year I shall be above all that. I've plucked out my jealousy of Katherine by writing her an insincere-sincere letter. Her books praised for a column in the Lit Sup[10]—the prelude of paeans to come. I foresee editions; then the Hawthornden prize next summer. So I've had my little nettle growing in me, & plucked it as I say. I've revived my affection for her somehow, & don't mind, in fact enjoy. But I've not read her book.

My book seems to me rather good. L.'s book seems to him (so I interpret) rather good. . . .

· · · · ·

Wednesday, 16 February   . . . Then there was Murry's farewell dinner at 46.[11] Clive gritty & bawling, Lytton observant & mute. The rest much as usual. I sat next [to] Murry, & let my prejudices run away with me for the first half. He posed, I thought; looked anguished & martyred. Yet the dinner was at his request. I kept thinking how he summed up us & held us worthless. Then, at the end, I asked after Katherine. Poor man! he poured himself out. We sat on after the others had gone.

"But I lacked imagination, he said. I never saw. I ought to have understood. I've always held one was free to do as one likes. But she was ill, & that made all the difference. And it was nothing—nothing at all."

This referred of course, without names, to the Bibesco Scandal,[12] with which London, so they say, rings.

"And I adore Katherine—She's absolutely the most fascinating person in the world—I'm wholly in love with her."

Apparently she is worse—dying? God knows. This affair seems to have brought on a crisis. She is desperately depressed, thinks her book bad, can't write; accuses herself; I imagine, is beside herself with jealousy. Murry asked me to write to her. She feels herself out of things, left alone, forgotten. As he spoke with great feeling, & seemed to be very miserable, & anxious to apologise (was it for this that he wished to see us all—to prove that there was nothing in it?) I liked him, felt with him, & I think there can be no doubt that his love for Katherine anyhow is sincere. All the rest seems of no great importance beside it. . . .

· · · · ·

Tuesday, 3 May 1921   Hamilton Fyfe in the Daily Mail says that Leonard's story P. & S.[13] will rank with the great stories of the world. Am I jealous? Only momentarily. But the odd thing is—the idiotic thing—is that I immediately think myself a failure—imagine myself peculiarly lacking in the qualities L. has. I feel fine drawn, misty, attenuated, inhuman, bloodless & niggling out trifles that don't move people. 'Limbo' is my sphere; so they say in the Daily News.[14] Then Romer Wilson has brought out a novel—to which Squire will certainly give the Hawthornden prize,[15] thus robbing Katherine of it: so I have some cause for pleasure. I write this purposely, to shame it out of me. A full stop in Jacob [*Jacob's Room*], owing partly to depression. But I must pull together and finish it off. I can't read it as it is. . . .

· · · · ·

Thursday, 15 September   It is the loveliest of evenings—still; the smoke going up straight in the quarry; the white horse & strawberry coloured horse feeding close together; the women coming out of their cottages for no reason, & standing looking; or knitting; the cock pecking in the midst of his hens in the meadow; starlings in the two trees; Asheham fields shorn to colour of white corduroy; Leonard storing apples above my head. & the sun coming through a pearly glass shade; so that the apples which still hang are palish red & green; the church tower a silver extinguisher rising through the trees. Will this recall anything? I am so anxious to keep every scrap, you see.

I have been dabbling in K. M.'s stories, & have to rinse my mind— in Dryden? Still, if she were not so clever she couldn't be so disagreeable. . . .

· · · · ·

Sunday, 12 March 1922   This book dwindles, now that I draw my stream off in the morning. Were it not for the irritation of suspense— Nelly & Lottie: the hospital; the operation, & my own raging toothache—by which I designate my desire to be writing out the preface to Reading,[16] I should let this page lie blank. Yet many portraits are owed to it—I have seen people—& people. Eliot, Clive, Violet,—if no one else. Of these Eliot amuses me most—grown supple as an eel; yes, grown positively familiar & jocular & friendly, though retaining I hope some shreds of authority. I mustn't lick all the paint off my Gods. He is starting a magazine; to which 20 people are to contribute; & Leonard & I are among them.[17] So what does it matter if K. M. soars in the newspapers, and runs up sales skyhigh? Ah, I have found a fine way of putting her in her place. The more she is praised, the more I am convinced she is bad. After all, there's some truth in this. She touches the spot too universally for that spot to be of the bluest blood. . . .

· · · · ·

Tuesday, 16 January 1923   Katherine has been dead a week,[18] and how far am I obeying her "do not quite forget Katherine" which I read in one of her old letters? Am I already forgetting her? It is strange to trace the progress of one's feelings. Nelly said in her sensational way at breakfast on Friday "Mrs. Murry's dead! It says so in the paper!" At that one feels—what? A shock of relief?—a rival the less? Then confusion at feeling so little—then, gradually, blankness & disappointment; then a depression which I could not rouse myself from all day. When I began to write, it seemed to me there was no point in writing. Katherine wont read it. Katherine's my rival no longer. More generously I felt, But though I can do this better than she could, where is she, who could do what I can't! Then, as usual with me, visual impressions kept coming & coming before me—always of Katherine putting on a white wreath, & leaving us, called away; made dignified, chosen. And then one pitied her. And one felt her reluctant to wear that wreath, which was an ice cold one. And she was only 33. And I could see her before me so exactly, & the room at Portland Villas. I go up. She gets up, very slowly, from her writing table. A glass of milk & a medicine bottle stood there. There were also piles of novels. Everything was very tidy, bright, & somehow like a dolls house. At once, or almost, we got out of shyness. She (it was summer) half lay on the sofa by the window. She had her look of a Japanese doll, with the fringe combed quite straight across her forehead. Sometimes we looked very steadfastly at each other, as though we had reached some durable relationship, independent of the changes of the body, through the eyes. Hers were beautiful eyes—rather doglike, brown, very wide apart, with a steady slow rather faithful & sad expression. Her nose was sharp, & a little vulgar. Her lips thin & hard. She wore short skirts & liked "to have a line round her" she said. She looked very ill—very drawn, & moved languidly, drawing herself across the room, like some suffering animal. I suppose I have written down some of the things we said. Most days I think we reached that kind of certainty, in talk about books, or rather about our writings, which I thought had something durable about it. And then she was inscrutable. Did she care for me? Sometimes she would say so—would kiss me—would look at me as if (is this sentiment?) her eyes would like always to be faithful. She would promise never never to forget. That was what we said at the end of our last talk. She said she would send me her diary to read, & would write always. For our friendship was a real thing we said, looking at each other quite straight. It would always go on whatever happened. What happened was, I suppose fault-findings & perhaps gossip. She never answered my letter. Yet I still feel, somehow that friendship persists. Still there are things about writing I think of & want to tell Katherine. If I had been in Paris & gone to her, she would have got up & in three minutes, we should have been talking again. Only I could not take the step. The surroundings—Murry & so on—& the small lies & treacheries, the perpetual playing & teasing, or whatever it was, cut away much of the substance of friendship. One was too uncertain. And so one let it all go. Yet I certainly expected that we should meet again next summer, & start fresh. And I was jealous of her writing—the only writing I have ever been jealous of. This made it harder to write to her; & I saw in it, perhaps from jealousy, all the qualities I disliked in her.

For two days I felt that I had grown middle aged, & lost some spur to write. That feeling is going. I no longer keep seeing her with her wreath. I dont pity her so much. Yet I have the feeling that I shall think of her at intervals all through life. Probably we had something in common which I shall never find in anyone else. (This I say in so many words in 1919 again & again.) Moreover I like speculating about her character. I think I never gave her credit for all her physical suffering & the effect it must have had in embittering her.

The Nation is probably sold over Massingham's head. L. has a violent cold. I have been in bed, 101, again. Fergusson threatens to cut my tonsils.

Sunday, 28 January   A certain melancholy has been brooding over me this fortnight. I date it from Katherine's death. The feeling so often comes to me now—Yes. Go on writing of course: but into emptiness. There's no competitor. I'm cock—a lonely cock whose crowing nothing breaks—of my walk. For our friendship had so much that was writing in it. However then I had my fever, & violent cold, was in & out of bed for a week, & still am below normal, I think. In casting accounts, never forget to begin with the state of the body.

K., so Ralph reports via Brett, died in 10 minutes of haemorrhage, walking upstairs with Murry who happened to be there. Brett is 'very hard hit' Ralph says.[19] I soon shant have Ralph's sayings to report. Does that make me melancholy? Like most of one's feelings mine on losing him are mixed. . . .

. . . . . .

Tuesday, 6 March   Poor Katherine has taken to revisiting the earth; she has been seen at Brett's; by the charwoman. I feel this somehow a kind of judgment on her for writing the kind of thing she did. Brett told me the story the other day & seemed so bare & rasped that I could not have taken this comfort from her had I wished. Nor do I wish seriously to obstruct any decent investigation of brains and nerves, seeing how much I've suffered that way myself. But then Brett is not scientific; she at once takes the old fables seriously, & reports some jargon learnt of Dunning, but no doubt diluted in transit, about day & night, birth, & *therefore* death, all being beautiful. She feels the 'contact' she says; & has had revelations; & there she sits deaf, injured, solitary, brooding over death, & hearing voices, which soon will become, I expect, entirely fabulous; & even now talking to her has a good deal robbed the image of K. M. of its distinctness. For it came distinctly back when I read her letters. And I saw her wink when poor Brett's note was handed in, & she said that little person can wait, or something like that. Now B. idolises her, & invests her with every quality of mind & soul. Do people always get what they deserve, & did K. M. do something to deserve this cheap posthumous life? & am I jealous even now?

No: I think one can be honest at my age. . . .

• • • • •

Friday, 17 October 1924   . . . The thought of Katherine Mansfield comes to me—as usual rather reprehensibly—first wishing she could see Southampton Row, thinking of the dulness of her death, lying there at Fountainebleau—an end where there was no end, & then thinking yes, if she'd lived, she'd have written on, & people would have seen that I was the more gifted—that wd. only have become more & more apparent. Indeed, so I suppose it would. I think of her in this way off & on—that strange ghost, with the eyes far apart, & the drawn mouth, dragging herself across her room. And Murry married again to a woman who spends an hour in the W.C. & so the Anreps have turned them out. Murry whines publicly for a flat in the Adelphi. Thats a sordid page of my life by the way, Murry. But I stick to it; K. & I had our relationship; & never again shall I have one like it. . . .

   . . . I have travelled on—as K. M. said to me, she saw me as a ship far out at sea. But K. M. always *said* affectionate admiring things to me, poor woman, whom in my own way I suppose I loved. . . .

Notes

&

**The Diary of Virginia Woolf,* ed. Anne Olivier Bell; assisted by Andrew McNeillie for vols. 2–5, 5 vols. (New York: Harcourt Brace Jovanovich, 1977–84). The selections here are from vol. 2: *1920–1924.*

1 Katherine Mansfield had written "It's very kind of you to have sent me a card. Yes, I'm back in England until August. I would be delighted if you'd care to come & see me one afternoon, but I am grown *very* dull" (quoted in Woolf's diary 2:43 n. 32). The story was "The Man without a Temperament," published in *Arts & Letters,* spring 1920.

2 Mansfield's husband, John Middleton Murry.

3 Murry's verse drama *Cinnamon and Angelica,* published in spring 1920, and his 1918 essay "The Defeat of the Imagination," republished 1919 in his *The Evolution of an Intellectual.*

4 *Leda and Other Poems* by Aldous Huxley, published May 1920.

5 Mansfield's *Prelude,* published by the Woolfs in 1918.

6 Mansfield had reviewed Woolf's *Night and Day* in the *Athenaeum* (edited by Murry), 26 November 1919.

7 Mansfield's *Bliss and other Stories* was to be issued by Constable in December 1920.

8 Roger Fry's *Vision and Design,* Mansfield's *Bliss,* Murry's *Aspects of Literature,* T. S. Eliot's *The Sacred Wood.*

9 John Davys Beresford, a well-regarded novelist, whose book *Revolution* Virginia Woolf reviewed in the *Times Literary Supplement,* 27 January 1921.

10 Mansfield's *Bliss* was reviewed in the *Times Literary Supplement,* 16 December 1920.

11 At 46 Gordon Square, home of Clive Bell.

12 Murry had been philandering with Princess Elizabeth Bibesco while Mansfield was lonely and sick with tuberculosis at Mentone.

13 "Pearls and Swine" in Leonard Woolf's *Stories of the East,* reviewed in the *Daily Mail,* 2 May 1921.

14 Virginia Woolf's *Monday or Tuesday* was reviewed there on 2 May 1921 under the heading "Limbo."

15 Woolf added the marginal note "he did."

16 Nelly and Lottie are servants of the Woolfs; the hospital and operation refer to Lottie's health problems; "Reading" refers to a piece on reviewing.

17 T. S. Eliot's quarterly *Criterion,* to which Virginia, but not Leonard, became a contributor.

18 She died at Fontainebleau on 9 January 1923, following a hemorrhage.

19 Dorothy Brett, at whose home Mansfield had stayed during her last visit to England in August 1922. Ralph Partridge was working for Hogarth Press, but was to leave it on 14 March 1923.

Vera Brittain

(1893–1970)

VERA MARY BRITTAIN was born to Thomas and Edith Brittain in
Newcastle, Staffordshire, where her prosperous father was a director
in his family's paper mill. She was educated at St. Monica's, Kings-
wood, and, having gained her father's reluctant consent, at Somerville
College, Oxford, where she won a scholarship in 1914. During the
First World War she served as a Voluntary Aid Detachment (VAD)
nurse in London, Malta, and France in 1915–19 and experienced a
long-lasting grief in the deaths of her fiancé and her brother, ordeals
movingly captured in her war diary for 1913–17, *Chronicle of Youth*
(1981). After the war she became an activist for women's right to
degrees at Oxford and during the twenties, writing regularly for the
feminist journal *Time and Tide,* she advocated even more extensive
legal and social enfranchisement for women. International acclaim
came with her autobiographical account of the war, *Testament of Youth*
(1933), ironically the book with which she was struggling at the time
of these diary excerpts. In 1937, she became a sponsor of the Peace
Pledge Union and a contributor to pacifist publications, and for the
rest of her life participated in pacifist endeavors. Her feminist activism
likewise extended over some fifty years, and its tenets were borne
out in her own life. In 1925 she had married George E. G. Catlin (later
Sir), a political philosopher and a professor at McGill University,
Canada, to whom she bore a son and a daughter. In order to pursue
her own work, however, she lived largely apart from him in England.
Brittain advocated close friendships among women and herself maintained a long-lasting friendship with novelist Winifred Holtby, me-
morialized in *Testament of Friendship* (1940). But as these 1932 excerpts
from her 1932–39 diary, *Chronicle of Friendship,* show,* her relations
with writer Phyllis Bentley proved to be quite another matter.

From *Vera Brittain's Diary*

1932

Friday May 6th Had early lunch & went off to King's Cross to meet
Phyllis[1] by the 1.55 from various parts of Yorkshire (Winifred's[2] familiar train). As the Halifax portion was right at the back I feared
I might miss her, & also was not entirely convinced that I should recognise her again, but in the end I met her without difficulty. She was
wearing a tweedy brown coat and hat and pince-nez and looked just
as school-mistressy as I expected but somehow less irretrievably plain
than I seemed to remember; not quite the "embittered spinster" of
last year but as if something had gone all through her & warmed her
up, even though it hadn't yet exactly made her unbend. Hair was
going grey though—too grey for 37; it wasn't last year. W[infred] said
it's the effect of writing *Inheritance* all in a year—certainly a performance in will-power alone.

She came up to me with the mixture of stiff shyness & determined
downrightness which I know now as the Yorkshire manner & said:
"it *is* you, isn't it?" I agreed that it was, & we went round together to
John O'London's to pick up her review books. We began to thaw even
in the taxi and much to my surprise (I had meant to do it but not
so soon) I found myself telling her about "Testament of Youth" and
Time & Tide's quarrel with Gollancz over reviews & advertisements, &
being listened to sympathetically. (A woman "bestseller" surely very
different from a man here; can't imagine a man wanting to talk about
any book but his own for at least three months.) Over tea we thawed
still more & discussed Lady Rhondda & *Time & Tide*.[3] . . .

Saturday May 7th Phyllis went to see Winifred in the morning at
Courtfield Gardens; W. told me afterwards she seemed very puzzled
as to why I had asked her to stay, and W. repeated my own remark
that it was "a daimon".

In evening we went to dinner at the Criterion & on to *The Miracle*
at the Lyceum. At dinner I tried to explain a little to Phyllis by saying
how I loved people to get on. . . .

Sunday May 8th   Did gardening & then took children to Oakwood Court while Phyllis spent the day with friends in Highgate. She finished her *John O'London* review in the morning—works with a kind of dynamic "I won't waste time" resolution which gets things done. After she had come in & gone to bed *Daily Dispatch* rang me up & wanted by to-morrow afternoon an article answering Margaret Kornitzer's book *The Modern Woman & Herself.* (I haven't read it but this didn't seem to matter as the Editor gave me a resume.) . . .

Monday May 9th   Woke up with a headache through hardly having slept owing to the rumpus in the kitchen.[4] Headache not improved by fact that it poured with heavy rain all day & that I had to finish *Daily Dispatch* article "Libelling Modern Woman" by 3.0. I did this, then raced out for half an hour in rain & came back to help maids prepare for party. (Phyllis out all day; didn't come till just before dinner.) Felt quite pleasantly hopeful about party as of the 30 people I asked, 29 accepted—interested, I suppose, to meet Phyllis but perhaps partly because of me too, as both the previous parties here have been good.

Mother and Aunt Lillie turned up to help with the food just after dinner & Phyllis to my delight appeared looking really nice in a very pretty black & silver dress that revealed to me the fact that she had a quite beautiful figure. After the orange and greens of the previous day, & Winifred's remarks about her clothes being terribly provincial and all hung about with beads & things, it was a pleasant surprise; also her face seemed better looking as on Saturday I hinted gently how becoming her horn-rimmed spectacles were, & she thereafter abandoned the pince-nez & stopped looking like a school-mistress. She looked animated too and happily expectant, like a pleased child.

. . . Everyone [at the party] *very* agreeable to Phyllis; I managed to get her introduced to them all & yet gave her a fair time for conversation with each. Ernest Davies suggested she should contribute a monthly article to the *New Clarion* when it comes out in June; Miss Davison talked to her for some time; & Clare & Ellen Wilkinson teased her very pleasantly about being a celebrity; "What does it feel like to have everybody talking about you?" asked Ellen; Phyllis blushed & protested that they weren't but Ellen went on "I hear your name & about your book wherever I go." Meanwhile Mrs Scott-

James and I stood by the mantelpiece watching. V. S. J.[5] (who had only seen Phyllis once before—an interview at V. S. J.'s house, when P. was apparently very plain & bustling & dogmatic) said very quietly: "What *has* happened to Phyllis Bentley? She's *quite* different. And she's got such a becoming frock on." I said, "Yes, isn't she different from last year. She's been getting more animated & self-confident ever since she came. It's great fun watching someone turn into a celebrity under your eyes." And V.S.J. remarked thoughtfully: "Yes—it's very pleasant, isn't it. Success *does* alter people. I'm ever so glad." . . .

I came back [afterwards] to find Phyllis standing by the table looking radiant & yet for some reason deeply moved. Quite suddenly she said: "I'm so happy! I've never been so happy as this in my life before. I've never enjoyed a party so much as this party." And I said: "It isn't often that one sees a dream coming true, is it? I've enjoyed it immensely too—seeing it come true & watching your success." She went on: "At least I've done one worth-while thing—written one good book. Of course I believed in it myself, but . . ." "Now you realise that other people believe [in] it too," I finished for her; "Well, it's a very enviable feeling—& it's made you quite different. Last year you had an inferiority complex; this year it's gone."

"I was very unhappy," she said, "when you saw me last year. *Trio* hadn't succeeded and I'd just been ill, & I was only starting *Inheritance* & felt I'd never finish it . . ." "But all that's over now," I said. "You've deserved your success & you've a right to enjoy it—if only *I* could say the same—but then again I'm nothing but a competent journalist . . ." But she took my arm & interrupted me. "Oh, don't talk nonsense! You're tired & you've got a headache; you won't feel like that in the morning. But I knew I should—and always shall—unless "Testament of Youth" succeeds.

As we went up the stairs she said again "Thank you—I do thank you" in her unadorned direct way, & I felt the party really had been worth-while.

• • • • •

Wednesday May 11th Very crowded day. Took Phyllis to the Marie Stopes Annual Luncheon at the Criterion; introduced her to Marie Stopes.[6] Canon Percy Dearmer spoke at the lunch; fine head; whole manner rather too intense & fanatical. Phyllis sat beside the (elderly male) representative of the *Star* who put in a paragraph about her afterwards. Tea at home and then both of us dropped in for a few minutes to Lady Harris's cocktail party in Hertford Street. . . .

Played with the children after tea & went to bed early while Phyllis went to dinner with the J. B. Priestleys & afterwards on with them to the Gollancz At Home to which I was *not* invited. I was still awake when she came back about 2.0 a.m. & she gave a most amusing account of the whole proceedings. . . .

Thursday May 12th Quiet day—Phyllis very tired after strenuousness of preceding day—also seems the kind of person with whom excitement goes all inside & turns to exhaustion. She had to broadcast just before tea; came back extremely pale so I put her to bed early. . . .

Friday May 13th In morning started drafting *Quiver* article on changes in work & leisure while Phyllis went to *Everyman* & arranged to answer their attack on her book & the long novel—also to the *New Statesman*, where Ellis Roberts definitely arranged for her to do novel reviews for a time in place of Viola Meynell.

We had tea together & then I went to St Pancras—she asked me to—to see her off. She looked very ill & pale & unhappily could only get a bad seat in a smoking carriage all the way to Halifax owing to the Whit Week-end crowds. She tried to thank me again for the week, and I to tell her why I asked her, but the crowds were too thick & she too tired for much intimate conversation. I did feel sorry she had nowhere more comfortable to sit & rest in for the long journey home. As I went out of the station I saw several copies of *Inheritance* on the book-stall with a small paper placard "A Great Novel: 5th Edition" fixed above them. Dropped around to nursing home to see Winifred on my way home but found she had gone out to tea & dinner with Stella Benson; very sorry not to see her.

• • • • •

Monday May 16th Finished *Quiver* article. Charming note from Phyllis saying she *was* ill all the way back to Halifax but had arrived alive & happy, & that I had altered her prospects & whole outlook on life. It ended with the words "Yours affectionately" scratched out & the phrase inserted: "No, I think I'd rather say: Yours with love."

Whit Monday. Gardened a good deal with children.

· · · · · ·

Sunday May 22nd   Children to Oakwood Court. Phyllis came back after supper, to occupy Gordon's[7] room until his return. Felt very pleased to have her there.

Monday May 23rd   Went on with Chapter IX. Long talk in W[inifred]'s room after supper between W., Phyllis & me, all about ourselves. P. referred yet again to our rapid talk (W.'s & mine) as "brilliant conversation". Said she thought I ought to feel utterly fulfilled, being so pretty & having such a "gift for life". I explained why I never could unless I wrote a really great book, & talked about the War which I had told something of last week. She repeated what she told me then, that she had never been anyone's mistress & that the scenes from *Inheritance* which seemed to show sex experience were all imagined.

· · · · · ·

Saturday May 28th   Phyllis out to lunch with Lady R[hondda]—went off looking nice in dark blue & red. Cicely Hamilton dropped in to tea, just come back from France; we talked about the French, war memorials & the War. P., back from lunch and rather tired, lay on W.'s divan in her dressing gown and listened; then went out to a sherry party at Charles Morgan & Hilda Vaughan's flat; taken there by Macmillan's London agent.

Sunday May 29th   Dispute over lunch about respective merit of critical & creative qualities in literature (already discussed with some animation by Phyllis and myself a day or two before in relation to the place in literature of Rebecca West) and the relation of both to inspiration & sincerity. For some reason or other it developed into a furious argument & ended in a row, with Phyllis & I both losing our tempers. I told her that she put *everything* in her novels & called that creative, & she said in retaliation (though she hasn't read anything of mine except my articles) that my over-critical non-creativeness was the great difference between her & myself. This struck hard because I'd been struggling all morning with a particularly vile part of Chap. IX, and I suddenly felt so near to tears I had to get up & pretend to play with John.[8] I said loudly to Winifred on the stairs that P. was "damned superior" & then P. came to my bedroom & tried to apologise for being horrid about my book, but I wouldn't have it & took John off to Oakwood Court without showing her the way to Queen's Gate, which I'd promised to do.

Just before supper, when I'd put J. to bed and Winifred & I were just going to the post, Phyllis came in; Winifred asked her to come with us but I remarked supper was just ready & I suppose conveyed without meaning to that we didn't want her. Anyhow we'd hardly finished our soup when Phyllis got up with her eyes full of tears, said she wouldn't stay for any more, & went off upstairs. Tried to persuade W. to go & fetch her back but she said that obviously *I* must, so I went up to find her in Gordon's room. She let me come in and I found her sitting in the arm-chair, crying quite hard; she began saying she'd been so happy with us but now she'd hurt me about my work & it was all dreadful; none of her personal relations ever did go right & she just couldn't stay if we were going to be cold & distant. I felt terribly sorry because she was obviously feeling it all so dreadfully whereas I had only been superficially annoyed by a too-acute & rather unfair criticism. Also I felt awkward because I don't really understand York-shire people (except Winifred now) nor how far one can go towards intimacy with them, but I sat beside her on the arm of the chair & took her hand & said I'd really only lost my temper & one shouldn't discuss a book one's actually working on.

Then she cried more than ever & all the repressed misery of her past life burst out in a flood—how grey, how negative it had been, how women hadn't loved her nor men married her; how writing had been the only thing & she was still defenceless against even a mere remark which suggested she might not have even that. I told her that *Inheritance* had settled that question for ever & she must try to believe that she was an established success & I at least had been interested & intuitively attracted by her even before she came. I also said I did understand the greyness & frustration & sorrow because though I hadn't had that particular grief I'd had others, & she said: "Yes, I could tell you about it because you *are* acquainted with grief." And she said she would try to believe that she was successful, & able to be loved & that it wasn't too late for her life to have a flowering time; "You see," she said, "I can't put beauty and charm & happiness into my books because I've never known them." And I insisted—and believe— that through her own achievement she is just at the beginning of knowing them & that they will come into the next book she writes.

So at last she stopped crying and I persuaded her to come down to supper; Winifred, calm, tactful, never surprised by anything, was sitting placidly in the window-seat reading the *New Statesman.* After supper we talked in the dark in my study till Winifred went to bed. Before going myself I showed Phyllis my poem "The Superfluous Woman" & I think persuaded her that I had felt like that—so much as she does—in 1920. Anyhow, she kissed me & said "Goodnight, my dear" & I began to feel as if I had known her always.

Tuesday May 31st   After dinner Phyllis & I went to J. B. Priestley's new play *Dangerous Corner* at the Lyric. Full of suspense and psychology; we both thought it good. After we got home drank hot milk & sat for ages talking in my bedroom.

Wednesday June 1st   In morning Louis Golding—who has been intrigued by idea of Phyllis for ages as he is magnanimously but definitely jealous of her best-selling era having so swiftly succeeded his own—rang up ostensibly to ask W. to dinner to-night but really (since he must have known W. would have to refuse) to ask her if she thought he could ask Phyllis at the last moment like that. W. told him to try & called Phyllis who went to the telephone very cheerily & said: "Well, Mr. *Magnolia Street,* what do you want of me?" She accepted the invitation to dinner, & agreed, after spending the afternoon reading books for her *New Statesman* review, to meet me for tea at Ridgeway's & together buy a red evening dress & a black velvet evening cloak.

After lunch Mother & I went to the Academy . . . and then had tea with P. at Ridgeway's. Quest for frocks very successful; after one or two boss shots [guesses] we went to Marshall's & got a beautiful dress in Persian red & a black velvet evening cloak with white fur collar. Brought the garments back & she dressed herself up in them; W. & I made her make up her lips & did up her eyebrows for her; the result was to make her face look really interesting & the frock showed up her nice figure to perfection. . . .

• • • • •

Sunday June 5th . . . After supper had long talk with Phyllis over study fire about effects of war & how they deprived worth-while things in the present of their value. She said two memorable things:

1) "Jesus was a great psychologist. He was thinking of people like you when he said: 'From him that hath not shall be taken away even that which he hath.'" 2) After I had said that no one was left who remembered the War for me, and even John belonged to Gordon & not to Roland,[9] she said: "But it's biologically true, isn't it, that the essential part of him was within you in the days when you were with your brother & your lover—and so in a way he belongs to them too." She seemed much moved & spoke of people like her father and youngest brother, whose lives had been thrown away in their life-time, without their having to die. Again kissed me goodnight & called me "my dear".

• • • • •

Friday June 17th . . . After breakfast we got on to subject of Phyllis's inhibitions again; I told her that when people obviously sought her out she must make some gesture of response or they in their turn would drift into the inferiority complex that is in everybody & think themselves not wanted. She said she'd do her best but after such long loneliness & restraint it was possible that gestures & caresses which were a tremendous effort to her meant hardly anything to the other person. She got back again on to her childhood, & how she sought other girls out & they wouldn't be friends, & was made afraid by being forced, before it was discovered that she was short-sighted, to jump & dive into space when she couldn't see where she was going or what she was doing—and thence on to the awful humiliation of going to dances when young & being snubbed or despised and any-how not danced with by men. (Personally I think that somehow this tyranny of dances in provincial towns should be stopped; seems to account for more youthful misery & inferiority complexes in intelligent women than anything else.) She ended by crying again & asking how she could possibly be expected to make gestures of seeking towards anyone at all after a girlhood like this. I went on insisting that it wasn't too late for some kind of happiness, some sort of flowering time to come, if only she could overcome the conviction—so deeply rooted in young bitter experience—that happiness was not for her.

For the rest of morning helped her pack up & looked over notes for my speech at the Conference on the Family. Saw Phyllis off to Charing Cross for a week-end at Hythe & then went to the Conference on "The Family in a Changing Society" at Friends' House. . . .

After dinner Winifred & I for about 2 hours discussed Phyllis, her dark, intense misery & the tragedy and grief of frustration, & whether there was anything we could do to help her, warm her, soften her, make her happier & more attractive. I felt deeply oppressed by the greyness & the negativeness of her present life, of which the needs & the sorrows seem incapable of alleviation by literary success (and even this in a way is limited; various distinguished readers of *Inheritance,* such as Lady Rhondda, don't like it—not that Lady R. is any judge of literature). . . .

. . . . .

Sunday July 10th Very hot & bright. Letters & diary in morning. Phyllis in to lunch. Afterwards gave her the blue-green enamel pencil which I got for her in Harrods' jewellery dept yesterday; wrote a card saying it was to remind her often of "the triumph of *Inheritance* & the summer of 1932". Winifred also gave her some woodcuts of old Chelsea, to look at when she felt homesick for London and this household. She said goodbye to the children & we all had tea at the Lombard; then we all saw her off in a taxi to Euston where she is meeting her Highgate friend & going off to a dull holiday in Ireland. She wouldn't let me go with her as she said she'd rather say goodbye to us in Chelsea where we belong.

Felt extraordinarily flat after she had gone; in some queer way she is one of the most stimulating people I have ever met, & her tendency to get easily depressed & feel shy and inferior doesn't prevent this. Tried to work after dinner but too depressed to do much. . . .

•   •   •   •   •

Monday July 18th   Spent day at British Museum reading *Annual Reg-isters* from 1900 onwards. I got in at S. Kensington Tube, & sat down to read Phyllis's novel *Carr* which I am just finishing, when a most strange coincidence happened. I noticed that the woman beside me—youngish middle-age, plain, rather red weather-beaten face, dressed in black leather coat & small black hat, was looking at my book in the rather inquisitive way that people in the Tube often do, when sud-denly she said, in a rather harsh voice with a slight North country accent (but not at all the same as Phyllis's), "Forgive me for interrupt-ing you, but I was at school with the girl who wrote that book you are reading."

Then occurred the following conversation (which I put down to retell to Phyllis as soon as I got to the B.M.):

Vera. Really! How interesting! I know her quite well myself; I'm a writer too & she's been staying with me in London. Were you at Cheltenham?

Stranger. Oh no; it was a little school in Halifax called Miss Rouse's. I lived in Halifax for 27 years & we knew all the Bentleys—Phyllis & her brothers. They were a very clever family, and they all wore glasses & had red hair.

V. All this interests me a good deal, because I only know P. B. as a famous writer who's just had a terrific success with her last book *Inheritance*. Have you read it?

Stranger. Yes, I read that; I thought it was awfully good. I didn't read her others because I go in for out-door things much more than reading, but I've noticed them coming out & been so interested be-cause I was at the same school. Has she been in London lately?

V. Yes, she's only just left; she's had a perfectly splendid time here going to literary parties & making speeches at dinners & so on. Do tell me what she was like when you knew her—I don't know her from the point of view of her early life at all. How old was she when you knew her at school & what was she like?

Stranger. She was a good deal younger than I was—quite little, about 12 I should say. She was a plain little girl & wore glasses, but had beautiful auburn hair, very curly. But the chief thing about her

was that she was terribly high-strung & excitable—used to take it out
of herself like anything by rushing up & down all over the place. Of
course she was clever; really brilliant at lessons & things; everybody
thought her clever. Is she just as excitable now?

V. Well—probably she is, but it doesn't appear much on the surface.
She seems self-possessed as a rule now, & rather reserved, but I suspect a good deal of excitableness inside ("How different, different,
different we all are in our maturity," I thought to myself, "and yet how
singularly the same—our essential characteristics not altered but
merely thrust inward by the onslaught of life"). Was she popular at
school?

Stranger. Yes—quite; well, no, perhaps not exactly. You see, she was
so highly strung & absolutely absorbed in lessons & work; she didn't
seem to have much *outside* life, if you know what I mean.

V. Do tell me your name, so that I can mention it when I next write
to her.

She told me that she was married now but her name was Irene
Clarkson, but that Phyllis would be more sympathetic & more likely
to remember her sister Lydia who was lame; she said she lived in
Wimbledon now, & asked me my name, but it obviously didn't convey
much when I gave it. By this time it was Holborn & I had to get out;
the general impression she left on me as I departed was a kind of
mingled pleasure & incredulity that the excitable little auburn-haired
girl had fulfilled what even then had seemed her destiny & become
so famous. By the time we'd finished talking the other people near us
in the train had become interested & we had quite a little crowd listening to our conversation. As I walked to the B. M. it struck me that
the picture of the clever little red-haired girl running up & down in
sheer excitement was rather a pleasing one, but not in the least like the
one Phyllis gave me of herself; perhaps, after all, she didn't appear to
her childhood's contemporaries quite as unfavourably as she imag-
ines. . . .

· · · · ·

Thursday December 1st Phyllis and I walked to Haworth.[10]. . . It was
a lovely clear day & the country outside Halifax was just like the
country round Buxton—stone walls, bronze sun-flecked moors &

running streams. But I couldn't really enjoy it because I felt dead tired & sick & had a pain, & even a fascinating conversation about sex and our own temperaments couldn't make me forget these things.

Lunched at the Black Bull at Haworth; fireless cold room, tried to eat eggs & bread & butter & tea without much success. Afterwards looked over the church & parsonage with all the Brontë relics; largest photograph that of the American gentleman who had given the money to the Brontë Society to found the museum: Charlotte's photograph relegated to side wall. . . . We took the bus to Keighley instead of walking as Phyllis had intended. There she gave me tea in a restaurant between two buses; I sat beside the fire & felt warm for the first time that day. Nice tea & toast but couldn't eat much. We talked about the queer way that we'd "fallen in love" with each other.

In the bus on the way back to Halifax tiny sickle of new moon shone over the moor and I wished we had been walking there together beneath it if only the wind had been less cold & I less tired. Went to bed early & was sick. Too tired.

Friday December 2nd   Woke up still feeling sick; made myself get up but couldn't eat breakfast. Long conversation with Mrs. Bentley about Phyllis; she actually seemed quite moved about how "good" we'd been to P. and said if she could ever do anything for me I must let her know.

Went in car with Phyllis to Huddersfield to hear her speak on "Yorkshire as a Novelist's County" to the Huddersfield Women's Luncheon Club there. Not nearly so good a room as the Halifax one; stuffy, noisy, crowded, odious with smell of food; couldn't touch lunch & don't know how I sat through it all without being sick. Phyllis, though not feeling very well herself, spoke excellently; very differently from her rather uninspired after-dinner speeches that I heard in the summer. The lecture was interesting and well constructed & she spoke in a charming deep voice & read Yorkshire dialect from the Brontës most attractively. She had an unexpectedly gracious and easy manner too. A very enthusiastic member of the Club next to me kept murmuring: "She's a *brilliant* woman! It's as good as a brainwash."

Afterwards had to be sick in the gentlemen's cloak-room; then went with Phyllis to have tea with Miss Sykes, the local solicitor whom Winifred knows, & was sick again; finally had to stop car on way home (we went a long way round, over some high moors by a wireless station) for the same purpose. By this time concluded I must be going to have a baby again; told Phyllis so when we got in & she seemed almost as upset as I felt. Lay down for a bit; then dressed & went with her to the opera as she seemed bitterly disappointed at going alone, but it was sheer purgatory & I had to go out after the 1st act of *The Valkyrie*. She got me a taxi but stayed herself, so I went back alone in the taxi & had some difficulty in finding the house. Mrs. Bentley very kind; got me some hot milk & I went to bed but was pretty sick in the night.

Saturday December 3rd   Sick most of the day & didn't go out. Couldn't go to opera party in evening that P. had arranged. Both she & her mother thought it was a baby; I privately felt too ill to think it that alone, but didn't want to worry them.

Sunday December 4th   In morning made myself get up & go for short walk with P. but couldn't eat; was beginning to feel faint & light-headed; lay down again in evening while P. very nobly packed for me. Felt a fool & a nuisance & *furious* with myself for being so dependent on her. Too ill even to go down & see her brother so decided to go home next day.

Monday December 5th   After breakfast left with many apologies for being such a disappointment; felt miserably conscious all the time that P. was secretly exasperated with me for acting so much out of character & spoiling everything. But she kissed me very fondly when she put me on the quick Pullman train & seemed only sorry. Journey home a Purgatory; smells of food, meals laid round me & males— including the Bishop of Halifax—smoking heavy cigars in my non-smoking car just finished me off; was sick all second half of journey, couldn't even take Bovril, felt indescribable.

Gordon, to whom P. had telegraphed, met me at King's Cross; awful half-hour taxi ride home, trying not to be sick & held up at every turn. . . .

As Dr Gray is [getting] married we decided to call in Dr Joan Malleson . . . [who] diagnosed acute gastritis plus colo-cystitis & prescribed various forms of treatment, not operative thank Heaven; I'd been so afraid I'd never finish "T. of Y." . . .

Tuesday December 6th–Tuesday December 13th Bed. Very queer at first; floating on a cloud, quite light-headed at times, the queerest dreams, nurse coming in to give me blanket baths & water-injections because I was so thirsty. Gradually stopped feeling sick and began to be able to take slops. . . . During week pulled myself together enough to write & have flowers sent to Mrs Bentley; wrote twice to Phyllis but apparently most deliriously & injudiciously. But did write her for S. K. Ratcliffe a testimonial about her lecturing for W. B. Perkins, the American lecture agent who inquired about her abilities.

Tuesday December 13th Got up, wrote letters, slightly corrected an article for the *Quiver*. Very charming letter from Storm Jameson.[11] . . . . But chiefly a very stiff little note from Phyllis begging me not to write till I'm quite well again & saying my last two letters were too wild for her to understand. Apparently they *were* very rude & reckless as W. had a letter from her in great distress about them. Wrote & apologised & said I thought I must have got them mixed with some of my queer dreams last week. . . .

Wednesday December 14th–Saturday December 17th Feeling ill, tired & utterly miserable. Starting life & work again with wobbly feet & aching back. Phyllis insists on quarrelling with me for my silly let-ters—on Friday I got the coldest and cruellest of little notes from her saying she now regarded me quite differently & didn't feel she could resume our friendship again on the same terms. Of *course* I was in the wrong—but must this end everything? I can't think *how* she can let two foolish letters count more than all the things I tried to do for her in the spring & summer, all the other letters I've written her, & the conversations we've had about things so dear and sacred to us both. I wrote a long letter trying to explain this, and saying that I, at any rate, couldn't turn it all off like a tap. But I don't suppose it will be any good; she seems determined to be proud & haughty & offended & bitter. I can't alter suddenly towards people like that. I don't under-

stand the unrelenting hardness of the Yorkshire temperament when
angry. But I am too miserable to write about it any more.

Have tried to do my Christmas shopping & wrap up cards & parcels
feeling ill & wretched & vainly remorseful. Half an hour's conversation would put all this misery & misunderstanding right at once.
If only her house were hers & not her mother's I'd take the first train
to Halifax and *make* her see me. But as it is, there seems to be nothing
I can do but hope she'll relent in time. Yesterday as I walked along
the King's Road I felt a familiar sense of heavy finality weighing me
down and recognised it for the feeling I used to have in the War when
somebody dear was dead—only this time not a person was dead,
but a relationship that promised such lovely things. Having such a
lonely past & such an inferiority complex, she is convinced that I
meant every word I said—and of course it was really one of my idiotic
flare-ups intensified by illness—half temper, half delirium. What a
miserable *fool* I am!

· · · · · ·

Monday December 19th   Winifred got a letter from Phyllis by first post
apparently capitulating and saying she didn't resent my letters any
more, but still rather cold & emotionally upset. No letter came for
me—but felt better & went to a party at the Mitchisons' in the evening. . . .

Got back to find a letter from Phyllis—cool & beginning "My dear
Vera" but it said that she no longer felt any resentment & realised I
had been more ill than she thought. But she seems emotionally quite
exhausted and it's obviously going to take much tact and gentle treatment to get back to where we were.

Tuesday December 20th   Phyllis has started heaping coals of fire already—sent me a most charming blue "Flappach" powder case, & two
most expensive-looking & intelligently-chosen toys for the children—a
toy piano for John & larger cuddly animal on wheels for Shirley. I
retaliated with a black suede bag with a white-edged flap & her initial
in marquisite in a corner. . . .

Thursday December 22nd   A much nicer letter from Phyllis this morning—collapsed & in bed after another dental episode plus emotion.

Says she was *bouleversée* [upset] by my letters, partly owing to financial demands on her by the family & partly to demands from the *Manchester Evening Chronicle* for more low-brow articles. But *Inheritance* has gone into a 9th edition in England & her two *Harper's* stories have been sold here to *John O'London* & the *Woman's Journal*. . . .

· · · · ·

Monday December 26th   Feeling of terrific relief at being on hither side of Christmas. Blessed release from posts & telephones. Spent most of day finishing an experiment in *vers libre* called "Evening in Yorkshire" & written to Phyllis which was worrying me all last week. Fear it isn't a good poem but it does say what I want to say to Phyllis & can't in letters any more (it's on the text of "Out of this nettle, danger, we pluck this flower, safety") but its badness doesn't matter as she'll probably only think it emotional & hysterical anyway. Wish I could write more poems & better ones. Sent W. a copy but all her poems are so much better than mine that I'm sure she'll think nothing of it either. . . .

· · · · ·

Thursday December 29th   My thirty-ninth birthday & pretty miserable to start with. G.—in spite of having bought me a present—absent-mindedly forgot it until I reminded him; W. left me a present but of course wasn't here to give it me, & no letters came at all. There was one from Phyllis but it just turned out to be a rather snooty little note thanking me coldly for the poem & saying she understood its main idea but couldn't feel adventurous—though she does seem to want to come here in January. Couldn't help contrasting this (unreasonably, perhaps, as I never told her when my birthday was) with my own efforts to find out the date of hers & make it agreeable. Wrote her a long letter about coming here & describing my birthday sensations—but I'm beginning to think it's all no good; she's too ill & neurotic & put off me to care any more about what happens to me. However, the day cheered up as it went on. . . .

· · · · ·

Saturday December 31st   Quite a good day for the last of the year. . . . A really quite charming letter came from Phyllis this morning—so much warmer than all have been of late; she seemed really sorry not to have known my birthday, and also said: "I'm terribly sorry I was so stupidly obtuse about the poem; but you see I just wept the whole morning over it, and I just felt I couldn't bear any more. Now I am stronger & better, and understand what you meant."

Also Gollancz's "Early Spring List" arrived to-day in the shape of his usual fat, intelligent and most exciting-looking mustard-coloured catalogue; it stated amongst other things that *Inheritance* & *Trio* go into cheap editions in March, and that Phyllis Bentley has a new novel in preparation provisionally entitled "As One". (News to me and I should think to everyone else.) W. & I tried to think what its rather intriguing vagueness could mean. . . . Anyhow, the thought of her new book having at least this much of life seemed somehow to irradiate the future. Gollancz *is* intelligent; oh! if *only* he'd take "T. of Y."!

G. went down to spend the day with Beatrice and Sidney Webb at Liphook; got back at 8.0. W. & I looked after the children & talked much about Phyllis, & how I'm to get "Testament of Youth" finished and published. I only hope I shall feel myself a more worth-while person at the end of 1933 than I do to-day.

Notes

Diary of the Thirties, 1932–1939: Chronicle of Friendship, ed. Alan Bishop (London: Gollancz, 1986), is the source of all selections included here.

1 Phyllis Bentley (1894–1977) from Yorkshire, who became a well-known and prolific novelist; her regional historical novels such as *Inheritance* (1932) gained her international popularity and respect.

2 Winifred Holtby. Holtby, a fiction writer and journalist, had been Brittain's good friend since their Oxford days.

3 Margaret Haig (Lady Rhondda) started the weekly periodical *Time and Tide,* a feminist periodical run by women, in 1920.

4 Amy Francis, Brittain's housekeeper, and Dorothy, her parlormaid, quarreled over Dorothy's boyfriend, who had offended Amy.

5 Violet Scott-James.

6 Stopes was the pioneering advocate of birth control and sexual reform who founded the world's first birth-control clinic in London in 1918.

7 Brittain's husband, George Edward Gordon Catlin.

8 Brittain's son.

9 Roland Leighton, Brittain's fiancé, who was killed in World War I.

10 Brittain is now paying Bentley a return visit in Yorkshire.

11 Storm Jameson, who became a good friend of Brittain's in the mid-thirties, was a Yorkshire novelist, critic, and social activist.

Elizabeth Raper

(d. 1778)

ELIZABETH RAPER was the only child of a prosperous country
gentleman, John Raper of Twyford House, Hertfordshire, and his
wife, Elizabeth Hale. Nothing is known of her childhood, but, according to her great-grandson reporting family lore, when she grew
up, she was "plain, 'short in figure, with the Raper face, and undecided complexion,' with a warm heart and still warmer temper,"
though "accomplished, musical, clever."★ She was also, to judge by
her 1756–61 diary, attractive to would-be lovers and encouraged their
advances; not surprisingly, the diary was kept partly in cypher. Yet
though Raper wanted very much to marry, marriage seemed to elude
her during the diary period, what with fortune hunters and deceivers
to plague her. At first in the selections here from 1756 to 1760, some
sort of understanding exists between her and Captain Howe, R. N.
(afterwards Admiral Lord Howe), so that she expects a formal declaration when he returns from his cruise. Captain Howe's brother's
wife, Elizabeth's dearest friend, has encouraged her hopes. But in the
first of many disappointments, her expectations come to nothing.
She later married a successful physician, William Grant, M.D., of
Inverness-shire, a man younger than she. Though she endured almost
as many disappointments in her attempts to bear a child (sixteen) as
in her courtings, she successfully bore Grant two children—John
Peter in 1774 and Elizabeth Raper in 1778—only to die a few weeks
after her daughter's birth. Before then, Raper had become a noted
housewife and cook, and bound with her diary is her receipt (recipe)
book for 1770 with instructions for food and other preparations such
as Lavender Water: "Half an ounce of oil of lavender, 6 penniworth
of ambergrease, mix them together and put to them a pint and half of
the best rectified spirits of wine, shake it well two or three times a
day, let it stand two or three months, then Philter it off." A free spirit,
Raper was also a very practical one.

From Elizabeth Raper's Diary

Sunday, [September?]¹ 1756 Dined at 5, and in the evening Mrs. Howe got the grand secret² from me. Cried and was pitied. What will come of it God knows. To bed at ten.

Thursday [September?] Up at 6. Finished packing, dressed and went down. Set out and got to Ballesdon by 3, found Uncle Page better, dined, and after coffee sauntered abroad, came in about 6, the 4 went to quadrille, I chose to walk round the wood. Mrs. Page, etc., laughed at me and said I should be frightened. She told me I should meet Captain Howe there, upon which I hid my blushes. Walked round to the right first. A river runs by the bottom and you walk by it some way. The whole wood and place together is immensely pretty; a great walk goes from the house to the wood and all round it. The moon shone very bright thro' the trees, the evening was quite calm and there only wanted the presence of *one* to make me think myself in heaven, but he being absent, I indulged myself in thought, and was lost in it during my hour's ramble. At 7 I returned to the house, but found the door fastened which I came out at; I then went round and found another which led me in. I turned wrong and lost my way, but turned back again and found it. They were all very glad to see me come in safe, I full of the beauties of the place I had just left, but don't think my words did it justice. Mrs. Davis then informed me that it was a favorite walk of Captain Howe's, and that the last time he was there he used to walk for hours in the wood every night, to which I answered that I fancied it was excessive fine by daylight.

Friday, 1st. October Up soon after 6, found my way down to the parlour where was Mr. Howe at breakfast. Soon after came Mrs. Howe, drank our dish of tea and at 7 I set out, got to Hertford a quarter before one, sent to order dinner; ate vastly. Came away before 3 and got to Thorley between 5 and 6, found my uncle vast glad to see us. My father and mother came and sat an hour, my aunt staid at Twyford. At 9 Mrs. H. and I went up; I sat with her till near 11; had a great deal of serious discourse, then Mr. H. came up, and I went, got to bed and contemplated.

Saturday, 2 October Got up at 7, washed, combed and came down to Uncle, discovered him and went up again, ordered dinner, dressed and sauntered about till near 10, when Mrs. H.'s bell rang. Made his T., breakfasted and sat with Mrs. H. all morning, had a great deal of talk. Between 1 and 2 my Aunt came with us, then went out, then took me in a corner and told me somewhat that made me very grave and concerned me a good deal. How it will end God knows. Between 2 and 3 came my father and mother, was very merry outwardly. Had a tete-a-tete with mother at owl-light, came down and found candles, could not see, got in parties. After 9 they went, at 10 Mrs. H. and I retired, sat with her till Mr. H. came up.

Sunday, 3 October At a quarter before 11 they brought word the coach was ready and I was obliged to part from my dearest friend. She promised to write directly if she heard any news of. . . . . . . and left me with great hopes.

Thursday, 7 October Got up at 7 after dreaming much to my satisfaction, but wish it had been real.

Wednesday Up at 8, had mighty good dress, waited impatiently for the post, had nothing by it but the news, saw nothing there but the Rhoda's safe arrival[3] at Margate.

Thursday Slept very ill, the wind so high all night that it disturbed both body and mind. Dreamt the Lord knows what, got up with a headache, worked and read all morning.

Friday Sat watching for the post, had a line from my dearest friend to enclose one from Miss Hanley that came after we left Hanslop. Skimmed the news and found nothing.

Wednesday Heard from Mrs. Howe That Dick [Captain Howe] was at Plymouth to refit and expected to go out again soon.

Saturday, Xmas Day Up at 10, washed combed, breakfasted, did a few odd jobs, and went to Thorley, where dined Mr., Mrs., and Miss Flack. The ladies drank T. and departed between 6 and 7. I to my Uncle in my favourite study and began to look over Euclid.

Sunday 26 December Attacked Euclid, drawed some of the figures, a little dull about an Angle, not to say a good deal so. Think I shall like the kind of thing, and much more so for a certain reason. Heigho! Ho! Read in the news that Knowles was arrived, but saw nothing of the Dunkirk.[4]

Friday, 31 December Fiddled about and did not much. Read in the news that Capt. Howe was left with the command of [a] squadron in the bay of Biscay.

Friday, 14th January 1757 Worked and attacked Euclid, immensely dull, could not keep up my attention to that or anything save one particular subject.

Saturday, 15th January Worked, made mince pies, eat up with vapours.

20th–21st January Did nothing nor heard nothing. Immensely dull and more out of spirits than ever, a new load and can't support the lump of dullness inseparable from me.

22nd January Did an immense deal of work. Tried Euclid again, in rather better spirits.

· · · · ·

29 March 1757 . . . The Dunkirk is not refitted yet and Dick is in Town. Damned mad in my mind, and do not care 3 straws if I never see him again;—damn all the sex![5]

9th January 1758 To the Parson's in the afternoon, disturbed Sam[6] in his study, romped and returned very grave to the parlor.

26th January Word was brought me Mr. Houblon and Mr. Lipeat were come. Stuffed up my alls and went to them, chatted very agreeably, a little after 12 Uncle came in, found the fire smoking, so invited them into the study. Mr. L. desired to see the great room whither I attended him but found it was more for his sense of feeling than his sense of sight, Kissing being his chief business there. That over, we adjourned to the study, drank chocolate, then the gentlemen went into the Observatory, I to order about dinner in case they should stay. In due time they came down again, L. came hopping before to get a kiss or two, thought the devil was in him, etc. They would not stay to dinner, so about ½ past 2 they went. L. contrived to be a little behind so as to take his leave, they gone he told me he would dine here. I went to writing as if the duce was in me; not done till 6, cards and to bed.

15 February . . . Heard from her [Mrs. Howe] that Dick was married to a Miss Hartop, thought I should have died, cried heartily, damned him as heartily, and walked about loose with neither life nor soul.

29 April About 12 set out for Moore Hall, the house like a Paradise, so neat, looked all over it, ate brown bread and cheese and butter, and drank hot elder wine, vast good, and came away at ½ past 2. Got home before 3, soon after came Sam, dined, immensely facetious, lost my shoe, told stories of sprights, drank coffee.

• • • • • •

21 August Went to Mrs. Radford's, young Dunn came too, walked in garden and sang till supper. Mr., Mrs. and Miss Jennings, Dr. Con and his lady, all there, and children, but went at 8; came in, supped, Mr. R. to club about 10, we walked into ye garden again (young D. stuck close by me and would not stir an inch from me, Lord help's). Sung again, at 11 in came Mr. R., Lyslie Cox and another, paid me many compliments, made me sing and then left us. At 12 Miss Wood and I came away, Dunn with us.

22nd August Up, Bkft. and to Town with Miss Radford, etc. (a billet doux from ——). Called on Miss D. and to Alder to meet Harry; dined him, Miss D., Dick and I at ½ past 12; not in spirits. At 5 Harry went, I wrote in the office, at 7 we came away, Dick with us. Called at Coleman St. and got down to the Bog before 9, supped at Dunn's, young D. came down, stayed till past 11, when he came home with us. Thought he would have eat me up almost.

23rd August A Billet doux before I was well up.

26th August Up, packed up my alls, Statue called, and at 11 2 Virgins and I to P.E.[7] Found all vast glad and all that, dined, talked, worked, walked, romped, supped, upstairs a great deal of kissing from my young he-cousin [Harry], romped and to bed.

1 to 9th September The Time spent in reading, working, eating, sleeping, walking, romping and kissing, and packed up our alls and away to the Bog.

• • • • •

21st [*September?*]   Set off to Chiselhurst. Mr. Hotham, 2 of his sons, at home, very clever people, walked in ye garden, a mighty pretty place. Dined before 3, after dinner *the* Mr. Hotham and I went all alone (there being no crowd) to walk in the wood and about, liked it much; sang to him in the Temple and we came in pretty good friends, drank coffee, soon after T.; then with much ado *the* Mr. Hotham brought down his Violincello and played to us. Then they made me sing I know not how many songs, after chatted very agreeably till 9, supped, were very sociable; came away at 11.

22nd [*September?*]   All invalids, could not go to church, but dressed and went out to dine at 1 with neighbour Friths; Miss Daweson there, I rather out of sorts, headache and ear, little dinner. Hotham and I jumbled not quite right, often quite the reverse, very facetious, after dinner sung too. Hotham made a song, very *entertaining* and infinitely *agreeable,* supped, were rather better, came away at 11, Hotham with us as far as home.

24th [*September?*]   Up, Bfkt. had scarce done when Mr. Hotham came, but could not stay he said, routed out a Bass and played to us, well. Then he staid to dinner, but was to go before dark, then it misled [*sic*], then it grew darkish, then wrote and sent home instead of going, soon very facetious, pretty good friends, romped, but not all that, supped, had a long argument, he and I, concerning matrimony, managing wives, what degree of learning a woman ought to have etc. etc., liked my conversation very well and believe he did not dislike it, both agreed though both differed. Not in bed till one. N. B. Miss Cleeve and I dressed up a Joan[8] and put it in his bed.

• • • • •

25th [*September?*]   Gave an infinity of orders, then to Fleetditch, picked up Mr. Cleeve and away to the Cocoa, the Pall Mall. Mr. Hotham there. . . . Dark by [time] that we got to Eltham, some hard language passed between Thing[9] and I, but fancy its not much to the purpose. Arrived safe at Foots Cray between 7 and 8. Mr. Hotham was determined on going several times, but somehow he staid all night. Read Hogarth's Analogies, supped, sung and came up to bed before one, I repaired to Mr. Hotham's room, pinned down his pillow exactly opposite to what it should be, sewed up his nightcap, and got into bed soon after one.

. . . . .

8th December   After bkft., Ed. came and I went to S's Lane, was asked to stay to dinner. Dined very agreeably, drank coffee and before 5 came away, my dear Statue with me. Took a coach in Cheapside and to King's Road. Mrs. G. going to make visits, he not at home, so Statue staid with me all alone. Mr. G. came in at 6 to T., wished him gone again and thank my stars he went.

. . . . .

25th December   Christmas Day. Up at 7, collick all night. Dressed, and before 8 went with Mrs. Hoy and Patty home, set them down and went on to Alder, picked up Statue and returned to Mrs. Hoy's soon after 9 and were conducted to the *dining* room and sat very snug. Bkftd. Mrs. Hoy obliged attend her business, so was forced to have a tete-a-tete in ye dining room; could not go to *church* not being well, so sat there till past 12, when we parted, and I went in the coach to the Temple. Took up Uncle and arrived at the Bog soon after one.

21st January 1759   After Bkfst. Pompey[10] and I walked as far as Islington with Harry, got back by 10. Dressed up and to Meeting with all the etceteras till night. At six A. went to bed, at 10 Mr. Hoy, by 11 Pompey; soon after came Statue and staid well past 3 Lord help's!

25th January   Pompey and I to town to buy mourning, saw Statue and got home by dinner. Found Harry there with a story of a Cock and Bull, made the Devil of work, and me very uneasy, played at cards and again after supper till near bed time. Had the honour of a tete-a-tete with him, did not like and went to bed.

26th January   Up before he went, intended going to Mrs. Cleeves but had ye headache too much for that. A. and Pompey went airing, I miserable at home. After dinner played crib; Parson came, tea etc. and all till bedtime.

27th January   Up and to Town, Pompey and I called in several places and heard several mighty disagreeable things, out of spirits and humourish, met Statue who followed me to Mrs. M.'s and there took a long *adieu,* I, not so much affected as I thought I should, as there were some circumstances I thought a little odd without knowing why.

30th April   Met Dr. Dimsdale in the lane. *****Mrs. Parsons and I went into the pastor where were the Dr. and Mr. King, the Dr. very much my humble servant and all that egad. Chatted very socially, some significant *squeezes* from the Dr. [Dimsdale].

26th May   Up before 7, dressed and to Stortford before 8 to Bkft. with Mrs. Dimsdale. Ye Dr. not up till some time after we got there. Bkft. over we all walked in the garden, the lover very pensive, kept close to me, sighed, squeezed and sighed again; his mother looked very arch but said not a word.

5th June   'Liver' [Dr. Dimsdale] close by me (begin to be sorry for him, but at present it proceeds no farther than pity).

25th June   Fear I shall play with the candle till I burn my fingers.[11]

26th June   My Partridges came.[12]

25th September   Up and dressed before 6. At ½ past came Liver with guns and dogs to call Jack to shooting, ordered some brkft., took him into the partridge house, he seemed very dull, but had not lost all love for the 'pattys' as I should have imagined he would, being mine, sighed and said it was some satisfaction to see that something was loved which was once his. I said they were now mine, and I loved them for my own sake, and that I should be very miserable if any accident was to happen to them. He said he did not pretend to have any share in them now. We were going on with such discourse which might have produced something more when Jack came to us; wished him hanged with all my soul. However, said *I* was glad he was come, and then we all three repaired to the Hall for victuals. By this time Mrs. P. was come down, half awake; soon after 7 the shooters went off. A long morning, dressed at 4, ere I was quite ready (for I'd been ordering and doing about dinner) the shooters came back; they had dined at the Dr's. Went down to them, looked miserably, which Liver took notice on, but that was *more* than I desired him to do. Jack had been drinking some wine that he liked mightily and came home half glazed and vast loving, which I was very sorry for, not being at all in the humour for *his* love; got rid on't as well as I could. Left them to drink a bottle of cyder whilst we dined, which was soon over with me; asked them if they'd have any cold dumpling, which would do as well as pudding to settle their love. *Liver* replied 'he did not want any for that he was *fixed*.' This I made a cat's paw on and plagued him eternally, threatened to discover him to the girls etc., tormented him all day, told him he should never see me feed the pattys any more, and in short were both very queer. However let him go to them lest he should *break his heart*. Mrs. Bur came to us all impatience to think I had been so long with two young men and she not. From the Pattys repaired to the long walk. Sat there some time, had a disputation on *love,* which I said I knew nothing on. Sung 'Why heaves my fond bosom,' 'Alexis and Damon' and 'Lavella,' all which *seemed* to touch Liver, but I'm not at all sure they did, as I suspect he's like the rest of his sex, detest them all, curse them with all my soul! Singing and chattering over we were preparing to go in. I changed my seat, Liver jumbled himself by me, would have kissed me and hugged me, but would not let him as he had been doing the same to Mrs. B. and with (seeming) equal pleasure. Had like to have been in possession of the grand secret but escaped, however not without an assurance that I should hear it another time, and when I told him about his being fixed, he repeated 'that he looked upon himself as engaged while a certain young lady was single.'

8th October   Wish I could put it out of my head as I think it impossible ever to do. Kissed and hugged me, think I am gratifying my present inclination at the expense of (perhaps) my future happiness. God knows how it will be in the end.

21st October   I imagine he will never speak plain and hints can never come to anything. . . .

15th   Met Statue, looks sadly, crossed over to speak to me and stood talking in the street sometime; was much shocked at the discourse and thought I could not have stood. He behaved very inconsistent and odd; at last we parted, I very miserable, *he* looked not much better. . . .

· · · · ·

14th December 1760   Ye 2 girls[13] gave me a letter from Cadwallader to Sal, read it as soon as I got home, a long one, the subject matter *me*. I think there was not 10 words about any other person, mighty smart and gallant, conveyed very *strong ideas,* more than I thought had been in him, read it to Mother. She thought it savoured of affection, read it to Father and *he* thought Do [*sic*]. Believe he will soon come down, shall see if he carries it on, rather in favour I think just now, but it won't do.

28th December   Cad has arrived at the Parsonage and does duty in church inimitably well.

24th January 1761   Set cakes into the oven, all very light, dined and to the Parson's to tea, carried him a cake with which he seemed much pleased. Well, he talked about Sam and told some secret history; I sat very grave and got the headache by the means. He went at 6, me to Quadrille, more talk, think it odd, but gave him his scope and talked myself, thinking I might as well throw in a hint (undesignedly) as he. Played till 8, all very sociable and friendly, seem to grow more and more so.

26th January   Worked and *mused* all morning, ruminated on the thing, am more and more astonished every time I think on't, suppose it is *so* but am amazed at it, wonder where 'twill end.

3rd March   Cad met me and ushered me into the parlour. He trembled all over, talked very pathetically a good while, could not answer him, at last plucked up courage and told him something that I think struck him very much, what he was moved by I can't say, but disappointed he certainly was, and I very much fear and question his sincerity as to his real love of me *only*. God only knows the *heart,* but I *fear*. How-ever, we went on some time, great expressions of love on his side, that is with great earnestness and positiveness, but I wish I knew his heart and soul; am afraid I shall find it like the Statue's.

5th March   Sal gave me a note and used all her eloquence to persuade me to let Cad speak. ½ consented at last.

6th March   Sal called and made me walk, left her at Aunt Prior's, while I went home and told Mother Cad's intention. Mother seemed disposed to do all she could in reason. Cad told me that he had spoken to Uncle, that he had told him much as I had before, but with this addition, that he wished with all his heart it could be practicable as a thing that would make him very happy if there was a possibility of it. Then Cad told me his resolution to leave Thorley directly in case he should not succeed, wished *me* soon to forget it, but *he* could never, that he hoped and wished me to meet with a man that would make me happy in every respect, that if he did not succeed in this he should never look for happiness again, that if I *should* live single, *he* should always be at my command (or something like that if not the very words), for he should have no thoughts of marrying, and a great deal more. Cad repeated his design of leaving the country, and said if he did it would be for my sake. This sort of conversation lasted to the stile, where we parted.

8th March   We had a great deal of very grave discourse. Cad said he had had a very civil letter from my Father, which he said had almost made him mad, as he could not build any hopes on it. He apeared excessively uneasy, I was not much better, for to see him so excessively unhappy worked me to death. To church. A christening happened that day, which showed a most [*sic*] of Cad's positiveness; little circumstances give strong ideas. (Mem. It may be so in regard to my temper as well as other's). Question the goodness of his temper, he is certainly positive, and very much so.

9th March   Muzzled ale the afternoon, had the fidgets confoundedly, this being the time when Cad was to meet Father.

10th March   Cad met me much dejected, I hardly know what I did, but into the parlor I went. Said I'd go up to Misses, Cad followed me, and into Mr. Horsley's room, where he bolted the door. I trembled from head to foot, he, to all appearance just like a mad thing. At last he spoke and told me what I had before read in his countenance. He gave me to understand that he and my Mother had agreed it was utterly impossible, and spoke in such a manner that I imagined he had himself given over all thoughts of its ever being so, nor did he give the least hint of any hopes from time, or that he even wished it. The only way I could account for this was his being in the utmost despair and hardly knowing *what* he said. Yet still I think it odd that he should drop no hint, nor express in his manner even a distant hope; this struck me, he said he would not write to me, nor should I to him, he would not be guilty of so dishonest an action, nor could he after the confidence my Mother had placed in him. He said we must now only look on each other as friends, and even when I asked if they had determined the impossibility of its ever being, he gave me no direct answer, nor did he so much as say that time would do any the least thing, but seemed to me to have chopt (rather than lost) all thought of its ever being. He gave me a good deal of very *prudent* advice, which I told him I thought very *prudent;* that he would not only advise me but persuade also to accept of any person that my friends approved, and that I thought I could be happy with. He wished I might meet a man that loved me as well as he did, in return I wished *him* very happy, and said I thought his best scheme would be to marry some woman with ready money, and he begged me to give him none of my advice, and seemed in great agitation. We had more of this discourse and adjourned to the nursery where were the 2 eldest girls, all very miserable, they and I really were so, I believe he too perhaps, and perhaps all from different motives. At last I got away, he seemed agitated to the greatest degree, but there seemed a mixture of crossness as well as grief. What would I give to see into his heart.

11th March   Up soon after 7; in a violent fright lest Cad should come to take leave of Uncle, and I not be out of the way, fidgeted immensely, but took care to keep clear of the Study, at 8 sent a note to *Anna,* had an answer from *Cad.* Kept out of the way still, at last went in to breakfast, in one continued fright. After that was over sent again to the Parsonage, heard that Cad had been to take leave and was going to set off for Town. Uncle went out soon after 9, I, after he was off, went into the Study again and gave a loose to my tears. Before 11 came Anna and Sall, both very dismal and found me worse than themselves. They declared they would not undergo such another morning for the world, that they thought they should never have got Cad to set out. They said but little about him, but I understood by their manner that his distress exceeded all description.

12th March   Up at 7 and to the Parson's to quilt. Very low and all of us queer. After breakfast Mr. Horsley made his motions intelligible, and they all walked off and left me alone with him. He talked to me very *tenderly* and affectionately, I was ready to die all the time, and could hardly drag out yes and no. The conversation lasted two hours, I believe he told me, amongst other things, that he *wished* me well as any one of his own daughters, and should as truly and sincerely rejoice at my happiness. The manner of his conversation, nay the very words, were excessively like his son; to be sure there's a very great likeness between them. After he had said a great deal of good and seasonable he himself broke up the party, for, as I believe, I should have staid to this time if he had not moved.

16th March   Home between 11 and 12. Uncle walked with me. I into Mother's room where she gave me a long account of what had passed between her and Cad. The sum of Conversation was that he seemed vastly surprised that so rich as Father and Mother were reputed to be, they could not give me in present about 200 a year, though they might not have ready money to spare. This, I say, astonished him greatly (and Mother dwelt on it) without considering that he had not any the least right to demand it, unless he thought everything due to his *personal* merit. However, as it could not be, it could not, and all that. Mother dropped something about a coach and that it was impossible for me in the Eye of the *World* to marry without one. *Supposing* we ourselves were willing and contented to live without any shew, yet common convenience in appearance must not be given up, and that it was a sad thing to be straitened. He said that was by no means his scheme, and that he could not think of marrying with only his present preferments, without any fortune from the woman in present, for that he could not maintain a wife and family. Mother says he seemed vastly vexed, and said he *wished* he had never spoken at all, and on her hinting something on the smallness of his income, as if (I suppose) nothing to speak *upon,* he told her he had not *designed* to speak so *soon,* that he was in no haste to marry, but intimated he should have no *objection* to being married if everything had fallen out as he thought; that it was no part of his scheme to marry without a sufficiency to live genteely, and a great deal more prudent stuff, by much *too* prudent in *my* opinion for any man so much in love as he had pretended to be. He professed great concern for me, as he said *I* should be very unhappy and he wished I did not like so well as I did, and intimated that he was sorry for unhappiness, yet he had gone no further than was just necessary for a man to do, only *sounded,* I suppose to know before he spoke, that his proposal was not *disagree-able* to me, and by what he said, the fool thought or for *prudent* reasons chose to make *Mother* believe, that I had swallowed the tempting bait, and was desperately in for it, Lord help him! he knows little of me. *Supposing* him indeed sincere in his affection to me; I could have *loved* and *valued* him, but upon my soul the moment I think him to *cool, I* am *off* without a *pang.* It may be thought, (and justly) that this account which I know to be fair and impartial, did not make in his favor to me. But to return he again repeated he wished he had not spoken at all; his sorrow for *me,* and his vexation for *himself;* so as I believe he got in a hole, wanted to get out, and did not know how, he gave up the point and seemed to conclude it was over. Mother said nobody knew what might happen, but that at *present* it could not be. To this he made no answer. She in the course of her talk flung another opportunity before him by saying things might happen, and hinted if he had no prospect of preferment? If he had chose to say the handsome thing, or to have made any reserve for hereafter—but he was *mute as a picture;* only when she touched on preferment he dragged out that he should try for it. They had more of this kind, but I think I have recollected the heads, at least the material ones that gave me my *idea,* I confess not the most pleasing, and very different from what I had before this tete-a-tete, though not so different neither from my real opinion when I suffered myself to judge impartially. But as my opinion could only be founded on my own conjectures, so I was willing to suppress those thoughts which were not for his honor, and rather uncharitable, supposing that *all mankind* were not (I will not say villainously but) mercenarily and so very *prudently* inclined. He asked my mother if she had any objection to his taking his leave of me or, after a little time, visiting as friends, to which she said, no, and laid no embargo on him, saying at the same time that she had too good an opinion of *me* to think I would ever do anything which she etc. or the world should condemn me for and think imprudent. Neither did she think that *he* would ever urge me to act contrary to what my friends would approve. But I'm tired of all this so will drop it, and only say my opinion is worse, and I don't think he can clear it up, not make things appear any better. Father never mentioned the thing to me at all.

Notes

❧

★*The Receipt-Book of Elizabeth Raper,* ed. Bartle Grant (London: Nonesuch Press, 1924), p. 5; also the source for the recipe quoted in this paragraph (p. 41). All the diary selections here have been taken from this edition.

1 Raper does not always give a full date or follow a consistent pattern when she does date entries.

2 Presumably, her hopes concerning Captain Howe. Mrs. Howe is his sister-in-law.

3 Possibly the *Rhoda* was Captain Howe's ship at the time.

4 The *Dunkirk* was Captain Howe's current ship.

5 He has chosen not to declare himself, and it hurts her for a long time, as her entry of 10 June 1760 shows: "Wish to God I could bury in oblivion all that passed 5 years ago, but alas! it's still fresh in my memory, fool that I am."

6 Sam Horsley, whom she also calls Cad or Cadwallader, son of the rector of Thorley; having recently taken orders himself, in 1760 he assumes the Living of Newington Butts, where Elizabeth's grandmother lives at "the Bog."

7 *Statue* is her nickname for young Dunn. *P.E.* designates Ponders End, where live an uncle of hers and cousins.

8 A *Joan* at the time was a close-fitting cap worn by women; they apparently put a dummy head wearing such a cap in his bed.

9 Another of her nicknames, but to whom it refers is unknown.

10 Young Mr. Dunn's sister.

11 She has gone walking with Dr. Dimsdale.

12 Tame partridges, given to her by Dr. Dimsdale; she also calls them the Pattys.

13 Anne (Anna) and Sarah (Sal) Horsley, sisters of Sam (or Cadwallader).

Clarissa Trant

(1800–1844)

CLARISSA SANDFORD TRANT was the daughter of an Irishman, Sir Nicholas Trant, and his English wife, Sally Horsington. She was born in Lisbon during the Napoleonic wars, while her father, a professional soldier, served as a lieutenant in the British army. After her mother died in 1806 she and her younger brother, Tom, were cared for by friends in England until her father, who had entered the Portuguese service, became governor of Oporto in 1811, when he sent for his children to rear them abroad. Trant, who traveled all over Europe with her father, could speak and read six languages; her diary often lapses into French and sometimes into Italian and German. Although she later rewrote much of her early diary for her daughter Clara, she left the period 1824–32 mostly unchanged. By this time, Trant's father had retired from the army, while her brother, whom she loved dearly, had entered it; and she was living in England, though often visiting with relatives and friends in Ireland. Although not wealthy, Trant was intelligent and well read, accomplished in drawing and music, and beautiful, and therefore many are the admirers she can write of. Her diary names at least twelve suitors before she marries, and others are implied. But no one has her heart except a Colonel Cameron of Bath who, as the selections here from 1824–31 show,* chose to break it. Trant shared the contemporary fears of spinsterhood, yet refused to marry for security alone. She held out for a spiritually compatible mate, whom she finally found in the Reverend John Bramston and married in 1831. Although Trant was often ill, it was a very happy marriage in which she bore three children—not only Clara (b. 1833) but Mary (b. 1841) and John (b. 1843)—before dying of pleurisy and other complications. She left a letter expressing the wish that her husband would remarry, and he did so, a year later.

From Clarissa Trant's Diary

5 January 1824 . . . J'ai dansé avec Mr. Southwell, Mr. Heyland and Captain V.; walked about the rooms with Major Cameron who is by far the most gentlemanly man I have met with for a long time. He was left for dead on the field of Waterloo and has lost his arm. He acted the part of a *preux chevalier*[1] to me in the course of the evening.

· · · · ·

12 January Major Cameron most unexpectedly made his appearance and I spent a very agreeable evening. He kindly offered to procure me a ticket for the next fancy ball but I declined. He is very pleasing and there is no nonsense about him.

· · · · ·

2 February Spent an hour at Stowey House, où j'ai fait mes adieux au Capitaine Coffin. Il m'a reproché de l'avoir toujours traité avec beaucoup de froideur, et il m'a dit en riant que j'avais l'air d'une lièvre affarouchée dès qu'il s'approchait de moi pour me parler. Je n'osais pas lui dire que ma timidité croissait avec mon estime—mais s'était pourtant vrai—au reste il est à croire que nous ne nous reverrons jamais.[2]

· · · · ·

26 August . . . This day week we dined at Fort William. Mr. Lloyd[3] is coming to spend a few days with us.

· · · · ·

30 August Anty went to town, my Father and I paid our visit at Carig Mahon, where we found Mr. Lloyd waiting to return with us. On our return from Cove we met the "Gossamer" and hailed our friends. Mr. Lloyd, my Father and I dined together and again we talked over Blois. In the evening I was taking my usual walk upon the rocks when I was joined by the former. I confess that from something which had occurred in the morning I began to feel rather uncomfortable at finding myself *tête-à-tête* with my old acquaintance. I could not help seeing that he liked me, but I certainly was unprepared for any serious declaration on his part. It is gratifying to me to think that my candour and sincerity did not offend his feelings and in losing a *lover* I have gained a friend. I did not conceal from him that I have not a sixpence in the world and I ventured even to remind him that it was his positive duty not to displease his indulgent father. I said many other wise things after I had *fully* explained the nature of my own feelings towards him and *now* that I know he cannot misunderstand me, I shall treat him with the ease and confidence of friendship. I cannot but feel most grateful for such an instance of *disinterested* affection.

31 August   Vingt-cinq ans—une belle fortune and highly connected—et moi pauvre—with nothing to be proud of but my Father—vingt-trois ans, *ni laide ni jolie!*[4]

I did not acknowledge a preference for another—but how could I when I have no positive assurance that it is mutual. To-morrow Mr. Lloyd returns to Beech Mount.

1 September   We were to have gone this day to a party at Mr. Bury's, but the weather was boisterous and we preferred remaining at home. Mr. Lloyd and I spent a great part of the morning alone, as my father and Anty were engaged with the papers; but I no longer felt any uneasiness, as it is so perfectly agreed between us that we are to be *friends* for ever more. He spoke to me with the most unreserved confidence of his family, &c.

2 September   Very rainy day. Mr. Lloyd read Italian to me whilst I was at work—he says that I have brought him to his senses, and promises to love my brother for the sake of his *friend*. He says (but what do not even former lovers say?) that his boyish attachment to me at Blois[5] lasted for two years—acknowledged his jealous disposition and paid some compliments to my character at the expense of my sex in general of whom I fear he has met the least favourable specimens during his long intercourse with the depraved society of Italy.

3 September   As usual we spent the morning in reading and talking Italian, and strolling among the rocks. We never allude to the conversation of Monday, but we could never have been so mutually at ease if this early *éclaircissement* [enlightening] had not taken place.

4 September   After breakfast we all went in the boat to Cg. Mahon where we parted from Mr. Lloyd—whose generous and delicate conduct I shall not soon forget. In the evening I had a long and painful conversation with my beloved father—he represented to me in the strongest terms the folly of which I had been guilty in refusing so advantageous an offer and told me what I knew to be the case[:] that if our situation with respect to pecuniary matters had been LESS DREADFUL , he would have urged me still more to consider the absolute necessity of my giving up romantic thoughts at this moment but the generous feelings of his heart prevented him from endeavouring to influence my decision on this ground.

I have acted as my heart told me I ought to act—but if I did not fancy that *one* person was interested in my happiness, I *would* have conquered every romantic feeling and taught myself to love Mr. Lloyd as my husband and as he deserves to be loved by *me* in return for his disinterested preference.

6 September   Walked to Hoddersfield. Thought over the events of last week. Am I indeed acting the foolish part of a romantic girl or have I acted as my beloved mother would have done in my place?

20th January 1825   Went to Church. Captn. Patterson spent the evening with us and was in better spirits than I had seen him since 1822, not that I am vain enough to suppose that what passed between us at that time could materially influence his general state of mind, far less am I inclined to derive any pleasure from such an idea. On the contrary it has been my constant endeavour to make him forget it, and I trust that I have succeeded in proving that I consider him in the light of a sincere and respected friend.

· · · · ·

26 January   Il Signore e venuto ma non ha voluto salire perché c'era gente: Che vuol dire tutto questo? Non so che pensare, e la mia povere teste e molto im brogliata.[6]

28th January[7]   Two weeks never to be forgotten in the annals of my life. Col. Cameron called to take leave previous to his going to Bath. I found myself placed in a situation so particularly embarrassing in receiving his daily visits with my Father's sanction, and still without knowing in what light to consider them.

Confined to my bed with illness.

29th January   My dearest Father enters into all my feelings with the utmost tenderness, but he wishes me not to be hasty and to suspend my decision.

8 p.m.   What is becoming of my resolution? and how have all my unhappy feelings disappeared? How can I doubt his sincerity after the solemn assurance of it which his letter this moment received has conveyed to me? May Heaven direct me for the best. We are to meet to-morrow.

C'en est fait de toi, pauvre Clara—et pour la vie![8]

30th January   The events of yesterday and to-day have crowded together so rapidly that I can scarcely persuade myself that the whole has been more than a happy dream. For the first time in our acquaintance of three years, we fully understand each other and I hope that henceforward all will be candour and openness between us. I am *very happy*. He goes to Bath this evening but will return in a fortnight.

4th February   Spent the day alone—thought over the events of the week which now, more than ever, appear to me like a dream. I have resumed all my usual employments. My visitors are all old friends, whose faces I have known from my early childhood, and the only trace which remains of *him* is the little note which my Father has by mistake locked up with other papers in his desk, and I am ashamed to ask for it.

My dear Father and I dined tête-à-tête and had a comfortable chat.

12th February   Tomorrow he returns—that is to say, if he has not forgotten.

13th February   He has not returned because his Father will not let him come back to London until he has written to my Father about business arrangements. He says his Father is very pleased with his choice.

14th February   A letter from the General [Cameron's father]. Many compliments for me but he asks if my Father can give me money. He[9] has none.

16th February   My Father has answered the letter to-day: no one will ever love me as he loves me. I am more than doubtful about the end of this story.

17th February   The post has come and no letter from Bath. "Then he will surely come himself" I said to my Father, my best confidant. But he is not here.

18th February   No news of Colonel Cameron. We shall see to-morrow whether in losing him I have lost much or little. I am stronger than I was yesterday. Never did I love my Father more.

19th February   The correspondence which has taken place between my Father and General Cameron had prepared me for the termination of all future intercourse between L. C. and myself, which from the knowledge that I have acquired of his character within the last fortnight, I have but too much reason to think would have led to much future unhappiness. The General offered to settle £10,000 upon me and £1,000 per an. upon his son, provided that my Father give me a proportionate quota of fortune. My Father whose experience of the world had enabled him long ere this—[sentence unfinished].

20th February   My dear Father was confined to his bed. I exerted myself to the utmost to be cheerful and I succeeded—still it is not *possible* that I should not feel. I dread the thought of returning to Ballyhonoon where every spot will remind me of that happy time when I believed Colonel Cameron to be in every respect worthy of the high opinion I had formed of him.

21 February   With a heavy heart I summoned up my courage to dine with Lady Torrens. . . . Lord Blantyre no sooner heard my name than he exclaimed, "Can it be a daughter of my old friend Trant?" He then told me that he had seen me when I was a year old, and we had a great deal of chat together. Lady Gordon and her interesting daughter came in the evening, and were extremely kind to me. Lord Thomas and the Ladies O'Brien also joined the party, we had some delightful music, and unconsciously my thoughts became more cheerful, and Clara was herself again.

22 February   How different I feel now. God! I thank Thee from my heart that this knowledge of him did not come too late. And my beloved Father says so often how glad he is that I am not going to leave him.

25 February Last night my Father showed me a most curious letter which he received a few days ago from his former *Aide de Camp*, Sarmento, the purport of which was nothing less than a proposition, couched in very diplomatic terms, of making me *Madame la Chargée d'Affaires* at the Court of D.[10] He honestly confessed that were he not driven by the dulness of his present *Séjour* [sojourn] to the desperate measure of choosing a wife, he should prefer a *vie de garcon* [bachelorhood]. So much for candour.

· · · · ·

19 October 1828, Sunday I never spent a pleasanter day on board a steam packet[11]—thanks to our *rencontre* with a most agreeable, well informed, and at the same time, truly religious young clergyman, a Mr. Bramston, who has been making a tour in Ireland for his amusement and who had been in Rome when we were there. . . .

30th October . . . I spent a pleasant day with the Waldegraves at Harptree. What was my surprise at hearing that our fellow passenger, Mr. Bramston, is brother to the lady who is going to be married to their clergyman, Mr. Davidson. He mentioned having come over in the packet with us. I wonder how he found out who we were.

· · · · ·

9th. May 1829 Walked with my brother to pay visits. In Bond Street we were joined by his acquaintance Captain H., and at a little distance further we passed close to Col. Cameron. I clung close to my dearest brother's arm and turned my head away. Thank God that I have a Father's and a Brother's protecting arm to support me. Never did I prize it more than at that moment. Colonel Cameron looked very ill, as far as I could judge from the distant glimpse which I had of his face before I recognised it. One look was quite enough for me.

· · · · ·

22nd May A note from poor Caddy Boyle[12] begging me to spend the morning with her. I went, and found her suffering under a trial such as has broken many a woman's heart. Quello á cui ella ha sagrificato i suoi primi affetti, per cui ha rifiutato tanti buoni offerti di matrimonio, quello va sposar una conoscenza, Lady Anne B; e questa sera ella deve incontrare i promessi Sposi at Devonshire House. Poveretta! La compiango di cuore, ma egli era indegno di lei.[13]

23rd May   I spent an hour in Hamilton Place with poor Caddy and Mr. J. Boyle. We were all sentimental and melancholy. The former and I started at seven o'clock and had a pleasant drive in the open carriage to Hampton Court, where Caddy was welcomed with a *Mother's* love, increased by the conviction that her mental sufferings were great at the moment. She did meet the happy pair last night at Devonshire House. Lady Anne, radiant with beauty and the consciousness of being an object of envy to her Companions, Lord B. proud of having been preferred by one of the loveliest women in London! Caddy saw him more in sorrow than in anger. *Ils se ressemblent beaucoup* in point of conduct—*ces Messieurs!*[14]

25th May   Returned from a visit to the Boyles at Hampton Court. Madalina Trant spent the day with us. She is growing every day prettier. We took her to the Panoramas, etc. Pandemonium very curious and well worth seeing. Water Color exhibition still more so. Copley Fielding's landscapes perfection itself! We seated ourselves near the door pour nous reposer [to rest ourselves], and I happened to raise my eyes just at the very moment when Col. Cameron entered. It is really singular that we should thus perpetually haunt each other. I begged my dear Brother to come away, which he consented to do, after looking at a few more pictures, but from the moment he entered the room, I had no more enjoyment, as I was afraid to turn my head, lest I should meet his eye. And yet why should I fear to do so? I have *nothing* to reproach myself with, thank God, as far as he is concerned, in all that is connected with our acquaintance. My thoughts, words and actions were dictated by the purest sincerity and candour. *Peut-il en dire autant?*[15]

· · · · ·

27th May   At ten o'clock Col. Cruise and Edward Wilmot joined our party and we walked to Hyde Park, where a most interesting Review took place in honor of the Dukes of Orleans and Chartres. The ground was covered with spectators, and *comme de raison* [of course], amidst 25,000 people I had the narrowest escape of coming in contact with Colonel Cameron. I am doomed to meet him wherever I go but I feel so independent and happy when I am leaning on my dear Brother's arm.

. . . . .

20th June Walked with Mrs. Audley, who, with her usual kindness, insisted upon paying for all my shopping. I was not well, and during the three nights I spent with her in Bath I scarcely closed my eyes. I could have fancied myself four years younger and many degrees lighter hearted, when seated at dinner with the very same group of sexagenarians, Old Maids and widows, and the same solitary half-witted Beau, Capt. S., who constituted our daily Society in the winter of 1823–4.

What a little fool I was! With all my *fancied* cleverness and knowledge of the world, what a novice I was, how unprepared for that most insidious mode of warfare upon a silly girl's heart, that of showing every species of the kindest interest in all I said and did, and yet not saying a word which could commit himself. And I thinking that very mode of acting was the very ne plus ultra of honorable and manly conduct. Why did I like him? Because he never paid me a commonplace compliment, never made me feel uncomfortable by paying those marked attentions which attract general notice, whilst he never lost any opportunity of endeavouring to convince me that I was uppermost in all his thoughts. But it is all over, and I forgive him. I only pray that I may never again be tempted to rely upon my own weak, erring judgment.

. . . . .

6th September[16] Went to Church at Carigaline, after which I mounted the Poney and trotted off towards home, my Squire walking by my side with a basket of vegetables on his arm. A storm came on and I was obliged to take refuge in a Cabin, where I left my hat and wig, and borrowed a peasant's cloak. Thus attired, I proceeded on my journey, and could not help laughing at the contrast between my rustic appearance *now* and my *self-satisfied* feeling when, leaning on Tom's arm, I displayed my new dress in the Queen of Portugal's Drawing-room. Little did I ween that I was within a few minutes of being overtaken and recognised by our good-humoured friend Mr. Burgess, or as we used to call him *M. Moustache,* who made his appearance at the Cottage door just as we had finished dinner, having only this morn. heard that we were in the neighbourhood of Cork, where he has just joined his Regiment (53rd).

Returned to the Cottage with my father, Major Eden and *M. Moustache,* qui parait s'amuser beaucoup dans notre Hermitage,[17] which must indeed be a contrast to his Mess-room; his voice is very sweet, and we make furieusement de la musique.[18]

16th September   My Father busy with his garden, and I was left to amuse Major Eden, who is without exception one of the least difficult persons to amuse that I ever met with. We took a long and pleasant walk together to Ringabella, then rowed up the river to Gortegrinnana. The family not at home. Returned by the rocks. Had a nice chat about Tom and old times.

22nd September   My Father, Major Eden, Anty and myself left the Cottage at one for my Uncle's, and we went to a dance.

The General and Lady Binham very kind to me. I introduced Major Eden to the former. Danced every quadrille, and *fancied* that I was still young because every-one was kind and good-natured to me.

Parted with my old friend, Major Eden, whom I liked very much.

23rd September   Major McCrohan, my Father's old Brigade Major at Oporto came to dine with us—the sound of his voice and his peculiar brogue, brought back all the days of my childhood and I could have fancied myself once more the Governor's Daughter—the merry-hearted little being I once was, if the noise of the steamboat passing under the window had not reminded me that I was in my Uncle's House and a peep in the glass that I am no longer quella che un tempo fui,[19] although I still hope that I am not less dear to a few partial friends than I was in those my bright days of youth and hope.

28th September   A most tragical accident occurred this morng. which has, thank God, terminated much better than we at first expected. Mr. Burgess had just taken leave of us at the Cottage and mounted his horse to return to the Barracks when the animal took fright at the sea, and galloped off full speed along the Cliffs—the saddle turning at the same moment, our poor friend was thrown upon the bank but not until he had been dragged some distance. . . . When he saw me he tried to persuade me that he was not hurt, and made very light of the injury which his knee had sustained; but he was in great pain, and my Father wrote to his Colonel to inform him of the circumstance.

29th September With some difficulty we prevailed on him to lie quietly on the sopha, and he is now so much better that he will be able to move to-morrow.

30th September Mr. Burgess very sentimental this morning *mais je fais semblant de ne pas m'en apercevoir. Au reste je ne peux pas faire toujours l'oreille sourde car je prévois que cet état des affairs ne durera pas toujours, at qu'il a bien de la peine à garder son secret.*[20] He wished to-day for another accident to detain him here, but he was not punished by the fulfilment of this wicked wish. I walked to Coolmore. Dined and slept there.

3rd October Just as we were sitting down to dinner, the *Etourdi*[21] arrived, looking as happy as if we had not met for 3 months instead of 3 days. He really is a most good-natured, warm-hearted fellow— but such a head! so scatter-brained!

4th October After a family council had been held upon the subject, it was settled that as the Hodders had laughed at my *prudery* in not allowing Mr. Burgess to accompany me to Church last Sunday, he might have the felicity of escorting me on this occasion. Accordingly off we started, and the *Etourdi* behaved most discreetly. As we were coming home, the conversation which I was exerting myself most ingeniously to turn upon the most indifferent subjects suddenly assumed a sentimental aspect, but I again averted the catastrophe, as I cannot see the use of coming to an explanation, when we are each going in different directions and Heaven knows when or where we shall meet again.

5th October The *Etourdi* ought to have returned to his regiment to-day, but as usual he very coolly sent an excuse, and I was doomed to spend another nonsensical morning varied by the arrival of Lady T. and her three gawky daughters. As usual, she was scarcely seated before she announced her determination of not allowing her girls to marry until after her death. *Tell that to the Marines.* Poor Woman, it is evident that her whole heart is set upon their disobedience to this precept. Walked with Mr. Burgess to Collins' farm. It is most amusing to observe all the manœuvres which he employs to find out my sentiments upon different subjects connected with his prospects in life without coming directly to the point.

I cannot accuse myself of acting with coquetterie towards him, but one *lesson* in my life has been enough to teach me how to carry on that kind of warfare without losing one iota of my self-possession, and I was not a little amused to-day when, after I had baffled his circumlocutions by my straightforward answers, he suddenly exclaimed, half laughing, half angrily, "Och, there is no getting anything out of you. You are so close—so guarded." "Ah," thought I, "*c'est du nouveau.*" [22]

7th October   Spent the day in packing up.

· · · · · ·

16th October   We spent a sociable, chatty evening over the fire. Mr. Burgess was very anxious to keep up an occasional intercourse with my Father by letter, but I did not encourage it. When the parting moment arrived he was really affected, and I felt *almost* sorry myself. We both stood near the door, when he grasped my hand, and giving it one long and *emphatic* shake, he ran out of the house and mounted his horse without saying a word. C'est dommage qu'il ne soit pas plus sage, plus âgé, plus riche, plus spirituel, mais il faut convenir qu'en affaires d'amour, je joue de malheur. No sensible person except Colonel Fagan ever took a fancy to me! C'est pourtant bien drole car je les prefère aux gens qui n'ont pas d'esprit, et qui se laisseraient mener par le nez. [23] We embarked for England at seven o'clock this morning on board the Superb. . . .

· · · · · ·

11th April 1831   Stephen Fitzgerald came to escort me to Devonshire Terrace where I spent a happy morning with the dear girls. As we were walking through High Street, Marylebone! of all streets in the world, *quelle horreur!* [horrors!] who should I see advancing from the other end but Colonel Cameron! There was no possibility of avoiding the disagreeable *rencontre* therefore I mustered up all my dignity (and on this occasion it was no difficult task) and passed him with averted head and unmoved countenance. I told my dearest Father how brave I felt.

28th July   In the evening, Sir Henry came to beg me to go and stay at Sutton Court with his mother and sister but I did not go.

30th July   He came again this morning. It did not seem to be seemly to receive him now I am alone, so I told him I had letters to write. He is an original—full of talent but too original. In the evening he wrote me a note, with the last number of the Foreign Quarterly. As an acquaintance he pleases me very well because his character is so refined and cultivated, but as a husband if he should be thinking of me, it would be a different matter. . . .

.   .   .   .   .

13th August   Mr. Bramston called & left a card for me.

14th August   I was sorry to miss this opportunity of seeing him as I had not forgotten his kindness on board the Steam packet in 1828. How singular that we should meet again. He is staying on a visit to his Sister in this neighbourhood [in Ireland]. . . .

.   .   .   .   .

27th September   When Lady Cork[24] and I were alone in the evening she told me something which if true is very flattering to me. Encore Mr. Bramston and the Steam Packet!

14th October   Wet morn. I thought it very uncertain that Mr. Bramston would come; however he did come—just as I had risen from my prayers and prayed that God would direct me, I saw him riding up to the house. Lady Cork's conversation had made me feel quite *conscious* and foolish, altho' indeed I can hardly believe what she told me; it is too flattering, even to my vanity. I felt my cheeks burning with awkwardness when I had to make my appearance in the Drawing Room.

Lord Mount Sandford was not up—it was reported that he had over-slept himself—but I have always suspected and I believe with truth that it was a *fox's sleep*—that he wished to give us an opportunity of chatting comfortably and quietly in the Drawing Room before breakfast.

Yet there was something so ridiculous in the circumstance attending our first and last meeting in 1828, the grunting of 700 pigs and the smell of steam and the horrors of seasickness were so blended with my recollections of his pleasant conversation that I could hardly help laughing. I found him as I expected very pleasing and gentlemanlike. We shall perhaps meet again.

15th October   Wte. to Fanny Fitzgerald declining her very kind invitation and to dearest Tom giving him an account of my unexpected rencontre with the "Spectre Bridegroom" who for the last three years has haunted me thro' the speculations of our mutual friends. He is much too amiable for such a faultfull wife as I should make.

16th October   He returns next month for his sister's marriage but we shall be gone. However of this I feel assured that if it is *His Will* that we should be better acquainted

> "He who brings forth the unexpected hour
> When hearts that never met before
> Shall meet, unite and part no more"

will give us the opportunity of knowing each other's character.

29th October   Wte. to Lord Cork and Tom. Lord Mount Sandford called on the Davidsons where he heard that Mr. Bramston will come to Harptree next week. Singular that after all the fluctuations in our plans, in which I have remained perfectly passive, *on principle,* we are likely to meet again after all.

9th November   Whilst I was talking today with the Palairets, how was I startled when the groom came running with a message from Lord M[ount] S[andford] to say that the young gentleman from Mrs. Davidson's was at Stowey. I trembled from head to foot and of course did not escape a little quizzing. Why did Lady Cork tell me anything about it! it makes me feel so conscious. Now it would be mock humility to doubt that he is trying to like me. But oh, how little does he know of my character! he gave me the Christian Year.[25] He is most kind. Lord Mount Sandford is delighted with him.

10th November   Letter from my precious brother announcing the joyful news of his coming to Bath to-morrow. Then I shall have the long wished for opportunity of making them known to each other. Thought over everything. Felt calm and quietly happy and yet very nervous.

This is an awful day. May God direct us both for our happiness. He dines and sleeps here.

11th November   He arrived about 2 o'clock. Lord Mount Sandford was out. I had shut myself up in my own room *dreading* yet wishing to see him again. I felt so convinced that a few days would decide my fate. We had a long conversation about his sisters—his sentiments on Religious subjects appear to me those of a most *sincere* and *unprejudiced* Christian. He would win by gentleness not by controversy and *bitterness*. Mr. C. Palairet dined with us. We spent the evening at the Vicarage. The little curé looked reproachfully at me but I had nothing to reproach myself with, as far as he is concerned.

Mr. Bramston read prayers in the eveg. We could neither of us *say much* when we separated that night, his heart was full and so was mine.

. . . . .

14th November   We met this morning at my dear Father's. A few words passed between us but those few said everything. He is all that my heart could desire in the guide, the friend, the protector of my future life. I feel such *repose,* such confidence in his affection, *quite different* from anything I ever felt before for anyone. . . .

15th November   Nothing can exceed the delight of my kind marriage-loving Hostess, at finding that I am at length going to be married. She actually cried with joy. *He* won her heart by his gentle manner and his "lovely eyes." I wish I had one good feature in my phiz to offer him in return, but I have only my teeth, and they will soon be gone, besides his are quite as white! He dined with us and my dearest Father was in high spirits. Lord Mount Sandford says he cannot say half he feels upon the subject.

At six o'clock he left us for London, after shaking hands most cordially with my beloved brother, who spent the evening with us.

I am too happy even now that he is gone.

. . . . .

1st December   Whilst I was at Cheltenham Colonel Cameron was married at Bath to [word illegible] to the disgust of his family. . . .

2nd December   I am not yet quite at home with him, but every hour makes me feel his value more and more. The dinner was less stiff than yesterday and in the evening we were able to talk. Lord and Lady C. are most kind.

3rd December   Wte. to thank Mrs. Bramston [his stepmother] and his sister for their kind notes. This day for the first time I heard him preach. I must not now say all I feel and think about him because my journal like my heart will ever be open to his inspection. The text was my own favourite verses of the 116th Psalm. Lady Cork asked him to read another sermon in the evening. They like him so much.

·   ·   ·   ·   ·

8th December   Tom and the *bien aimé* [beloved] have settled it between them that our marriage shall take place with God's blessing on Thursday, the 5th of January. I try to fancy it a great way off. He is most kind and never reminds me of it when he can help it. May God be with us both in that awful hour! Wrote to his [step] Mother whom I expect to love very much.

·   ·   ·   ·   ·

16th December   Drove to Mells, asked Elizabeth Horner to be one of my bridesmaids. I often feel inclined to ask myself "Is it really you, Clara, who are going to be married?" It seems to me as if it were some other person. . . .

Notes

୶

*These selections are taken from *The Journal of Clarissa Trant: 1800–1832*, ed. C. G. Luard (London: John Lane, 1925).

1 *J'ai dansé avec:* I danced with; *preux chevalier:* a gallant knight. Trant is in Bath at this time.

2 I said my farewells to Captain Coffin. He reproached me with having always treated him very coldly and told me laughingly that I have the look of a shy rabbit as soon as he comes near to speak to me. I didn't dare tell him that my timidity increases with the esteem in which I'm held—but that was nevertheless the truth—besides, presumably we'll never see each other again.

3 The Trants are now in Ireland, staying with "Anty"—Miss Lawler—a close family friend. Mr. Lloyd is an acquaintance from Blois.

4 That is, Mr. Lloyd is twenty-five and wealthy while she is poor, twenty-three, and neither ugly nor beautiful.

5 In 1816–17; she was sixteen at the time.

6 The gentleman [unidentified, but probably Col. Cameron] has come but did not want to come up because there were people here: What does it all mean? I don't know what to think about it, and my poor head is much perturbed.

7 Trant's editor has chosen to translate the entry for this date, most of which Trant wrote originally in German.

8 That's it for you, poor Clara—for life.

9 That is, her father.

10 D. probably means Denmark. Count Christopher de Maraes Sarmento became Portuguese minister at the Court of St. James in 1832.

11 The Trants are returning to England, from a visit in Ireland.

12 Caroline Boyle, one of Trant's best friends. She never married.

13 He to whom she has sacrificed her first affections, for whom she has refused so many good offers of matrimony, is going to marry one of her ac-

quaintances, Lady Anne B.; and this evening she will have to meet the engaged couple at Devonshire House. Poor little thing! I pity her from my heart, but he is unworthy of her.

14   They're much alike in point of conduct, these men!

15   Can he say as much?

16   Trant has returned to Ireland at this time.

17   He [Mr. Burgess] seems to enjoy himself greatly in our hermitage.

18   We make music together with a vengeance.

19   That which I once was.

20   But I pretend not to notice. However, I can't always turn a deaf ear because I foresee that this state of affairs will not last forever and [hope] that he takes great pains to keep his secret.

21   Madcap: Mr. Burgess.

22   This is something new.

23   It's a pity that he's not older, wiser, richer, more clever, but it seems inevitable that in matters of the heart I have bad luck. . . . Nonetheless it's quite funny because I prefer them to men who have no spirit and let themselves be led by the nose.

24   Lord and Lady Cork were among Trant's most intimate friends in Ireland; her godfather, Lord Mount Sandford, lived nearby them.

25   John Keble's book, *The Christian Year,* was published in 1828.

Frances Stevenson

(1888–1972)

FRANCES LOUISE STEVENSON (afterwards Countess Lloyd-
George), the daughter of John Stevenson and his wife, Louise Arman-
ino, won scholarships to Clapham High School, then to London
University (Royal Holloway College), where she took a degree in
classics. She also became a suffragist, while secretly sympathising with
the more militant suffragettes. In the determining event of her life,
after teaching in a boarding school for girls at Wimbledon, she was
hired in 1911 to coach Megan, the nine-year-old daughter of David
Lloyd George, during the summer holidays. By the following Christmas, at his invitation she had become a secretary at the Treasury.
She had also become Lloyd George's mistress, beginning a relationship
that endured until his death in 1945, despite the friction with her
family that at first ensued. Only in 1943, when Lloyd George was
eighty years old and became a widower, could they marry, for although he was estranged from his wife throughout his liaison with
Stevenson, he would not imperil his political party by seeking a divorce. An official secretary on the government payroll from 1913
to 1922, Stevenson moved with Lloyd George to the Ministry of Munitions and the War Office; and when he became prime minister, she
and J. T. Davies became his joint principal private secretaries—the
first time a woman had held such a prestigious post. Always actively
involved in Lloyd George's career, Stevenson helped compose his
speeches, negotiated with important people on his behalf, and accompanied him on foreign missions like the peace conference at Paris in
1919. From 1914 to 1944, she also kept a diary so focused on him that
it could later be published as *Lloyd George: A Diary by Frances Stevenson.*★ Though her own life had to remain peripheral to his, she evinces
no real sense of deprivation in her diary, as these 1914–22 selections
show. Rather, he is central to her existence and almost above reproach.

From Frances Stevenson's Diary

20th November 1914   C. has just gone to W. Heath[1] to spend a 'virtuous weekend'. However we managed to have an evening there together this week on Wednesday—quite unexpected, but enjoyed to the very fullest. C. was rather conscience-stricken on the way down, as he was dying to get away from the House, & could not give his mind to Budget discussions. He says he accepted any proposal which was quickly dealt with, & persuaded them to leave Beer till today, which he assured them would serve just as well. He is very tired this evening after a very hard day.

The Budget speech was a great success, though I could not go to hear it owing to a Red Cross Exam. Bonar Law on Monday night sent a note to the P.M. begging him not to allow the Budget to be brought in, as it would provoke bitter and dangerous opposition. However, C. flatters himself that by a very artful & ingenious speech he has brought round the House—or most of it—to his way of think-ing, & thinks he will be able to see the thing through.

Mamma went to the Budget Speech instead of me, & thoroughly appreciated it. C. also got her a ticket for Lord Roberts' Funeral. She needs to have her mind occupied just now, as she is worrying about Paul.[2] I think she is getting more reconciled to the relations be-tween C. & me, as she recognises it is an honest love which will last, & not just a passing passion. She and C. get on very well together.

I dined with Dorothy Brown[3] on Tuesday. She wished to know whether my feelings towards her brother were any different as he is still very unhappy. I told her that I had not changed my mind. I cannot explain how things really are, but feel that I am doing right in refus-ing to see him, since he may forget & marry someone else. I am sorry he is unhappy.

C. again referred to the love-letters he sent me two years ago, when he was wooing me: he says he wishes we could read them over to-gether now. But they are destroyed. They were indeed very beautiful, but the things he says to me now are more beautiful still. Sometimes I am so happy that I tremble for fear it will not last. Our love will always last, but there is the dread that he might be taken from me. He is never tired of talking of that summer when he used to come to Allenswood, & we both felt there was something between us, though it was not yet expressed—and of the following autumn, when we used to meet once a week, and I hovered between doubt and longing, dread and desire: and of the time in the House of Commons, when I left him because I would not agree to his proposals, but returned soon after to say that I could not face life without him, & would do what he wished. I have never regretted the decision. It has brought me two years of happiness, & if Fate wills will bring me many more.

30th November The work is a little more slack today, though C. has been busy this afternoon with the Separation Allowances and Pensions Committee. I am to keep his papers for this Committee, which I am glad to do as I shall know what is going on. A well-known lady of the Mrs. Humphrey Ward type, sent him suggestions for dealing with the case of the 'unmarried wives', to avoid treating them on the same plane as the legal wife. She said (or words to that effect) that it would be an incentive to immorality. C. pushed the papers away with an exclamation of disgust. "Who is she,' he exclaimed, 'to talk of immorality! Why, her husband lived on immorality. He was President of the Divorce Court.'

C. is in very good spirits after a week-end rest. Yesterday I went down to W. H. & spent the afternoon with him, & we had a jolly good time. We have both been reading Wells' last book The Wife of Sir Isaac Harman and C. thinks it is his most brilliant work. Wells has modified his views considerably, though, since he wrote Anne Veronica!

C. made a clinking speech on Friday. He had prepared the first part of it ages ago—somewhere in August—& we thought it would never really come off, as it was continually postponed. It was a most difficult subject to handle, much more to make interesting, but it has been highly praised. The L.C.J.[4] was watching him intently from the Gallery. He is extraordinarily fond of C.—one would almost say he is jealous—not of C., but of C.'s other friends. C. & I were counting up yesterday—as far as we could remember he has made 22 big speeches since I have been working for him here. We began with the Marconi speeches in 1913. I remember him sending for me when I was in Scotland, when I had only been there a few days, urging me to come back, for a great trouble had come upon him & was gripping him, so that he could not sleep at night, and he wanted me to be there with him. I had no idea what the trouble was, nor would he tell me until I came back, & even then I could not grasp the extent of it, did not realise the menace of the Marconi campaign. I do not think I fully understood all it meant until the thing was over. I only know that all that spring I did my best to drive the shadow away from him & make him as happy as I could. He says he will never forgive Massingham[5] for deserting him at that time. He (C.) is one who can never forgive an act of treachery or an act of deceit, however much he may want to. . . .

We really thought that, after the hundreds of letters containing suggestions for new taxes that we have received during the last few weeks, the sources of new taxation had been exhausted. But this evening we received still another—a man who thinks that the women of the country are not paying enough towards the War, suggests that there should be a tax on corsets!

· · · · ·

17th January 1915   I fear my diary has got very behindhand. The last three weeks have been so busy and happy that I have not had the opportunity for writing things down. C. returned from Wales on Dec. 29th and from then till now I have been with him at W.H., coming up every day to town, & going back in the evening. It has been like an idyll, but alas! came to an end yesterday, when the family returned from Criccieth, & I returned home. The longer we are together, the more our love and affection seems to increase, so that it is all the more difficult to part. But we have resolved not to be miserable at parting, for 'my true love hath my heart, & I have his' and happy memories will buoy us up till 'the next time'. . . .

· · · · ·

21st January   C. is not very well today. He has been working very hard, but personally I think he is suffering from too much 'family'. He was very upset on Monday because not one of them had remembered that it was his birthday on Sunday. They did not think of it

until Sir George Riddell came in at 7.30 in the evening & wished him
many happy returns, & then it suddenly occurred to them. He always
remembers their birthdays, however busy he is, and goes to a lot of
trouble to get them something which will please them—he takes
a delight in doing it. 'They take me for granted', he said to me rather
bitterly. 'They treated me as someone who must be just tolerated
because I provide money for everything they want. But they don't
seem to remember that it is through me that they have their education
and position and that if it were not for me they would get very little
notice taken of them.'

C.'s plan for an attack in the East of Europe is progressing favoura-
bly. K. is keen on it, and so is the Prime Minister, but Winston[6] is
opposed to it for reasons afore-mentioned. People are beginning to
get rather dissatisfied with Winston. . . .

It is just two years since C. & I were 'married', and our love seems
to increase rather than diminish. He says I have taken the place somewhat of Mair,[7] 'my little girl whom I lost' as he always calls her. He
says I remind him of her & make up a little for her loss. I have always
wanted to make this loss seem a little lighter to him, and he seems
now to be able to speak of her with less pain than he used to. . . .

· · · · ·

11th March   The last fortnight has been too dreary and unhappy to
write of. I am down here [at Walton Heath] to recover from the effects
of it. My people have been trying to separate us—trying to make
me promise that I will give up his love, the most precious thing of
my life. They do not understand—they will never understand—they
do not see that our love is pure and lasting—they think I am his
plaything, & that he will fling me aside when he has finished with
me—or else they think that there will be a scandal and that we shall all
be disgraced. I know they are fond of me, and think it is for my good
that they are doing this, but I have always held different ideas from
theirs, & it was bound to come to this, or something akin to this,
sooner or later. I am willing to pay dearly for my happiness, but I will
not give it up. I fear that in the end I shall have to leave home, for
they will never cease to urge their views upon me, & it will be almost
intolerable. Besides which, they will never speak of C. except in

unfriendly & contemptuous tones & that I will not endure. I cannot
give up the hold upon life, & the broader outlook, which I have gained
since C. & I came together. I can't help *hating* myself for making
Mamma so miserable. The thought haunts me all day long, and I
would do anything to prevent it. But what *can* I do? Some years ago,
Harold Spender said to C. 'You are the most lonely man I know.' I
think I have changed all that now, & I cannot think that I have done
wrong. I am not vicious or evil, and my only fault, in this matter[,]
and his, is love. 'Love justifies many audacities.' I think the justification for these audacities is the length of love's duration & I know
C. and I belong to each other for ever. I should be so happy were it
not for the fact that I am causing unhappiness to two people whom I
love and who have been so good & loving to me.[8]

In addition to distress of mind, I have been ill, which increased my
misery. Finally C. insisted that I should come down here & have
absolute rest for a few days, & be free from worrying surroundings. I
agreed to all this the more willingly as I could see that C. was making
himself ill through worrying about me—several times I thought he
was on the point of breaking down; but he has been better since I
have been down here & have shown signs of recovering.

I do not think I can ever repay him for his goodness to me the last
fortnight or three weeks. He has been husband, lover & mother to
me. I never knew a man could be so womanly & tender. He has
watched and waited on me devotedly, until I cursed myself for being
ill & causing him all this worry. There was no little thing that he
did not think of for my comfort, no tenderness that he did not lavish
on me. I have indeed known the full extent of his love. If those who
idolise him as a public man could know the full greatness of his heart,
how much more their idol would he be! And through it all he has
been immersed in great decisions appertaining to this great crisis, until
I have trembled for his health, & loathed myself for causing him
trouble at this time.

In the midst of all this he found time to prepare and deliver a speech
at Bangor, which many think is the greatest speech of his life. He
says that the anxiety and trouble helped him to make a great speech,
for when his mind is disturbed his whole nature is upheaved, and

it stimulates him to greater power of expression. He is very pleased
that the Nation should have praised it, saying that as an orator he
is unequalled. He tells me that from his youth it has always been his
ambition to become a great orator rather than a statesman or politician. And it does now seem as though his ambition has been fulfilled.
He deserves that it should be, if ever any man did. I do not think
that there is any man in England who is working more unselfishly for
our victory in this war, than he is. He does not cease from one week
to the next to devise some means for advancing our interests. . . .

Paul is under orders to go to France. They were to have left Southampton on Tuesday, but there appears to be some difficulty in getting
the troops off, & they have not yet gone, but may leave at any moment. Mamma and Dada are naturally upset about it, & it seems very
hard for them that their troubles should come all at once. I do not
want to add unduly to their trouble, so must make up my mind to a
little self-sacrifice for some time to come so as not to upset them
too much. Nevertheless I will never, never, give C. up. 'Leave all for
love!'

C. tells me that Italy is coming in in April.[9] That is good news.
Things will begin to move then.

25th March   Paul went to France last Sunday week. I went home for
the weekend, and was glad I did so, as Mamma was very upset about
it. She is quite sure he will never come back. She is very bitter as to
the disappointment that one's children bring. She says, 'Everything is
turning out so differently from what we had expected. Dad & I have
had 27 years of happiness, and now we have got to pay for it.' Poor
Mother! She cannot realise, & I fear she never will, that parents cannot
control their children's lives forever—that children exist for their
own and the next generation, and not for that of their parents, which
is past. However, it is hopeless to argue with her; but I fear she will
never be happy unless she takes a wider view. What is more, if she is
not careful, she will lose the sympathy and respect of her
children. . . .

. . . . .

31st January 1916   . . . D. & I manage to spend a good deal of time
together now that the flat is in existence.[10] He comes along there

to dinner from the House of Commons, and walks home across the Park. I gave him a birthday dinner on his birthday, & we managed by dint of manoeuvring to spend the following weekend together. On the Sunday we motored down to Eastbourne, & I stayed on the pier while D. went to see Lord Murray, who was staying down there recovering from various heart attacks.

Last Thursday D. spent the evening with me, as he was off to France the following day. I was very depressed, as D. had had a communication from some psychic individual telling him to beware the 28th & 29th of January, & I can never quite bring myself to disbelieve in these psychic people. D. too loathed going away, though I think he always itches for an exciting time when there is one coming. He says though that he could face disgrace with me now, and still be quite happy. 'I can understand Parnell[11] now for the first time', he said to me on Thursday night. Although it would be bitter grief for me were I to be the cause of his disgrace, yet it is comforting to know that he feels like that. 'I shall love you the whole time I am away, Pussy', were his parting words to me. 'And I shall long to get back again to you.' Oh, how I long to see him back again safely. I spoke to Mr. Davies at G.H.Q. (France) on the telephone this morning, & he said they would be in London tonight at 11.0. I am to go straight to Walton Heath & wait for D. there

· · · · ·

8th February 1916 D. had Gwynne, the Editor of The Morning Post to lunch. 'Since all the Liberal papers are attacking me', he said, 'I must keep someone on my side.' Gwynne told him: 'There are only two men in the country whom I believe in at the present time—yourself and Carson.'[12] D. referred to Carson's disappearance for the time on the grounds of ill-health. 'Ah', said D., 'he has married a young wife and it is telling upon him.'

D. dined with me and told me of the above conversation. He said he has been thinking, all the way to Chester Square, of how he wished he could marry me. But we both agreed that we must put that thought out of our minds, for it only leads to bitterness and discontent, and sometimes to injustice and folly. However, he has sworn to marry me if he ever finds himself in a position to do so, & I am content with

that. Not that I wished him to promise it, for I am happy as we are—
we have our little home now, where we can spend many evenings
together in solitude—and how sweet the evenings are! The only thing
we lack is children, but I often think that if I were married & had
children, then I should not be able to keep in touch with D.'s work to
the extent that I do now, & perhaps should be less happy. At present
all our interests lie together; he does nothing but what I know of
it; I almost know his very thoughts. I don't suppose I should see nearly
as much of him if I were married to him. . . .

• • • • •

26th July . . . It is a long time since I kept a record. I lost heart after
being ill: was very depressed and rundown for a long time, & D. &
I had no courage to face the future—the result of my illness—& D.
sent me down to Walton Heath to recuperate. I was feeling very bitter
& sore with things in general, when one night I had a dream. I
dreamed that D. had been killed, & the horror that that filled me with
drove out every other feeling. I knew then that I loved him better
than anything in the world, & that if he were dead nothing else would
matter. It is extraordinary what a difference this dream made to my
mental attitude. That is all past, however, & we are now just as we
always were, & he says if I had not come to the War Office he would
not have come. But here we are, and D. seems to be getting on very
well with everyone. It was rather depressing at first, until we got
into things—we felt just like children going to a new school, & D.
knew he would have great difficulties to cope with. But everyone here
seems very pleasant and anxious to help, & D. is tackling things with
great vigour. They seem to rely on him to put everything right, in
spite of the fact that some of his colleagues in the Cabinet do their best
to undermine his influence secretly. . . .

I am sharing some of the reflected glory. People have just woken up
to the fact that Ll. G. has a lady Secretary, or rather, that the Sec. of
State for War has a lady Secretary. I have people calling to interview
me, & I have my photograph in the papers! . . .

• • • • •

11th November Col. Stern drove D. & me & Grace Stonedale down
to college[13] for the afternoon. I was very jolly, & D. was very merry. It

quite took him out of himself and away from all his troubles and probably did him good, as the war is beginning to prey upon his mind. We were very busy all the morning with a statement which he is preparing on the Situation for the Paris Conference, & which is a very gloomy & threatening document, & an indictment of the whole policy of the war. Grace remained at college, and Col. Stern drove D. and me back to Walton Heath, where we finished the Document, which was to be submitted to the Prime Minister before being trans-lated into French. Little Miss Davies—typist—was also there, & D. & I tried to make her feel at home, as Mrs. Ll.G. had been rude to her in the morning, & she had been very upset by it. It is extraordinary how everyone dislikes Mrs. Ll.G. Mr. J. T. Davies was talking to me about her this morning: he says that sometimes when he is feeling particularly unfriendly to her, he tries to find some redeeming feature about her which will compensate for all her unlovely qualities. But it is impossible to find one. I have often felt the same too. She is simply a lump of flesh, possessing, like the jellyfish, the power of irritating. But I am being very nasty. I try as much as possible to re-frain from commenting upon her, as she has good reason to dislike me. But she has no pride. D. has told her time & again that he does not want her in London, that he would much prefer her to live at Criccieth—when she has been making a fuss about me. I am sure I would not remain with a man who showed so plainly that my pres-ence was not wanted.

Little Miss Davies was telling me how everyone worships D. in Wales. She says that she is quite sure they would not mind if they were told to worship him in the Chapels, instead of the Almighty!

• • • • •

11th May 1919   Spent a very happy day wandering about the woods, though was annoyed by Mrs. ——, who expected D. to pay a lot of attention to her, & I was cross in consequence. She is a most self-satisfied person, talks a lot & loves the sound of her own voice. Of course all women are fascinated by D. & he in turn is nice to most of them, & once having started they expect him to go on. The silly ones get their heads turned immediately & there is no doing anything with them. It is most amusing to watch. But I got rather angry with Mrs. —— having had rather too much of that sort of thing lately. However D. & I made it up in the evening. . . .

· · · · ·

23rd May   D. & I had a long talk. I know Stern would marry me if I gave him the slightest encouragement & if he thought I would leave D. It is a great temptation in a way for although I don't love him we are good friends & I know he would be very kind to me. It would mean a title & wealth, whereas now I may find myself old & friendless and having to earn my own living, if anything should happen to D. People will not be so anxious to marry me in 10 years' time. On the other hand I know I should not be happy now away from D. & no-one else in the world could give me the intense & wonderful love that he showers on me. He was very sweet about it, & says he wants to do what is best for me. But I can see that he would be unhappy if I left him, so I promised him I would not.

25th May   D. told me this morning that he had definitely made up his mind that he could not let me leave him. So that is final, & I am very glad. I need not worry about it any more. It would be very foolish to spoil for material prospects the most wonderful love which ever happened. . . .

· · · · ·

29th June   We said goodbye to Paris, & returned home. We have had a wonderful time there, & we left with many regrets. D. hates returning home. He has been well looked after in Paris—has had every comfort—the best food—the best attendance. He has been able to entertain at will. When at Downing St., or Walton Heath it is another matter. There is never enough to go round & what there is, is very inferior. I have never seen anyone with such a capacity for making a place uncomfortable as Mrs. Lloyd George. Her meanness forces the household to economise in coal & food, & everything that makes for comfort. The servants would be a disgrace to any house, & the P.M. is rightly ashamed of them. But it is no use his protesting—he says he gave that up long ago, because it had no effect & only caused unpleasantness. . . .

. . . . .

26th November   We had a perfectly wonderful day yesterday. Went
down to Cobham Tuesday evening, & played golf at Burhill yesterday
morning. It is a beautiful course & it was a lovely sunny morning.
The pro & I beat D. & Ernie[14] hollow, so I am rather pleased with
myself. I want to be really good at golf as D. has been so sweet about
my learning & takes such a patient interest in my progress. Came
up in the evening in time for dinner. Dined at the Cazalets—Mrs. C.
& Thelma are both sweet—kind and sincere. But it is extraordinary
how not one of these women wants Nancy Astor to get in. They
all dislike her.

29th November   Nancy Astor elected the first woman M.P. I am beginning to understand why she has so few friends. I used to think
it was jealousy, but I know now that it was true when they told me she
was treacherous & not to be trusted. In spite of her repeated protesta-
tions of friendship & goodwill to me, I find that she takes every
opportunity of saying spiteful things about D. & myself. It is almost
incredible, but it is true. Anyhow, she will get her reward in the House
of Commons! I do not think any *wise* woman would choose to sit in
the House!

   D. & Mrs. Ll.G. on very bad terms. D. is giving a big weekend
party at Cobham, including the American Ambassador & Mrs. Davies, and Mrs. Ll.G., instead of helping is doing all she can to *hinder*
D.'s arrangements. She simply hates him to enjoy himself & will
not lift a finger to make the Cobham house comfortable.

   Sir James Guthrie has painted a wonderful likeness of D. He had
the last sitting this morning. Mrs. Ll.G. went up to look at it, & when
D. asked her what she thought of it she said—'I can't lay my finger
on anything bad in it!'

. . . . .

23rd December   D. has gone away today, & it *is* wretched without
him. I get such a terrible feeling of loneliness when he goes, & feel
almost frightened at his being so far away. However, as D. says, we
have not done badly this year. We had all that time at Paris together, &
then a month at Deauville, & as he says, we see each other every day

& almost every hour of the day. But I suppose that only makes it
all the more hard when he does go away.

He made an extraordinarily good speech in the House last night. I
behaved very badly. I was feeling very tired & had a splitting headache,
& D. had annoyed me over a trifling little thing, & I quite forgot to
say anything to him about his speech, or to compliment him on it. I
usually leave a little note on his table in the House in case I don't
see him at once, & so that he may get it directly. But this time he
didn't. And when he came back to Downing St. after 11.0 he came up
to me & said: 'You haven't said a word to me about my speech—not
a word. And you know how I count on your words to me after my
speeches.' I felt a perfect pig at once, & did my best to make up for it,
& it ended quite happily. But I hate myself for having behaved like
that.

24th December   Just off down to Wallington for a family party at
Xmas. Have been simply overwhelmed with presents, until I feel
quite ashamed of myself. Have had some most beautiful things, &
people have been so kind.

Notes

Lloyd George: A Diary by Frances Stevenson, ed. A. J. P. Taylor (London: Hutchinson, 1971). It is the source for all diary selections here.

1   Stevenson refers to Lloyd George as C. while he is chancellor of the exchequer and afterwards as D. (David). Walton Heath is Lloyd George's modest home, about fifteen miles from London. He had another home at Criccieth in North Wales, where Mrs. Lloyd George (Margaret Owen) spent much of her time.

2   Stevenson's brother, a soldier.

3   Sister to Stuart Kelson Brown, whose proposal Stevenson had rejected shortly before meeting Lloyd George and who would later marry a friend of hers.

4   Lord Chief Justice.

5   Henry W. Massingham, an editor opposing Lloyd George's conduct of the war.

6   K. probably refers to King George V; *Winston* is Winston Churchill.

7   Lloyd George's deceased daughter (1890–1907).

8   Stevenson added, after this, an undated memo to her from Lloyd George which says, as its first line, "Go *now* a little beyond the House of Lords," and as its second, "I am off to Walton."

9   Actually, Italy entered the war on 23 May 1915.

10   She left her parents' home at Wallington in 1915 for a flat in London.

11   Charles Stewart Parnell, leader of the Irish Home Rule Party, sacrificed his role and split his party by marrying Kitty O'Shea, whose husband had divorced her for her adultery with Parnell.

12   Edward Henry Carson, Irish Unionist leader and attorney general in 1915.

13   Royal Holloway College, at Englefield Green.

14   Ernie Evans, one of Lloyd George's other secretaries.

Loran Hurnscot

(d. 1970)

ALTHOUGH LORAN HURNSCOT (pseudonym for Gay Stuart Taylor) has left no childhood records, she has written in her diary of her unhappy marriage and love affair and her subsequent release from the limitations of nature through a religious conversion. In 1920 she married "Hubert Tindal" (Hu), whom she had known for less than three months and who suffered from arrested tuberculosis. Although both were agnostics and they shared some similar interests, theirs was an inauspicious marriage, for she disliked housework, and he had never yet earned any money. Indeed, after a week of marriage she returned to a flat shared with two girlfriends, "Pernelle" and "Bee," and he to his mother's home outside London. But when Tindal decided to start a small publising house near London despite his poverty, she gave up her newspaper job to join him in the venture. Sexually their marriage had been a failure from the start, its consummation deferred and disappointing, and after she rejoined him, they continued to sleep apart, rarely engaging in sexual relations. Retrospectively, she conjectured that Tindal had been an unacknowledged homosexual; she recognized early that he was a misogynist. Hurnscot met "Barny Blythe" (the writer A. E. Coppard) when her husband decided to publish Barny's first book of short stories and provocatively sent her to stay overnight at his cottage during his wife's absence, but only two years later did they become lovers. Barny took a cottage nearby, where they could meet, and Hubert, who would later become jealous and punitive, encouraged their affair, provided Hurnscot promised not to leave him. As these selections from 1923–25* show, the love affair proved also an ordeal. In the published diary for 1922–58, originally written up from a pocket diary soon after the events, the names of participants and places have been changed. Taylor's own pseudonym, Loran Hurnscot, is an anagram based on Sloth and Rancour—to her, her besetting sins.

From Loran Hurnscott's Diary

9th December 1923 Last week I stayed with Barny. Tonight he is in Paris. Tomorrow he will be in Italy. I feel terribly divided from him.

Last week Nicholas Aran stayed here. I fell asleep in my chair, and half woke to hear my cold husband talking of sex and women and pleasure in a cold brutal way that revolted me till I remembered that about all these things he knows less than nothing. I pretended to be asleep until there was a point where I could fairly wake up. But it was startling and horrible to me that this man and I had once imagined we loved. I don't wonder that no other woman has ever cared for him—my own sex has wiser instincts than I have. Nicholas said to me later that my "ignoramus of a husband" had better go to some studio parties and learn something.

18th December Hu has gone to Cornwall, to his mother. On Sunday Pernelle and I went for two days to the hut.[1] Barny had given me the key. It was strange to find everything as we had left it on that last morning—for I went to stay with him, the night before he went, and our last words seemed still to be hanging in the air. The familiar tables and chairs and disordered bookshelves almost drew tears from Barny's foolish girl.

19th December Tonight suddenly, in this dim-lit room, as I sat at the piano, I had the sharpest remembrance of him as I knew him first. It was in the old dreary winter days when we lived in the workshop, rose at five in the morning, and worked till we were too tired to work any more. Hu and I had been married for nearly ten months; I was a girl who looked a child—I used often to be ashamed of my childish appearance—and all my joy in life had turned to loathing. I was a very unhappy young creature. One afternoon I heard a knock at the door. I thought it was the baker, and went to open it. For one fantastic moment I stood on the step, looking down into the clear, light-brown eyes of this lovely person. Perhaps in that moment I felt we should be lovers one day. He was wearing a brown suit, and had that gypsy look of which Hu had told us. He had even said gloomily, "You're sure to fall in love with him."

That evening we worked late, collating the magazine we were

printing, and this serene, contented-seeming person worked with us, talking and laughing and singing to us, until midnight. He stayed for the weekend, and on the Sunday we went for a picnic up Lansey Hill, and over to Brandesley. And a change came over me that day; the settled misery of life with Hu broke up into a state of joy and expectation. Certainly I didn't think consciously of love between us. He was so gay and charming and uncapturable that I simply welcomed the good mood he brought, without any backwash of feeling. And tonight, remembering him as he was then, I thought that no woman could keep him her lover for long. His freedom is his charm, and it would die, in chains.

20th December I asked Pernelle what she lived by. She said, by being in love. Well, so do I, but it's a dangerous basis. Like saying you live in a train; perpetually going somewhere and never arriving.

21st December When I say there is no life for me without Barny, what do I mean? If we quarrelled for the last time, if he never came back from Italy, I suppose I'd go on living just the same. But the one thing that for me "makes sense" would have gone. There's been torment and sadness in our love, but there's been a fulfilment too, more than I ever dreamed of.

22nd December As happy as it's possible to be without him. He writes that I am too far away, and he is "savagely bored."

24th December Went to stay with Pernelle in her new flat. This morning an express letter from Hu's mother saying he has had a relapse and wants me to go to him at once. She enclosed a dictated note from him; it meant the end of the G.L.,[2] of everything. I left Waterloo at eleven, with a train journey of over six hours. In my carriage were three respectable bourgeois women, shrivelled with chastity, and a pimpled young man in bright tan boots. I shut my eyes against them and thought only of Barny. Hu? Wretched Hu, dogged by this horrible disease? Yes, I know. And I know too that all he wants is to have me enslaved to him—he's like a sort of parasite and I the weak unwilling host. It's never love, it's a vindictive desire to use and chain me, and perhaps infect me with T.B. He was *excited,* over that September scare.

At Barstock I picked up the threads of my sadder life, and thought only of Hu who is my burden instead of Barny who is my joy. I ran straight up to see him. He was sweet and wistful, and even seemed glad that I had come. The relapse is serious. We'll have to sack the men and sell the press. He wants me to stay here for some time. . . . [3]

7th January 1924   I am in a very bitter state. The end of every hope and plan is that I am tied to an invalid whom I do not love. I have tenderness for him, and pity, but there's no love, there's sometimes panic fear and sometimes hatred. Well, I conceal my bitterness. Short of finally breaking with Barny, which I cannot and will not do, for it is only he that makes this dreadful existence possible at all, I am drearily unwilling to do everything I can for this Hubert I once loved—or imagined I did.

On New Year's Day I went back to Shotton Green, for Hu had been much better during the three days before I left. I started in the dark. Light was beginning to glimmer on the eastern slopes of the black hills, and dawn slowly broke as the train puffed up to Okehampton. I could not believe I was going back to Barny, beloved Barny who had arrived late, in the dark, at the hut in the woods, and found no one there—for I had no means of letting him know I couldn't be there, as he was already on his way back to England. At last the long journey was done. I was at the back gate, wheeling my bicycle in. It was just getting dark, and I was watching intently for a glimmer of light. There was one in the kitchen. He *must* be there. I tiptoed round to the front of the house. Beside the garden door I stood for a moment, looking in at my house. He was sitting in an easy chair, with a candle beside him on the table, and a bare wooden tray with a teapot and a mug. I ran in, and was clasped in his arms.

It was heaven. All the horrors fell away. One step, and I was in a different world. With my darling once more, even the concrete surroundings, the familiar chairs and tables and lamps and curtains, seemed touched with light and infinitely blessed. We had tea together beside the fire, talking and caressing. We were too loving then for the fiercer raptures that came later. I was very tired, so I went to bed early, and Barny brought a supper of cold meat and celery and fruit to bed on a tray.

Night was enchanting, and our desires insatiable. But they died down at last, and we slept enfolded, in a blessed peace. It was full morning when we woke, to a new day to be lived though with pleasure instead of misery. I wrote some letters, we made meals together, and did our household jobs together in happy friendship. Once, while we sat together by the fire, he laid his head against mine and whispered, "It's a foolish thing to say—but I would die for you." Perhaps in certain moods he would. But meanwhile he'll clean my shoes or pump up my bicycle tyres. And I adore his tenderness, his perfect willingness to be of service. He's indeed a man to make a woman happy. I said to him how untrue the Byronic couplet was of him,[4] and he said he thought it was very true of most men.

Next morning, after we had slept very chastely, a wire came. Hu had had another relapse and I was wanted at Barstock. In that first moment I had nothing but coarse, wicked, pitiless thoughts. Lord, I knew cruelty then, as the wise men know one knows it. *"When one is in love one has no love left for anyone."* It would have been so different if Hu had ever been gentle or tender or even humanly kind to me. But I know the cold bully behind his facade, as no one else on earth knows it. I know the tyrannical way he uses his own weakness as another instrument to bully with. Still, that mood went. Poor frustrated Hu, with this vile disease gaining on him inch by inch. Never well or buoyant or happy, always dogged by defeat and catastrophe. Poor little helpless boy, I must go to him.

. . . And now I'm back in the prison-house again. I have to sleep in Hu's room in case he wants anything in the night, and I'm with him all day. I go to bed weary with despair. . . .[5]

17th January Hu was so much better last week that he asked me to come home and arrange for his return.

27th January I came back from Cornwall to get the house at Shotton Green ready for Hu, and to try to sell the press. Why it occurred to nobody at Barnstock that if we sold the press, the house would have to be vacated too, I can't think. Matthew Robson is thinking of buying it, but his purchase would be conditional on possession of the house. But Hu says he must have the house till Lady Day, and if Robson would not agree, we should have to let his offer go. This is imbecility. Nobody seems to want the press. . . .

31st January   I have been to the hut—and that was heaven. My mother-in-law has wired for me to go to Barstock yet again, because Hu had a haemorrhage, and though at first I thought I would go, there was a railway strike and I was in the middle of selling the press, so I refused. Then they wired that he was going back to the sanatorium, and after all the thousand and one plans of the last week or so, for getting houses furnished or unfurnished, this news came as a relief. On Tuesday I went to Exeter and brought him back in a car to the sanatorium. I left him in bed, looking sad and rather feverish, though the journey was not such an ordeal as I'd thought it would be. I got home late, and Barny welcomed me and put me to bed. Robson is going to take over gradually, and will move in when I move out, in about a fortnight.

7th February   To the hut for two marvellous days. The sky was grey and the woods were dim, but that did not matter. And yet again, we quarrelled. My period was due and at present I'm not in the mood to take risks. He was angry and bitter. But presently I was in his arms again, and his bitterness passed, and there was a new world. To-night, at home in a fireless kitchen, by an oil lamp, I am thinking of the strange story we are living through, a paragraph at a time; our wilful stormy love, my unhappy marriage and resolve not to have children; Hu's illness and lovelessness, Barny's poverty and middle age; the little woodland hut where we've known such wild hours. Sometimes I've thought that in his complete disregard of money or security or comfort, there's a certain beauty—one could take it for granted in a younger man, but not in him.

5th March   On the 12th of February I moved to the cottage at Winterblow, on a wan and misty day. . . .

· · · · ·

18th March   A bad "black" bout. I had a letter from Hu, telling me that his friend Dr. Landon had died two days before. "The poor devil was conscious for the last twenty-four hours, and yelled for the last two." This worked on my mind horribly, for I knew his motive in telling it. Just now, Barny came over with an important cheque to be signed. He was on a bicycle, hatless, a buff scarf around his neck. I almost embraced him in the road. He came to tea and unpacked my pictures, then sat beside the fire smoking—a charming, bright-eyed *balanced* person. *He* says that I had him on approval for a year, before I decided to fall in love with him, but I think I've loved him all the time, though not so continuously as now.

26th March   Irony and shame. I had a letter from my mother-in-law condoling with me over the dreadful worried weekend I must have spent, waiting to hear if Hu's lung will collapse—for he is just starting A.P. But though I had worried about him all the week, on Saturday I dropped this sense of existence as nothing but pain and horror and disease, and went once more to Hodmer Wood. We went for a walk down a lane beyond Oxmore Farm, which curves down into a valley, past a grove of yews, and then back by Berridge and the wood. It was a bright pure day of spring, the trees were bare but green buds were showing on the hawthorn. Once we saw a sea-purple patch of field violets, on a sheltered slope at the edge of a wood. It's an exquisite time of year, for the sun shows up the subtle colours of the tree trunks. . . .

Well, we loved, and we had to make love. The world with its laws and codes and its horrors was forgotten, leaving only the little high house, and love between my darling and me.

31st March   I ought to have left Hu long ago, before it became impossible. Last week he was vilely insulting—said he would like to bring an action against Barny for debauching me—that I had become absolutely vicious, had a vicious look, I disliked all normal people, and led the life of a person with a secret vice. His mind is a positive sink of jealous hysteria. But I can't treat him only with pity. These outbursts terrify me.

He had had bad news; the lung would not collapse, and Dr. Westerleigh had told him he would get rapidly worse if he could not get his resistance back. This I suppose was the cause of his hysteria. I am deadly sorry for him as he lies there and sees his resistance going— but when he shouts insults at me I can only feel shattered and long to be out of his presence. What remains of our relations is a very terrible thing. He knows he can rely on my pity to answer his claims as far as I can, to bring the things he needs, to visit him (and be shouted at), even to take a house and nurse him if he wants it—he knows I can't answer him as one would a normal man: "Oh, go to hell." I'm in a horrible position. There's no strength like that of the weak man.

On my return I went to the hut and on my arrival I got a queer distasteful shock. I went in without knocking, as I always do, and as I opened the inner door Barny darted furtively to the dresser, and put down a small parcel so that the address was not visible. He turned an indescribably hang-dog look on me, and said in a jaunty voice, "Hullo, my dear, I didn't hear you come in." I remembered Mrs. Jenkins saying of him and his wife, "Of course they've neither of them given up the secretiveness of their class," and I asked him bluntly what he was trying to hide. "I'll show you," he said, with a great air of candour. I had evidently interrupted him in the middle of addressing it, for it read: Mrs. Bobette Harty, something or other road, Beakenham. I had heard of her before: a local company director's young wife who admires Gilbert Frankau, and who writes him gushing letters about his books. And he was lending a Tchekhov to her. I don't know. I don't know. But that furtive gesture was the ugliest thing I had ever seen in him.

4th April   Deep calls to deep, and cheap calls to cheap. My first thought is fidelity, but not my second. If Barny indulges in mental masturbation with half-baked females like Bobette Harty and Mrs. Evie Knickerbocker, why should I save him from jealousy? A postcard came from Nicholas Aran, saying he wanted to come and see me when the G.L. was finished. (I am translating one volume and he the other.) I left it on the mantelpiece. Tom Forrest-Smythe came today, to ask me to go round the cathedrals of southern England for a ten-day holiday. I can't go—I don't want to go—but I shall tease Barny, who is already jealous of him, with the idea. We both rail at everyone else as a possible enemy. I go off into gloom over his Hartys and Knickerbockers—and he over Lloyd, Tom, Aran and Robson, because he says I would give myself to any man who stirred me. Well, let him believe it.

. . . . .

18th April   Hu has told Dr. Westerleigh of my relation with Barny. I
had often thought—and said—that he ought to know, I'd even tried to
write to him several times, but I couldn't get it written. Hu has now
seen a nerve specialist, who said that worry over it had contributed to
his loss of resistance. Hu told him he was sure I wouldn't give the
man up, even if I knew it had a bad effect on him. Of course the
wretched man can only give a partial account, because he fancies I
love him—God knows why—he daren't confess to himself that only
pity has prevented me from breaking away from him finally, long
ago. So because I am sorry for him, and because he thinks I have
wronged him, I must leave the cottage and the hills and my love, and
return to domestic slavery to a bad-tempered invalid who will do
nothing but shout and bluster at me. But unless and until my relation
with Barny comes of itself to an end, I shall not give him up. I've
thought and thought, tried to look at it all in a dozen ways. But the
simple cruel fact remains that I can't give up a man I love for a man I
hate.

Yesterday I met Barny on the edge of the wood and we went to
Brandesley. Had tea at the Worcester Tea Rooms, and dinner at a little
hotel overlooking the river, where a full moon rose above the water
and the budding willows. I went home with him, though I hadn't
meant to, and walking across Sudley Common I said, "I hope you
have lots of milk, for I'm thirsty." "Just what I was saying to myself,"
he said. "I said, Will she want a fire? Don't know. Will she want anything to eat or drink? Yes, milk." I felt overcome by the sweetness
of the darling creature, always instinctively thoughtful for one. Over
and over again, he's been lovely to me. . . .

. . . . .

1st September   No record of the last four months. I had a talk with
Dr. Waterleigh, who understood the situation better when I told him
that if a cure were discovered for T.B., I would leave Hubet for good if
I knew he was cured—I was most unhappy with him and it wasn't a
normal marriage in any way.

He asked me if I could act a part, and if I would pretend to have
given up this man for six months, to see if it had any effect on Hubert's

health. I said I would. I was strongly tempted to ask him whether Hubert had ever told him that the whole idea of this pattern of married adultery had been his own, but I rather felt he had not done so, that perhaps a certain shame had kept him silent, and that he might feel miserably humiliated if I were to tell Westerleigh the truth.

At first Hu whined rather, and said he didn't know if he could "accept the sacrifice," but within a week he had forgotten all about it and was venting his furies on me in the old abusive way. This at least was instructive—for if I *had* given Barny up, I should have been in the wildest misery, and he would obviously have taken it as his due. So I had no scruple over getting the roundabout put up in a grass-grown gravel pit sheltered by tree and bushes, far enough from the house, over taking Mrs. Wright into my confidence, and having Barny over several times in secret. . . .

The summer went on, polarised in its old abnormal way between hell with Hu and heaven-and-hell with Barny, and far too little ordinary common earth. Also, I began my real acquaintance with jealousy. One day, in a friendlier mood, I said to Hu, "In fact, I'm simply terrified of what life's going to do to me." "What's there to be terrified of?" he said impatiently. But a breath of the future was upon the present in that moment. For I was virtually a prisoner, and to be a prisoner is not an attractive condition, especially as I became unhappily aware that Barny was finding some renewed interest in his wife, who had taken on a little belated charm, simply as a kind of infidelity to me. He was also meeting one or two women who had written to him about his books.

Suddenly, last month, when Hu had got no better and no worse, I began to look as if I were in for another nervous breakdown, of the sort I had three years ago. I simply don't know what happened. I was in Hu's room, he was bawling at me, and I found myself beating madly on the window with my flat hands—perhaps I was at last *shouting back!* And things changed very rapidly. The doctors decided that perhaps I had too stimulating an effect on Hu, and that we had better try what six months' separation would do. When I left, he said that he would miss me and he thought I would miss him. How *can* he think these things? We're like two trees of different species, that poison the ground for each other.

4th September   Yesterday at the hut I said to Barny, "When are you going to Vennor?" "Not for some time," he said. So I went to see his wife. A shadow passed the window. "Here *he* is," she said. The old tormenting mistrust of him came up and I went home in a whirl of suspicious thoughts.

30th September   "Men prize the thing ungained more than it is?" that's what my present state amounts to. Sandhills [sanitorium] was such daily hell to me that any escape from it was heaven. But freedom from Sandhills is not heaven, it is only normal. My life has swung between such extremes for so long that I can't see how to get it on to a reasonable level. Barny is having a bad time—stories refused—a damnable series of disappointments. It rains ceaselessly. And I may get called back to Sandhills at any time.

2nd October   Went to see Barny's wife. We talked till three, then she shared her bed with me, and we talked till morning. It looks as though Barny has been fooling both her and me. No doubt I was unwise to go there and find out the discrepancies between what he says to her and what he says to me. But it's done now, and so is my peace of mind. What he has told me is: that their relation has been improved by their separation and by a new spirit of frankness between them, but that there was no lover-like feeling in him for her, in fact, he was bored by her, but he wanted her to be happy; and to keep her so, and to get some work done without bothering to cook and shop, he went over to Vennor. I believed this—I hadn't even bothered to be jealous of her, though I didn't care for her coming to the hut. But to her he has said that I quite understand and even hold sacred the relation between them (a little too much, this, for my ribald sense!), and in spite of my jealousy I am too wise to attempt to alter it, knowing how fatally it would react on mine with him. He has said in so many words that he came home to Vennor in order to have sex relations with her, and he has gone to a deal of trouble to make these relations exciting, writing out details of all his past love affairs, and making her do the same, then reading them over as a sexual stimulus. I was never cynical enough about my relation with him to find this an easy thing to accept—in fact it horrifies all that was tender and romantic in me—I want only to break with him at once. Lie upon lie of his came up—so trivial, so disillusioning. . . . Oh no, too endless and wearying a catalogue. I am sick with disgust. I want to end it at once. . . .[6]

7th October   I'm too weak—I haven't the courage. I went over one day when he was out, packed up my possessions, took away his aphrodisiac-diary, tore my photographs in two and left them on his table. Then I found he still had the key to my cottage, that I'd had cut for him a few weeks back. So I went to fetch it. It was a perfect autumn day; at every turn of the road I was aware of all I meant to forgo for always. The tawny forest, the serene sky, twisted my heart with anguish. He was not there, and I sat below the hut, waiting for him. Presently I heard a tune whistled, loudly and sweetly, down on the track, and a figure came in sight. I did not recognize it as Barny until he was coming up the path. I walked down to him and said, "I've come for the key." "What's the matter?" he said. "I've talked with your wife." His face grew ugly and sullen. He said, "I'm not going to say anything. You must believe what you like."

Heaven knows why I stayed the night. All my feelings were in conflict. I made up my mind to go away at once, to let my cottage, to write to Hu, saying I wanted to return a different answer to his letter. (He had written to me just after I left Sandhills for this doctor-suggested "six months' separation," asking me if I would not now give up "this disastrous relationship," and saying that if I would do so, he would let me have money to go abroad for some time.)

Yet when the time came for us to part on the hill, I couldn't endure it. "Don't let us say that anything is finished," I said. "It's only that I'll go away for a time. I'd like to feel that my love for you was over. Let things stay suspended for a time. I just don't *know.*"

I went back to the cottage, and on another golden day I sat in a deck-chair in my weedy garden, writing long letters to Hu and to Minna Blythe. Then I discovered that I had left my watch at the hut. I wrote him a note, asking him to send it to Monica's. Then the self-betraying part of my mind resolved to go to London via Combe Marley and to collect it on the way. I put the letters in my bag and said I would post them in Combe Marley.

He came along the little passage as I mounted the steps and walked in. "It's my watch," I stammered, and then I broke down and cried, and he took me in his arms, whispering, "Don't go, darling—I love you, don't go." And again my recollection is hazy, and though I still wanted to, it seemed I could not break with him. "What's the use," I had said to him in bed that morning, "of hanging on just for these scraps and crumbs of love?" "One day you'll know there's a use even in scraps and crumbs of love," he answered. "Yes, but you're twenty years older than I am," said my mind. For I had no pleasure in not being able to break—I felt ashamed and disappointed—nothing was beautiful any more—I had been a deluded fool—I knew that I would end it quite ruthlessly if ever I became strong enough to do it. But he declared in his skipping superficial way that we were happy enough as we were—all he wanted was to get some work done and for us to stay lovers, and in weakness and anger I gave way to his "Don't go. Let us be as we were."

And of course the storm between us did not stop sex between us— it even seemed to have wakened it more strongly than ever. It was exciting, and sensually satisfying. But it did not change the bitter coldness of my heart.

8th October   Alone at the cottage, I find that I still mean to end it. I'm honest at least in saying that I don't *want* to love him any more. The longer things drag on, the more disillusioning our final parting will be. I've read his "literary aphrodisiacs," which are written in what he calls "the language of the rut," and I am full of self-disgust, for they are filthy and coarse to the last degree.

15th October   When, I wonder, did I begin to love Barny less? Quite possibly as soon as the overwhelming stimulus of the Sandhills separation was removed. All the way through, we've had to fight so desperately for its continuance—in placid circumstances, would it have lasted a year? But something made us take up every challenge to it. Now there's no challenge, nothing to fight for—and my inmost feelings have turned savagely against it. . . .

21st October   . . . I went to Sandhills for a weekend. Hu was, so far as a sick man can be, jubilant. But he told me that he had left me his money in his will on condition that I gave up Barny, and this seemed to me so vile a thought, so much the essence of all I hate in Hu, and it seemed to me so repellent to *gain money* by leaving a man I had so passionately loved, that I brooded over it after leaving him, and decided it was impossible to accept money from him any more. These two men are both in their ways impotent, and that explains everything: Barny sexually (yes, I could call it a repertory of tricks, in a hostile mood), so he has to have infidelities to reassure himself; Hu in life, so he bullies with his temper and bullies with his money. . . . [7]

On my way home from London I went to the hut. He came across the field to meet me, at the edge of the wood, and I felt in spite of everything that he was my own darling love again. "Well, have you come back to me?" he said. "I've come to tea," I mocked. "Have you come back to me?" he insisted. I told him what had been happening: that is, I told him Hubert had been threatening me about money; I never told him about the altered will—and asked him if he would live with me in London if I got a job. He said he would. But two days later, at the hut, his answer was different. His wife could not bear it— she was taking it terribly to heart—it was the last symbolic unbearable thing to her. He could not do it. I was embittered, devastated. I was giving up every sort of security for him—had told Hubert and his evil money to go to the devil—but he would take no risks.

21st November In London and at the cottage. I went to see Barny four days ago at the hut. The moment I touched the latch there was a scuffling noise inside—he opened the door and took me in his arms, almost sobbing and clearly stirred to the depths. He had just written me a letter telling me how tormented he felt, and asking me to give up the idea of London and to live with him at the hut. But what *can* come of it all?

28th November He wrote to me two desperate letters while I was away, full of misery and love, and an apparently overwhelming desire for me. In spite of everything, I believe he does love me. And I love him, though never again in the old way. I've thought I'd let my cottage and buy a caravan, and live on the proceeds, in the wood with him.

11th December   Have bought a caravan and hope to let my cottage by the new year. It's a fantastical thing that after all the storms, all the resolves to break away from Barny, I am now going to live with him altogether. Well, the first of October took something that won't be again. I am cold and cynical now, and I know there's nothing to spoil, because it's spoiled already. There'll be times of misery, times of tearing doubt and unhappiness, times of frank and bitter jealousy when he goes to London to meet other women. The best of love, the best of our time together, is already over.

Notes

❧

*These selections are taken from *A Prison, a Paradise* (New York: Viking, 1959).

1 Barny's rented cottage nearby.

2 Unexplained; refers to a book she is translating, along with Nicholas Aran.

3 Hurnscot later added to this, recalling not only an event, but her exact thoughts at the time,

> It was on Christmas Day that my mother-in-law and I were together in the dining-room. . . . She paced up and down . . . and suddenly began to cry out, over and over, "Oh, I hope he dies, I hope he dies, I hope he doesn't live." She had had sixteen years of an invalid son; he had had (as she told me) far more than his share of the family assets; and I suppose she was beginning to tire. Each day I used to go for my prescribed hour's walk in the lanes . . . thinking of this outburst. I had expected the life of day-beds and temperature-charts and crises to go on and on, perhaps for . . . ten or fifteen years. . . . But "If *she* wants him to die . . . if his own mother sees no solution for our burdens except in his death . . . Then where am I?"

4 Perhaps an allusion to "Man's love is of man's life a thing apart, / 'Tis a woman's whole existence" (*Don Juan*, canto 1, stanza 194).

5 Hurnscot later added to this to say that Hu had earlier asked Barny to live in their house at Shotton Green and watch the press and its staff of three while Hurnscot was away nursing him, at first offering no pay, then agreeing to only two shillings an hour.

6 Hurnscot later added a realization to this entry, following a description of Barny's "restless promiscuity" and of her own romanticizing for two years— her "whole false mysticism of sexual love, and of myself as a blissful part of Nature"—a realization that came with her conversion: that "man cannot remain as a blissful part of Nature, the structure of the universe forbids it. . . . But

that primitive ecstasy which lights up the whole of the outward creation is in the end the most immediate of pointers to divine ecstasy."

7   Hurnscot's later addition to this entry points out that Hu told her Barny would abandon her if she were left without money, a claim she suspected was true but nonetheless objected to as a form of blackmail. (Hu did cut her out of his will.)

III

Of Marriage and Motherhood

Lady Anne Clifford

(1590–1676)

ANNE CLIFFORD, Countess of Dorset, also later of Pembroke and Montgomery and Baroness Clifford, was the only surviving child of George Clifford, third earl of Cumberland, and his wife, Margaret Russell. An accomplished woman, Russell educated her daughter unusually well, even for awhile providing her with the poet and historian Samuel Daniel as tutor. Clifford's father (d. 1605) involved her in courageous litigation for years because, though his vast northern estates were already entailed upon his child irrespective of sex, he bequeathed them to his brother and his brother's male heirs. Clifford fought in the courts for possession of her rightful inheritance, with her mother's assistance until her mother died, and then alone. Her spendthrift first husband, Richard Sackville, second earl of Dorset (whom she married in 1609), needing money for clothes and amusements, enlisted the help of James I to demand that she desist for a cash settlement, but Clifford refused. To coerce her agreement, Dorset even took away their young daughter, Margaret (b. 1614), to live with his family; but neither that strategem nor refusing to share the marriage bed, as these selections from 1616–17 show,* shook the redoubtable Clifford. Nor, if one can believe her extant diary for 1616–19 (plus a portion of 1603), did they turn her against him, any more than did his frequent absences from home or inviting his mistress, Lady Peneystone (or Peniston), to their home at Knole. Clifford bore Dorset five children, but only two girls survived. Widowed in 1624, she married Philip Herbert, fourth earl of Pembroke, in 1628, to use his influence in her cause, but soon separated from him. Her thirty-eight-year struggle for her inheritance ended when her uncle's son died without male issue so that in 1643 the estates, a great part of Westmoreland and Yorkshire, reverted to her, to be ruled by her firmly but wisely for the rest of her long life.

From Anne Clifford's Diary

April 1616 Upon the 1st came my Coz. *Charles Howard* and Mr. *John Dudley* with letters to shew that it was my Lord's pleasure that the men and horses should come away without me and so after much falling out betwixt my Lady and them all the folks went away there being a paper drawn to shew that they went away by my Lord's direction and contrary to my will.[1]

At night I sent 2 messengers to my folks to entreat them to stay. For some 2 nights my Mother and I lay together and had much talk about this business.

Upon the 2nd I went after my folks in my Lady's coach she bringing me a quarter of a mile in the way where she and I had a grievous and heavy parting. . . .

Upon the 10th we went from *Ware* to *Tottenham* where my Lord's coach with his men and horses met me and came to *London* to the lesser *Dorset House*.

Upon the 11th I came from *London* to *Knole* where I had but a cold welcome from my Lord. My [daughter] Lady *Margaret* met me in the outermost gate and my Lord came to me in the Drawing Chamber.

Upon the 12th I told my Lord how I had left those writings which the Judges and my Lord would have me sign and seal behind with my Mother.

Upon the 13th my Lord and *Thomas Glenham* went up to *London*.

Upon the 17th came *Tom Woodgatt* from London but brought me no news of my going up which I daily look for.*

Upon the 18th *Baskett*[2] came hither and brought me a letter from my Lord to let me know this was the last time of asking me whether I would set my hand to this award of the Judges.

*Upon the 17th my Mother sickened as she came from Prayers, being taken with a cold chillness in the manner of an ague which afterwards turned to great heats and pains in her side, so as when she was opened, it was plainly seen she had an Imposthume [abscess].

Upon the 19th I returned my Lord for answer that I would not stand to the award of the Judges what misery soever it cost me. This morning the Bishop of *St. David's* and my little Child were brought to speak to me.

About this time I used to rise early in the morning and go to the Standing in the Garden, and taking my prayer Book with me beseech GOD to be merciful to me in this and to help me as he always hath done.

May 1616   Upon the 1st *Rivers* came from *London* in the afternoon and brought me word that I should neither live at *Knole* nor at *Bolebrooke.*

Upon the 2nd came Mr. *Legg*[3] and told divers of the servants that my Lord would come down and see me once more which would be the last time that I should see him again.

Upon the 3rd came *Baskett* down from *London* and brought me a letter from my Lord by which I might see it was his pleasure that the Child should go the next day to *London,* which at the first was somewhat grievous to me, but when I considered that it would both make my Lord more angry with me and be worse for the Child, I resolved to let her go, after I had sent for Mr. *Legg* and talked with him about that and other matters and wept bitterly.

Upon the 4th being Saturday between 10 and 11 the Child went into the litter to go to *London,* Mrs. *Bathurst* and her two maids with Mr. *Legge* and a good Company of the Servants going with her. In the afternoon came a man called *Hilton,* born in *Craven,* from my Lady *Willoughby* to see me which I took as a great argument of her love being in the midst of all my misery.

Upon the 8th I dispatched a letter to my Mother.

Upon the 9th I received a letter from Mr. *Bellasis* how extreme ill my Mother had been and in the afternoon came *Humphrey Godding's* son with letters that my Mother was exceeding ill and as they thought in sore danger of death—so as I sent *Rivers* presently to *London* with letters to be sent to her and certain cordials and conserves.

At night was brought to me a letter from my Lord to let me know his determination was, the Child should go live at *Horseley,* and not come hither any more so as this was a very grievous and sorrowful day to me.

Upon the 10th *Rivers* came from *London* and brought me word from Lord *William* that she [my mother] was not in such danger as I fear'd, the same day came the Steward from *London,* whom I expected would have given warning to many of the servants to go away because the audits was newly come up.*

Upon the 11th being Sunday before Mr. *Legge* went away I talked with him an hour or two about the business and matters between me and my Lord, so as I gave him better satisfaction and made him conceive a better opinion of me than ever he did.

A little before dinner came *Matthew*[5] down from *London,* my Lord sending me by him the wedding ring that my Lord Treasurer and my old Lady were married with–all and a message that my Lord would be here the next week, and that the Child would not as yet go down to *Horsley* and I sent my Lord the wedding ring that my Lord and I was married with; the same day came Mr. *Marsh*[6] from *London* and persuaded me much to consent to this argument.

The 12th at night *Grosvenor*[7] came hither and told me how my Lord had won £200 at the Cocking Match and that my Lord of *Essex* and Lord *Willoughby* who was on my Lord's side won a great deal and how there was some unkind words between my Lord and his side and Sir William Herbert and his side. This day my Lady *Grantham* sent me a letter about these businesses between my Uncle *Cumberland* and me and returned me an answer.

All this time my Lord was in *London* where he had all and infinite great resort coming to him. He went much abroad to Cocking, to Bowling Alleys, to Plays and Horse Races, and [was] commended by all the world. I stayed in the country having many times a sorrowful and heavy heart, and being condemned by most folks because I would

*Upon the 10th early in the morning I wrote a very earnest Letter to beseech him that I might not go to the Little House that was appointed for me, but that I might go to *Horsley* and sojourn with my Child, and to the same effect I wrote to my Sister *Beauchamp*.[4]

not consent to the agreements, so as I may truly say, I am like an owl in the desert.

Upon the 13th being Monday, my Lady's footman *Thomas Petty* brought me letters out of *Westmoreland,* by which I perceived how very sick and full of grievous pains my dear Mother was, so as she was not able to write herself to me and most of her people about her feared she would hardly recover this sickness, at night I went out and pray'd to GOD my only helper that she might not die in this pitiful case. The 14th *Richard Jones* came from *London* to me and brought a letter with him from *Matthew* to the effect whereof was to persuade me to yield to my Lord's desire in this business at this time, or else I was undone for ever.

Upon the 15th my Lord came down from *London* and my *Coz. Cecily Neville,* my Lord lying in Leslie Chamber and I in my own. Upon the 17th my Lord and I after supper had some talk about these businesses, *Matthew* being in the room where we all fell out and so parted for that night. Upon the 18th being Saturday in the morning my Lord and I having much talk about these businesses, we agreed that Mr. *Marsh* should go presently down to my Mother and that by him I should write a letter to persuade her to give over her jointure presently to my Lord and that he would give her yearly as much as it was worth.

This day my Lord went from *Knole* to *London.**

Upon the 20th being Monday I dispatch'd Mr. *Marsh* with letters to my Mother about the business aforesaid. I sent them unsealed because my Lord might see them.

*N.B.—My Lord was at *London* when my mother died but he went to *Lewes* before he heard of her death.

Upon the 20th went my Child to *W. Horsley* with *Mary Neville* and Mrs. *Bathurst* from London. *Mary Hicken*[8] was with her, for still she lain in bed with Lady *Margaret.*

Upon the 24th being Friday between the hours of 6 and 9 at night died my dear Mother at *Broome* in the same chamber where my Father was born, 13 years and 2 months after the death of Queen *Elizabeth*

My Brother *Compton*[9] and his wife kept the house at *West Horsley* and my Brother *Beauchamp* and my sister his wife sojourned with them so as the Child was with both her aunts. Upon the 22nd Mr. *Davy's* came down from *London* and brought me word that my Mother was very well recovered of her dangerous sickness. . . .

Upon the 28th my Lady *Selby* came hither to see me and told me that she had heard some folks say that I have done well in not consenting to the composition. Upon the 29th *Kendall* came and brought me the heavy news of my Mother's death which I held as the greatest and most lamentable cross that could have befallen me. Also he brought her will along with him wherein she appointed her body should be buried in the Parish Church of *Anwick* which was a double grief to me when I consider'd her body should be carried away and not interred at *Skipton,* so as I took that as a sign that I should be dispossessed of the inheritance of my forefathers.

The same night I sent *Hamon* away with the will to my Lord who was then at *Lewes.* . . .

Upon the 31st came Mr. *Amherst* from my Lord and brought me word that my Lord would be here on Saturday. The same day Mr. *James* brought me a letter from Mr. *Woolrich* wherein it seemed it was my Mother's pleasure her body should be conveyed to what place I appointed which was some contentment to my aggrieved soul.

June 1616   . . . At this time[10] my Lord desired to have me pass my rights of the lands of *Westmoreland* to him and my Child, and to this end he brought my Lord *William Howard* to persuade me and then my Lord told me I should go presently to *Knole,* and so I was sent away upon half an hour's warning leaving my Coz. *Cecily Neville* and *Willoughby* behind me at *London* and so went down alone with *Kath.*

---

and 10 years and 7 months after the death of my Father, I being 26 years old and 5 months and the Child 2 years old wanting a month. . . .

There was much Bull Baiting, Bowling, Cards and Dice, with suchlike sports to entertain the time [at Lewes].

Buxton about 8 o'clock at night so as it was 12 before we came to *Knole*.

Upon the 15th came the Steward to *Knole* with whom I had much talk. At this time I wrought very hard and made an end of one of my cushions of Irish stitch work.

Upon the 17th came down Dr. *Leyfield, Ralph Couniston* and *Basket* [*sic*], *D. L.* bringing with him the conveyance which Mr. *Walter* had drawn and persuaded me to go up and set my hand to it which I refused because my Lord had sent me down so suddenly 2 days before.

Upon the 19th my Lord came down for me and Dr. *Layfield* with him when my Lord persuaded me to consent to his business and assured me how kind and good a husband he would be to me. . . .

Upon the 30th, Sunday, presently after dinner my Lady *Robert Rich*, my Coz. *Cecily Neville* and I went down by barge to *Greenwich* where in the Gallery there passed some unkind words between my Lady *Knolles* and me. I took my leave of the Queen and all my friends here. About this time it was agreed between my Lord and me that Mrs. *Bathurst* should go away from the Child and that *Willoughby* should have the charge of her till I should appoint it otherwise. He gave me his faithful promise that he would come after me into the North as soon as he could and that the Child should come out of hand so that my Lord and I were never greater friends than at this time.

* * * * *

January 1617 . . . Upon the 8th we came from *London* to *Knole*. This night my Lord and I had a falling out about the land.

Upon the 9th I went up to see the things in the closet and began to have Mr. *Sandy's* book read to me about the Government of the Turks, my Lord sitting the most part of the day reading in his closet.

Upon the 10th my Lord went up to *London* upon the sudden, we not knowing it till the afternoon.

Upon the 16th I received a letter from my Lord that I should come up to *London* the next day because I was to go before the King on Monday next.

Upon the 17th when I came up, my Lord told me I must resolve to go to the King the next day. Upon the 18th being Saturday I went presently after dinner to the Queen to the Drawing Chamber where my Lady *Derby* told the Queen how my business stood and that I was to go to the King so she promised me she would do all the good in it she could. When I had stay'd but a little while there I was sent for out, my Lord and I going through my Lord *Buckingham's* chamber who brought us into the King, being in the Drawing Chamber. He put out all that were there and my Lord and I kneeled by his chair sides when he persuaded us both to peace and to put the whole matter wholly into his hands, which my Lord consented to, but I beseech'd His Majesty to pardon me for that I would never part from Westmoreland while I lived upon any condition whatsoever. Sometimes he used fair means and persuasions and sometimes foul means but I was resolved before so as nothing would move me. From the King we went to the Queen's side. I brought my Lady *St. John* to her lodgings and so we went home. At this time I was much bound to my Lord for he was far kinder to me in all these businesses than I expected and was very unwilling that the King should do me any public disgrace.*

Upon the 19th my Lord and I went to the Court in the morning thinking the Queen would have gone to the Chapel but she did not, so my Lady *Ruthven* and I and many others stood in the Closet to hear the sermon. I dined with my Lady *Ruthven*. Presently after dinner she and I went up to the Drawing Chamber where my Lady *D.*, my Lady *Montgomery*, my Lord *Burleigh*, persuaded me to refer these businesses to the King. About 6 o'clock my Lord came for me so he and I and Lady *St. John* went home in her coach. This night the Masque was danced at the Court but I would not stay to see it because I had seen it already.

Upon the 20th I and my Lord went presently after dinner to the Court, he went up to the King's side about his business, I went to my Aunt *Bedford* in her lodging where I stay'd in Lady *Ruthven's* chamber till towards 8 o'clock about which time I was sent for up to the King into his Drawing Chamber when the door was lock'd and nobody suffered to stay here but my Lord and I, my Uncle *Cumberland*, my

---

*The Queen gave me warning not to trust my matters absolutely to the King lest he should deceive me.

Coz. *Clifford*, my Lords *Arundel, Pembroke, Montgomery*, Sir *John Digby*. For lawyers there were my Lord Chief Justice *Montague* and *Hobart Yelverton* the King's Solicitor, Sir *Randal Crewe* that was to speak for my Lord and I. The King asked us all if we would submit to his judgment in this case. My Uncle *Cumberland*, my Coz. *Clifford*, and my Lord answered they would, but I would never agree to it without *Westmoreland* at which the King grew in a great chaff. My Lord of *Pembroke* and the King's Solicitor speaking much against me, at last when they saw there was no remedy, my Lord fearing the King would do me some public disgrace, desired Sir *John Digby* would open the door, who went out with me and persuaded me much to yield to the King. My Lord *Hay* came to me to whom I told in brief how this business stood. Presently after my Lord came from the King when it was resolved that if I would not come to an agreement there should be an agreement made without me. We went down, Sir *Robert Douglas* and Sir *George Chaworth* bringing us to the coach, by the way my Lord and I went in at *Worcester House* to see my Lord and Lady and so came home this day. I may say I was led miraculously by GOD's Providence, and next to that I trust all my good to the worth of nobleness of my Lord's disposition for neither I nor anybody else thought I should have passed over this day so well as I have done.

Upon the 22nd the Child had her 6th fit of the ague in the morning. Mr. *Smith* went up in the coach to *London* to my Lord to whom I wrote a letter to let him know in what case the Child was and to give him humble thanks for his noble usage towards me at London. The same day my Lord came down to *Knole* to see the Child.

Upon the 23rd my Lord went up betimes to London again. The same day the Child put on her red baize coats.

Upon the 25th I spent most of my time in working and in going up and down to see the Child. About 5 or 6 o'clock the fit took her, which lasted 6 or 7 hours.

Upon the 28th at this time I wore a plain green flannel gown that *William Punn* made me, and my yellow taffety waistcoat. *Rivers* used to read to me in Montaigne's Plays and *Moll Neville* in the Fairy Queen.

Upon the 30th Mr. *Amherst* the Preacher came hither to see me with whom I had much talk. He told me that now they began to think at *London* that I had done well in not referring this business to the King and that everybody said GOD had a hand in it.*

· · · · · ·

April 1617 . . . The 5th my Lord went up to my closet and said how little money I had left contrary to all they had told him. Sometimes I had fair words from him and sometimes foul, but I took all patiently, and did strive to give him as much content and assurance of my love as I could possibly, yet I told him that I would never part with *Westmoreland* upon any condition whatever. Upon the 6th after supper because my Lord was sullen and not willing to go into the nursery I made *Mary* bring the Child to him into my chamber, which was the 1st time she stirred abroad since she was sick.

Upon the 7th my Lord lay in my chamber. Upon the 8th I set by my Lord and my Brother *Sackville* in the Drawing Chamber and heard much talk about my businesses and did perceive that he was entered into a business between my Lady of *Exeter* and my Lord *Roos* of which he will not easily quit himself.

Upon the 11th my Lord was very ill this day and could not sleep so that I lay on a pallet. The 12th Mrs. *Watson* came here, with whom I had much talk of my Lord's being made a Knight of the Garter. This night I went into *Judith's* chamber[11] where I mean to continue till my Lord is better.

The 13th my Lord sat where the gentlemen used to sit. He dined

---

*All this time of my being in the country there was much ado at *London* about my business in so much that my Lord, my Uncle *Cumberland*, my Coz. *Clifford* with the Chief Justice of the Council of both sides on divers times with the King hearing it go so directly for me, he said there was a law in *England* to keep me from the land.

There was during this time much cock fighting at the Court where the Lords' cocks did fight against the King's. Although this business was somewhat chargeable to my Lord yet it brought him into great grace and favour with the King so as he useth him very kindly and speaketh very often to him than of any other man.

abroad in the great Chamber and supped privately with me in the Drawing Chamber and had much discourse of the manners of folks at court.

The 14th I was so ill with lying in *Judith's* chamber that I had a plain fit of a fever.

The 15th I was so sick and my face so swelled that my Lord and *Tom Glenham* were fain to keep the table in the Drawing Chamber and I sat within. *Marsh* came in the afternoon to whom I gave directions to go to Mr. *Davis* and Mr. *Walter* about the drawing of letters to the tenants in *Westmoreland* because I intend sending him thither. This night I left *Judith's* chamber and came to lie in the chamber where I lay when my Lord was in *France,* in the green cloth of gold bed where the Child was born.

The 16th my Lord had much talk about these businesses, he urging me still to go to London to sign and seal but I told him that my promise so far passed to my brother [in-law] and to all the world that I would never do it, whatever became of me and mine.

Upon ye 17th in the morning my Lord told me he was resolved never to move me more in these businesses, because he saw how fully I was bent. . . .

The 20th being Easter Day my Lord and I and *Tom Glenham* and most of the folk received the Communion by Mr. *Ran,* yet in the afternoon my Lord and I had had a great falling out, *Mathew* [*sic*] continuing still to do me all the ill office he could with my Lord. All this time I wore my white satin gown and my white waistcoat.

The 22nd he came to dine abroad in the great Chamber; this night we played at Burley Break[12] upon the Bowling Green.

The 23rd Lord *Clanricarde* came hither. After they were gone my Lord and I and *Tom Glenham* went to Mr. *Lune's* house to see the fine flowers that is in the garden.

This night my Lord should have lain with me but he and I fell out about matters.

The 24th my Lord went to *Sen'noak* again. After supper we played at Burley Break upon the Green. This night my Lord came to lie in my chamber. . . .

The 26th I spent the evening in working and going down to my

Lord's Closet where I sat and read much in the Turkish History and Chaucer.

The 28th was the first time the Child put on a pair of whalebone bodice.

My Lord went a hunting the fox and the hare. . . . About this time my Lord made the Steward alter most of the rooms in the house, and dress them up as fine as he could, and determined to make all his old clothes in purple stuff for the Gallery and Drawing Chamber.

May 1617 Upon the 1st I cut the Child's strings off from her coats and made her use togs[13] alone, so as she had two or three falls at first but had no hurt with them.

The 2nd the Child put on her first coat that was laced with lace, being of red baize.

The 3rd my Lord went from *Buckhurst* to *London,* and rid it in four hours, he riding very hard, a hunting all the while he was at *Buckhurst* and had his health exceeding well.

The 7th my Lord Keeper rode from *Dorset House* to *Westminster* in great pomp and state, most of the Lords going with him, amongst which my Lord was one.

The 8th I spent this day in working, the time being very tedious unto me as having neither comfort nor company, only the Child.

The 12th I began to dress my head with a roll without a wire.

I wrote not to my Lord because he wrote not to me since he went away. After supper I went with the Child who rode the piebald nag that came out of *Westmoreland* to Mrs. ——. The 14th the Child came to lie with me, which was the first time that ever she lay all night in a bed with me since she was born.

The 15th the Child put on her white coats and left off many things from her head, the weather growing extreme hot. . . .

The 17th the Steward came from *London* and told me my Lord was much discontented with me, for not doing this business, because he must be fain to buy land for the payment of the money which will much encumber his estate.

· · · · ·

June 1617 . . . The 30th still working and being extremely melancholy and sad to see things go so ill with me and fearing my Lord would give all his land away from the Child.

July 1617 The 1st still working and sad.

Notes

*These selections are taken from *The Diary of the Lady Anne Clifford,* ed. Victoria Sackville-West (London: William Heinemann, 1924). Many of Clifford's later annotations are also included here, and Clifford's style of dating the entries is retained.

1   *My Lord* is her husband; *my Lady* is her mother, to whose home she has come to discuss a demand from George Abbot, archbishop of Canterbury, that Clifford accept a settlement of her inheritance claim. The paper referred to, still extant, specifies over the signatures of witnesses that she wishes to go to London but her husband will not allow it, so that she remains at Knole under duress.

2   Mr. Peter Baskett, gentleman of the horse to Dorset.

3   Mr. Edward Legg, steward to Dorset.

4   Her sister-in-law Anne (daughter of Robert, Earl of Dorset, and wife of Lord Beauchamp), temporarily a guardian of Clifford's child.

5   Mr. Matthew Caldicott, Dorset's favorite.

6   Attendant upon Lady Margaret, her daughter.

7   Mr. Grosvenor, gentleman usher to Dorset.

8   Presumably Lady Margaret's nurse, with whom the child sleeps until she is three years old.

9   Her brother-in-law, Sir Henry Compton.

10   That is, after 8 June. Clifford is in London at the time.

11   Probably Mrs. Judith Simpson, a household servant, with whom elsewhere in the diary Clifford goes walking in the park.

12   Barley-break, a country game played by three couples, one couple serving as catcher of the others, who may separate or "break" (change partners) to avoid capture but if caught become catcher in turn.

13   *Strings* at the back of a pinafore (or the like) were used to control a toddler; *togs* are coats, i.e., clothes.

Fanny Boscawen

(1719–1805)

FRANCES EVELYN (Fanny) BOSCAWEN, daughter of William Evelyn and Frances Glanville of St. Clere, Kent, was the great-great-niece of John Evelyn, the diarist; the wife of Admiral Edward Boscawen, whom she married in 1742; and one of the better known figures of eighteenth-century London. Her circle of friends included Samuel Johnson, David Garrick, and Sir Joshua Reynolds; and James Boswell praised her in his biography of Johnson for her agreeable manners and conversation. She has been credited, along with her friend Elizabeth Montagu, with the distinction of originating bluestocking assemblies, where conversation and discussion were substituted for the usual card playing. In 1748, she began a letter journal for her husband while he was away with the fleet, planning to send him sections of it whenever the chance occurred. Although she continued writing to him until he returned home in April 1750, all that remains is what she wrote in 1748, at least half of it having survived a voyage to India and back and the wreck of the admiral's flagship in a hurricane. As her diary for 1748 reveals,* she was devoted to her husband and their children: at the time of the extant diary, Edward Hugh (b. 1744), Frances (b. 1746), and Elizabeth (b. 1747). She later bore two additional surviving sons: William Glanville (b. 1751) and George Evelyn (b. 1757). Unfortunately, however, out of the eighteen years of her married life, at least ten were spent anxious for the admiral's welfare while he was away on active service, and, three months after his final return to England as a national hero, he died at their new home at Hatchlands in 1761. His adoring wife was to survive him for forty-four years.

From Fanny Boscawen's Diary

12th July 1748   . . . If my husband were here, I should like to explore
the country "all in my chaise and pair," but as it is, I seldom sally
forth without some company to induce me, for, my gardens being
large,[1] nothing can be pleasanter than to sit and walk in them and see
all my olive branches flourishing round me. If you would know our
way of life, I can tell it you very exactly. As soon as I am up (which is
not so early as if my lord were at home) I sally forth into the garden,
the boy in my hand, and by the time his shoes are wet through with
dew (which never gives us any cold) we come in to breakfast. The
instant breakfast is over, we retire into another room to say our lesson—a ceremony never omitted nor broke into, whether I have company or not—by which means he has made a considerable progress
since we came into the country, and, if he had but half as much application as he has genius and capacity, he would read soon. But this
same application is an ingredient seldom found in the composition of
such a sprightly cub.

But to return to my journal: after I have instructed my son, we
usually take a little walk together, either on the Green or in the garden—the weather determines. Then come in and sit close to business
for an hour and a half. Mine lies chiefly at my desk, where a number
of correspondents, *et mon cher mari par-dessus tout,*[2] find me continual
employment. Then half a quarter of an hour's dressing, then dine
exactly at 2. After dinner, sit awhile (whatever you may think to the
contrary); then walk in the garden, where we have a charming green
parlour, stored with chairs. Here we fix before 4, the table, workbas-
ket, and book. The latter is my province, as the former is Julia's.[3]

Hard by, there is a grove. Here my son and his sister make hay
beside us, Mrs. Smythe[4] having presented the former with a rake,
fork and spade, and I treated him with a large wheelbarrow. We likewise stole a haycock from our neighbour, Sir John Elwell, which
has amused the young ones for these three weeks past, and the rule
is—and it is very strictly kept to—that the hay never peeps out into
our green parlour, but stays in the grove, which is full of dead leaves

and twigs, so that it could not be kept neat, which the rest of the garden is in an eminent degree.

The haymakers have interrupted the thread of my narration, which goes on to tell you that, still in the same green retreat (if the weather permits), we drink tea at 6. And here I should be very ungrateful if I did not thank my dearest for the charming Dutch kettle he gave me, which is quite the comfort of one's life.

After tea, we see the young ones safe settled with their maids on the lawn, and then we sally forth to take our long walk, either on foot or *en carosse* [by coach]. If the latter, the babes are of the party, but the former is much the most frequent.

Sometimes, we get in by 8 to see the young ones put to bed: (Bess, in that situation, is a sight) and sometimes not till 9, which is the hour of supper, after which I read and Julia knots till 11, when we retire, she to dream of her parents and I of my husband.

19th July   I could not even sleep last night, so much elated was I, for yesterday I received a letter from Mr. Stephens to say the *Syren* Man of War would sail express to you and carry you orders to return. I assure you, my dear, you have deprived me of a night's rest, for I employed it in thinking when and where (not how) I should receive you!

20th July   I have the same complaint to make to-day, for I have laid awake above half the night thinking of your coming home; when it will happen. Sure, in March or April. God grant my children may look as they do now. Just such rosy countenances, and my boy just as orderly and well behaved as he is now.

You can't imagine what a triumph I had on that subject yesterday. I must relate it to you. Mr. Mason[5] has told me he had a boy a little older than mine. I asked if he was bigger; he said, not stouter, but a great deal taller. Yesterday, we were there and this tall boy proved to be half a head shorter than mine, to the great astonishment of his father. But here my triumph did not stop, for the Mason boy did nothing he was bid to do, nor minded father nor mother: would not speak to your son, nor play with him: whereas mine obeyed my very looks, was very talkative and civil, only asked Mrs. Mason if she was that boy's mother and, upon being answered yes, he said, "why doesn't he mind what you say to him?" In short, there could not be a greater contrast between these two children—as well in figure as behaviour—so much so, that I thought Mason and his wife seemed mortified (for theirs, too, is a darling) and the former cried out, "What a joy it must be to the Admiral to see such a lovely, such an extraordinary, child!"

21st July   This whole day I dedicate to my dearest husband without any one interruption, except teaching my boy. I shan't allow myself a book or anything that may hinder me, for this packet must be sealed to-night, and to-morrow I carry it up to Mr. Cleveland, to go by the *Syren* or *Charmer*.

Now to tell you some news of this place, which consists of a burying and a wedding. The former is of that poor wretch, Lord Forester, long since buried to everything that he ought to have lived for. He died at Egham, where it seems he had taken up his dwelling above a year.

The wedding is no less than the great Sir. W. W. Wynn, who was married last Saturday to Miss Frances Shackerly, youngest daughter of Mr. Shackerly, who lives in the road from hence to Egham. The bridegroom arrived only on the Friday; threw himself at Mistress Shackerly's feet and said he would not rise till she consented he should be married the next day. She begged him to stay a fortnight only, till preparations were made, clothes bought, etc., but he was inflexible and all she could obtain was for him to put off his weepers (his wife not having been dead above 6 weeks). For my part, I commend his impatience, for 'tis certain he has no time to lose. The lady he has married is about 26; is his Goddaughter, for there has always been a great friendship between him and her father, to whom he declared his intentions about 3 weeks ago; but they did not imagine he proposed to have executed them till his deep mourning was expired. He says his late lady enjoined him to marry immediately and, with that view, left him her whole estate.

On Sunday Fred Evelyn[6] dined with me. We carried him back to Eton, and your son was vastly delighted with seeing the place where he is to go to school. As I was leading him along King Henry's Square, he said to me, "Mama, I'll make haste and read my book, that I may come and play with all these little parsons," meaning the scholars, who were just then crossing the Square in their gowns. My boy was vastly pleased too with seeing his Grandfather's name engraved on the stone in the Cloisters, and he spelt it, I assure you, as well as I could do and without the least hesitation.

The Fredericks are at Maisonette, Tunbridge Wells, where Lucy writes me word she proposes to produce a boy in about 2 or 3 months, but I hope he (Charles) will write to you by this opportunity, as he may tell you of many things which I omit; for my letters are full of nothing but childish talk, that "to-day we did this and yester-day, that." But as I am neither informed nor qualified to talk of great events, I think tittle tattle may be acceptable, and when it concerns those who have the greatest share of your affection, it even grows important. You know P.P.'s Memoirs are entitled "The importance of a man to himself." Mine might properly enough be called, "The im-portance of a wife to her husband, of children to their father."

Indeed, my dearest, these tender names draw tears from my eyes, and I do not believe you will read them with greater indifference. God grant you the joy of seeing them! Seeing them answer your utmost desires! Seeing them everything you could wish, and conformable to the highest picture your fancy could paint. Hitherto, my prayer is heard, and the children improve daily in beauty.

With me, 'tis not so. Beauty and I were never acquainted. But May I not hope, dear husband, that you will find charms in my heart, the charms of duty and affection, that will endear me as much to you as if I were in the bloom of youth and beauty. But I must return to my trifles, for talking thus from my heart kills me, and my tears blot my writing! I will go into the garden and take a turn or two. When I have composed myself, I will come to you again. . . .

• • • • •

6th August On the Saturday, the third day of the Smythes' reign, I carried them about 8 miles to Mrs. Hart's, who lives on t'other side Ascot Heath, who has a fine garden and *ferme ornée a la Southcote*[7] (but not equal to his, in my opinion). Mrs. Clayton preferred it greatly. But a fine cascade, which falls and roars only when company stays, disgusted me, who should be apt to form my villa for myself, not strangers.

I do not enter into a particular description of these places, because I cannot help flattering myself that you will one day see these things without me. Next May, I flatter myself, you will return, and the little leisure you will have for the country will, I suppose, be spent here. You cannot imagine how many schemes I form to receive and entertain you. It has kept me awake many an hour. I adorn myself, I dress my children, I decorate my house. You arrive! I figure to myself your looks, your words. As for mine, they will be few—I shall be past speaking. Sometimes I cannot determine whether I shall be dressed in blue, or white, or yellow, or red, or green. My last resolves were white, I think, for sure 'twill be another marriage and I once more a bride, happier than the first time by as much as I am enriched with 3 beautiful infants, as well as the means of maintaining and endowing them. Thus have we gained great riches since our marriage, and hope we shall not be less rich in love and affection, esteem and friendship for each other.

Notes

❧

*Selections here come from Cecil Aspinall-Oglander, *Admiral's Wife: Being the Life and Letters of the Hon. Mrs. Edward Boscawen from 1719 to 1761* (London: Longmans, Green, 1940).

1   Boscawen had rented a furnished house at Englefield Green, on the borders of Windsor Great Park, for the summer of 1748.

2   And my dear husband, above all.

3   Boscawen's cousin and good friend, Julia Evelyn.

4   Kate Evelyn Smythe, another cousin of Boscawen's, who comes to visit with her husband, Sydney Smith.

5   From the Admiralty.

6   Her nephew, the son of Sir John Evelyn and Mary Boscawen.

7   Farmhouse decorated in the style of Southcote (referring to Philip Southcote, the decor of whose Woburn Farm neary Chertsey she admired).

Ellen Weeton

(1776–1845)

ELLEN WEETON was the daughter of Thomas Weeton of Lancaster, a privateersman killed at sea in 1782, and his wife, Mary Rawlinson. At twenty-one, on her mother's death, Weeton took over the small school her widowed mother had opened at Upholland to support herself and her two children. Then she became a governess and a companion, always denying herself so that her adored brother, Tom, could be trained to law. In 1814 she married a near-bankrupt widower, Aaron Stock of Wigan, upon the recommendation of Tom, who gained £100 under the terms of their mother's will for arranging the marriage. Stock wanted her meager savings to reestablish his cotton-spinning firm. Though more than once Weeton fled home with their daughter, Mary (b. 1815), because Stock had brought in a mistress, she left him only after more than seven years of verbal and physical abuse that included beatings, confinements to her room on bread and water, imprisonments, and being turned out onto the street. Tom helped Stock force a deed of separation on her (without her reading it) in 1822 by threatening her with starvation, further imprisonment, or a Lunacy Commission hearing. The separation banished her from Wigan and its environs and limited her to three annual supervised visits with her child; her compensation was her former governess's salary (£70 per annum), an inadequate sum only irregularly paid. Weeton refused, however, to remain separated from Mary, and because Stock had placed Mary in Mr. Grundy's Academy for Young Ladies outside Wigan, regularly walked almost eight miles each way to view Mary on the school grounds or to join the file of school children en route to chapel. Finally, in 1827, Stock left Wigan and Mary was returned to her mother, possibly through the good offices of Hope Chapel, which Weeton had joined. Weeton kept diaries and letter journals from 1807 to 1825; parts of the bitter pages she wrote from 1818 to 1825 are included here.*

From Ellen Weeton's Diary

Occasional Reflections, A.D. 1818

A.D. 1818   An intention of marking a few domestic events, but more
particularly the religious state of my mind, induced me to attempt a
kind of Diary. But so painful and heart-rending have been the occur-
rences of the few days which have yet passed in the New Year, that
agitation, anguish, and despair, have driven all thoughts of religion
away. Have mercy! have pity on me, Oh my Father! and enable me to
sustain thy chastening hand with more submission and humility.
Forsake me not at this trying time, and help me to see which way I
should act, so as to please Thee and save my own soul.

It is Thy Will that I submit to the tyranny of him who so cruelly
uses me, and abuses the power which he has over me? Oh, that I could
say that it were any other than my own husband. He that should
nourish, cherish, and protect me; he that should protect me, so that
even the winds should not blow too roughly on me—he is the man
who makes it his sport to afflict me, to expose me to every hardship,
to every insult. Or am I right in struggling to free myself from his
griping hand?

Bitter have been the years of my marriage, and sorrowful my days.
Surely the measure of them is full! My life, my strength, cannot sustain many more such.

5th January   Turned out of doors into the street! In the anguish of my
mind, I broke out into complaints; this only was my fault. I took a
chaise to Leigh; my brother not being at home, dismissed it and
stopped two nights. He brought me home with an intention to effect
either a reconciliation or a separation. He could do neither. Mr. Stock
wants me either to remain at home pennyless, as an underling to his
own daughter, or to be kept by anyone that will take me. I cannot
agree to such a reconciliation, or such a separation, whilst he has
plenty of money. I am obliged totally to withdraw myself from any
domestic affairs, in obedience to my husband's orders; to live in an
apartment alone; not to sit at table with the family, but to have my
meat sent to me; and amuse or employ myself as I can.

When and how will this end?

10th January   Still in my solitary confinement. Had a new cloak brought home, and the first thought on seeing it, was, Well! I have made sure of this, however (having long wished for a Winter garment of this description, and not had it in my power to obtain it). Alas! . . . how presumptuous! That very night might my soul have been required of me, disease have seized me, or fire have destroyed both it and me, and all else I possessed. But Thou, O Father, hast been very merciful. Yes! although my husband makes me, as it were, a prisoner in my own house, I have a Peace which he knows nothing of, a Joy which he cannot take away. Oh! that his heart would soften, and that he might repent.

16th January   My brother came with a view to assist, if in his power, to put an end to the unhappy state in which Mr. Stock and me were. It was done. My hopes are not very sanguine; but should this peace be of short continuance, or should it be more lasting than before, may I bear it meekly. . . .

· · · · ·

1821[?][1]   Repeatedly turned out destitute; twice imprisoned—the first time for a first offence of the kind; the 2d., *perfectly innocent,* having myself been beaten almost to death; several times obliged to flee for my life; the time when I broke the windows, if I had not by that means forced my way in, I must have been out all night, on the cold and wet pavement of a dark November night. I had then been turned out only for complaining, whilst enduring exceedingly unkind treatment. I was threatened with being sent to a Lunatic Asylum, only for asking for food. Cloaths I could not procure until I got them on credit; and that I did not attempt, only for the last year that I was with him. The second time I was in prison, was on a false oath; yet you said I acknowledged that I struck the man. I did not strike the man, and how you could construe the passage so, I know not. I should like to see that letter again, for I took no copy; for, owing to anguish of body from that dreadful beating, and a distraction of mind at being at the point of being a 2nd. time sent to prison by my husband out of revenge for my procuring a warrant for him, I could not copy it.

With my bruises thick upon me—bruises such as the Doctor said would have mortified had I not been so extremely thin—was I imprisoned for two days, and you would not bail me out! Oh, oh, you unnatural being. I had no money, and no provisions were sent to me, and I was obliged to beg of the person in whose custody I was! I was just on the point of being sent to Kirkdale house of Correction for the want of bail (since you would not do it), when J. Latham and G. Oakes[2] of Holland, came over and bailed me out. Oh! this was a climax of misery! 'Tis strange I did not lose my senses, to think that I should have such a husband and such a brother!

At 8 o'clock that night, my bruises still undressed, and pitiably emaciated, I had to walk with these men to Holland, 4 miles. The night was dark, wet, and winterly; but I was now among friends, and I was nursed, and soothed, and comforted. Mrs. Braithwaite's door was open to me, if my brother's was not—and her door is often open to the friendless.

I soon returned to my miserable home, for I dared not stay long away, now expecting nightly or daily to be murdered—or worse, sent to a Lunatic Asylum in my right mind; for so I was threatened; and I had no help to expect from you (for so you had assured Mr. Stock)! I had to resign myself. I expected to be again turned out, although Mr. Stock lived in another house, and to be driven out destitute as I had often been, so that I kept myself locked up day and night in my bedroom, going out only by stealth in the evening, to fetch provisions, and let Dr. Hawarden's see that I was in Wigan, and alive. On returning one night, I found my room on fire, and my bed burnt! I most solemnly declare that I was not in the house when the fire commenced. In my opinion it was done to procure my transportation, or perhaps even hanging; for I had no help to expect from you. I wish it had been investigated. I could easily have proved my innocence, and have brought home the charge to the guilty.

I had now no bed! As I was reduced lower and lower in affliction, I often exclaimed—what next? After lying some nights on a Sofa, rolled in blankets, I again found shelter at the kind Mrs. Braithwaite's of Holland.

· · · · ·

1st July 1823   Packed up Mary's doll, to send it to her with all its cloathes, and took it to Edward Melling, to take to her father's in Wigan the following morning. . . .

2d July Wednesday   When Edward returned, he brought the doll back with him, informing me that he called at a shop near Mr. Stock's (as I had directed him) to inquire first if Mary was still at home, and was there informed that Mary was, on Monday morning, 30th. inst.[3] sent off by the Coach in a hasty and rather mysterious manner. For the remainder of the day, I was almost inconsolable, so bitter and inveterate a spirit is so perpetually manifested against me by my husband. However, I began to take comfort that my child was from under the care of such a father, for she is better anywhere than with him.

3rd July   H. Latham told me he was going to St. Helens, and I instructed him to discover whether Mary was at Parr Hall or no; at night he called on his return and told me she was there. I was now quite easy about her.

•   •   •   •   •

21st October   Set off from home about 10 o'clock, to walk to Parr Hall, to see my little darling Mary, whom I had not seen since May 23d. I told no one where I was going. Not being well acquainted with the road beyond Billinge, I walked near a mile in tracing and retracing. About half past 12, I arrived there. When Mr. Grundy entered the room, he looked so grave and solemn, not the least smile embellished his features, that I thought it was a prognostication of a refusal to see my child. However, I brought a cheerful countenance, and kept it, which seemed to impart some of its influence to Mr. Grundy, for, by degrees the cloud on his brow disappeared, and he brightened his eyes and relaxed his mouth, and became very chatty and agreeable. He touched upon no topic relating to me or my child; a mother's anxiety touched my heart, for I began to fear they were conveying Mary away somewhere, she was so long in coming. In about a quarter of an hour, my little sweet one came into the parlour, looking very pale and very thin. She looked glad to see me. In a short time, dinner came in to me on a single plate. Mary was called away to dine with

her schoolfellows. This was unusual; she had always before dined
with me, in the little parlour in which I now was, except twice when
I had gone with her to the large dining-room. I suppose it was some
order of Mr. Stock's, to degrade me in the eyes of my child. However,
I ate my dinner, asking no reasons, nor making any observations. I
had come to enjoy for a short time, the company of my child, and
strove to the utmost to drive away the approaches of dejection on
being treated in so unmerited a manner. Mary came to me as soon as
she had dined, but was soon called away again, to prepare for a walk.
Mr. Grundy evidently wanted me to depart—unfeeling being! Knowing that I had walked 7 or 8 miles, and had to walk as many more, I
surely wanted resting time. I appeared not to observe his manner,
or take his hints, for I determined to stay as long as I thought proper.
Mary coming in again with her bonnet, I desired she might remain
with me, as my stay could not be so long, and she was suffered to do
so, Mr. Grundy scarcely leaving us for five minutes; in obedience, I
dare say, to Mr. Stock's instructions. It is a matter of indifference
to me whether we are alone or all the world is present. I neither mean
to run away with the child, nor to say anything to her that I fear to
have known; the greatest openness, and the strictest integrity, have
ever marked my conduct, and ever shall. At half past three, I took
leave, Mr. Grundy and Mary accompanying me a little way. Heaven
bless her! a time may come when this distressing mode of seeing
her may be done away with. If not—Thy will, O my Father, be done.
With thy help, I can resign myself cheerfully, for, in a few years,
death will silence us all, and then what matters it?

On leaving Mr. Grundy and Mary, I went with alacrity and speed,
and arrived at home about half past 5, very little fatigued. Thanks
be to Him who gives me spirit and strength.

•   •   •   •   •

13th November   My father in law was buried here this day, about one
o'clock, in rather a pompous manner, his previous circumstances
considered. I expected this would be the case, Mr. Stock thinking
probably he could blind the world to his undutiful neglect by a hearse,
3 chaises, and a dinner for 40 people at the interment of his father.
The cost of two thirds of this would have made the old man very

comfortable during some months of his life, and have been better spent. . . .

As Mr. Stock did not cause any one to inform me of his father's death, or send me any mourning, I have therefore thought it advisable not to wear any. I can feel the same respect for the old man, without any ostentatious shew, and I can ill bear the expence.

I was in hopes this event might soften his heart a little, and that something like humanity would touch it; but—he could not finish the funeral dinner before he began to pick a quarrel with his brother William at the table, before all the company, by insulting his wife! 'William,' he said, in an abrupt, peevish, sleering manner, 'whether are you or your wife president?' Mr. Stock has made many attempts to prejudice Wm. against his wife, and on this occasion, she was not invited; but as many other female relatives were even more distantly related than she, Wm. was hurt that she should be neglected, and brought her with him, and seated her by him at the dinner table; for she has ever conducted herself in a most respectable manner. This public insult wounded Wm. deeply; he was so confused, he scarcely knew what he replied, but said, 'My wife is president, because I choose to make her so; and I shall always take my wife's part as long as I live.' Saying this, he rose, greatly agitated, from the table before he had quite finished dinner, and taking his wife, quitted the room. She burst into a flood of tears; Mrs. Perkins, too, one of Mr. S's sisters, could not restrain herself, but left the room to give vent to her grief, but soon after returned. Wm. and his wife came to me at my lodgings, and returned no more to the funeral party; their minds were so deeply hurt, that they were some time before they could become composed. I could not help but weep with them, having myself so acutely suffered from the same malignant spirit. Wm., with all a Christian's meekness, prayed for his brother; his wife, in the true spirit of charity, joined him; and so most sincerely and earnestly did I, that the Almighty would turn him from the evil of his ways, ere his days were ended.

• • • • •

29 December Packed up a few toys for my little Mary, and wrote a note to Mrs. Alston, requesting her to give them to her; and to intreat Mr. Stock to let me see my child during this vacation.

. . . . .

6th January 1824   Having heard nothing respecting my child, walked over to Wigan this morning, and heard that Mr. Stock was still inflexible, and was exceedingly angry with Mrs. Alston for sending the toys to Mary at his house; at which, she is so offended, that she considers me as extremely ill used.

. . . . .

2d February   I have long contemplated writing a History of my life, and yet have deferred it from month to month, from what must appear a very strange reason by any one who sees the quantity of my writings—the reluctance I feel to attempt writing. Whether it proceeds from indolence, or some other undefinable motive, I cannot say; but whether I have a letter to write, a journal, or an account, it seems to task me; and yet the activity of my mind perpetually urges me to it. It is a strange contradiction! but are we not all strange contradictory beings.

   This day I arranged my books and writing materials on my table, determining to begin, when such a depression of spirits seized me at the melancholy retrospect, that I could not commence. I wept, I trembled, and my soul utterly refused comfort; like Rachel, I wept for my child. I tried to pray, to sing a hymn, but could do neither. I passed the whole of the day in melancholy inaction; the next day the same. I attempted to sew, I put it away again; I took my flageolet, but it pleased me not, my mind was not in tune; and living by myself, I had not a human being to speak to. If I had, it would often make me more chearful and would help greatly to restore my composure when my spirit is cast down.

4th February (Wednesday)   This morning I was enabled to overcome my unwillingness to commence my history, and made a beginning, since when, I have proceeded by little and little; but if I get on no quicker hereafter, I shall be a long time finishing it. It is for my daughter's sake I am desirous to do it, and on her account I feel it absolutely necessary.

12th February   I think of my Mary from day to day, and mean immediately to make another attempt to see her, let Mr. Grundy treat me as he may. I think he means well upon the whole, but Mr. Stock has taken so much pains to prejudice his mind against me, that he is influenced to obey Mr. S.'s tyrannical directions much more decidedly than he ought to be if he were really a Christian; which I hope he is, almost.

18 February, Wednesday   Left home a quarter before 10 o'clock this morning, to go to Parr Hall. I walked by the way of Winstanley, the Bear in the Ring, Senela Green, & Black brook. I had just sat down in the parlour, when Mr. Grundy came in, looking exceedingly solemn. Whether he really grieves for the loss of his wife, or no, I cannot say. I am not inclined to give him credit for it. I fancy the jewel is within, enclosed in a case of *black shagreen*. We had a good deal of conversation respecting my seeing Mary. Mr. Grundy informed me that he was awkwardly situated in regard to her, but would endeavour to procure some precise instructions, and for the present Mary should be immediately introduced to me. She came, little darling, as soon as she was summoned, and embraced me most affectionately. She is extremely tall for her age, and very thin and pale, but says she is well. I staid with her till a quarter past 3, and then left, perhaps never to see her more; for her father, in his mad passions, declares if I do not cease attempting to see her, he will place her where no one but himself shall ever know. Poor Mary, what is to become of her?

I got home at 1/2 past 5, very little fatigued.

As I told Mr. Grundy that if I had not much more liberty of seeing my child, I should certainly return to Mr. Stock and run whatever risk I may of having my life sacrificed by his brutality,[4] and requested him to inform Mr. Stock of my determination, perhaps ere another year has elapsed, I may have breathed my last. Oh, my Father! look with pity on thy oppressed servant; extend thy protecting arm over me, and put into my heart what Thou wouldest have me do. If I go to my husband, go with me; if I should not go, put such obstacles in the way as shall entirely prevent my attempting it; be with me at all times, for if Thou forsakest me, I am lost. Oh, be with me, and protect me.

· · · · ·

30 April, Friday   Having waited for 2 or 3 days for fair weather, that I might walk over to Parr Hall to see my little daughter once more before I went to London,[5] I set out this day at 10 o'clock. The morning was fair and bright, but the wind blew quite a hard gale, and I had great difficulty in forcing my way through it, for it blew right in my face. I had for some weeks been rather weak and indisposed, and, on setting out today, almost despaired of accomplishing so long a journey on foot; but a mother's heart can do great things. The farther I proceeded, the more light and active I felt, and I arrived at Parr Hall at half-past 12. Miss Hammond, the teacher who was engaged on Mrs. Grundy's death, opened the door, and as I followed her through the writing room, my little Mary, who was there, advanced to me immediately, and we retired together to the little back-parlour where I always sit when at Parr Hall. Feeling apprehensive that Mr. Stock may remove my child some time when he thinks I am quite unprepared for such a blow, and she may be placed where I could not discover her, I had prepared a card with a direction for Miss Dannett of Up-Holland, and gave it to her now, telling her, that if ever she were removed to any other school, she must take an opportunity, in private, of writing to inform me where she was, and with whom, and to direct for Miss Dannett (for if my name was on the direction, it might be intercepted at the Post Office); and be very careful with whom she intrusted it, to put it there.

The child is so young that I fear she will hardly be able to manage such a business, should there be occasion. This is the beginning of my instruction to her to do anything in secret; but after much hesitation and mature deliberation, I have come to the decision that if I had taken no such precaution, I should have been sadly wanting in duty as a mother. That it should be necessary, must lie at Mr. Stock's door; and on his head be the guilt. If he would act as a husband and a father ought to do, there would be no occasion to keep anything secret from him; it would be a crime to attempt it. I told Mary to put the card at the bottom of her box, and shew it no one; and if any one should see it, I think they would not know what it meant. I staid with her until 4 o'clock, and then returned home, less fatigued with a 12 or 14 miles walk than might have been expected.

· · · · ·

28th August   Walked to Parr Hall to see Mary, my dear, dear, child Mary, and spent some hours with her most delightfully, walking in the garden together a long time. Whether I must ever see her again, is doubtful, for Mr. Grundy told me that Mr. Stock had again enjoined him not to let me see her without his previous permission. I fear I shall be forced back again to my husband's house, for I will not very long be so treated; Mary's welfare demands that she either never goes home, or that her mother should be there. I walked back with great ease, and little or no fatigue, and perfectly safe. 14 miles.

• • • • •

22nd March 1825   Set off to Liverpool on foot at 1/2 past 8 o'clock, and prevailed with Mrs. Price[6] to accompany me from Seymour St. to Mr. Perkins, 14 Roscoe Lane, brother-in-law to Mr. Stock, to request his mediation, and that of Mrs. Perkins, to prevail with Mr. Stock to let me have more liberty in seeing Mary, and to increase my income. Mrs. Perkins was not at home. Mr. Perkins was so kind and friendly, that I was quite rejoiced and grateful; he promised me to make the attempt.[7] I returned home, feeling as if God had prospered my going out this day, as well as on Sunday.

• • • • •

29th March Tuesday   As Mary had requested me last Sunday but one to buy a few prunes and some Spanish Juice for her, I had no way of conveying them to her but by taking them myself to the old woman at the cottage, near Parr Hall gate; so this morning I purchased, and took them. It was a lovely morning, and I had a very pleasant walk. I sat about 1/4 of an hour with the old woman, who promised to take up the parcel to the Hall, and give it to the cook, which she said was the only way, for otherwise Mary would not get it. When I had arrived within a quarter of a mile of St. Helens on my return, I heard a horse following; the rider was on the trot, but slackened pace when he came up with me. I had my parasol up, and never turned my head to look at him, but kept my face covered with my parasol whilst he was approaching. I was imagining it might be Mr. Grundy following me, to give me some information or other, and when for a minute he walked by my side, I peeped a little under my parasol, and saw the legs of a fine horse, and the accoutrements of a well saddled one, but raised my eyes or uncovered my face no further—how fortunate that I did not! for, when he had got a few yards before me, I ventured to look out, and—beheld Mr. Stock! dressed in a beautiful dark puce-coloured coat, and every thing else corresponding. He was either tipsy, or one of his nervous agitations had come upon him; he wriggled and twitched upon the horse most comically, pulling the horse to stop, and whipping to make it go. At length, the harrassed animal tried what a trot would do, and away they went, jogglety, jogglety, and were soon out of my sight. Mr. Stock never saw my face, and whether he knew me, I cannot say; I suspect he did.

It was very unlucky I should be overtaken so short a way from Parr Hall; had I been nearer Prescot, I should not have cared; he will suspect my errand, and the old woman at the cottage will be prevented admitting me again. I dare say he was at Parr Hall whilst I was at the cottage—it cannot be helped now!

It was Mary herself who told me, that her aunt Perkins last Christmas, when she was at Mr. Stock's house for a part of Mary's holidays, urged him every day to alter his present system as regarded his wife and child. I had not an opportunity of asking Mary more particularly what it was precisely that her aunt said to her father, but it raised my hopes so much, that 2 days after, I walked to Liverpool and called upon them.

· · · · ·

10th April Sunday   At one o'clock in the afternoon, I took a walk to St. Helen's to meet my little darling again; an unusual trepidation and anxiety seized me as I went, but exerting as much fortitude as possible, I endeavoured to divert my thoughts by the beauties of the scenery; for indeed, my indulgent Father had gilded the prospect by a glorious sun and a clear atmosphere. I proceeded to the farther part of St. Helen's, but had not met my child. My knees trembled so, that I went into one of a row of cottages where a fruit shop was kept, and requested leave to sit down. A very neat-looking young married woman was in, and was very civil indeed. As I sat waiting, I told her my situation as regarded my child, and she seemed to pity me much. I said I was afraid that when Mr. Grundy and Mr. Stock found that I made a practice of meeting her on the way to Chapel, they would prevent her going; but I had no other method left, and I considered it to be my duty to see her in any way I could. I was afraid that this might be the last time; and I added, 'Judge then what must be my feelings at this moment,'—for I was very faint.

Bye and bye Miss Jackson, the head teacher, came past, and the whole train of boarders; my anxiety confused my sight, and I could not recognize my Mary. I sat in a corner by the window, so that they could not see me; for I was afraid the young woman might suffer some unpleasant treatment on my account if they saw who afforded me shelter; for such is Mr. Stock's unceasing bitter and dreadful persecution against me, and I should be sorry that a single human being should lose so much as a penny on my account, or have one uneasy moment.

When the whole of the Parr Hall family had passed, I issued forth and hastened to overtake them, that I might be quite sure whether Mary was there. I asked Miss Hammand, one of the teachers who walked last, whether Mary was there; she replied that she was at the front, with a very haughty, forbidding nod, which I cannot soon forget. Oh, my Father, have pity, have pity on thy suffering servant! Thou knowest that from my fellow creatures I deserve not this cruel treatment.

I hastened forward and saw my Mary next after Miss Jackson; the change from Winter habiliments to Summer ones, had been one means of preventing my knowing her. Miss Jackson spoke and looked kindly. Heaven bless her for it! but it is in her very nature. We were soon at Chapel, and I determined on entering, that I might enjoy the sight of my child another hour. Miss Jackson directed me to the Pew next Mary's. During service, Mary became very faint; poor child! I know thy feelings are harrassed. One of the young ladies, apparently about 14, looked at me with a peculiar degree of compassion. On coming out, Mr. Grundy and Wm. Woodward[8] had got their heads together, talking in a low tone. Mr. Grundy perhaps was afraid that Wm. Woodward might tell Mr. Stock that he had seen me at Chapel in Mr. Grundy's pew, as if Mr. G. encouraged me, and so perhaps he was explaining.

I took leave of Mary at the Chapel door, timid and spiritless, afraid of going to too great lengths; yet Mary's indisposition would well have justified me in going part of the way homeward with her. I re-

pented ever since that I had not; but I have not the spirit of a mouse. I
was just arrived at the outskirts of St. Helen's when two young
women speaking to me by name requested I would go with them
home to tea. I hesitated a moment, not knowing them, but their looks
were kindly, and I, expressing myself pleased with the friendliness of
their manner, accompanied them. They led me near a mile, and I
began to wonder where they were taking me to. At length, they made
up to a gentleman's house and grounds. Will they lead me to the
front door, thought I; but I inquired not. At last they entered a cottage
in an out-building, where was an elderly, sickly-looking woman,
laid on a sopha, and there I sat down.

They had heard of my situation, and offered me the calling there at
any time when I wished to meet with Mary at Chapel, as it lay between St. Helen's and Prescot, and in Summer is a very pleasant way
through fields. The Almighty raises me Comforters among the poor,
if I want friends among the rich. . . .

8th June   The storminess of the weather is still such as wholly to
prevent my going out, except a few errands; the wind, as well as rain,
is violent. I find from the papers, that there was a tremendous thun-
derstorm at Manchester the night that I was at Conway. It seems to
have let loose an amazing quantity of wind. For amusement I have
been obliged to resort to a circulating library (Pool and Harding's).
'Brighton on the Steyne,' a satirical work, was the first I got hold of. I
would not have wasted my time with it, had I known what kind of
composition it was; a great deal of profligate sentiment is elicited, and
the vilest conduct towards women, particularly wives, treated with
the utmost levity, as a very trivial kind of offence; nay even as afford-
ing much amusement; and characters ranking high as to title and
warlike achievements, are little, if at all, censured for the most diabol-
ical conduct towards women, when, if there be one crime of greatest
magnitude, it is that!

If man injures man, the injured has a great portion of power to
defend himself, either from natural strength of body, of [or?] resolution, of [or?] the countenance of many of his fellows, or from the
laws; but when man injures woman, how can she defend herself? Her

frame is weaker, her spirit timid; and if she be a wife, there is scarce
a man anywhere to be found who will use the slightest exertion in her
defence; and her own sex cannot, having no powers. She has no hope
from law; for man, woman's enemy, exercises, as well as makes those
laws. She cannot have a jury of her peers or equals, for men, every
where prejudiced against the sex, are her jurors; man is her judge.
Thus situated, thus oppressed, she lives miserably, and by inches sinks
into the grave. This is the lot not merely of a few, but of one half, if
not two thirds of the sex! That a man who will use a woman with
cruelty, is a coward, a despicable villain, may be asserted by one of his
own sex who has perhaps some share of probity. He is so. But then,
according to that assertion, there is a prodigious number of cowards
and of villains; I may justly say, seven eighths. I scarcely go into a
house in which there is not a fornicator, a seducer, an adulterer, a ty-
rant. Even here—see a poor suffering creature in the person of Mrs.
Hughes. She is consuming with a vile disorder, given to her by her
wretch of a husband. She is in continual pain, and must die; she cannot
be cured. To see such a sweet, innocent, mild-tempered woman, in
such constant agony, rouses the utmost indignation against the fellow
who could prove himself so like a fiend; yet this is not an uncommon
case. My own experience of the world shews me many such. What
numbers of men murder their wives; and that, by the most cruel of all
means—slow torture.

Notes

❧

*These selections are taken from vol. 2 :*1811–1825* of *Miss Weeton: Journal of a Governess, 1807–1825*, ed. Edward Hall, 2 vols. (London: Oxford University Press / Humphrey Milford, 1936–39).

1   Letter-journal entry to her brother Tom; undated by editor but numbered 390.

2   She had done a favor for Oakes many years previously.

3   Mary was already a boarding pupil at Mr. Grundy's Parr Hall, but paid visits to her father. Weeton's *inst.* perhaps signifies *ult.*, for *ultimo*, meaning in the last (the preceding) month.

4   Weeton did not return to Stock.

5   A visit intended as a pleasure trip. Weeton had not returned to Stock.

6   A friend of long standing.

7   Weeton followed up this visit with an impassioned letter begging that he would directly intervene with Stock. She also wrote (unsuccessfully) to Stock asking for £200 a year for life and freedom equal with his to see Mary.

8   Stock's brother-in-law.

Jane Carlyle

(1801–1866)

JANE BAILLIE WELSH CARLYLE was the only child of a prosperous Scottish surgeon, Dr. Welsh of Haddington, whose heiress she
became when he died in 1819 (though she later made over most of
her income to her mother). A bright, strong-willed child devoted to
her father, she was so distressed by his death that she became sickly
for years. Precocious as well, she insisted on being thoroughly educated and was sent to the Haddington school to learn Latin, where
eventually she fell in love with one of the masters. But though for him
she turned down many other suitors, he married another woman in
1823. He had, however, introduced her in 1821 to the historian and
philosopher Thomas Carlyle, who, attracted by her brilliance, pro-
cured books for her and wrote her letters intended to guide her intellect. Recognizing Thomas's superior intelligence, Jane returned his
interest, and her respect for him gradually extended to love. They
were married in 1826 and lived in Scotland and London at different
periods, settling finally in Chelsea, London, in 1834. Their childless
marriage was beset with financial difficulties and the strains of Thomas's constitutional irritability plus her frequent depressions, and
she was oftentimes lonely while he worked. Although their finances
improved as Thomas's literary reputation grew, and Jane gradually
formed her own circle of London friends, happiness eluded her.
Thomas, who brooked no criticism of his ways, began to socialize
with Lord and Lady Ashburton at Bath House, where Jane felt unwanted even if invited along. She and Thomas became seriously
estranged, as these excerpts from her 1855–56 diary show.* Jane destroyed all her other diaries (except a fragment for 1845) before her
sudden death from stroke or heart failure, but those pages recording a
year of distress she deliberately or accidentally kept, and at least posthumously they aroused Thomas's remorse.

From Jane Carlyle's Diary

21 October 1855   I remember Charles Buller saying of the Duchess de Praslin's murder, 'What could a poor fellow do with a wife who kept a journal but murder her?' There was a certain truth hidden in this light remark. Your journal all about feelings aggravates whatever is factitious and morbid in you; that I have made experience of. And now the only sort of journal I would keep should have to do with what Mr. Carlyle calls 'the fact of things.' It is very bleak and barren, this fact of things, as I now see it—very; and what good is to result from writing of it in a paper book is more than I can tell. But I have taken a notion to, and perhaps I shall blacken more paper this time, when I begin quite promiscuously without any moral end in view; but just as the Scotch professor drank whiskey, because I like it, and because it's cheap.

22 October   I was cut short in my introduction last night by Mr. C.'s return from Bath House. That eternal Bath House. I wonder how many thousand miles Mr. C. has walked between there and here, putting it all together; setting up always another milestone and another betwixt himself and me. Oh, good gracious! when I first noticed that heavy yellow house without knowing, or caring to know, who it belonged to, how far I was from dreaming that through years and years I should carry every stone's weight of it on my heart. About feelings already! Well, I will not proceed, though the thoughts I had in my bed about all that were tragical enough to fill a page of thrilling interest for myself, and though, as George Sand has shrewdly remarked, 'rien ne soulage comme la rhétorique.'[1]

23 October   A stormy day within doors, so I walked out early, and walked, walked, walked. If peace and quietness be not in one's own power, one can always give oneself at least bodily fatigue—no such bad succedaneum [substitute] after all. Life gets to look for me like a sort of kaleidoscope—a few things of different colors—black predominating, which fate shakes into new and ever new combinations, but always the same things over again. Today has been so like a day I still remember out of ten years ago; the same still dreamy October weather, the same tumult of mind contrasting with the outer stillness;

the same causes for that tumult. Then, as now, I had walked, walked, walked, with no aim but to tire myself.

25 October   Oh, good gracious alive; what a whirlwind—or rather whirlpool—of a day! Breakfast had 'passed off' better or worse, and I was at work on a picture-frame, my own invention, and pretending to be a little work of art, when Mr. C.'s bell rang like mad, and was followed by cries of 'Come, come! Are you coming?' Arrived at the second landing, three steps at a time, I saw Mr. C. and Ann in the spare bedroom hazily through a waterfall! The great cistern had over-flowed, and was raining and pouring down through the new ceiling, and plashing up on the new carpet. All the baths and basins in the house were quickly assembled on floor, and I, on my knees, mopping up with towels and sponges, &c.

In spite of this disaster, and the shocking bad temper induced by it, I have had to put on my company face to-night and receive. —— and —— were the party. Decidedly I must have a little of 'that damned thing called the milk of human kindness' after all, for the assurance that poor —— was being amused kept me from feeling bored.

My heart is very sore to-night, but I have promised myself not to make this journal a 'miserere,' so I will take a dose of morphia and do the impossible to sleep.

31 October   Rain! rain! rain! 'Oh, Lord! this is too ridiculous,' as the Annandale farmer exclaimed, starting to his feet when it began pour-ing, in the midst of his prayer for a dry hay time. I have no hay to be got in, or anything else that I know of, to be got in; but I have a plentiful crop of thorns to be got out, and that, too, requires good weather. To day's post brought the kindest of letters from Geraldine,[2] enclosing a note from Lady de Kapel Broke she is staying with, invit-ing me to Oakley Hall. This lady's 'faith in things unseen' excited similar faith on my part, and I would go, had I nothing to consider but how I should like it when there. I had to write a refusal, however. Mr. C. is 'neither to hold nor bind' when I make new visiting ac-quaintances on my own basis, however unexceptionable the person may be. The evening devoted to mending Mr. C's trowsers among other things! 'Being an only child,' I never 'wished' to sew men's trowsers—no, never!

1 November   At last a fair morning to rise to, thanks God! Mazzini[3] never says 'thank God' by any chance, but always 'thanks God,' and I find it sound[s] more grateful. Fine weather outside in fact, but indoors blowing a devil of a gale. Off into space, then, to get the green mould that has been gathering upon me of late days brushed off by human contact.

5 November   Alone this evening. Lady A, in town again; and Mr. C. of course at Bath House.

> When I think of what I is
>   And what I used to was,
> I gin to think I've sold myself
>   For very little cas.

6 November   Mended Mr. C.'s dressing gown. Much movement under the free sky is needful for me to keep my heart from throbbing up into my head and maddening it. They must be comfortable people who have leisure to think about going to Heaven! My most constant and pressing anxiety is to keep out of Bedlam! that's all. . . . Ach! If there were no feelings 'what steady sailing craft we should be,' as the nautical gentleman of some novel says.

7 November   Dear, dear! What a sick day this has been with me. Oh, my mother! nobody sees when I am suffering now; and I have learnt to suffer 'All to myself.' From 'only childless' to that, is a far and rough road to travel.

> Oh, little did my mother think,
>   The day she cradled me,
> The lands I was to travel in,
>   The death I was to dee.

[?] November   'S'exagérer ses droits, oublier ceux des autres, cela peut être fort commode; mais cela n'est pas toujours profitable et on a lieu souvent de s'en repentir. Il vaudrait mieux souvent avoir des vices qu'un caractère difficile. Pour que les femmes perdent les familles, il faut qu'elles aillent jusqu'à l'inconduite, jusqu'au désordre. Pour les y

pousser, it suffit souvent qu'un homme gâte toutes ses bonnes qualités et les leurs par des procédés injustes, de la dureté et du dédain.'[4]

It is not always, however, that unjust treatment, harshness, and disdain in her husband drives a woman *jusqu'au désordre* [to disorderly conduct], but it drives her to something, and something not to his advantage any more than to hers.

To-day has been like other days outwardly. I have done this and that, and people have come and gone, but all as in a bad dream.

· · · · ·

20 November   I have been fretting inwardly all this day at the prospect of having to go and appeal before the Tax Commissioners at Kensington to-morrow morning. Still, it must be done. If Mr. C. should go himself he would run his head against some post in his impatience; and besides, for me, when it is over it will be over, whereas he would not get the better of it for twelve months—if ever at all.

21 November   O me miseram![5] not one wink of sleep the whole night through! so great the 'rale mental agony in my own inside' at the thought of that horrid appealing. It was feeling like the ghost of a dead dog, that I rose and dressed and drank my coffee, and then started off for Kensington. Mr. C. said, 'the voice of honour seemed to call on him to go himself.' But either it did not call loud enough, or he would not listen to that charmer. I went in a cab, to save all my breath for appealing. Set down at 30 Hornton Street, I found a dirty private-like house, only with Tax Office painted on the door. A dirty woman-servant opened the door, and told me the Commissioners would not be there for half-an-hour, but I might walk up. There were already some half-score of men assembled in the waiting-room, among whom I saw the man who cleans our clocks, and a young apothecary of Cheyne Walk. All the others, to look at them, could not have been suspected for an instant, I should have said, of making a hundred a year. Feeling in a false position, I stood by myself at a window and 'thought shame' (as children say). Men trooped in by twos and threes, till the small room was pretty well filled; at last a woman showed herself. O my! did I ever know the full value of any sort of woman— as woman—before! By this time some benches had been brought in, and I was sitting nearest the door. The woman sat down on the

same bench with me, and, misery acquainting one with strange bed-
fellows, we entered into conversation without having been introduced,
and I had 'the happiness,' as Allan termed it, 'of seeing a woman
more miserable than myself.' Two more women arrived at intervals,
one a young girl of Dundee, 'sent by my uncle that's ill;' who looked
to be always recapitulating inwardly what she had been told to say
to the Commissioners. The other, a widow, and such a goose, poor
thing; she was bringing an appeal against no overcharge in her individual paper, but against the doubling of the Income Tax. She had
paid the double tax once, she said, because she was told they would
take her goods for it if she didn't—and it was so disgraceful for one in
a small business to have her goods taken; besides it was very disad-
vantageous; but now that it was come round again she would [not?]
give. She seemed to attach an irresistible pathos to the title of *widow,*
this woman. 'And me a widow, ma'm,' was the winding up of her
every paragraph. The men seemed as worried as the women, though
they put a better face on it, even carrying on a sort of sickly laughing
and bantering with one another. 'First-come lady.' called the clerk,
opening a small side-door, and I stept forward into a *grand peutêtre.*[6]
There was an instant of darkness while the one door was shut behind
and the other opened in front; and there I stood in a dim room where
three men sat round a large table spread with papers. One held a
pen ready over an open ledger; another was taking snuff, and had
taken still worse in his time, to judge by his shaky, clayed appearance.
The third, who was plainly the cock of that dung-heap, was sitting
for Rhadamanthus[7]—a Rhadamanthus without the justice. 'Name,'
said the horned-owl-looking individual holding the pen. 'Carlyle.'
'What?' 'Carlyle.' Seeing he still looked dubious, I spelt it for him.
'Ha!' cried Rhadamanthus, a big, bloodless-faced, insolent-looking
fellow. 'What is this? why is Mr. Carlyle not come himself? didn't he
get a letter ordering him to appear? Mr. Carlyle wrote some nonsense
about being exempted from coming, and I desired an answer to be
sent that he must come, must do as other people.' 'Then, sir,' I said,
'your desire has been neglected, it would seem, my husband having
received no such letter; and I was told by one of your fellow Commissioners that Mr. Carlyle's personal appearance was not indispens-

able.' 'Huffgh! Huffgh! what does Mr. Carlyle mean by saying he
has no income from his writings, when he himself fixed it in the beginning at a hundred and fifty?' 'It means, sir, that, in ceasing to write,
one ceases to be paid for writing, and Mr. Carlyle has published
nothing for several years.' 'Huffgh! Huffgh! I understand nothing
about that.' 'I do,' whispered the snuff-taking Commissioner at my
ear. 'I can quite understand a literary man does not always make
money. I would take it off, for my share, but (sinking his voice still
lower) I am only one voice here, and not the most important.' 'There,'
said I, handing to Rhadamanthus Chapman and Hall's account; 'that
will prove Mr. Carlyle's statement.' 'What am I to make of that?
Huffgh! we should have Mr. Carlyle here to swear to this before we
believe it.' 'If a gentleman's word of honour written at the bottom
of that paper is not enough, you can put me on my oath: I am ready
to swear to it.' 'You! you, indeed! No, no! we can do nothing with
your oath.' 'But, sir, I understand my husband's affairs fully, better
than he does himself.' 'That I can well believe; but we can make nothing of this,' flinging my document contemptuously on the table.
The horned owl picked it up, glanced over it while Rhadamanthus
was tossing papers about, and grumbling about 'people that wouldn't
conform to rules;' then handed it back to him, saying deprecatingly:
'But, sir, this is a very plain statement.' 'Then what has Mr. Carlyle to
live upon? You don't mean to tell me he lives on that?' pointing to
the document. 'Heaven forbid, sir! but I am not here to explain what
Mr. Carlyle has to live on, only to declare his income from literature
during the last three years.' 'True! true!' mumbled the not-most-
important voice at my elbow. 'Mr. Carlyle, I believe, has landed income.' 'Of which,' said I haughtily, for my spirit was up, 'I have
fortunately no account to render in this kingdom and to this board.'
'Take off fifty pounds, say a hundred—take off a hundred pounds,'
said Rhadamanthus to the horned owl. 'If we write Mr. Carlyle down
a hundred and fifty he has no reason to complain, I think. There,
you may go. Mr. Carlyle has no reason to complain.' Second-come
woman was already introduced, and I was motioned to the door; but
I could not depart without saying that 'at all events there was no use in
complaining, since they had the power to enforce their decision.' On

stepping out, my first thought was, what a mercy Carlyle didn't come himself! For the rest, though it might have gone better, I was thankful that it had not gone worse. When one has been threatened with a great injustice, one accepts a smaller as a favour.

Went back to spend the evening with Geraldine when Mr. C. set forth for Bath House. Her ladyship in town for two days.

28 November —Took the black silk—presented me with last Christmas to Catchpool, that it might be made up. 'Did you buy this yourself, ma'am?' said Catchpool, rubbing it between her finger and thumb. 'No, it was a present; but why do you ask?' 'Because ma'am, I was thinking, if you bought it yourself, you had been taken in. It is so poor; very trashy indeed. I don't think I ever saw so trashy a moire.'

4 December I hardly even begin to write here that I am not tempted to break out into Jobisms about my bad nights. How I keep on my legs and in my senses with such little snatches of sleep is a wonder to myself. Oh, to cure anyone of a terror of annihilation, just put him on my allowance of sleep, and see if he don't get to long for sleep, sleep, unfathomable and everlasting sleep as the only conceivable heaven.

11 December Oh dear! I wish this Grange business[8] were well over. It occupies me (the mere preparation for it) to the exclusion of all quiet thought and placid occupation. To have to care for my dress at this time of day more than I ever did when young and pretty and happy (God bless me, to think that I was once all that!) on penalty of being regarded as a blot on the Grange gold and azure, is really too bad. *Ach Gott!* if we had been left in the sphere of life we belong to, how much better it would have been for us in many ways!

24 March 1856 We are now at the 24th of March, 1856, and from this point of time, my journal, let us renew our daily intercourse without looking back. Looking back was not intended by nature, evidently, from the fact that our eyes are in our faces and not in our hind heads. Look straight before you, then, Jane Carlyle, and, if possible, not over the heads of things either, away into the distant vague. Look, above all, at the duty nearest hand, and what's more, do it. Ah, the spirit is willing, but the flesh is weak, and four weeks of illness have made mine weak as water. No galloping over London as in seven-leagued boots for me at present. To-day I walked with effort one little mile, and thought it a great feat; but if the strength has gone out of me, so also has the unrest. I can sit and lie even very patiently doing nothing. To be sure, I am always going on with the story in my head, as poor Paulet expressed it; but even that has taken a dreamy contemplative character, and excites no emotions 'to speak of.' In fact, sleep has come to look to me the highest virtue and the greatest happiness; that is, good sleep, untroubled, beautiful, like a child's. Ah me!

·   ·   ·   ·   ·

11 April   To-day I called on 'my lady' [9] come to town for season. She was perfectly civil, for a wonder. . . .

21 April   I feel weaklier every day, and my soul also is sore vexed— Oh how long! I put myself in an omnibus, being unable to walk, and was carried to Islington and back again. What a good shilling's-worth of exercise! The Angel at Islington! It was there I was set down on my first arrival in London, and Mr. C. with Edward Irving was waiting to receive me.

The past is past, and gone is gone.

29 May   Old Mrs. D. said to me the other day when I encountered her after two years, 'Yes, ma'am, my daughter is dead: only child, house, and everything gone from me; and I assure you I stand up in the world as if it was not the world at all any more.'

Mr. B. says nine-tenths of the misery of human life proceeds according to his observation from the institution of marriage. He should say from the demoralisation, the desecration, of the institution of marriage, and then I should cordially agree with him.

Notes

❧

*These selections are taken from vol. 2 of *Letters and Memorials of Jane Welsh Carlyle*, ed. J. A. Froude, 2 vols. (New York and London: Harper and Bros., 1883). The rest of her extant diary for 1855–56 may be found in vol. 2 of *New Letters and Memorials of Jane Welsh Carlyle*, ed. Alexander Carlyle (London: John Lane, 1903).

1 Nothing is so comforting as rhetoric.

2 Geraldine Jewsbury, her closest friend.

3 Giuseppe Mazzini (1805–72), the Italian republican patriot.

4 To exaggerate one's own rights, to forget those of others, that can be very useful; but it is not always profitable and often obliges one to repent. Often it would be better to have vices than a demanding personality. For women to lose their families, they have to go as far as misconduct, even disorderly conduct. To push them into it, it often suffices that a man ruin all his good qualities and theirs by unjust treatment, harshness and disdain.

5 Oh, wretched me!

6 A great perhaps.

7 In Homer's *Odyssey*, Rhadamanthys, along with his brother King Minos, dispenses justice among the dead in the paradise of the Elysian plain.

8 One of Lady Harriet Ashburton's homes was the Grange at Addiscombe, where Jane had been invited to accompany Thomas to a house party.

9 Presumably Lady Ashburton.

Hester Thrale

(1741–1821)

HESTER THRALE, the only child of John and Hester Salusbury, was educated unusually well for her day, studying romance languages, Latin, and literature; her training bore fruit in her frequent writing from 1776 on. Her father's absence during her childhood attempting to improve his fortunes in Nova Scotia (his Welsh estate was heavily mortgaged) strengthened her ties to her mother, and they always remained close. At twenty-two, by her mother's choice she married Henry Thrale, an Oxford man ten years her senior but the owner of a brewery in Southwark, plus substantial other property, and M. P. for Streatham. Samuel Johnson became a close family friend with whom in 1774 she visited Wales and whose letters she published in 1788. At his suggestion, Thrale in 1776 began her loquacious *Thraliana,* as her diary till 1809 was titled; after 1779 it replaced her *Family Book* diary, begun in 1766 to record her twelve children's histories. Only five daughters survived early childhood, one (Harriet) subsequently died, and the three eldest of the four who remained (Hester Maria, b. 1764; Susan, b. 1770; Sophy, b. 1771; and Cecilia, b. 1777) were to be a source of grief when Thrale determined to remarry after Henry's death in 1781. Her choice, to the consternation not only of her daughters but also of friends like Johnson and Fanny Burney, was Gabriel Mario Piozzi (1740–1809), formerly singing master for Hester Maria (nicknamed Queeney by Johnson for her imperious ways). As these 1782–84 excerpts show,* Thrale at her daughters' insistence first sent Piozzi away, but then obtained grudging permission to recall him after suffering a nervous breakdown nursing Sophy through a near-fatal illness. She married Piozzi in 1784, and they remained in Italy until 1787. Eventually Cecilia lived with them for awhile, but relations with the other girls remained cool and worsened greatly when the Piozzis adopted Gabriel's nephew as heir.

From Hester Thrale's Diary

26 September–1 October 1782 . . . Here I have finished the Epitaph for my Husband, I mean the Transcribing it—& now I am going to leave Stretham for three Years, where I lived—never happily indeed,. [*sic*] but always easily: the more so perhaps from the total Absence of Love and of Ambition

> Else those two passions by the way
> Might chance to show us scurvy Play.[1]

Now! that little dear discerning Creature Fanny Burney says I'm in love with Piozzi—very likely! he is so amiable, so honourable, so much above his Situation by his Abilities, that if

> Fate had'nt fast bound her
> With Styx nine Times round her
> Sure Musick & Love were victorious.[2]

but if he is ever so worthy, ever so lovely, he is *below me* forsooth: in what is he below me? in Virtue—I would I were above him; in Understanding—I would mine were from this Instant under the Guardianship of his:—in Birth—to be sure he is below me in birth, & so is almost every Man I know, or have a Chance to know;—but he is below me in Fortune—is mine sufficient for us both? more than amply so. does he deserve it by his Conduct in which he has always united warm notions of Honour, with cool attention to Œconomy; the Spirit of a Gentleman with the Talents of a Professor? how shall any Man deserve Fortune if he does not? but I am the guardian of five daughters by Mr. Thrale, and must not disgrace *their* Name & Family—Was then the Man my Mother chose for me of higher Extraction than him I have chosen for myself? No.—but his Fortune was higher—I wanted Fortune *then* perhaps, do I want it *now?* Not at all. but I am not to think about myself, I married the first Time to please my Mother, I must marry the second Time to please my Daughter— I have always sacrificed my own Choice to that of others, so I must

sacrifice it again:—but why? Oh because I am a Woman of superior
Understanding, & must not for the World degrade my self from my
Situation in Life. but if I *have* superior Understanding, let me at least
make use of it for once; & rise to the Rank of a human Being conscious of its own power to discern Good from Ill—the person who
has uniformly acted by the Will of others, has hardly that Dignity
to boast. but once again I am Guardian to five Girls; agreed—will this
Connection prejudice their Bodies, Souls, or Purse? my Marriage
may assist *my* Health, but I suppose it will not injure *theirs:*—will his
Company or Companions corrupt their Morals; God forbid, if I did
not believe him one of the best of our Fellow Beings I would reject
him instantly. Can it injure their Fortunes? and could he impoverish
(if he would) five Women to whom their Father left 20,000£ each—
independent almost of Possibilities?

To what then am I Guardian? to their Pride and Prejudice? & is
anything else affected by the Alliance?

Now for more solid Objections. Is not the Man of whom I desire
Protection a Foreigner? unskilled in the Laws and Language of our
Country certainly. Is he not as the French say *Arbitre de mon sort?*[3]
& from the Hour he possesses my person & Fortune have I any power
of decision how or where I may continue or end my Life? Is not the
man upon the Continuance of whose Affection my whole Happiness
depends—*younger* than myself,[4] & is it wise to place one's Happiness
on the Continuance of *any* Man's Affection?—would it not be painful
to owe his appearance of Regard more to his Honour than his Love?
& is not my Person already faded, likelier to fade soon than his? on
the other hand is *his* Life a good one? & would it not be Lunacy even
to risque the Wretchedness of losing all Situation in the World for
the sake of living with a Man one loves, and then to lose both Companion and Consolation. When I lost Mr. Thrale, every one was
officious to comfort & soothe me: but which of my Children or
quondam friends would look with kindness upon Piozzi's Widow? if I
bring Children by him must they not be Catholicks, & must not I
live among People, the *ritual* part of whose Religion I disapprove?

These are *my* Objections, these *my* Fears: not those of being cen-

sured by the World as it is called—a Composition of Vice & Folly.
though 'tis surely no good Joke to be talked of

> by each affected She that tells my Story
> and blesses her good Stars that *She* was prudent.[5]

These Objections would increase in Strength too, if my present
State was a happy one. but it really is not: I live a quiet Life, but not a
pleasant one: My Children govern without loving me, my Servants
devour & despise me, my Friends caress and censure me, my Money
wastes in Expences I do not enjoy, and my Time in Trifles I do not
approve. every one is made Insolent, & no one Comfortable. my
Reputation unprotected, my Heart unsatisfied, my Health unsettled.

I will however resolve on nothing, I will take a Voyage to the
Continent in Spring; enlarge my Knowledge, & repose my Purse:
Change of Place may turn the Course of these Ideas, and external
Objects supply the room of internal Felicity. If he follows me, I may
reject or receive at Pleasure the Addresses of a Man who follows on
no *explicit Promise,* nor much probability of Success, for I wd. really
wish to marry no more without the Consent of my Children, (such I
mean as are qualified to give their Opinions:) & how should *Miss
Thrale*[6] approve of my marrying *Mr.* Piozzi? here then I rest, & will
torment my Mind no longer, but commit myself as he advises to the
Hand of Providence, & all will end all 'ottima Perfezzione,[7] & if I *am*
blest with obtaining the Man—the only Man I ever could have loved,
I verily believe it will be only because the Almighty will not leave
such Virtue as his—unrewarded.

· · · · · ·

4 November[8]   . . . Sir Richard Musgrave has sent me proposals of
Marriage from Ireland. His Wife is dying at least if not dead, & he is
in haste for a better—He will get *me* to be sure!! a likely matter! when
My Head is full of nothing but my Children—my Heart of my beloved Piozzi! . . .

I had looked ill or perhaps appeared to fret so much that my eldest
Daughter would—out of Tenderness perhaps—force me to an expla-

nation. I could however have evaded it if I would, but my heart was
bursting, & partly from instinctive Desire of unloading it—partly
I hope from principle too, I called her into my Room & fairly told her
the Truth: told her the Strength of my Passion for Piozzi, the Imprac-
ticability of my living without him; the opinion I had of his Merit,
& the Resolution I had taken to marry him, of all this She could not
have been ignorant before; I confessed my Attachment to him &
her together, with many Tears & Agonies one Day at Streatham; told
them both that I wished I had two hearts for their Sakes; but having
only one I would break it between them, & give them *ciascheduno
la Metà.*[9] *After that* conversation She consented to go abroad with me,
& even appointed the Place, (Lyons,) to which Piozzi meant to follow
us: He & She talked long together on the Subject; yet her never mentioning it again, made me fear She was not fully apprized of my Intent;
& though her Concurrence might have been more easily attained
when left only to my Influence in a distant Country, where She would
have had no Friend to support her different Opinion—yet I scorned
to take such mean Advantages; & told her my Story *now* with the
Winter before her in which to take her Measures, her Guardians at
hand—all displeased at the Journey—and to console her private Distress I called into the Room to her my own Bosom Friend, my beloved Fanny Burney; whose interest as well as Judgment goes all
against my Marriage—whose Skill in Life and Manners is superior to
that of any Man or Woman in this Age or Nation; whose Knowledge
of the World, ingenuity of Expedient, Delicacy of Conduct, & Zeal
in the Cause will make her a Counsellor invaluable; & leave me destitute of every Comfort, of every Hope, of every Expectation.

Such are the Hands to which I have cruelly committed thy Cause—
my honourable, ardent, artless Piozzi! yet I should not deserve the
Union I desire, with the most disinterested of all human Hearts; had I
behaved with less Generosity, or endeavoured to gain by Cunning
what is witheld only by Prejudice, had I set my Heart upon a Scoun-
drel, I might have done virtuously to break it & get loose: but the
Man I love, I love for his Honesty; for his Tenderness of Heart, his
Dignity of Mind, his Piety to God, his Duty to his Mother, & his

Delicacy to me, in being united to this Man only, can I be happy in this World; & short will be my Stay in it, if it is not passed with him.—

Saturday 16 November   For him I have been contented to reverse the Laws of Nature, and request of my Child that concurrence which at my Age (and a Widow) I am not required either by divine or human Institutions to ask even of a Parent: the Life I gave her She may now more than repay, only by agreeing to what She will with difficulty prevent; & which if She does prevent, will give her lasting remorse— for those who stab *me* shall hear me groan—whereas if She will— but how can She?—gracefully, or even compassionately consent; if She will go abroad with me upon the Chance of his Death or mine preventing our Union; & live with me till She is of Age—Perhaps there is no Heart so callous by Avarice, no Soul so poisoned by Preju- dice, no Head so feather'd by Foppery; that will forbear to excuse her when She returns to the Rich & the Gay—for having saved the Life of a Mother thro' Compliance extorted by Anguish, contrary to the receiv'd Opinions of the World.

19 November   What is above written, tho' intended only to unload my heart by writing it, I shew'd in a Transport of Passion to Queeney & to Burney—sweet Fanny Burney cried herself half blind over it; said there was no resisting such pathetic Eloquence, & that if She was the Daughter instead of the Friend, She should be even tempted to attend me to the Altar. but that while She possessed her Reason, nothing should seduce her to approve what Reason itself would con- demn: that Children, Religion, Situation, Country & Character— besides the Diminution of Fortune by the certain Loss of 800£ a Year were too much to Sacrifice to any One Man; if however I were re- solved to make the Sacrifice *A la bonne Heure!*[10] it was an astonishing Proof of an Attachment, very difficult for Mortal Man to repay.

   I will talk no more of it.

• • • • •

1 December   The Guardians have met upon the Scheme of putting our Girls in Chancery[11]; I was frighted at the Project, not doubting the Lord Chancellor would stop us from leaving England; as he would

certainly see no Joke in three young heiresses his Wards quitting the
Kingdom to frisk away with their Mother into Italy: besides that I
believe Mr. Crutchley proposed it merely for a Stumbling block to
my Journey, as he cannot bear to have Hester out of his Sight. Nobody
much applauds my Resolution in going; but Johnson & Cator said
they would not concur in Stopping me by Violence, & Crutchley was
forced to content himself with intending to put the Ladies under
legal Protection as soon as we should be across the Sea. This Measure
I much applaud; for if I die or marry in Italy, their Persons & Fortunes
will be safer in Chancery than any how else; Cator said *I* had a right
to say that going to Italy would benefit the Children as much as they
had to say it would *not,* but I replied that as I really did not mean
any thing but my own private Gratification by my Voyage, nothing
should make me say I meant *their* Good by it: & that it would be like
saying I eat Roast Beef to mend my Daughter's Complexions. The
Result of all is that we certainly *do go,* I will pick up what Knowledge
& Pleasure I can here this Winter to divert myself & perhaps my
Compagno fedele[12] in distant Climes and future Times, with the Recollection of England & its Inhabitants: all which I shall be happy and
content to leave *for him. . . .*

29 January 1783   Adieu to all that's dear, to all that's lovely. I am parted
from my Life, my Soul! my Piozzi: Sposo promesso! Amante ador-
ato! Amico senza equale.[13] If I can get Health & Strength to write my
Story here, 'tis all I wish for now! Oh Misery![14] The cold Dislike of
my eldest daughter I thought might wear away by Familiarity with his
Merit, and that we might live tolerably together or at least part
Friends, but No: her Aversion increased daily, & She communicated it
to the others; they treated *me* insolently, and *him* very strangely—
running away whenever he came as if they saw a Serpent: and plotting
with their Governess, a cunning Italian how to invent Lyes to make
me hate him, and twenty such narrow Tricks. by these means the
notion of my partiality took air—and whether Miss Thrale sent him
word slyly, or not I cannot tell; but on the 25: Jan: 1783. Mr. Crutchley
came hither to *conjure me* not to go to Italy: he had heard *such* Things
he said, & by *means* next to *miraculous.* The next day Sunday 26. Fanny

Burney came, said I must marry him instantly, or give him up; that
my Reputation would be lost else—I actually groaned with Anguish,
threw myself on the Bed in an Agony which My fair Daughter beheld with frigid Indifference: She had indeed never by one tender
Word endeavoured to dissuade me from the Match; but said coldly
that if I *would* abandon my Children, I *must:* that their Father had not
deserved such Treatment from me; that I should be punished by
Piozzi's neglect, for that She knew he hated me, & that I turned out
my Offspring to Chance for his Sake like Puppies in a Pond to swim
or drown according as Providence pleased: that for her Part She must
look herself out a Place like the other Servants, for my Face would
She never see more—nor write to me said I? I shall not Madam replied
She with a cold Sneer—easily find *out your Addresse:* for you are
going you know not whither I believe. Susan & Sophy said nothing at
all; but they taught the two little ones to cry where are you going
Mama? will you leave us, and die as our poor papa did? there was no
standing *that,* so I wrote my Lover word that my Mind was all distraction, and bid him come to me the next Morning my Birthday. 27
Jan. mean Time I took a Vomit, & spent the Sunday Night in Torture
not to be described—my Falsehood to my Piozzi, my strong affection
for him; the Incapacity I felt in myself to resign the Man I so adored,
the Hopes I had so cherished, inclined me strongly to set them all
at Defiance, and go with him to Church to sanctifie the Promises I
had so often made him—while the Idea of abandoning the Childen of
my first Husband, who left me so nobly provided for, and who depended on my Attachment to his Offspring, awakened the Voice
of Conscience, and threw me on my Knees to pray for *his* Direction
who was hereafter to judge my Conduct.

His Grace illuminated me, His Power strengthened me; and I flew
to my Daughter's bed in the morng & told, told her my resolution
to resign my own; my dear, my favourite purposes; and to prefer my
Children's Interest to my Love. She questioned my Ability to make
the Sacrifice; said one Word from him would undo all my[15]. . .

· · · · ·

14 April Here[16] I am settled in my Plan of Œconomy, with three
Daughters, three Maids and a Man: my Lover is leaving England, and

I wait here patiently for my own Release: living if possible on *1000£*
Pr. Ann that I may save Money enough to pay my Debts, and fly
to the Man of my Heart. . . .

My daughter does not I suppose much delight in *this* Scheme, but
why should I lead a Life of delighting her who would not lose a
shilling of Interest, or an Ounce of Pleasure to save my Life from per-
ishing? when I was near losing my Existence from the Contention
of my Mind, and was seized wth. a temporary Delirium in Argylle
Street, She & her two eldest Sisters laughed at my distress, and observed to dear Fanny Burney—that it *was monstrous droll: She* could
scarcely suppress her Indignation.—. . .

[?] *April*   Terrible Accounts from poor Cæcilia and Harriett; I fear
those poor Babies will dye, notwithstanding the Efforts of Jebb &
Pepys to relieve them:—Thank Heav'n they are with Dear Mrs. Ray.[17]

Harriett is dead, my other Girls Fortunes increased, their Insolence
extream, and their hardness of Heart astonishing: When the Baby
was to be moved to Streatham for the Air—it will kill her said I—She
will be nearer the Church Yard replies the eldest, coldly.

My poor Piozzi was ill in Consequence of his Agitation I guess: a
sore Throat Pepys said it was, with four Ulcers in it: the People about
me said it had been lanced, & I mentioned it slightly before the
Girls.—Has he cut his own Throat? says Miss Thrale in her quiet
Manner. This was less inexcusable because She hated *him,* & the other
was her Sister: though had She exerted the good Sense I thought her
possessed of, She would not have treated him so. had She adored
& fondled & respected him as he deserved from her hands for the he-
roic Conduct he shewed in January,[18] who knows but She might have
kept us separated? but never did she once caress or thank *Me,* never
treat *him* with common Civility except on the very day which gave her
hopes of our final parting. Worth while to be sure it was, to break
one's Heart for *her.* The other two are however neither wiser nor
kinder; all swear by her I believe, and follow her Footsteps exactly.
Mr. Thrale had not much heart, but his fair Daughters have none
at all. Henrietta's Death however was inevitable; She came home with
a slight glandular Swelling in her Neck which was succeeded by the
Measles & Hooping Cough: these united fell very heavy on an Infant

so tender, & falling on her Lungs particularly, produced an Abscess which was the immediate Cause of her Death. Cator & Johnson sent for me from Bath, I was ill when their Messengers came, had that moment taken a Vomit, & called for the Chamomile Flowers & the Post Chaise I think all in a Breath. I set out at 3 o'Clock & ran to Reading by 11 at night: lay down for two or three Hours, & away again till I got to Streatham School on *Easter Sunday* Morning 20: April 1783 by 9 oClock: having first written to Piozzi & Miss Burney whom I hoped to get a Sight of now I was so near them.

Dear Miss Burney was however out of Town, and Piozzi was prudent, & feared to raise fresh Clamours by such Indulgence of an idle Desire, which could only have increased our Sorrow in the End—so I saw neither of them. Cecilia however was mending, and it was now very delightful to me to find She would not die too, as we had been in great Anxiety for both. I returned on the Wednesday 23d. and not one of my three eldest Daughters said even *how do you do?* but going on just as I left them, appeared diligent as they always are about their Work, their Drawing, Accounts, or other Studies for Improvement: of which to do them Justice they have a very singular Avidity.

. . . . .

3 June I have altered—that is new written my Will to day; & left the Estate unentailed, to my eldest Daughter & her heirs for ever: only charging it pretty heavily with Legacies which however she will now be empowered to pay by selling the Estate if She pleases, and what signifies entailing it on People who have already more than does them good? if I cannot live to enjoy my Estate with the husband of my Choice, they may take it that please—I care not.

. . . . .

14 August I was reading to the Girls to day More's Acct. of The King of Prussia's Severity to his favourite Valet who unable to endure it, shot himself.—he was *an Ape* says the eldest to shoot himself because the King was rough wth. him—the King was a cruel Wretch (said the other two,) he had *a Right* to do as he did (replied Hester)—so here a wise Fellow would Fancy he saw *Character*—but tis only *Opinion.* The two youngest have for ought I see Hearts as impenetrable as their Sister, they will all starve a favourite Animal, all see with Unconcern the Afflictions of a Friend: and when the Anguish I suffered on their Account last Winter in Argylle Street nearly took away my Life and Reason, the younger ridiculed as a Jest, those Agonies which the eldest despised as a Philosopher. When all is said, they are exceeding valuable Girls:—beautiful in Person, cultivated in Understanding and well principled in Religion: high in their Notions, lofty in their Carriage, and of Intents equal to their Expectations; wishing to raise their own Family by Connections with some more noble—and Superior to every Feeling of Tenderness which might clog the Wheels of Ambition. What however is *my* State? who am condemned to live with Girls of this disposition—to teach without Authority, to be heard without Esteem; to be considered by them as their Inferior in Fortune, while I live by the Money borrowed from them; and in good Sense when they have seen me submit my Judgment to theirs, tho' at the hazard of my Life & Wits.

Oh 'tis a pleasant Situation! & whoever would wish as the Greek Lady phrased it *to teize himself & repent of his Sins:*—let him borrow his Children's money, be in Love against their Interest & Prejudice, forbear to marry by their Advice;—and then shut himself up and live with them.—. . .

. . . . . .

11 September   The hardness of my companion's Hearts however increases my Willingness to leave them: when we were at Portland, (the three Girls, Harry Cotton[19] & myself;) we climbed a Precipice the which with much ado *they* conquered; but *My* Strength failed me within about Six Yards of the Top; when seeing them safe, I intreated their Assistance, and threw them by my Request into a most vehement & unmanageable Fit of Laughter: Harry Cotton however tried to compose his Countenance, & turning to the Ladies I heard him say, *As to helping her that's all Stuff you know.*—Mrs. *Thrale* (to me) *won't you come up?* I bore wholly on my Elbow and Thumb, but was incapable of stirring as any Change of Position must have inevitably produc'd a Fall from the Heighth, which I could never have recovered:—I beseeched Sophy at last to call a Fellow who kept Sheep upon the Hill, and he came just in Time to save me, while the Misses & the Macaroni Gentleman laughed delighted at my Distress—protested they could not help it &c. and when I gave the Clown five Shillings for his Assistance said Six Pence was enough—perhaps it might said I; but *I am not used to have my Life rated at so low a Price.* & that was all the Reproach I gave them for a Behavior too savage to be repeated—

But Oh that I had wings like a Dove (thought I,) and then would I flee away & be at rest! . . .

· · · · ·

19 November   Heavens! a new Distress! my Child, my Sophia will not dye: arrested by the Hand of God—apparently so: She will die without a Disease—Fits, sudden, unnacountable, unprovoked; Apoplectic, lethargic like her Father. Woodward and Dobson are called: they say her Disorder should be termed *Attonitus.*[20] 'tis an instant Cessation of all Nature's Pow'rs at once. I saved her in the first Attack, by a Dram of fine Old Usquebough given at the proper Moment—it reviv'd her, but She only lives I see to expire with fresh Struggles.

Oh spare my Sophia, my Darling, oh spare her gracious heaven— & take in Exchange the life of her wretched Mother!

She lives, I have been permitted to save her again; I rubbed her while just expiring, so as to keep the heart in Motion: She knew me instantly, & said you warm *me* but you are killing *yourself*—I actually was in a burning Fever from exertion, & fainted soon as I had saved my Child.

Hester has behaved inimitably too, *all* our Tenderness was called out on this Occasion: dear Creatures! they see I love them, that I would willingly *die* for them; that I *am* actually dying to gratifie their Humour at the Expence of my own Happiness: they can *but* have my Life—let them take it! . . .

30 November   Sophia will live and do well; I have saved my Daughter sure enough, perhaps obtained a Friend: they are weary of seeing me suffer so, and the eldest beg'd me Yesterday not to sacrifice my Life to her Convenience; She now saw my Love of Piozzi was incurable She said, Absence had no Effect on it, and my Health was going so fast She found, that I should soon be useless either to her or to him.—It was the hand of God & irresistible She added, & begged me not to endure any longer such unnecessary Misery.—

So now we may be happy if we will, and now I trust some other cross Accident will [not] start up to torment us; I wrote my Lover word that he might come & fetch me, but the Alps are covered with Snow, & if his Prudence is not greater than his Affection—*my* Life will yet be lost, for it depends on his Safety: Should he come at my Call, & meet with any Misfortune on the Road—Death with accumulated Agonies would end me—May Heaven avert such insupportable Distress!

21 December   He will *not* come; he is safe and happy at the Palace of the Prince de Belgioioso, who loves him, & acknowledges his Merit— he is too happy there to think very much of me I suppose; dear Piozzi! I might have known long ago that he is more wise than kind, yet love him I must, and with unequalled Tenderness—had he written to *me,* as I have done to *him,* nothing could have witheld me from running thro' frost or thro' fire to console *him.*

I wrong him positively, he has not had my Letters.[21] . . .

· · · · ·

27 January 1784   On this Day Twelvemonth—Oh dreadfullest of all Days to me! did I send for my Piozzi, & tell him we must part. The Sight of my Countenance terrified Dr. Pepys, to whom I went into the parlour for a Moment; and the Sight of the Agonies endured in the Week following would have affected anything but Interest, Avarice and Pride personified—with such however I had to deal, so my Sorrows were unregarded—seeing them continue for a whole year indeed, has mollify'd my stony-hearted Companions; & they *now* relent in earnest, & wish me happy: I would *now* therefore be *loath to dye;* yet how shall I recruit my Constitution so as to live? The pardon certainly did arrive the very Instant of Execution—for I was ill beyond all power of Description when my eldest Daughter bursting into Tears bid me call home the Man of my heart, & not expire so by slow Tortures in the presence of my Children, who had my Life in their power.—

You are dying *now* said She; I know it replied I, and I should die in peace had I but seen him *once, once again.* Oh send for him said She, send for him quickly; he is at Milan Child replied I,—a thousand Miles off:—well, well, returns She, hurry him back, or I myself will send him an Express—at these words I revived, & have been mending ever since.

This was the first Time that any of us had named the name of Piozzi to each other, since we had put our Feet into the Coach to come to Bath. I had always thought it a point of Civility & Prudence never to mention what could give nothing but Offence, & cause nothing but Disquiet; while they desired nothing less than a Revivial of old Uneasiness, so we were all silent on the Subject, & Miss Thrale thought him dead.

I will be so here I mean *silent,* & quitting for a Moment the Idea which never quits me, will mention a few odd Things of another Nature. . . .

Notes

လ

*These selections are taken from vol. 1: *1776–1809* of *Thraliana: The Diary of Hester Lynch Thrale*. ed. Katharine C. Balderston, 2d ed., 2 vols. (Oxford: Clarendon Press, 1951).

1 Matthew Prior, *Alma,* canto 3, ll. 547–48.

2 Alexander Pope, *Ode on St. Cecilia's Day,* ll. 90–92.

3 The master of my destiny.

4 Thrale errs; Piozzi was born in 1740. She later added a note to say "he was ½ a Year *older* when our Registers were both examined."

5 Nicholas Rowe, *The Fair Penitent,* 2.1.35–36.

6 Her eldest daughter, Hester Maria ("Queeney").

7 In ultimate perfection.

8 Thrale was now living in Brighton, having rented out her house at Streatham. She lived temporarily in various places afterwards.

9 Half to each one.

10 Right, very good!

11 Mr. Thrale's will had so stipulated. The will also named Hester (an executrix) and Mr. Thrale's other executors—Dr. Samuel Johnson, John Cator, Jeremiah Crutchley, and Henry Smith—as the girls' joint guardians. Mr. Thrale's will thus complicated Thrale's plan to take her three eldest daughters abroad.

12 Faithful companion.

13 Promised groom! Adored lover! Unequalled friend!

14 Thrale cut two leaves from her diary at this point. They likely included her parting interview with Piozzi and possibly the scandalous stories that were circulating about them.

15 Thrale removed another leaf here.

16 Thrale had settled in at Bath by now.

17   At Russell House, the school Mrs. Ray ran with Mrs. Fry in Streatham.

18   Piozzi returned her mother's love letters to Miss Thrale then.

19   Thrale's nephew, the son of Sir Lynch Salusbury Cotton.

20   Whatever Thrale may mean by *Attonitus* (Latin for "struck by thunder, senseless"), Dr. Samuel Johnson's letters imply that Sophia's attack was merely hysterical, according to the editor of *Thraliana* (see 1:580 n. 2).

21   Piozzi delayed coming to England until July.

Mary Hardy

(1733–1809)

MARY HARDY was the youngest daughter of Robert Raven and Mary Fox Raven of Whissonsett, near Fakenham, Norfolk, where Ravens had been living for several generations. Robert Raven, who was a churchwarden, seems to have been a prominent townsman and farmer. As would be normal for a yeoman's daughter, Mary was probably educated at a dame school at Fakenham, four miles away, the school to which she later sent her own daughter. In 1765 she married a young farmer, William Hardy, at Whissonsett. Their first child, Raven, was born in 1767; a second son, William, in 1770; and their daughter, Mary Ann, a month before Hardy's diary for 1773–1809 opens. Mary was an able helpmate to William, who held maltings and a small farm in Coltishall and in the adjoining parish of Horstead as tenant and soon became a prominent man in the two parishes. In 1781 he bettered himself by purchasing a brewery at auction with its dwelling house and acreage at Letheringsett, and Letheringsett Hall became the family home thereafter. For thirty-five years, Mary Hardy never missed making a daily entry in her diary unless incapacitated by illness and has left a remarkable record of domestic life, including such tantalizing items as the announcement that "We borrowed Mr. Davy's Washing Mill & washed 3 weeks linnen without a work woman" (19 April 1791).* But Hardy was also fascinated by crimes, accidents, and natural disasters, which she regularly reports from the weekly newsprints and local gossip. Apparently she craved some excitement. Her marriage, however, was successful and her life secure and satisfying, but for the tragedy she laconically records in these extracts for 1786–87. Her eldest son, Raven, who had shown great promise of success while studying for law at North Walsham, died despite the careful nursing of his devoted mother. Fortunately, at least the other two children survived and prospered.

From Mary Hardy's Diary

6 August 1786, Sunday   I attended the School[1] both foornoon and aft. All went to our Church aft. The children began to try to sing.

9 August, Wednesday   I and Raven rid to Brinton afternoon to speak to a young man apprentice to Mr Brereton he having a scrophila in his neck the same as Raven.

12 August, Saturday   A very wet day. Mr Hardy at home all day, made a dam in the orchard. Wm. set of for Cromer even 6 with a letter for Mr. Buck to let Raven stay a little while to try to cure his neck it being very bad.

16 August, Wednesday   Mr Hardy set of morn 9 with Mr Purdy of Kelling, Mr. King of Holt and Mr Coe of Dalling for Foulsham to see old John Bullocks stock out of the greasing grounds. I bathed.

21 August, Monday   A fine day. Mr Hardy I & Raven walked up to Holt afternoon, drank tea at Mr Daveys. Mr Hardy went to Bowling Green after tea. Heard Mr Cremer of Beeston was dead. I bathed.

26 August, Saturday   Wm. Lamb went to Hempton. J. Ram shearing till even, then went to Bodham with beer. Raven very poorly. Wm Freary died this morng about 10 o'clock. Mr Hardy went to Cromer to meet Mr Buck to git leave for Raven to stay a little longer.

2 September, Saturday   Raven very poorly. Mr Buck sent him some writings to copy.

7 September, Thursday   Mr Hardy went to Holt foornoon to the sale of Mr Colls estates only a few cottages were sold.

16 September, Saturday   A very fine day. I & Raven walked up to Holt afternoon, drank tea at Mr Bartells. Our men had their Harvest frolic at Mays. Mr Hardy[,] Wm & Mr Burrell came home from Norwich even 10. Mr B. put his shoulder out of the way in coming home. A great riot at Norwich yesterday, a great deal of mischief done, one man killed & several limbs broke[.] Hubbard got his election by a majority of 70. A Crutiny[2] is talked of.

20 September, Wednesday   The Revd John Murrell married to Miss Garret of Brinton.

24 September, Sunday   A fine day; all went to our church foornoon.
Mr Burrell preached; the Bride and Bride Maid at Church. 6 young
gentlemen came to see Raven from Walsham, dined and drank [tea]
here. Mr and Mrs Bensley drank tea here. I attended the school till
past 4.

6 October, Friday   Recd a supenea to appear at Norwich in a Trial
between J. Burrell and Richd. Rouse. It was given in favour of Rouse
with £90 damages.

10 October, Tuesday   A close showry day. Maids went away. Mr Hardy
at home all day. Jos. Christmas came to town to be our malster. Mr
and Mrs Emery went out of town. Thos. Newman took R. Lounds
farm. Ann Claxton came as upper maid.

October 29, Sunday   All went to our church foornoon except Raven
who was very bad. Mr Burrell was instituted to this Rectory on
Thursday last and read the 39 articles etc. I attended the school a little
while.

November 9, Thursday   Sent for Mr Bartell to open the sore on Raven's
neck, it discharged a great deal of bloody water and he was very
poorly. Raven's Birthday aged 19.

19 November, Sunday   A very cold morn, a great deal of snow and
sleet fell in the afternoon. Sister Raven and children Mr Hardy & Wm.
at our church foornoon. Mrs Burrell came a little while after noon
to see Raven. Thos. Youngman went to Norwich for Dr. Donne. He
was not at home. Mr. Alderson came in his stead in the eveng. Raven
very bad all day. Mr. Bartell visited Raven twice.

27 November, Monday   I and Wm. rid up to Holt foornoon bought 6
st. 9 lbs. Beeff at ⅔ per st. Wm. had his tooth pulled.

28 November, Tuesday   Mr Buck & Mr Cubit dined here. Mr Hardy
went with them up to Holt after dinner. The Stage Coach & Harness
sold. Young Cubit came home & slept here.

11 December, Monday   A tolerable day. Raven very poorly. Mr Hardy
and Wm. went morn 10 to Mr. Chad's at Thurstford from thence
to Gunthorp to Mr. Tillson's sale; bought a pair of leather baggs for
8/–, 4 tea napkins 3/–, books ⅙.

12 December, Tuesday   Raven began to take Hemblock inwardly.

13 December, Wednesday   Dr. Pleasence came in the eveng to see Raven. A very stormy night, wind very high.

11 January 1787, Thursday   A small rime frost beautifull day. Mr Hardy & I rid to Sherington afternoon to Woodrows & exchanged our Black cow & old Dankhorse for two young polled cows, gave him 4/s 3d in exchange.

15 January, Tuesday   Mr Hardy at home all day. Raven much as yesterday. His neck measured 24 inches.

20 January, Saturday   Recd letter from Wegan Joseph Hardy very ill.

23 January, Tuesday   Began to poultice Raven's neck again with white bread and White Lylys and grounsell.

27 January, Saturday   Raven much as usual, began taken antimony and sarcerparella.

6 February, Tuesday   Mr Bartell came to see Raven laid 2 little costick plasters to his neck to open the sores.

7 February, Wednesday   A fine day. Mr. Bartell came to see Raven opened a place in his neck with an lancet. It discharged only a little blood. The costicks did no good, he grows weaker every day and his cough very bad and raise a good deal of phlem.

8 February, Thursday   A sharp rime frost very fine day. Mr Bartell came to see Raven. We began to apply hemlock to his neck instead of poultice. He continue much as yesterday.

11 February, Sunday   Mr Cubit from N. Walsham to see Raven, staid here all night. Raven very bad but came down to dinner.

12 February, Monday   O how shall I write it. My poor Raven died this morng abt 5 o'clock. Sent for Bro. Raven from Whissonsett, he came even 4 and staid all night.

16 February, Friday   Bro. Raven and Mr. Thos. Fox came to dinner. My poor dear Raven was buried. Our own labourers carried him, Sherington singers came.

18 February, Sunday   A very fine day. Wm. & M. A. & Sister Raven
went to our Church afternoon. Mr Burrell preached. A great many of
Holt people at Church. Mr & Mrs Burrell drank tea here.

26 February, Monday   A close mild day. Mr Hardy and I rid out for air
aftern. on to Biddens Brecks.

Notes

*Taken from *Mary Hardy's Diary,* ed. B. Gozens-Hardy, Norfolk Record Society Publications, 37 (Norfolk, Eng.: Norfolk Record Society, 1968), p. 78. All selections from Hardy's diary come from this edition.

1   Presumably Sunday school. All her Sunday entries report attendance at school.

2   Possibly a dialect word, perhaps meaning "a mob."

Elizabeth Gaskell

(1810–65)

ELIZABETH CLEGHORN GASKELL, who would become the novelist known as Mrs. Gaskell, was the daughter of William Stevenson, keeper of the treasury records and formerly a Unitarian minister and an editor. Because her mother, Elizabeth Holland, died when Gaskell was one month old, she was reared by her maternal aunt, Mrs. Lumb, at Knutsford in Cheshire, a setting Gaskell would later idealize for her novel *Cranford* (1853). She was educated at boarding schools at Burford and Stratford-upon-Avon. In 1832 she married the Reverend William Gaskell, an intelligent and liberal-minded man who was then minister of the Cross Street Unitarian Chapel in Manchester and from 1846 to 1853 professor of English history and literature at Manchester New College. They lived in Manchester, where she helped her husband with his pastoral duties by teaching and organizing relief work. It seems to have been at his suggestion, to distract her from her grief when their infant son died in 1844, that she undertook to write her first novel, *Mary Barton, a Tale of Manchester Life* (1848), one of the earliest novels to describe the conditions of the working class. It was an immediate success and earned her the regard of Dickens. Six other condition-of-England and provincial novels followed, as well as collections of tales and a *Life of Charlotte Brontë* (1857), who had become her good friend. Gaskell's was a happy and companionate marriage in which she bore six children, though only four daughters survived. When the first of these children, Marianne (b. 1834), was six months old, Gaskell, who saw motherhood as one of her most sacred duties, began a detailed diary (1835–38) of Marianne's progress "as a token of her Mother's love and extreme anxiety in the formation of her little daughter's character."* The diary included also some account of her second child, Margaret Emily (Meta, b. 1837), but the excerpts here reflect only 1835.

From Elizabeth Gaskell's Diary

To my dear little Marianne I shall "dedicate" this book, which, if I should not live to give it her myself, will I trust be reserved for her as a token of her Mother's love and extreme anxiety in the formation of her little daughter's character. If that little daughter should in time become a mother herself, she may take an interest in the experience of another; and at any rate she will perhaps like to become acquainted with her character in its earliest form. I wish that (if ever she sees this) I could give her the slightest idea of the love and the hope that is bound up in her. The love which passeth every earthly love, and the hope that however we may be separated on earth, we may each of us so behave while sojourning here that we may meet again to renew the dear and tender tie of Mother and Daughter.

10th March 1835, Tuesday Evening   The day after to-morrow Marianne will be six months old. I wish I had begun my little journal sooner, for (though I should have laughed at the idea twelve months ago) there have been many little indications of disposition, &c., already; which I can not now remember clearly. I will try and describe her *mentally*. I should call her remarkably good-tempered; though at times she gives way to little bursts of passion or perhaps impatience would be the right name. She is also very firm in her own little way occasionally; what I suppose is obstinacy really, only that is so hard a word to apply to one so dear. But in general she is so good that I feel as if I could hardly be sufficiently thankful, that the materials put into my hands are so excellent, and beautiful. And yet it seems to increase the responsibility. If I should misguide from carelessness or negligence! *wilfully* is not in a mother's heart. From ignorance and errors in judgment I know I may, and probably shall, very often. But, Oh, Lord! I pray thee to lead me right (if it be thy will) and to preserve in me the same strong feeling of my responsibility which I now feel. And you too, my dearest little girl, if, when you read this, you trace back any evil or unhappy feeling to my mismanagement in your childhood, forgive me, love!

Marianne is now becoming every day more and more interesting. She looks at and tries to take hold of everything. She has pretty good ideas of distance and does not try to catch sunbeams now, as she did two months ago. Her sense of sight is much improved lately in seeing objects at a distance, and distinguishing them. For instance, I had her in my arms to-day in the drawing room, and her Papa was going out of the gate, and she evidently knew him; smiled and kicked. She begins to show a decided preference to those she likes; she put out her little arms to come to me, and would, I am sure, do so to her Papa. She catches the expression of a countenance to which she is accustomed directly; when we laugh, she laughs; and when I look attentive to William's reading, it is quite ridiculous to see her little face of gravity, and earnestness, as if she understood every word. I try always to let her look at anything which attracts her notice as long as she will, and when I see her looking very intently at anything, I take her to it, and let her exercise all her senses upon it, even to tasting, if I am sure it can do her no harm. My object is to give her a habit of fixing her attention.

She takes great delight in motion just at present—dancing, jumping; shutting and opening the hand pleases her very much. I had no idea children at her age made such continued noises; she shouts, and murmurs, and talks in her way, just like conversation, varying her tones, &c. I wish we could know what is passing in her little mind. She likes anything like singing, but seems afraid of the piano; to-day she even began to cry when I began to play.

In general I think she is remarkably free from fear or shyness of any sort. She goes to anyone who will take her. Staring at strangers to be sure, and being very grave while they are in the room, but not crying or clinging to me. I am very glad of this, as, though it is very flattering and endearing to me, yet I should be sorry if she were to get the habit of refusing to go to others.

Then as to her "bodily" qualifications. She has two teeth cut with very little trouble; but I believe the worst are to come. She is very strong in her limbs, though, because she is so fat, we do not let her use her ankles at all, and I hope she will be rather late in walking so that her little legs may be very firm. I shall find it difficult to damp the energies of the servants in this respect, but I intend that she shall teach herself to walk and receive no asistance from hands, &c. She lies down on the floor a good deal, and kicks about; a practice I began very early and which has done her a great deal of good. She goes to bed *awake;* another practice I began early, and which is so comfortable, I wonder it is not more generally adopted. Once or twice we have had grand cryings, which have been very very distressing to me; but when I have convinced myself that she is not in pain, is perfectly well and that she is only wanting to be taken up, I have been quite firm, though I have sometimes cried almost as much as she has. I never leave her till she is asleep (except in extreme cases), and as she is put to bed at a regular time (6 o'clock) she generally gets very sleepy while being undressed. While the undressing is going on, I never like her to be talked to, played with, or excited; yet sometimes she is so very playful when she ought to be put down, that a turn or two up and down the room is required to soothe her, still putting her down awake. Sometimes she will cry a little, and when I turn her over in her cot she fancies she is going to be taken up and is still in a moment, making the peculiar little triumphing noise she always does when she is pleased.

Crying has always been a great difficulty with me. Books do so differ. One says "Do not let them have anything they cry for"; another (Mme. Necker de Saussure, "Sur l'Education Progressive," the nicest book I have read on the subject) says: "Les larmes des enfans sont si amères, la calme parfaite de l'ame leur est si nécessaire qu'il faut surtout épargner des larmes."[1] So I had to make a rule for myself, and though I am afraid I have not kept to it quite as I ought, I still think it a good one. We must consider that a cry is a child's only language for expressing its wants. It is its little way of saying, "I am hungry, I am very cold," and *so,* I don't think we should carry out the maxim of never letting a child have anything for crying. If it is to have the object for which it is crying I would give it it *directly,* giving up any little occupation or purpose of my own, rather than try its patience *unnecessarily.* But if it is improper for it to obtain the object, I think it right to withhold it steadily, however much the little creature may cry. I think, after one or two attempts to conquer by crying, the child would become aware that *one* cry or indication of a want was sufficient, and I think the habit of crying would be broken. I am almost sure even my partial adherence to this plan has prevented many crying fits with Marianne. I have somewhere read that a child gets bad habits, *first by being irritated* and then by finding that crying causes the irritation to cease. I think this is very true. I think it is the duty of every mother to sacrifice a good deal rather than have her child *unnecessarily* irritated by anything—food given irregularly or improperly, dress uncomfortable, even to an uneasy position. I think this rule should be attended to.

But though I keep laying down rules, I fear I have not sufficiently attended to them, though I hope I have been conscientious hitherto in discharging my duty to her. Still, I sometimes fear there is too much pride in my own heart in attributing her goodness to the success of my plans, when in reality it is owing to her having hitherto had such good health, and freedom from pain, a blessing for which I cannot be too thankful. Still, I put down everything now because I have thought a good deal about the formation of any little plans, and I shall like to know their success. I want to act on principles *now* which can be carried on through the whole of her education. I have written a great deal to-night, and very unconnectedly. I had no idea the journal of my own disposition and feelings was so intimately connected with that of my little baby, whose regular breathing has been the music of my thoughts all the time I have been writing. God bless her!

4th August 1835, Tuesday Evening   It seems a very long time since I written anything about my little darling, and I feel as if I had been negligent about it; only it is so difficult to know when to begin or when to stop when talking, thinking, or writing about her.

In a few days she will be eleven months old; and in some things I suppose she is rather backward; in walking and talking, for instance. *I* fancy she says Mama, but I think it is only fancy. She can stand pretty steadily, taking hold of something, for a few minutes, and then she pops down. But as I am not very anxious for her to walk or talk earlier than her nature prompts, and as her Papa thinks the same, we allow her to take her own way.

She has various little accomplishments of her own—clapping hands, shaking hands—which are very pretty, though I sometimes fear we rather try to make her exhibit too much to strangers. We must take care of this as she grows older. She understands many words and sentences, "Where are the cows?" "the flies?" &c., &c., &c. I am very much afraid of her catching cross or angry expressions of countenance or even one that is not quite happy. I find her own changes so directly to the expression she sees. If we / I could but consider a child properly, what a beautiful safeguard from evil would its presence be. Oh! I do hope and intend. . . . [2]

How all a woman's life, at least so it seems to me now, ought to have reference to the period when she will be fulfilling one of her greatest and highest duties, those of a mother. I feel myself so unknowing, so doubtful about many things in her intellectual and moral treatment already, and what shall I be when she grows older, and asks those puzzling questions that children do? I hope I shall always preserve my present good intentions and sense of my holy trust, and then I must pray to be forgiven for my errors and led into a better course. . . . [3] afraid of pleasure being associated with the faces of pain they pull. Perhaps this is foolish, but I will put everything down relating to her.

She has been to Knutsford and Warrington since last I wrote in this journal. and oh! after her visit to Warrington she was very, very ill, and I was very much afraid we should have lost her. I did so try to be resigned; but I cannot tell how I sickened at my heart at the thought of seeing her no more here.

> Her empty crib to see,
> Her silent nursery,
>   Once gladsome with her mirth.

I am sometimes afraid of using expressions of gratitude to God, for fear I should get into the habit of using them without sufficiently feeling them, but I think there is no danger when I say that I bless and thank my Father, and hers, for not taking away the blesing he gave; and oh! may I not make her into an idol, but strive to prepare both her and myself for the change that may come any day.

After her illness her temper had suffered from the indulgence that was necessary during her illness; but as she grew strong it wore away, and I think she is now as sweet-tempered as ever in general; though at times her little passions are terrible and give me quite a heavy heart.

I should say impatience will be one of her greatest faults; and I scarcely know the best way of managing it. I certainly think being calm oneself and showing that the impatience makes no difference in the quickness or slowness of her actions, and never disappointing her when *unnecessary,* are good rules; but then, in every little case it is so difficult for an undecided person like me to determine at once; and yet *every body* and every book says that decision is of such conse-quence to the comfort and consequently to the temper of a child; and that it is almost better for *the time* to go on with a treatment that is *not bad,* rather than by changing to a better, let the child see your wavering. I only mean for the time. I must take care to have presence of mind to remember and adopt the better method every future occa-sion.

There is another thing I try to attend to and make the servants attend to: never, by way of distracting her attention, to call it to a thing that is not there, and never to promise her anything uncondi-tionally without performing it.

Of course, she now knows all those whom she is in the habit of seeing. I do not think she is remarkably shy, although more so than she was. But certainly most people take children in such a brusque, injudicious manner that no wonder they are often shy.

And now I shall conclude to-night, and I do not intend to be so long again without writing about my dear little girl.

4th October, Sunday Evening   I see it is exactly two months since I last wrote in this book, and I hope my little girl is improved both in "body and mind" since then. She suffered a good deal from the changes of weather we have had, and I have found it necessary to leave off milk as an article of diet at present. She lives on broth thick-ened with arrow root, and I think this food strengthens her; but she is still a delicate child, and backward in walking. I hope she will not be hurried by any one in her attempts at trotting about; for the more I see and hear of children the more I am convinced that, when they feel their limbs strong enough to begin to walk, they will constantly be trying their powers, and that, till Nature prompts this, it is worse than useless to force them to their feet.

She is, I believe, a small child of her age, though tall, and she has looked (and been too, alas!) very delicate since that sad, sad illness in the summer. I am going to clothe her in flannel waistcoats and long sleeves to her frocks this winter, and to keep her in *well-aired* rooms. . . . Oh! may I try not to fasten and centre my affections too strongly on such a frail little treasure; but all my anxiety, though it renders me so aware of her fragility of life, makes me cling daily more and more to her.

I think her disposition has improved since I wrote last; she is not so impatient (perhaps it was the remains of her former illness). She does not throw herself back in the passionate way she used to do so seven or eight weeks ago, and she bears her little disappointments better. The fewer she can have of these the better, I think, and I try to avoid exciting her expectations, even when they are pretty certain of being gratified for the excitement (which is always so great in a child) is injurious, and produces a degree of impatience. There are and always will be enow of disappointments to enure a child to bearing them, and they will increase with years and with the power of enduring, and what I mean to say is that, all that can be averted by a little forethought on the part of the parents or nurse, without interfering with the necessary degree of quiet but resolute discipline should be attended to and removed. . . . It is quite astonishing to see the difference bodily feelings make in Marianne's temper and powers of endurance. I was in a great measure prepared for this by Combe's Physiology; but I had no idea how every change of temper might be deduced from some corresponding change in the body. Mothers are sometimes laughed at for attributing little freaks of temper to teething, &c., but I don't think those who laugh at them (I used to be one) have had much to do with children. I do not mean to say that the habit of self-control may not be given, and that at a very early age, but I think that, with certain states of the body, feelings will arise which *ought* to be controlled, and that everything physical tending to produce those peculiar states of the body should be avoided, with as much care as we would anything moral tending to produce moral evil. I wish I could act upon this conviction myself; want of sleep invariably brings on an irritable state of excitement; and want of food, though I may not have the sensation of hunger, has in general the same effect. I should describe Marianne as a child with whom excitement should be particularly avoided; and yet it is very tempting to see the little cheek flush and the eye dilate, and the childish lip look so eloquent. She is very much tired, and consequently more irritable, after a certain degree of play and novelty, and besides her sensibilities seem to me very acute. If she sees others laughing when she is grave and serious, or is not aware of the joke, she bursts into tears; I fancy it must be a want of sympathy with her (at the time) serious and thoughtful feelings which makes her cry; but it must be a morbid feeling, I should think, and one that for her happiness had better be checked, *if I but knew how.* Then unexpected pleasure has occasionally made her cry: seeing her Papa after an absence of a few days; and I thought tears were not a common manifestation of joy in children so young, not thirteen months old yet. I feel very ignorant of the best way of managing these sensibilities, so beautiful when healthy and so distressing when morbid. Perhaps, as her body becomes stronger, her mind will too. There is a laugh of hers which is almost sure to end in a cry. She is in general very gentle, rather grave, especially with strangers, and remarkably observing, watching actions, things, &c., with such continued attention. She is very *feminine,* I think, in her quietness, which is as far removed from inactivity of mind as possible. . . .

William told me the other day I was not of a jealous disposition; I do not think he knows me. In general, Marianne prefers being with me, I hope and think; yet at times she shows a marked preference for Betsy, who has always been, as far as I can judge, a kind, judicious and tender nurse. To-night Marianne was sadly tired, and I would fain have caressed and soothed her while Betsy was performing various little offices for her on her knee, and M. A. absolutely pushed me away, fearing I should take her. This was hard to bear; but I am almost sure I have never shown this feeling to anyone; for I believe Betsy fully deserves and returns her love, and, having more bodily strength, can amuse her more than I can in different ways. There will come a time when she will know how a mother's love exceeds all others; and, meanwhile, I will try never to put myself in rivalry with another for my child's affections, but to encourage every good and grateful feeling on her part towards every one, and particularly to-wards a faithful and affectionate servant. I have been much gratified these few days past by the beginning of self-restraint in the little crea-ture; she has sometimes been washed in water either too hot, or too cold, and taken a dislike to it. This week past I have in general got up to wash her myself, or see by the thermometer that the water was the right heat (from 85 to 90), and Betsy and I have tried to distract her attention and prevent her crying; this last two days she has tried hard to prevent herself from crying, giving gulps and strains to keep it down. Oh! may this indeed be the beginning of self-government!

Lord! unto thee do I commit this darling precious treasure; thou knowest how I love her; I pray that I may not make her too much my idol, and oh! if thou shouldst call her away from "the evil to come," may I try to yield her up to him who gave her to me without a mur-mur. I hope I may say thou also knowest how truly I wish to do my duty to her. Help my ignorance, O Lord; strengthen my good pur-poses, and preserve a due sense of my holy trust, which I now ac-knowledge with fear and trembling. . . .

Notes

❧

*Taken from *"My Diary": The Early Years of My Daughter Marianne* (London: privately printed by Clement Shorter, 1923), p. 5. All selections from Gaskell's diary come from this edition.

1   Children's tears are so bitter, yet the perfect repose of their spirit is so necessary that one should especially spare them tears.

2   The manuscript has been cut away here.

3   It has also been cut away here.

Lady Cynthia Asquith

(1887–1960)

CYNTHIA MARY EVELYN ASQUITH was the third of the seven
children of Hugo Charteris, Lord Elcho, later the eleventh earl of
Wemyss, and his wife, Mary Wyndham. In the tradition of her class,
she was educated at home. Fortunate not only in birth and intelligence
but in looks, she grew up a beauty who would be painted by Mc-
Evoy, Sargent, and Augustus John. In 1910 she married Herbert (Beb)
Asquith, a barrister and second son of Prime Minister Herbert Asquith. She bore him three sons: John (b. 1911), Michael (b. 1914), and
Simon (b. 1919). After Beb enlisted in the Royal Field Artillery in
1914—he was to spend a good deal of time in England recovering
from wounds, illnesses, and shell shock—Cynthia and her two babies
began what she called "cuckooing," staying temporarily in the homes
of others while her town house was let. She also undertook volunteer
war work, mainly in hospitals, though not at the expense of a social
life that included many male admirers and evident pleasure in flirta-
tions. Her diary began because of a pact with a male friend that each
would keep one, though only she persisted. At the end of the war
she became J. M. Barrie's secretary and remained in that role for
twenty years; she later wrote his biography (*Portrait of J. M. Barrie*)
and her own autobiography (*Remember and Be Glad*). But her life was
clouded by her brothers' deaths in the Great War and the agonizing
discovery that her eldest son, John, precocious in his musical ability,
was autistic (though autism at the time was not a diagnosed condition). The dreadful realization of his abnormality, as these excerpts
from her published 1915–18 diary indicate,* grew but slowly as each
attempt to find some way to tutor him into normal life failed. Finally
sent to live permanently apart with a governess, John, perhaps fortunately, died young in 1937. Asquith's editor has deleted from her
diary the most painful references to him.

From Cynthia Asquith's diary

Tuesday, 11th May 1915 A lovely day, and by the evening I was devoted to Brighton. Another letter from Beb—he still hadn't heard from me.

The D. H. Lawrences arrived at one o'clock and we went out on a bus and had lunch at a filthy little shop. They decided to stay the night and we engaged another little room in my lodgings. Aileen Meade[1] arrived while we were out—we had the most ridiculous discussion about the lodgings which exhausted us and convulsed Lawrence. I rather wanted to change, but Aileen's sentiment for Charlie's old gardener[2] (reinforced by finding a photograph of Charlie on the wall) made it impossible for her to contemplate sending her Antonia anywhere else, so I acquiesced and decided to leave the children, at least for the present.

Mrs Lawrence rested on the sofa, and Lawrence and I took Aileen to the station. We couldn't get a taxi, and thought we should never catch the train. It was a tiring day, spent mostly on asphalt in the sun, but I found the air a wonderful tonic and felt unusually well. We all had tea with the children. The Lawrences were riveted by the freakishness of John, about whom they showed extraordinary interest and sympathy. The ozone had intoxicated him and he was in a wild, monkey mood—very challenging, just doing things for the sake of being told not to—impishly defiant and still his peculiar, indescribable detachment. We all went out with the children till their bedtime and then we returned to our lodgings about five minutes away, had a short rest, and then a dinner of whiting and cold chicken—Lawrence and I had bought asparagus, and so on, on the way home from the station. We had delightful dinner talk. . . .

Wednesday, 12th May We all breakfasted with the children. They went out and we sat on in the funny little sitting room, so packed with ornaments, and had a philosophical discussion—very interesting. He is a fierce believer in the absolute and the actual, 'twice two making four' independently of the human mind. I wish I could repeat, but alas I can't.

About eleven we three walked on to the top of the cliff where it was lovely and we lay there for about two hours and had one of the talks I shall always remember, though alas I could no more record it than a thrush's song! He was most interesting and earnest about John, round whom we talked most of the time. He thinks him very abnormal and that he will require most careful treatment. He thinks he is what he calls a 'static challenge', and that his throwing of food, and so forth, on the floor is symbolic of real Descartism, the negation of all accepted authority. He said dry, conventional authority, verbal bullying, must never be applied to him. He considers Nurse exactly right for John's nature, but I'm afraid he thinks I am quite wrong and that there will always be conflict between us. He considers me not positive enough, and that John would see lack of conviction—what he wants is a simple positive nature. He thinks—rather like Whibley[3] calling Mamma cynical—that my so-called tolerance is really based on profound skepticism and a sort of *laisser-faire* cynicism. I tried to argue but I think he has extraordinary insight, and, of course, it is the idealists who are hard, and if everyone were as acquiescent and 'philosophical' about people as my mother and I, I suppose the world wouldn't move much. He quite alarmed me about John and rather depressed me about myself.

We went into town and lunched at Fullers. Thrilling talk the whole time. They are tremendously interested in my autobiography and all my family, and they are most skilful cross-examiners. They went off after lunch, and I returned to a very happy evening with the children.

• • • • •

Sunday, 22nd August Wore my black-and-white gown. It was much dewdropped.[4] Letty and I had exquisite vision of Adele[5] in hat and stays. Really her legs are poems and, if I had such knees and feet, I feel I should be safe from all the 'slings and arrows of outrageous fortune'. They would be an unfailing source of consolation.

Mamma, Letty,[6] and I had very hot walk to church. I liked the new minister, with his sandy head and harsh voice. Sermon rather touching in its ugliness and simplicity. Extraordinary luncheon party of some of Papa's golf cronies. These invasions are rather trying. We went up to play tennis at Craigielaw at 3.30.

We returned late to a huge tea party—Countess Torby, Lady de Trafford, Margot, and the George Hopes. George Hope is very good-looking. His wound doesn't show at all, though it has blinded one of his eyes. John had great success at the piano. It really is extraordinary how he chooses the notes and gently caresses them, all the time making most eerie Puck faces. To my consternation I heard him say— I could almost swear to it—'I'm going to play Schumann.'

Monday, 23rd August . . . We returned to tea. Mr Asquith came, very mellow and asked about John. Puffin had given a glowing account of his musicalness. If I were Margot[7] I would whitewash the Prime Minister's face. He is so much attacked for callousness because he looks rosy and well. Played with the children when I got in, and then went for a short walk with Adele. She also discussed family finances with great intelligence. I like her more and more. Papa had gone away in the morning so we had no Hell, but some letter game and fairly early to bed.

. . . . .

Sunday, 12th September . . . It was Mr Asquith's birthday: we had a cake for him, and he came to tea to see his grandchildren. They presented him with flowers. Michael looked very pretty, was very coquettish with his grandfather, and had a great success at tea. John silent and absorbed in his own thoughts. . . .

. . . . .

Monday, 4th October Bibs[8] dined with Mamma and me. She was rather a stormy petrel and took objection to Mamma using the word 'second-rate'. As a treat—Bibs, John and I all slept in my bed. It was a very exhausting one. John woke for good before six, was exquisitely amused by the situation, and it was like having a bicycle and a puppy in bed with one. When I woke up his arms were tight round my neck.

. . . . .

Saturday, 23rd October We took John to the Zoo, and entirely failed to make him even see a lion or a tiger. He cut them dead. I wonder if there is anything wrong with his eyes. Felt in a mood of black-bitter nausea about the war. I'm afraid Lawrence's views are beginning to soak in. . . .

. . . . .

Saturday, 25th December Got up early to see the children opening their stockings. It was like the nightmare of a spoilt child. They have lovely things—Michael broke the Tenth Commandment and coveted John's. We got through our Christmas somehow, though we all felt sufficiently dejected and the weather added the last touch. It simply poured. We got quite wet going to church.

Bibs was horizontal with a sprained ankle, but we conveyed her to the Christmas tree at the hospital. We took John and David[9] with us. First there were carol-singers, then the tree with Dr Halliwell dressed up as Father Christmas—a noble performance, he made jokes in 'ye olde English' for quite three quarters of an hour. John was wonderfully pip-pippish at 'enter Father Christmas'. He was altogether wildly excited and clapped his hands at each burst of applause, wriggling and jiggling about all over the room. He loves crowds. It was a nice party. . . .

. . . . .

Sunday, 27th February 1916 Snow still falling. I walked to Didbrook with Mamma before lunch—very heavy going through snow. She talked of Yvo[10] all the time, planning a little memorial of his letters, etc.

After lunch Beb perpetrated a most horrible atrocity. He has always been bothering about John's hair being too long and, suddenly, when I was out of the room, he hacked about two inches off on one side. He brought the hair in to show me. I rushed in and found poor John looking a figure of fun. I have seldom been more unhappy and never more angry: I wept and made an awful scene before Nurse. It really was an abominable thing to do. We had always taken so much trouble about the cutting of his hair, and he had such a good medieval club head, just what I wanted. Now the whole ear—a feature I consider obscene—is exposed, and it will take months and months for the hair to grow right again. Damn! Beb was full of irritating sophistries, not nearly contrite enough. He tried to be funny and said we could each look at the side we preferred. Poor nurse is miserable. God—I am angry!

. . . . .

Tuesday, 21st March . . . Travelled down to Windsor by 4.30. Found children had arrived all right. Evelyn[11] has lent us this house while she is in Ireland. We have got her housemaid and a Belgian refugee, Jean Baptiste, is acting as a kind of butler. I have got my own cook and it is an appalling thought to be ordering and paying for one's own food after so long a holiday. I interviewed before dinner, and tried to be clever about meticulous war economies—'margarine', no lump sugar . . . Had a very straightforward solitary dinner and went to bed early very tired.

· · · · ·

Thursday, 23rd March Snow falling again to my disgust. At six I went off to call on Miss Weisse,[12] having had the inspiration of trying to explain John to her. I felt all the old tremor on driving up to the door. She was really very nice and very interested—said she thought it sounded 'anxious', but that it might be quite all right, and realised my great hopes by offering to take him for half an hour every day. I am to take him for diagnosis at 9.30 next Tuesday. It will be most interesting. . . .

· · · · ·

Monday, 17th April . . . Miss Weisse came to tea. Before getting on to mine, I let her have her head on the topic of *her* son Donald Tovey. She—poor thing—is *utterly* miserable about his engagement contracted in Edinburgh. At the best I suppose it would have been hard to bear, and there seem to be no extenuating circumstances—elderly, kittenish, commonplace, and unmusical.

John was the next topic. She recommended musical drill of some sort, and seriously advised my taking him to a child specialist. This I had already decided to do. He is nearly five and must be taken in hand. Sometimes I feel miserably worried about his abnormality. I don't *think* Miss. W. is really afraid for him *ultimately,* but of course as she says, arrested development, if only temporary, interferes with a boy's career. . . .

· · · · ·

Thursday, 20th April I went off and scoured the bargain basement at Self-ridges and then, in great excitement, to Park Street for my appointment with Dr Cantley. Found John there—Nurse had brought

him up for the day—he was quicksilver with excitement. I went into
the doctor by myself first. He had my letter and asked me with a
smile, quite a kind one, if I had been studying psychology. When John
came in, of course he behaved in his *most* eccentric way—wriggling,
giggling, twitching and making faces. Cantley stethoscoped and
examined him naked, finding him physically perfectly all right. He
said he was a 'neurotic' type, but would prescribe nothing, opining
that he would become more normal. But saying—what is obvious—
that he must now have some form of tuition and discipline besides
Nurse—something that will control, take him out of himself, and
gradually coax him more on to the same plane as his fellow-creatures.
I felt rather re-assured—I don't quite know why. Nurse and I took
him to Stewarts, where he revelled in a lunch of Scotch broth, ham
roll, banana, and cake. We discussed his unnormality more frankly
and thoroughly than we ever had before. I thought her wonderfully
understanding and sensible—she *is* a dear. I left them munching and
went off to lunch with Bluetooth. [13]

My spirits had risen and I was quite merry. . . .

· · · · ·

Saturday, 13th May . . . Met John at Dr Shuttleworth, the specialist
recommended by Miss Weisse. John answered above his average.
The doctor disquieted me on the whole. He said, 'You can't go by
looks', and there *might* be indubitable 'intelligence' permanently without control. I feel cold terror about John now more and more often.
It is just because the word 'stupid' is so inapplicable and because of
a strange completeness about him as he is, that makes one despair of
any reason why he should ever change. Oh God, surely nothing so
cruel can really have happened to me myself? I must just hope and
wait and hope.

· · · · ·

Monday, 12th June Nannie told me a lady in their house, contemplat-
ing Michael, had pronounced him to be 'just lovely'. Whereupon he
had torn off his hat and said, running his finger through his curls,
'He's got lovely hair, too.' Beb and I had a shrimp tea with them. The
governess recommended by Dr Shuttleworth had just arrived, so I
took her for a walk afterwards, as I wanted to describe John to her. She

is quite young and seems very, very nice—gentle and intelligent. She came in with me and watched the children going to bed. John took a fancy to her and was in much his best form—really more or less normal on the surface. She thought him fascinating and I could see she was surprised. I expect she thinks I am the exact *converse* of the fatuous mother who thinks her ordinary child a genius.

· · · · ·

Sunday, 25th June   Had a long talk with the governess—like her very much. She is convinced that there is nothing *mentally* wrong with John, though of course he is undeniably eccentric. She considers him superhumanly obstinate and self-conscious. Luckily, she and Nurse are getting on very well, but she said she would have a much better chance of effecting improvement if she were to have him more to herself. I agreed and devoted much thought to domestic politics, finally arranging for her and John to have their meals apart in her lodging. At present they all eat together, and naturally it is rather difficult for her to correct him before Nurse, and *constant* drilling is the only way to get him out of his inverted way of talk, etc. I really think I already see *some* improvement, and she says she is getting his attention at lessons. I told her I wanted her to stay on after July. What am I to do? I *can't* have three women for two children.

· · · · ·

Sunday, 9th July   Pilgrimage to Littlehampton to see the children. John was supposed to be in a very naughty mood, but I really do see an improvement in him. His voice is much more normal and he answers more. His strange charm quite unimpaired. He has grown immense.

· · · · ·

Wednesday, 19th July   Arrive Littlehampton 12.47 and was met by both children, looking very well—Michael too lovely. I lunched with him. He has come on a lot and talks very precisely and grammatically: 'Yes. No. I will . . . I like . . . etc.' I asked him if he would send love to Daddie—'love' means kiss to them—and he replied, 'No, Daddie got bristle'. When John cried, he said, 'I'm ashamed of zoo'.

Miss Quinn seemed very satisfied with John's progress, but I can't say there is any startling difference on the surface.

•   •   •   •   •

Monday, 31st July   Grilling hot again. As soon as I had had breakfast,
I went along to see John doing his lessons. He did his drill quite
nicely, and some writing and counting all right—only somehow it
gives you the impression of a *tour de force* like a performing
animal. . . .

•   •   •   •   •

Friday, 18th August   I am sitting out at Pixton. After the constant
brace of Brighton it is like sitting in a greenhouse. Children both
asleep when we arrived. Had a talk with Miss Quinn. John has been
doing his lessons well, but otherwise, in general conduct, Miss Quinn
thinks he has 'gone back'. She doesn't have him so much to herself
here, and is hinting that she ought to have him right away by herself
somewhere. If I stay on at Brighton, I think I shall let her bring him
there. I shall never have the nerve to *say* it to Nurse—I think I shall
have to wait till I'm away and write it.

Sunday, 18th February 1917   Foggy, muzzy day. Got up with rather
speckled spring face. We all breakfasted together. There were war
scones made with barley instead of wheat—very good. I took John
out from eleven till nearly one, and very exhausting I found it. I don't
wonder his governess needs a siesta. Beb walked with us nearly as
far as the Copper Horse.

I went for a walk with Evelyn after luncheon, and had a long John
talk. She thinks his governess (in spite of some faults) is doing good
work, but thinks it essential to have someone else in charge of John, a
governess not being capable of the two functions—the mental training, and the dressing and undressing, and so on. She advocated
Polly.[14]

I was feeling deadly depressed and bothered. On paper certainly I
can make out a desperate case. The sore past—two war terrors—
the sickening worry of John—bad health—a load of debt—and now,
last but crushing straw, I must give up Polly to John. Evelyn told
me I ought to be with John—so I ought and so I will, a great deal. I
shall go down Fridays to Sunday, but I must be in London a good
deal. In the circumstances I can't sit in the country alone with John. It

only makes me ill with distress and I don't think I'm very good for him. I must do some war work in London.

• • • • •

Sunday, 18th March   Made my postponed journey to Brighton. Michael very busy helping me pack. I left the room for a few moments to find my box filled with every possible portable object—towels, fire irons, etc. He was rather hurt when I took them out.

I am staying with the Seymours. Horatia [Seymour] was in bed, but I lunched with Lady Seymour, and arranged that she should be a Mrs Pipchin and board John and his two attendants. It will be much nicer for them than lodgings, but it will not be for long as she is probably going to let her house. Then I think I shall try and send them to Eliza's cottage. I really can't afford lodgings and the flat. Dined alone with Lady Seymour. She is terribly delicate on the subject of money and couldn't negotiate with me as to terms. Horatia was the agent next day and I agreed to pay £14 10s for everything.

• • • • •

Sunday, 1st April   I had a talk with John's governess after dinner. I feel more and more despairing about any real change in John. Improvement in behaviour means little to me. It is an awful shadow over my life. I may forget and be merry, but happy I can never really be while it is there. Why? Why? Why? is all that rises from one's heart and brain.

Monday, 2nd April   . . . I took John out in the garden after lunch, having bought him a ball. He had quite a good idea of kicking. After tea Lady Seymour and I had him in the drawing room. Have been through the accustomed cycle of feelings. First miserable despair, with almost horror, then his great charm intervenes and I become soothed, almost reassured. Lady Seymour very nice about him. We get on very well together. I am really rather fond of her. After dinner, at her request, I read half Dickens' 'Haunted Man'. Beloved Dickens. As usual he warmed the cockles of my heart.

Tuesday, 3rd April   Snowed in the night. Lovely sunny, cold morning. John and his governess took me to the station in the bus and John looked strained and pale. He minds my going very much now. I went to Cadogen Square and ate the remains of Sockie's and Bibs' lunch. Shopped at Harrods. . . .

· · · · ·

Tuesday, 10th April . . . I had a letter from John's governess saying she would leave at the end of the month she was so disheartened by all the changes—all no doubt because she and Polly cannot work together. It's very disappointing.

· · · · ·

Friday, 20th April . . . Lawrence came to see me. He has not moved from Cornwall for over a year, so it had been a long interval. He looked better. I still found great interest and vividness in his face and voice, and he wove the most interesting theories round the John mystery. He thinks him the logical conclusion of generations of frustration and conforming to an unreal plane. The result being that John is quite off the plane I have violated myself in order to remain on. He is certain his state is spiritual not mental and a case for exorcism, and said I could cure him by getting off the false unreal plane of 'buses, Lloyd George's speeches and so on, to which I was now clinging. He said the first time he saw John he had noted the revolt in his eyes, the subconscious antagonism. He believed he could help. He talked about the war—assured me Beb wouldn't be killed if I didn't want him to be and reproached me for 'subscribing to the war' to the extent of working in a hospital. . . .

· · · · ·

Saturday, 28th April Polly brought John to lunch in the flat. It was tantalising and painful. The two boys looked so delicious together and one felt poignantly what fun one ought to be having with them. Michael was so sweet, trying to entertain John and offering him his toys one after the other. 'Will you play ball with me? No?' John knocked him down. Poor Nurse looked very wistful and it made us unhappy.

Nannie cooked us a delicious lunch. We had early tea and Polly, John, his governess and I went down to Stanway[15] by the 4.55.

· · · · ·

Wednesday, 24th October Woke up to terrible morning misery. The dreary detail of the John tragedy blackens life. One can never dismiss it from one. It is a past, present, and future nightmare. I loved my idea of that baby more than I have ever loved anything—and it was just something that never existed! . . .

Thursday, 25th October   Took John to see Forsythe, the brain specialist recommended by Katharine.[16] Mamma came to assist me. He said it was not at all a usual case. If something had gone wrong *before* his birth, then nothing could be done, but it was *possibly* a case of what he calls introversion when training might help. He is going to read my book about John[17] for data, and will look out for a governess for me. In the meantime, I must get another hospital nurse.

·   ·   ·   ·   ·

Tuesday, 18th December   Mary[18] and I talked a lot about John in the evening, and she was most darling. I gathered someone had been critical of me, and had said she couldn't imagine not concentrating on him if he were her child. I said if I believed him to be really curable, I would never leave him, but I had long really inwardly realised the hopelessness of the case and determined to keep the cruel sorrow within certain limits—not to *allow* it to blacken the whole of life for me, but to keep myself sane for Michael, and the best way to do that was to fix one's thoughts as much as possible on the latter.

·   ·   ·   ·   ·

Tuesday, 22nd January 1918   Woke up at three and couldn't get to sleep again for ages. John's governess pressed about twenty-five sheets of letters into my hand—a great portion of it was in rhyme (her jungle jangles she calls it). It had been written in a rage—she said at three o'clock in the morning—it must have been the intensity of her thinking about me which aroused me from my slumbers. It was an indictment (for which she remorsefully apologised) . . . what amused me was her indignation over the books I had asked her to order for me at the library: Keats' *Letters*, Morley's *Recollections*, and Balzac. She wanted to know what on earth they had to do with my sons? She has had a letter from Mamma saying she thought she had found an ideal farm for John a mile from Stanway.

Very sentimental talk with the governess before she went home, in which she told me how she longed to die. I compelled myself to kiss her for which she has been dumbly asking all these days. Poor dear, she has such a craving for affection. . . .

Wednesday, 23rd January   John and his governess walked me as far as the park, and then I bicycled to Mrs Cullen's to have my hair cleaned. We met Papa and he gave John fourpence. He is constantly giving him little tips and is being very sweet to and about him. I had written a long letter to John's governess, having felt incapable of responding to hers by word of mouth. Mine was not a success. She wrote to me three times in the course of this day! I lunched with Freddie and Brenda[19] at Claridge's to say goodbye to Freddie, who is going off to—what he calls—the 'Le Touquet Salient'.

Tea with John—he really is improving

· · · · ·

Wednesday, 13th February   I travelled up to London by the eleven something, feeling oh! so ill and depressed. Tea with John and his governess—John certainly looked worse again. . . .

· · · · ·

Sunday, 10th March   Foggy morning. Walked with John and his governess. I met Aunt Madeline and talked to her for a bit. . . .

John's governess and I—at her suggestion—did planchette after I got home. It wrote briskly, answering my unspoken inquiry as to who the force was by 'I am Blackwood'; a question as to whether John would get well by, 'Your dearest hopes will be realised'; and giving a lot of typical (to spiritualism I mean) sentiments, such as 'I love you more than I could on earth' and so on. I had dinner in bed—felt strangely happy and *exaltée*—why? 'You approach the most critical points in your development—beware of the pitfalls of intellect' and words to the effect of 'Think less and pray more' were scribbled by the pencil! Ugh!

· · · · ·

Tuesday, 7th May   John's birthday—I don't know what to think of him. At times I was telepathised by his governess's confidence—at other times fell back into despondency. Somehow or other she has taught him to read quite a lot. . . .

· · · · ·

Saturday, 20th July John and his governess met me at Eynsham at about five. John looking pale—temporarily, according to her, owing to digestive trouble—but huge and sturdy with great footballer's legs. His expression much better—at least he wears his best one much more continuously. I was astonished by his reading, and the great thing is the delight he takes in it and the wish to show off his accomplishment. He picks up a book directly and starts off like the Ancient Mariner, and when he is alone in a room he reads to himself. He puts mechanical toys together very well too. He is very, very darling and so loving—much less hysterical.

· · · · ·

Tuesday, 20th August Walked with Bones[20] before lunch. He has angelically been wading all through my soppy children's biography because he wants to make a précis of John's case to send to a doctor friend of his in Austria. . . .

Thursday, 22nd August . . . Long hair-combing talk[21] on John's governess with Mamma. My last letters seem to have incensed her, and she is writing rabidly to Mamma as well as me. She really is *impossible*, but also indispensable. Mamma too angelic. She is a blessed being— a witness to God if ever there was one.

· · · · ·

Thursday, 19th September . . . Terrible ordeal—went to see John and his governess in their new flat in Chelsea. It's surprisingly nice for the price. John looked well and was very sweet, but I see no sign of fundamental change and feel very sick at heart. Was going to bed in sulky misery, but Desmond[22] persuaded me to dine with him at the last moment and I am very glad he prevented me from turning my face to the wall. . . .

Notes

*These selections are taken from *Lady Cynthia Asquith: Diaries, 1915–1918*, ed. E. M. Horsley (London: Hutchinson, 1968).

1   Aileen Broderick Meade was a cousin of Asquith's and mother of Antonia Meade.

2   Presumably a former servant of Charles Meade, Aileen's husband.

3   Charles Whibley, an honorary fellow of Jesus College, Cambridge, whom Asquith admired and took as a literary mentor.

4   *To dewdrop* signifies "to report a compliment."

5   Adele Grant Essex, the second wife of the seventh earl of Campbell.

6   Lady Violet Elcho, wife of Asquith's brother Hugo, Lord Elcho.

7   Mr. Asquith is Prime Minister Herbert Henry Asquith; Puffin is his son Anthony, stepbrother to Asquith's husband; and Margot is the prime minister's second wife.

8   Asquith's sister Irene.

9   David Charteris, twelfth earl of Wemyss and Asquith's young nephew (b. 1912).

10   Yvo Charteris, Asquith's brother, who died heroically in action in 1915.

11   Evelyn Charteris De Vesci, Asquith's paternal aunt.

12   Dr. Sophie Weisse, musician and teacher, who developed the genius of her son, Sir Donald Tovey, a musical scholar, pianist, and composer.

13   The Right Honorable Harold Baker, M.P.

14   Polly Cliffe, Asquith's maid.

15   Stanway House, near Cheltenham in Gloucestershire, is the family seat of the Charterises.

16   Katharine Asquith, wife of Asquith's brother-in-law Raymond.

17   The diary of John that she kept as a record for his doctors.

18   Probably Mary Herbert, Asquith's closest friend.

19   Lord Freddie Blackwood and his wife.

20   Richard Smallbones.

21   *Haircombing* signifies women's chatting with each other in their bed-rooms at bedtime.

22   Sir Desmond MacCarthy, dramatic and literary critic.

Ivy Jacquier

(b. 1890)

IVY JACQUIER was the daughter of François Jacquier, a French
Catholic sent to London by his family to learn banking, who married
a Protestant Englishwoman. Accordingly disinherited by his father,
François planned to remain permanently in England, where his first
four children (Adele, Tony, Leon, and Violet) were born. When his
father, however, subsequently recalled him to Lyons to work in the
family's private bank, the Jacquiers returned to France, where Ivy and
five years later her sister Doris, the sibling to whom she was closest,
were born. The Jacquiers continued to live in an English way in Lyons,
and the children, who were bilingual, attended the Church of England and English schools. Intending to become an artist, Ivy continued her studies in Dresden, Paris, and Eastbourne. In 1921 she married a Scotsman named Skinner (referred to only as "A") in her diary,
and they settled first in Worcester, England. She disliked Worcester,
which reminded her of living in an Arnold Bennett novel, but at
the time of the diary entries for 1922 selected for inclusion here,★ her
distaste for her surroundings was in abeyance while she rejoiced in
the birth of her first child, Sara Sophie ("Sally"). Jacquier's diary for
1907–26 provides little information about her outer life, for it is mod-
eled on the French-style *journal intime,* a record of interior events;
such a diary registers moods, perceptions, antipathies, enthusiasms
freely, but rarely facts and activities. In her outer life, Jacquier continued with her art after her daughter's birth, producing watercolor,
tempera, and gouache portraits and figures and exhibiting them both
in London and in Paris.

From Ivy Jacquier's Diary

1922

Jan 1.   We had a lovely Christmas at Vi's.[1] Most depressing day today back in Worcester. Always New Year's Day is anti-climax. Men cannot create atmosphere. One must do all that . . . and what if one have a bad day on? Later I thought gloriously to have lost the sense of the eternal loneliness of everyone. But it has returned yesterday and today. One simply cannot be taken care of. One has got to be all alone for anything that matters. It is practically to deny oneself to shirk this loneliness. I reflect also on the force of legitimacy and the power of marriage. The many years of shared experiences together, even fiery feeling falls a little flat before that. Romance is really easily outwitted. (At Vi's, domestic poetry, poetry domesticated.) In Géraldy's play "Aimer" on the eve of going with her lover the woman finds he has, for the moment, forgotten she had lost a child. She realises that life is to begin all over again, without a past . . . and she shirks the issue. Faithfulness is easier to practise.

Jan 13.   I am so dependent on A. Almost panicky when he is not there. Afterwards I must regain independence. But the calm trustfulness of this time rivets us. Is it the baby that I lust after things so, beautiful things? Now it is a Queen Anne chest I have seen; three days ago for a carved red amber flagon of the 16th century, Doris described me in a letter from India. La vie est riche. Today Peggy Gillet sent me a little lacquered yellow vanity case with lipstick. Kate Hardy is hurt. Why does one ever remonstrate? People cannot, and will not, change themselves. If they are worth while . . . well, put up with them. I shall be less stupid next time. It is not good to offend on the last lap; yet, I thought people profit, and I believe I still can. But soon probably I shall not; and I too love adulation and warm constant approval.

Jan 17.   A.'s birthday. He is nervy over his birthday just as Doris and I are. Today I felt oh! the nothing done; all the effort and waste of small creative powers, and nothing to leave behind. Is that why people want children? But I want the glory of living, and not to live by proxy, even through a child.

．　．　．　．　．

Jan 22.　Fell in love with two Chinese black wood chairs, dark, silky, and intricate: uncomfortable, but how I wanted them! To desire possessions like this is distinctly pathological. I buy them. I culled a woman the other day by knowing she would like dry toast for tea, and giving it her. It is Miss Binyon. Doris is coming back from India. I am glad. Later, I re-read the 'married' diary, and realise the phrases, how I have come a long way . . . and am in good waters, satisfied, myself, and happy. I think A. is calm because satisfied, happy because he feels he is in his logical development to places he wants to reach . . . and, I can say it, I believe he thinks our life together has fulfilled many things and brought to blossom powers in him . . . and that he is not wasting time. For me I feel quiet: fed. And above all untrammelled. Above all interested in life. Even in the episode of giving birth so soon to be mine. A. is touching and inspires me with fearlessness: it leaves one free.

Jan 24.　Sara Sophie Jacquier Skinner, born at 2.20 a.m., much better than losing an appendix. Dr. Moore-Ede was a gem; I enjoyed the experience.

Feb 23.　BARKERS, BUCKINGHAMSHIRE I have tried to recapture the unmarried state in the sultry silence of this February evening at Barker's with Violet.[1] The silence . . . the trains, the ssss of the gas; the Englishness of it all. But the train's whistle in the countryside gave it me . . . that feeling of loneliness inseparable from celibacy . . . and the dread of nature. Landscape . . . and animals: why do they frighten? It is as well I remember the pains of the unmarried for Doris's sake: and never to forget any experience. In my glass since "Petrouska's" birth I seem materialistic, with a shorter neck, almost oriental.(I perceive I am trying to avoid the word 'coarse'.)

Mar 7.　Why do I not write my diary any more? I shall so like to re-read it later . . . and for "Petrouska", i.e. or Sara Sophie. For to her turn all my thoughts. I want to adorn her. (To sell my ambers and three dresses and buy the first pearl of a pearl necklace for her. To have her made a bed with my two old gilt carved lions set in the head and foot.) I think to myself if she is like me (and sometimes I feel I hold myself in my arms)—these many years of diary will help. I was not kissed and stroked enough . . . never enough. She shall have all that. When back from visits she shall be tucked up in bed. And the tangible word: "Oh! I am excited at having you again, Petrouska" shall be said literally. We are all bound by thongs of reserve. She still seems so near to me I could cry when she does . . . and often it is as if the crying was in my inside. She is nearly an obsession. I dream of her at night. Love is a load; love is heavy. When I look back to the nine months of carrying "Petrouska" they seem suffused with health, creativeness, imagination, that amply supplemented life in Worcester. Was it marriage or "Petrouska"? I cannot tell. I have never had one without the other, that is the trouble. Marriage as an experience is nearly all to begin again. I regret nothing however. As soon as one has a relationship with a man understanding is at an end. So the months one is camarade are a gain. I feel a reaction . . . as though I must make good to "Petrouska" for not having been absorbed in her all the time before, by being absorbed now! I pretended I thought her ugly when they showed her me. It makes me ill to think I ever pretended. One is primitive. When I am very tired, to sit and give her her bottle refreshes one as contact with some vital force. Are people so? After either a human hand alone seems to drag one back. "L'amour c'est une question d'épiderme."[2] That is true . . . as far as it goes.

Mar 12. Creativeness . . . at least capacity to make my life is with me again. So not banished by having a baby? I feel more intelligent this year than ever before. I suppose 32 is the hey-day? I feel also the lack of construction in my education, being essentially self-educated. The world is a wonderful place. Two hours ago I felt bored. And now I am afire again. Oh! to feel a latent power, as a torch, still alight; and now to a purpose . . . that of "Petrouska's" greater joys. I want her to be five now, this minute, to read her the Butcher and Lang Odyssey. One night when still in bed I cried with refreshment over George Moore's "Abelard". To cry because of beauty is a wonderful sensation. But why did George Moore temper [tamper?] with the inevitableness of the true story?

Mar 17. What a play one is to oneself. Sooner than I had dared to hope I feel elastic and springy in brain. "Petrouska" has a lovely peal [pearl?] skin lighted as though from within. At night. She has been brought in and laid across my knees just as I was going in to her and had got out of bed. She is healthy and expresses such harmonious effects with her hands. I read Katherine Mansfield. She is a new writer. I am refreshed by a new one, and one so of our own generation: talking like Jacquiers. A. is so happy in his work. All his energies converge.

Mar 27. Maternal emotion is morbid. I read Katherine Mansfield, diabolically clever . . . but irritatingly close to one's generation. Yet vulgar, with no vision. One has spite against her; she is of us. But clever, never by any chance great, seeing only facile beauty, journalistically. Alive to the things one thrills to, but not enhancing really. A few bad days. Readjustment.

Mar 30. Loneliness. I lie and read politics with a heavy cold. A. rushes back from a meeting, rushes out to dinner, I resume the thread of my thoughts. Tonight I say to myself I will get a very good nurse and travel, leaving "Petrouska". And to think that I probably would not have the guts to travel and develop along my own lines while A. is so busy. Also to be always happy would not suit me. These miserable days help me in reality to concentrate. How I want Mrs. Wilson to like me. She came yesterday. I believe she has suffered. She cannot bear the the agony of the "Abelard and Héloise" letters. She is passionate. She is young. She is 65. And she reads Katherine Mansfield. She is the wife of Canon James Wilson here. Almost I felt her wanting to cull me. Than quickly I talk of books, fool that I am. This awful reserve. I loathe reserve. It is Mother who never allowed us to be introspective to her. I must talk to "Petrouska"! "You are me in 1912." Had Dr. Moore-Ede for her. I like him: a little strange, his piercing gaze and always, rather embarrassingly so at times, his embracing the woman's point of view.

Apr 2. One needs to be frantically spoilt and adulated after a baby. And one is not.

Apr 3. To love one's child is as painful and has all the vulnerability of being in love. This sort of passionate protectiveness hurts one. One has no outlet; to hug tight . . . for this Sally is too tiny. As I heard Bach's Mass in B minor today I thought of the hat I should wear to my first English race-meeting. And all day was miserable. Sally alone, Sally more than ever, because with a cold she is so appealing. A. is in town. He worries me by his reserve. Why cannot I accept man's spasmodic affection and leave my own, chronically, organically, affectionate? Every year Easter depresses me.

Apr 4.   A. leaves for Scotland.

Apr 17.   I write this book more often when I am unhappy. Tonight I am a bit lonely but it is all on a loom of happiness. Sometimes I want to revert with A. to pre-marriage days. C'est mal comprendre la vie.³ Nothing is stationary, and all things have their season . . . and their reason. Women abhor change and like them all I want passion to be static; stable. I wish for someone big to give me ideals; to make me stand on tip-toe. Marriage *has* beauty. I have a need of ideals. This life of little luxuries has not enough. God! Give me a soul.

Apr 18.   Mrs. Wilson. A violet velvet dress and a violet waist-coat and her mobile experienced face. She says the only education is by example. Then it is that I must begin to educate myself for Sally. I told her about my need for 'ideals'. She agrees. I feel everywhere lack of structure. Colour we have. But no bone. Jouir, jouir.⁴ The very word renunciation is almost archaic.

Apr 19.   Oh! how feminine I am. I want, and do not want, to leave. I am packed, car ordered, then I countermand it. I will go by a later train. Why? Because I miss A.? Because I go to an empty house in London? Because Sally smells so lovely? I belong to the age of dependent women.

Apr 20.   LONDON   "A. I miss you. Sally I miss you." Though London is lovely.

Apr 26.   A gorgeous week after all. A. meets me from Scotland, and the last days are best of all. The trees in the park are in bud. We stay at the Alexandra Hotel and as we cross the road suddenly I nearly burst with enjoyment. A child reminds a man of bonds. To meet away is good.

May 8.   WORCESTER   Mon Dieu, this sudden heat in Worcester in this house reminds me of last year. Blossom everywhere, lovely yellow roses like at the "Sleeping Princess" at Christmas. Yesterday was our wedding day: a happy year. But I do not want to relive anything.

June 12.   One works for the far future with children: probably for after one's death: certainly for when they have children. I remember seeing in the one written page of this very book Mother gave me to use, the line she had left: "I am always very lonely." What bores women are with their loneliness! A. is away. Lying in the garden hammock I think that when he is here my self is ouatée: cotton-wooled. Also how one day soon I shall be taking up my own personality. As men do . . . after the first few months. Shall I have any intimacy with Sally; even when she is 18? Route funeste où je m'engage.[5]

· · · · ·

June 18.   Discovery: that love is not all in life even for women. I say it again and again and to sleep drew out a chart. If we faced love as men do we would be happier. As episodes, accesses. Life is not meant for love alone. We are hipped by the old saws of women about life turning on love, etc., etc. Je veux surmonter ma fémininité.[6] Love is not the whole of life. One ought to use men as they do us, as a means of experience to more knowledge. (Not more men because one is fairly monogamous.) To realise what A.'s given me for instance. A fuller life, more established, more rounded,. . . and then be self-supporting, a person, not a wife. Love like my creative powers comes and goes. I think often I shall never paint again—and it comes back.

· · · · ·

July 9.   Doris has been here and there have been days of bubbling laughter and complete bien-être.[7] With these three life is really complete. The house has rocked to music, often mere sound but with a tone to it.

July 18.   Doris is gone to London, A. away for the night. The night is a perfect late-summer one, throbbing; but summer wanes already. We have had such lovely days—with A. and Sally and Doris; what more could I want? The one so quietening and reassuring, health-giving, generous. The other one such a tiny replica of A. with benign little twinkling eyes and a double chin. And last Doris needing us both, appealing, as she does not always, to the protective; nervy, nerve-ridden. The few years before a girl marries are hell indeed: make one ill.

. . . . . .

Dec 15.   Here[8] I lose self-respect and grow nervy. It is not a healthy life. Why? over-eating, over-heating, not enough air, not enough exercise, agitation from Mother spreading all over the house. We bought a Persian vase today, Doris and I; but no respect and a full stomach. Oh! preserve me from envy and bitterness concerning the riches of others[.] I wonder how I recognised A. in the false values that surround us here. Often these days I have thought of him, for he is health and air and freedom from myself, to me.

Dec 18.   I am enjoying France. I think of last Christmas at Violet's house. It was delicious and had poetry. Sally has such a kind funny little face. I have bought her a musical box for Christmas.

Dec 29.   I am enjoying France. Time goes so quickly. A. joined us here on 23rd. It was lovely. In the evening we had a tree for the two babies, Sally and François,[9] up at Léon's house. Sally beat her heels up and down. The tree shimmered against the blue dining-room wall. She tore at her parcels. Christmas night Germaine and Doris played, both in white.

Dec 31.   The year's out. For me: Sally's birth. Not being able to nurse her. Going away and coming back to her. Going away from A. and meeting him in London after twelve days. Hopping across Hyde Park Corner arm-in-arm with Vi and him, and crying, "Oh! I love London!" Then receiving my friends in my house, my furniture, buying my tallboy: and our table. Our piano. Beauty in Paris: a terracotta statue on mahogany in a shop in the Rue de la Boétie. An ivory figure—and the dilapidated chateau we passed in the train. Then—revelling in the unmarried state—then being married. Then the self-analysis of meeting A. again, and the belonging—to sensation. France, and silks, and today St. Germain, where we go with the full and complete recognition of tradition. (Is it because I am nearly 33 and a parent?) The Beaujolais little hills are excruciatingly beautiful and blue.

Notes

❧

*These selections are taken from *The Diary of Ivy Jacquier: 1907–1926* (London: Gollancz, 1960).

1 Her sister Violet's home.

2 Love is a matter of touch.

3 It's a question of not understanding life very well.

4 Enjoy, enjoy.

5 It's a dismal course I have been taking.

6 I want to transcend my femininity.

7 Well-being.

8 Staying at her parents' home in France.

9 The son (b. 17 June 1922) of her sister Gladys and Gladys's husband, Léon.

IV

IN WARTIME

———————————————

Sarah Macnaughtan

(d. 1916)

OF SCOTTISH DESCENT, Sarah Broom Macnaughtan was the daughter of Peter Macnaughtan, J.P. She took such care to hide her birth date that even her obituary notice in the London *Times* could not reveal it, but she may have been born in the 1850s. She had independent means and never married. A minor novelist, Macnaughtan attained some public success in the Edwardian period and was actively associated with the women's suffrage movement, though never a militant. But her most distinguished achievement was her wartime services. Having had some training as a nurse, she first tended the victims of Balkan atrocities; then, during the Boer War, she went to South Africa as a volunteer with the Red Cross. At the outbreak of the Great War, she joined Mrs. St. Clair Stobart's Red Cross women's unit as head orderly; when the unit was ordered to evacuate beleaguered Antwerp, she stayed on to continue her work independently. After Antwerp fell, Macnaughtan joined Dr. Hector Munro's Ambulance Corps, with a base at Furnes. Horrified by the neglect of the wounded at the railway terminus, she established her first soup kitchen at Furnes Railway Station with the help of three Belgian nursing sisters, and when that station was largely shelled out, started another kitchen at Adenkirke Station, labors for which she was rewarded with the Order of Leopold. In June 1915 she returned to England to give thirty-five lectures encouraging workers at munitions centers, refusing to accept any pay for them. In October she joined an Anglo-Russian hospital group; after a wearisome wait in Russia for permission to proceed to active service, in 1916 she left for Persia, where she fell seriously ill and returned to England to die. Indeed she had been ill when she first came to Belgium, but disguised that fact and earned a reputation for unflagging hard work. The following account of her soup kitchen at Furnes comes from the 1914–15 diary that she herself (like many other women who had wartime adventures abroad) arranged for publication.★

From Sarah Macnaughtan's Diary

21 November 1914   I am up to my eyes in soup! I have started my
soup-kitchen at the station,[1] and it gives me a lot to do. Bad luck to
it, my cold and cough are pretty bad!

It is odd to wake in the morning in a frozen room, with every pane
of glass green and thick with frost, and one does not dare to think
of Mary and morning tea! When I can summon enough moral courage
to put a foot out of bed I jump into my clothes at once; half dressed,
I go to a little tap of cold water to wash, and then, and for ever, I
forgive entirely those sections of society who do not tub. We brush
our own boots here, and put on all the clothes we possess, and then
descend to a breakfast of Quaker oat porridge with bread and margarine. I wouldn't have it different, really, till our men are out of the
trenches; but I am hoping most fervently that I shan't break down,
as I am so "full with soup."

Our kitchen at the railway-station is a little bit of a passage, which
measures eight feet by eight feet. In it are two small stoves. One is
a little round iron thing which burns, and the other is a sort of little
"kitchener" which doesn't! With this equipment, and various huge
"marmites" [cooking pots], we make coffee and soup for hundreds of
men every day. The first convoy gets into the station about 9.30
a.m., all the men frozen, the black troops nearly dead with cold. As
soon as the train arrives I carry out one of my boiling "marmites"
to the middle of the stone entrance and ladle out the soup, while a
Belgian Sister takes round coffee and bread.

These Belgians (three of them) deserve much of the credit for the
soup-kitchen, if any credit is going about, as they started with coffee
before I came, and did wonders on nothing. Now that I have bought
my pots and pans and stoves we are able to do soup, and much more.
The Sisters do the coffee on one side of eight feet by eight, while I
and my vegetables and the stove which goes out are on the other. We
can't ask people to help because there is no room in the kitchen; besides, alas! there are so many people who like raising a man's head and
giving him soup, but who do not like cutting up vegetables.

After the first convoy of wounded has been served, other wounded
men come in from time to time, then about 4 o'clock there is another

trainload. At ten p.m. the largest convoy arrives. The men seem too stiff to move, and many are carried in on soldiers' backs. The stretchers are laid on the floor, those who can "s'asseoir" [sit up] sit on benches, and every man produces a "quart" or tin cup. One and all they come out of the darkness and never look about them, but rouse themselves to get fed, and stretch out poor grimy hands for bread and steaming drinks. There is very little light—only one oil-lamp, which hangs from the roof, and burns dimly. Under this we place the "marmites," and all that I can see is one brown or black or wounded hand stretched out into the dim ring of light under the lamp, with a little tin mug held out for soup. Wet and ragged, and covered with sticky mud, the wounded lie in the salle of the station, and, except under the lamp, it is all quite dark. There are dim forms and frosty breaths, and a door which bangs continually, and then the train loads up, the wounded depart, and a heavy smell and an empty pot are all that remain. We clean up the kitchen, and go home about 1 a.m. I do the night work alone.

24 November   We are beginning to get into our stride, and the small kitchen turns out its gallons and buckets of liquid. Mrs.____has been helping me with my work. It is good to see anyone so beautiful in the tiny kitchen, and it is quaint to see anyone so absolutely ignorant of how a pot is washed or a vegetable peeled.

I have a little electric lamp, which is a great comfort to me, as I have to walk home alone at midnight. When I get up in the morning I have to remember all I shall want during the day, as the villa is a mile from the station, so I take my lantern out at 9.30 a.m.!

I saw a Belgian regiment march back to the trenches to-day. They had a poor little band and some foggy instruments, and a bugler flourished a trumpet. I stood by the roadside and cried till I couldn't see.

1 December   Mrs. Knocker and Miss Chisholm and Lady Dorothy went out to Pervyse[2] a few days ago to make soup, etc., for Belgians in the trenches. They live in the cellar of a house which has been blown inside out by guns, and take out buckets of soup to men on outpost duty. Not a glimpse of fire is allowed on the outposts. Fortunately the weather has been milder lately, but soaking wet. Our three

ladies walk about the trenches at night, and I come home at 1 a.m.
from the station. The men of our party meanwhile do some house-
work. They sit over the fire a good deal, clear away the tea-things, and
when we come home at night we find they have put hot-water bottles
in our bed and trimmed some lamps. I feel like Alice in Wonderland
or some other upside-down world. We live in much discomfort,
which is a little unnecessary; but no one seems to want to undertake
housekeeping.

I make soup all day, and there is not much else to write about. All
along the Yser the Allies and the Germans confront each other, but
things have been quieter lately. The piteous list of casualties is not so
long as it has been. A wounded German was brought in to-day. Both
his legs were broken and his feet frost-bitten. He had been for four
days in water with nothing to eat, and his legs unset. He is doing
well.

On Sunday I drove out to Pervyse with a kind friend, Mr. Tapp. At
the end of the long avenue by which one approaches the village,
Pervyse church stands, like a sentinel with both eyes shot out. Nothing is left but a blind stare. Hardly any of the church remains, and
the churchyard is as if some devil had stalked through it, tearing up
crosses and kicking down graves. Even the dead are not left undis-
turbed in this awful war. The village (like many other villages) is just
a mass of gaping ruins—roofs blown off, streets full of holes, not a
window left unshattered, and the guns still booming.

[?] *December* Unexpected people continue to arrive at Furnes. Mme.
Curie and her daughter are in charge of the X-ray apparatus at the
hospital. Sir Bartle Frere is there as a guest. Miss Vaughan, of the
Nursing Times, came in out of the dark one evening. To-day the King[3]
has been here. God bless him! he always does the right thing.

6 December My horizon is bounded by soup and the men who drink
it. There is a stir outside the kitchen, and someone says, "Convoi."
So then we begin to fill pots and take steaming "marmites" off the fire.
The "sitting cases" come in first, hobbling, or carried on their com-
rades' backs—heads and feet bandaged or poor feet maimed. When
they have been carried or have stiffly and slowly marched through the

entrance to the train, the "brancard" [stretcher] cases are brought in and laid on the floor. They are hastily examined, and a doctor goes round reading the labels attached to them which describe their wounds. An English ambulance and a French one wait to take serious cases to their respective hospitals. The others are lifted on to train-stretchers and carried to the train.

Two doctors came out from England on inspection duty to-day. They asked if I had anything to report, and I made them come to the station to go into this matter of the different-sized stretchers. It is agony to the men to be shifted. Dr. Wilson has promised to take up the question. The transport service is now much improved. The trains are heated and lighted, and priests travel with the lying-down cases.

8 December   I have a little "charette" [cart] for my soup. It is painted red, and gives a lot of amusement to the wounded. The trains are very long, and my small carriage is useful for cups and basins, bread, soup, coffee, etc. Clemmie Waring designed and sent it to me.

To-day I was giving out my soup on the train and three shells came in in quick succession. One came just over my head and lodged in a haystall on the other side of the platform. The wall of the store has an enormous hole in it, but the thickly packed hay prevented the shrapnel scattering. The station-master was hit, and his watch saved him, but it was crumpled up like a rag. Two men were wounded, and one of them died. A whole crowd of refugees came in from Coxide, which is being heavily shelled. There was not a scrap of food for them, so I made soup in great quantities, and distributed it to them in a crowded room whose atmosphere was thick. Ladling out the soup is great fun.

12 December   The days are very short now, and darkness falls early. All the streets are dark, so are the houses, so is the station. Two candles are a rare treat, and oil is difficult to get.

Such a nice boy died to-night. We brought him to the hospital from the station, and learned that he had lain for eight days wounded and untended. Strangely enough he was naked, and had only a blanket over him on the stretcher. I do not know why he was still alive. Everything was done for him that could be done, but as I passed through one of the wards this evening the nurses were doing their last kindly duty to him. Poor fellow! He was one of those who had "given even their names." No one knew who he was. He had a woman's portrait tattooed on his breast.

19 December   Not much to record this week. The days have become more stereotyped, and their variety consists in the number of wounded who come in. One day we had 280 extra men to feed—a batch of soldiers returning hungry to the trenches, and some refugees. So far we have never refused anyone a cup of soup; or coffee and bread.

I haven't been fit lately, and get fearful bad headaches. I go to the station at 10 a.m. every morning, and work till 1 o'clock. Then to the hospital for lunch. I like the staff there very much. The surgeons are not only skilful, but they are men of education. We all get on well together, in spite of that curious form of temper which war always seems to bring. No one is affable here, except those who have just come out from home, and it is quite common to hear a request made and refused, or granted with, "Please do not ask again." Newcomers are looked upon as aliens, and there is a queer sort of jealousy about all the work.

Oddly enough, few persons seem to show at their best at a time when the best should be apparent. No doubt, it is a form of nerves, which is quite pardonable. Nurses and surgeons do not suffer from it. They are accustomed to work and to seeing suffering, but amateur workers are a bit headlong at times. I think the expectation of excitement (which is often frustrated) has a good deal to do with it. Those who "come out for thrills" often have a long waiting time, and energies unexpended in one direction often show themselves unexpectedly and a little unpleasantly in another.

In my own department I always let Zeal spend itself unchecked, and I find that people who have claimed work or a job ferociously are the first to complain of over-work if left to themselves. Afterwards, if there is any good in them, they settle down into their stride. They are only like young horses, pulling too hard at first and sweating off their strength—jibbing one moment and shying the next—when

it comes to " 'ammer, 'ammer, 'ammer on the 'ard 'igh road," one
finds who is going to stick it and who is not.

There has been some heavy firing round about Nieuport and south
of the Yser lately, and an unusual number of wounded have been
coming in, many of them "gravement blessés" [seriously wounded].

One evening a young French officer came to the kitchen for soup. It
was on Wednesday, December 16th, the day the Allies assumed the
offensive, and all night cases were being brought in. He was quite a
boy, and utterly shaken by what he had been through. He could only
repeat, "It was horrible, horrible!" These are the men who tell brave
tales when they get home, but we see them dirty and worn, when
they have left the trenches only an hour before, and have the horror of
battle in their eyes.

There are scores of "pieds gelés" [frozen feet] at present, and I now
have bags of socks for these. So many men come in with bare feet,
and I hope in time to get carpet slippers and socks for them all. One
night no one came to help, and I had a great business getting down a
long train, so Mrs. Logette has promised to come every evening.
The kitchen is much nicer now, as we are in a larger passage, and we
have three stoves, lamps, etc. Many things are being "straightened
out" besides,[4] my poor little corner and war seems better understood.
There is hardly a thing which is not thought of and done for the sick
and wounded, and I should say a grievance was impossible.

I still lodge at the Villa Joos, and am beginning to enjoy a study of
middle-class provincial life. The ladies do all the house-work. We
have breakfast (a bite) in the kitchen at 8.30 a.m., then I go to make
soup, and when I come back after lunch for a rest, "the family" are
dressed and sitting round a stove, and this they continue to do till a
meal has to be prepared. There is one lamp and one table, and one
stove, and unless papa plays the pianola there is nothing to do but
talk. No one reads, and only one woman does a little embroidery,
while the small girl of the party cuts out scraps from a fashion paper.

The poor convoy! it is becoming very squabbly and tiresome, and
there is a good deal of "talking over," which is one of the weakest
sides of "communal life." It is petty and ridiculous to quarrel when
Death is so near, and many things are so big and often so tragic. Yet

human nature has strict limitations. Mr. Ramsay MacDonald[5] came out from the committee to see what all the complaints were about. So there were strange interviews, in store-rooms, etc. (no one has a place to call their own!), and everyone "explained" and "gave evidence" and tried to "put matters straight."

It rains every day. This may be a "providence," as the floods are keeping the Germans away. The sound of constant rain on the window-panes is a little melancholy. Let us pray that in singleness and cheerfulness of heart we may do our little bit of work.

23 December   Yesterday I motored into Dunkirk, and did a lot of shopping. By accident our motor-car went back to Furnes without me, and there was not a bed to be had in Dunkirk! After many vicissitudes I met Captain Whiting, who gave up his room in his own house to me, and slept at the club. I was in clover for once, and nearly wept when I found my boots brushed and hot water at my door. It was so like home again.

I was leaving the station to-day when shelling began again. One shell dropped not far behind the bridge, which I had just crossed, and wrecked a house. Another fell into a boat on the canal and wounded the occupants badly. I went to tell the Belgian Sisters not to go down to the station, and I lunched at their house, and then went home till the evening work began. People are always telling one that danger is now over—a hidden gun has been discovered and captured, and there will be no more shelling. Quel blague! [What a joke!] The shelling goes on just the same whether hidden guns are captured or not.

I can't say at present when I shall get home, because no one ever knows what is going to happen. I don't quite know who would take my place at the soup-kitchen if I were to leave.

25 December   My Christmas Day began at midnight, when I walked home through the moonlit empty streets of Furnes. At 2 a.m. the guns began to roar, and roared all night. They say the Allies are making an attack.

I got up early and went to church in the untidy school-room at the hospital, which is called the nurses' sitting-room. Mr. Streatfield had arranged a little altar, which was quite nice, and had set some

chairs in an orderly row. As much as in him lay—from the altar linen
to the white artificial flowers in the vases—all was as decent as could
be and there were candles and a cross. We were quite a small congre-
gation, but another service had been held earlier, and the wounded
heard Mass in their ward at 6 a.m. The priests put up an altar there,
and I believe the singing was excellent. Inside we prayed for peace,
and outside the guns went on firing. Prince Alexander of Teck came
to our service—a big soldierly figure in the bare room.

After breakfast I went to the soup-kitchen at the station, as usual,
then home—*i.e.,* to the hospital to lunch. At 3.15 came a sort of
evensong with hymns, and then we went to the civil hospital, where
there was a Christmas-tree for all the Belgian refugee children. Anything more touching I never saw, and to be with them made one blind
with tears. One tiny mite, with her head in bandages, and a little
black shawl on, was introduced to me as "une blessée [a wounded
person], madame." Another little boy in the hospital is always spoken
of gravely as "the civilian."

Every man, woman, and child got a treat or a present or a good
dinner. The wounded had turkey, and all they could eat, and the children got toys and sweets off the tree. I suppose these children are
not much accustomed to presents, for their delight was almost too
much for them. I have never seen such excitement! Poor mites! without homes or money, and with their relations often lost—yet little
boys were gibbering over their toys, and little girls clung to big parcels, and squeaked dolls or blew trumpets. The bigger children had
rather good voices, and all sang our National Anthem in English.
"God save our nobbler King"—the accent was quaint, but the children
sang lustily.

We had finished, and were waiting for our own Christmas dinner
when shells began to fly. One came whizzing past Mr. Streatfield's
store-room as I stood there with him. The next minute a little child in
floods of tears came in, grasping her mother's bag, to say "Maman"
had had her arm blown off. The child herself was covered with dust
and dirt, and in the streets people were sheltering in doorways, and
taking little runs for safety as soon as a shell had finished bursting.
The bombardment lasted about an hour, and we all waited in the

kitchen and listened to it. As such times, when everyone is rather strung up, someone always and continually lets things fall. A nun clattered down a pail, and Maurice the cook seemed to fling saucepan-lids on the floor.

About 8.15 the bombardment ceased, and we went in to a cheery dinner—soup, turkey, and plum-pudding, with crackers and speeches. I believe no one would have guessed we had been a bit "on the stretch."

At 9.30 I went to the station. It was very melancholy. No one was there but myself. The fires were out, or smoking badly. Everyone had been scared to death by the shells, and talked of nothing else, whereas shells should be forgotten directly. I got things in order as soon as I could and the wounded in the train got their hot soup and coffee as usual, which was a satisfaction. Then I came home alone at mid-night—keeping as near the houses as I could because of possible shells—and so to bed, very cold, and rather too inclined to think about home.

26 December   Went to the station. Oddly enough, very few wounded were there, so I came away, and had my first day at home. I got a little oil-stove put in my room, wrote letters, tidied up, and thor-oughly enjoyed myself.

A Taube came over and hovered about Furnes, and dropped bombs. I was at the Villa, and the family of Joos and I stood and watched it, and a nasty dangerous moth it looked away up in the sky. Presently it came over our house, so we went down to the kitchen. A few shots were fired, but the Taube was far too high up to be hit. Max, the Joss' cousin, went out and "tirait [fired]," to the admiration of the women-kind, and then, of course, "Papa" had to have a try. The two men, with their little gun and their talk and gesticulations, lent a queer touch of comic opera to the scene. The garden was so small, the men in their little hats were so suggestive of the "broken English" scene on the stage, that one could only stand and laugh. . . .

27 December   Bad, bad weather again. It has rained almost continu-ously for five weeks. Yesterday it snowed. Always the wind blows, and *something* lashes itself against the panes. One can't leave the windows open, as the rooms get flooded. It is amazingly cold o'nights, I can't sleep for the cold.

We have some funny incidents at the station sometimes. A particularly amusing one occurred the other day, when three ladies in knickerbockers and khaki and badges appeared at our soup-kitchen door and announced they were "on duty" there till 6 o'clock. I was not there, but the scene that followed has been described to me, and has often made me laugh.

It seems the ladies never got further than the door! Some people might have been firm in the "Too sorry! Come-some-other-day-when-we-are-not-so-busy" sort of way. Not so Miss____. In more primitive times she would probably have gone for the visitors with a broom, but her tongue is just as rough as the hardest besom, and from their dress ("skipping over soldiers' faces with breeches on, indeed!") to their corps there was very little left of them.

It wasn't really from the dog-in-the-manger spirit that the little woman acted. The fact is that Belgians and French run the station together, and they are all agreed on one thing, which is, that no one but an authorised and registered person is to come within its doors. Heaven knows the trouble there has been with spies, and this rule is absolutely necessary.

Two Red Cross khaki-clad men have been driving everywhere in Furnes, and have been found to be Germans. Had we permitted itinerant workers, the authorities gave notice that the kitchen would have to close.

In the evening, when I went to the station, another knickerbockered lady sat there! I told her our difficulties, but allowed her to do a little work rather than hurt her feelings. The following day Miss____ engaged in deadly conflict with the lady who had sent our unwelcome visitors. Over the scene we will draw a veil, but we never saw the knickerbockered ladies again!

31 December The last day of this bad old year. I feel quite thankful for the summer I had at the Grange. It has been something to look back upon all the time I have been here; the pergolas of pink roses, the sleepy fields, the dear people who used to come and stay with me, and all the fun and pleasure of it, help one a good deal now.

Yesterday was a fine day in the middle of weeks of rain. When I came down to breakfast in the Joos' little kitchen I remarked, of course, on the beauty of the weather. "What a day for Taubes!" said Monsieur Max, looking up at the clear blue sky. Before I had left home there was a shell in the street close by, and one heard that already these horrible birds of prey had been at work, and had thrown two bombs, which destroyed two houses in the Rue des Trèfles. The pigeons that circle round the old buildings in Furnes always seem to see the Taubes first, as if they knew by sight their hateful brothers. They flutter disturbed from roof and turret, and then, with a flash of white wings, they fly far away. I often wish I had wings when I see them.

I went to the station, and then to the hospital for slippers for some wounded men. Five aeroplanes were overhead—Allies' and German—and there was a good deal of firing. I was struck by the fact that the night before I had seen *exactly* this scene in a dream. Second sight always gives me much to think about. The inevitableness of things seems much accentuated by it. In my dream I stood by the other people in the yard looking at the war in the air, and watching the circling aeroplanes and the bursts of smoke.

At the station there was a nasty feeling that something was going to happen. The Taubes wheeled about and hovered in the blue. I went to the hospital for lunch, and afterwards I asked Mr. Bevan to come to the station to look at some wounded whose dressings had not been touched for too long. He said he would come in half an hour, so I said I wouldn't wait, as he knew exactly where to find the men, and I came back to the Villa for my rest. As I walked home I heard that the station had been shelled, and I met one of the Belgian Sisters and told her not to go on duty till after dark, but I had no idea till evening came of what had happened. Ten shells burst in or round the station. Men, women, and children were killed. They tell me that limbs were flying, and a French chauffeur, who came on here, picked up a man's leg in the street. Mr. Bevan sent word to say none of us was to go to the station for the present.

At Dunkirk seven Taubes flew overhead and dropped bombs, killing twenty-eight people. At Pervyse shells are coming in every day. I can't help wondering when we shall clear out of this. If the bridges are destroyed it will be difficult to get away. The weather has turned very wet again in the evening. We have only had two or three fine days in as many months. The wind howls day and night, and the place is so well known for it that "vent [wind] de Furnes" is a byword. No doubt the floods protect us, so one mustn't grumble at a sore throat.

1 January 1915   The station was shelled again to-day. Three houses were destroyed, and there was one person killed and a good many more were wounded. A rumour got about that the Germans had promised 500 shells in Furnes on New Year's Day.

In the evening I went down to the station, and I was evidently not expected. Not a thing was ready for the wounded. The man in charge had let all three fires out, and he and about seven soldiers (mostly drunk) were making merry in the kitchen. None of them would budge, and I was glad I had young Mr. Findlay with me, as he was in uniform, and helped to get things straight. But these French seem to have very little discipline, and even when the military doctors came in the men did nothing but argue with them. It was amazing to hear them. One night a soldier, who is always drunk, was lying on a brancard in the doctor's own room, and no one seemed to mind.

3 January, Sunday   I have had my usual rest and hot bath. I find I never want a holiday if I may have my Sundays. I spent a lazy afternoon in Miss Scott's room, she being ill, then went to Streatfield's service, dinner, and the station. A new officer was on duty there, and was introduced to the kitchen. He said, "Les anglais [the English], of course. No one else ever does anything for anybody."

I believe this is very nearly the case. God knows, we are full of faults, but the superiority of the British race to any other that I know is a matter of deep conviction with me, and it is founded, I think, on wide experience.

6 January   I went to Adenkirke two days ago to establish a soup-kitchen there, as they say that Furnes station is too dangerous. We have been given a nice little waiting room and a stove. We heard to-day that the station-master at Furnes has been signalling to the enemy, so that is why we have been shelled so punctually. His daughter is engaged to a German. Two of our hospital people noticed that before each bombardment a blue light appeared to flash on the sky. They reported the matter, with the result that the signals were discovered.

There has been a lot of shelling again to-day, and several houses are destroyed. A child of two years is in our hospital with one leg blown off and the other broken. One only hears people spoken of as, "the man with the abdominal trouble," or "the one shot through the lungs."

Children know the different aeroplanes by sight, and one little girl, when I ask her for news, gives me a list of the "obus" [shells] that have arrived, and which have "s'éclaté" [burst], and which have not. One can see that she despises those which "ne s'éclatent pas [do not burst]." One says "Bon soir, pas des obus [Good evening, no shells]," as in English one says, "Good-night, sleep well."

10 January   Prince Alexander of Teck dined at the hospital last night, and we had a great spread. Madame Sindici did wonders, and there were hired plates and finger-bowls, and food galore! We felt real swells. An old General—the head of the Army Medical Corps—gave me the most grateful thanks for serving the soldiers. It was gracefully and delightfully done.

I am going home for a week's holiday.

14 January   I went home *via* Calais. Mr. Bevan and Mr. Morgan took me there. It was a fine day and I felt happy for once, that is, for once out here.

Some people enjoy this war. It think it is far the worse time, except one, I ever spent. Perhaps I have seen more suffering than most people. A doctor sees a hospital, and a nurse sees a ward of sick and wounded, but I see them by the hundred passing before me in an endless train all day. I can make none of them really better. I feed them, and they pass on.

One reviews one's life a little as one departs. Always I shall remember Furnes as a place of wet streets and long dark evenings, with

gales blowing, and as a place where I have been always alone. I have
not once all this time exchanged a thought with anyone. I have lived in
a very damp attic, and talked French to some kind middle-class people,
and I have walked a mile for every meal I have had. So I shall always
think of Furnes as a wet, dark place, and of myself with a lantern
trudging about its mean streets.

Notes

❦

*These selections are taken from the first published edition of Macnaughtan's 1914–15 diary, *A Woman's Diary of the War* (London: Thomas Nelson and Sons, 1915). A relative also published a more extensive version of Macnaughtan's diary: *My War Experiences in Two Continents,* ed. Mrs. Lionel Salmon (London: John Murray, 1919).

1   At Furnes.

2   Mrs. Knocker, Mairi Chisholm, and Lady Dorothy Fielding were members of Dr. Hector Munro's Ambulance Corps. Knocker and Chisholm did more than carry soup; around the end of November, on their own, they set up a first-aid station in the cellar at Pervyse, close to the battle line.

3   Albert I of Belgium.

4   This comma perhaps belongs more properly later in the sentence, after *corner.*

5   The statesman who became first Labour prime minister in 1924.

Florence Farmborough

(1887–1978)

FLORENCE FARMBOROUGH was the fourth child in a family of six children. Her parents raised no objections to her desire to live abroad, and in 1908, at twenty-one, she went to Kiev in Russia. After two years she moved to Moscow, to live with the family of Dr. Pavel Sergeyevich, a famous heart surgeon, and to teach English to his two daughters, sixteen-year-old Nadya and her nineteen-year-old sister, Asya. Soon after Farmborough's return from a holiday in England in 1914, England and Russia were at war with Germany. With the help of Sergeyevich as a member of the medical staff, she and her two pupils became volunteer nursing assistants at a hospital opening in Russia under the patronage of Princess Golitsin. But because Farmborough wanted also to become a nurse in a frontline unit, she undertook Red Cross training, at the conclusion of which Segeyevich arranged for her to be accepted in 1915 as a surgical nurse by the "Tenth Otryad of the All-Russian Zemski [Provincial] Soyuz."* Her Red Cross unit was soon sent to active duty at the front, where she remained for the rest of the war except when she participated in heartbreaking retreats with the army or was granted a rare leave. The work was arduous and discouraging, but she sustained her desire to remain of service. In 1917, upon the Russian revolution, that service was over. With Russians deserting the Romanian front, her current unit was ordered to return to Moscow by whatever means they could. In the ordeal of returning, disillusioned and weary, she marveled at "how much a human being can endure without any outward sign of having been broken up into pieces." Finally, having sold her camera at half its value to pay for a ticket to Vladivostok, she returned to England in 1918 via Siberia and America. Farmborough kept a detailed diary for 1914–18, portions of it written up after the event from notes. The selections here describe her harrowing experiences in 1915.

From Florence Farmborough's Diary

30th January 1915 Preparations for my departure are well under way.
I am breathlessly impatient to be off, but there is much to be done
and the Unit itself is not yet fully organised. My nurse's dresses,
aprons and veils have been made already, and I have bought a flannel-
lined, black leather jacket. An accessory to this jacket is a thick sheep-
skin waistcoat, for winter wear, whose Russian name, *dushegreychka,*
means 'soul-warmer'. I hear that our Unit will be stationed for a time
on the Russo-Austrian Front in the Carpathian Mountains and that
we will have to ride horseback, as direct communication can be established there only by riding; so high boots and black leather breeches
have been added to my wardrobe. . . . At the moment of my departure, Anna Ivanovna, my Russian 'mother', bade me kneel before her.
Taking from her pocket a little chain, she fastened it round my neck.
Then she blessed me, kissed me three times, 'In the name of the
Father, of the Son and of the Holy Spirit', and wished me 'God speed'.
I, too, was a soldier, going to war, for thus did all Russian mothers
to their soldier sons. The little chain, with a small icon and cross
attached to it, has already been blessed by a priest.

•　•　•　•　•

Saturday, 11th April[1] We travelled a long way since we left our train
and reached Grodzisko on 16th March. Our itinerary has taken us
through Przhevorsk, Lantsut, Rezheshchuv, Shchani, Ropchytse,
Dembitsa, Yaslo, Krosno to Gorlitse, where we arrived today, exactly
a month after leaving Moscow. Gorlitse is a poor, tormented town,
under constant fire from the Austrian guns. For over five months, its
inhabitants have been obliged to lead the existence of night birds.
Their days are spent in the cellars, for the slightest movement in the
streets could bring a shower of bullets. After dusk, they come creeping out, begging sympathy and food from each other and from the
soldiers—the Russian soldiers; for Gorlitse and all of the above-
mentioned towns were captured from the Austrians during the early
months of warfare in the autumn of 1914. The people are half-starving
and that is what takes up most of our time. Every evening, the mobile kitchens of the Red Cross Unit are sent into the town and daily

provide no fewer than 300 portions of food. We are hoping, in due course, to send 500 portions, for the misery among these unfortunate Austrian subjects is quite appalling.

Sunday, 12th April   The Sisters and personnel of our *Otryad's* 2nd Flying Detachment have left us today to drive to the place destined for their future work. We have already chosen our hospital; it is a well built house, with several nice, airy rooms. Everything is being scrubbed, painted and white-washed; the operating room will be a splendid sight when finished; our *apteka* [pharmacy] is already full of medicinal and surgical material and there are rows of labelled bottles on the shelves. We have no idea how long we shall be here; it might be six months—or six hours! The site is very beautiful for we are practically surrounded by the lovely, undulating ranges of the Carpathians. I love watching them at night, when the mountains lie mysteriously quiet and passive, outlined clearly against the night sky and overswept by the moon's luminous radiance.

Wednesday, 15th April   We have had a busy day; some 50 wounded men have been sent to us. We dressed their wounds and sent them on to Yaslo, where they will be sorted out and despatched to various parts of Russia. The booming of cannon is often heard, but spasmodically, and sometimes at long intervals. The soldiers tell us that they are well looked after and well fed in the trenches, but they all voice their dismay that German troops and heavy guns have been sent to this section of the Front. 'We are not afraid of the Austrians,' they explain, 'but the German soldiers are quite different.' We had heard that the Germans had transferred both man-power and guns to the Austrian Front, a sure sign that they consider the fortifications of their Allies to be inadequate. A sure sign, too, that an enemy offensive is imminent. We can do nothing but wait and watch.

· · · · ·

Wednesday, 22nd April   So much has happened. I am dreadfully tired. We are *retreating!* In that one word lies all the agony of the last few days. We were called from our beds before dawn on Saturday 18th. The Germans had launched their offensive! Explosion after explosion rent the air; shells and shrapnel fell in and around Gorlitse. The roar of the rival cannons grew increasingly intense. Rockets and projectors were at work. Patches of lurid, red light glowed here and there where fires had been kindled by shells. Our house shook to its very foundations, its windows rattling and quivering in their hinges. Death was very busy, his hands full of victims. Then the wounded began to arrive. We started work in acute earnest. At first we could cope; then, we were overwhelmed by their numbers. They came in their hundreds, from all directions; some able to walk, others crawling, dragging themselves along the ground. We worked night and day. And still they came! And the thunder of the guns never ceased. Soon their deadly shells were exploding around our Unit; for hours on end, the horror and confusion continued. We had no rest and were worn out with the intensity and immensity of the work. The stream of wounded was endless. Those who could walk were sent on immediately without attention. 'The Base hospitals will attend to you,' we told them; 'Go! go! quickly!' The groans and cries of the wounded were pitiful to hear. We dressed their severe wounds where they lay on the open ground; one by one we tended them, first alleviating their pain by injections. And all the time the bombardment of Gorlitse was continuing with brutal ferocity.

On Sunday, the violence of the thunderous detonations grew in length and strength. Then, suddenly, the terrible word *retreat* was heard. At first in a whisper; then, in loud, forceful tone: 'The Russians are retreating!' And the first-line troops came into sight: a long procession of dirt-bespattered, weary, desperate men—in full retreat! We had received no marching-orders. The thunder of the guns came nearer and nearer. We were frightened and perplexed; they had forgotten us! But they came at last—urgent, decisive orders: we were to start without delay, leaving behind all the wounded and all the equipment that might hinder us. A dreadful feeling of dismay and bewilderment took possession of us; to go away, leaving the wounded and the Unit's equipment! It was impossible; there *must* be some mistake! But there was no mistake, we had to obey; we had to go. '*Skoro! Skoro!* [quickly]' shouted familiar voices. '*Skoro! Skoro!* echoed unfamiliar ones from the hastily passing infantry. 'The Germans are outside the town!'

Snatching up coats, knapsacks, any of our personal belongings which could be carried—we started off quickly down the rough road. And the wounded? They shouted to us when they saw us leaving; called out to us in piteous language to stop—to take them with us; not to forsake them, for the love of God; not to leave them—our brothers—to the enemy. Those who could walk, got up and followed us; running, hopping, limping, by our sides. The badly crippled crawled after us; all begging, beseeching us not to abandon them in their need. And, on the road, there were others, many others; some of them lying down in the dust, exhausted. They, too, called after us. They held on to us; praying us to stop with them. We had to wrench our skirts from their clinging hands. Then their prayers were intermingled with curses; and, far behind them, we could hear the curses repeated by those of our brothers whom we had left to their fate. The gathering darkness accentuated the panic and misery. To the accompaniment of the thunder of exploding shells, and of the curses and prayers of the wounded men around and behind us, we hurried on into the night.

We had hoped to stop in Biyech, if only for an hour or two, but it was quite impossible. Infantry, cavalry, artillery were pressing forward. This was no place, or time, to think of rest or food. The enemy was close behind; his shells were falling ever nearer and nearer, claiming many victims. We reached Yaslo on Monday morning, but there, too, were confusion and chaos; and with that huge wave of retreating men and vehicles we were swept forwards, ever eastwards. There was no alternative . . . *Retreat* had us in its grip.

We came to a place called Skolychin and, miraculously, an empty house was found to be available. We were ordered to halt and open a dressing-station immediately. I don't know where the food came from, but even while we were unpacking some of the bales which contained first aid equipment, a cup of hot tea and a slice of black bread and cheese were put in our hands. Mechanically, we ate and drank; then, refreshed, we prepared to receive our wounded. They were already at our door, clamouring for help and food. Many there were who could no longer walk, and could scarcely speak, their bodies sorely wounded and their minds numbed by the severity of these wounds, yet their strength of will had been such as had enabled them to traverse many painful versts[2] in those first tragic hours of retreat. It is only today that we have heard that the bombardment of Gorlitse was quite unequalled as yet in the present War's history. But our men have suffered enormous casualties; it is said that our 3rd Army has been cruelly decimated and that the 61st Division, to which we are attached, has lost many thousands of its men.

Monday, 20th April   Weary and dustladen we looked at each other, conscious of the calamity at our Front. There was no time for questions, or for explanations; the sullen and continuous tramping of retreating feet on the roads told its own tale. What is happening there? What will soon happen here? The stricken faces and frightened eyes of the wounded told us. They were exhausted beyond words, too exhausted to groan as their wounds were dressed. Gun-carriages, batteries, motor lorries lumbered in and out of the streams of marching soldiers. Dust hung about the road in a thick grey mist; the sun beat down mercilessly. Now and then ambulance vans would pull up in front of the house and the orderlies would hastily drag the occupants out and deposit them on the ground near the entrance. Cries and groans accompanied this performance, but we were too busy to leave our posts and, beyond a much-needed admonition to the orderlies to use their hands more gently, the newcomers and their sufferings had, for the time-being, to be ignored. The wounds were dreadful: bodies and limbs were torn and lacerated beyond repair. Those in a hopeless condition were set apart and not sent on with the more promising cases to the Base. All those who could still walk, unless obviously in need of treatment, were dismissed at once without examination. But there were few of these, for the 'walkers' preferred to walk on. Not even a mug of tea could tempt some of them to turn off from the road for a few minutes' rest. This was no time for resting, with the enemy at one's heels.

Into our 'dressing-room' hurried the tall figure of Alexander Mikhaylovich, one of the Divisional surgeons. A few whispered words and he was gone. Alexander Mikhaylovich's usually careworn face had taken on a more serious expression, but he was silent and we went on working. After a few minutes, he looked up and said: 'In half an hour's time, I want two sisters to be ready to return to Biyech. There are many wounded there and we must open a dressing-station at once.' Then came eager voices: 'May I go?' 'May I go?' We were all so anxious to be the chosen ones. My anxiety to be one of the two was so intense that I was speechless and could do nothing but clasp and unclasp my hands. 'Vera Vasiliyevna is on duty and must, therefore, remain here; Olga Ivanovna, as dispenser, will take my place here in my absence. Sister Florence and Sister Anna will be ready to leave at 6:30 p.m., that is in half an hour.' I could scarcely refrain from crying aloud my thanks to him. Anna seized me and together we rushed off to the wagon on which our stores of material for dressings were packed. Hastily collecting several large drum-shaped, air-tight boxes, which held our sterilised dressings, we placed them, with bundles of wadding, bandages and the like, on two large sheets and tied them all together. We packed, too, the most necessary liquids, instruments, candles, gloves, splints. Our equipment complete, we donned our leather coats and clambered into a huge, dirty-looking lorry which was waiting for us. It was a divisional vehicle and the chauffeur, a stranger, offered no information. Anna and I were both feeling the same excitement at unknown dangers. She was squatting down in her corner, with hands tightly folded on her lap and eyes bright with excitement, staring across the open country. Alexander Mikhaylovich came out of the house. His first glance told him that we and our equipment were ready; he nodded approval and carefully, but with some difficulty, because of his stoutness, climbed up and took his seat. The divisional officer suddenly appeared and jumped in, followed by two orderlies. During the journey there was no conversation, only a few instructions given by the divisional surgeon to the chauffeur in an undertone. We were far from comfortable; the straw upon which we were sitting was coarse and scanty. Alexander Mikhaylovich, too, was not happy; every time the car bumped and jolted, which was often, he was tossed up and down like a rubber ball. The evening was growing cool and a keen east wind was rising. We saw innumerable soldiers; their faces all turned in one direction and wearing grim, dogged expressions. Some were hurrying, others stumbling. Many of them looked at us in amazement, wondering what was impelling us to return to the scene of disaster. Small bands of wounded, with blood-stained bandages round head or arm, met us. There were those, too, who were limping painfully, who, noticing the *kosinka* [head-veil] of a Sister, would stop, and with inarticulate sounds point beseechingly to their wounded limbs. But we could not stop and explanations in that continuous din were of no avail; we could but point towards the road we had traversed, trying to make it clear to them that help was at hand if they would only continue their journey. Saddest of all sights was to see wounded men exhausted, lying by the side of the road—unable to drag themselves any further. We saw too, how more than one soldier would stop to speak, to try to assist them to rise; then, finding that it was useless, would look awhile, sorrowing, and pass on. Nearing Biyech, we met a hooded van containing wounded and our car drew up for a moment while the divisional doctor interrogated the driver. It seemed that all was quiet in the town save for an occasional shell from the enemy; the inhabitants were sheltering in their cellars, but many badly wounded men were there, unable to leave owing to lack of Red Cross assistance and transport.

At last we pulled up at the gate of a large white monastery. Alexander Mikhaylovich, considerably shaken after his rough ride, hastily got down from the lorry and, passing down the small front garden, disappeared through the white doorway. After a few minutes he beckoned us to follow him. In the doorway stood a black-robed priest; his face was stern and very pale, but so calm and passive was his manner, it was evident that this was not the first time that he had encountered a uniformed contingent. We followed him from room to room as he explained, in broken Russian, that we were at liberty to make what use we pleased of the monastery with its scanty supply of furniture. We told him that only water and basins were necessary and he at once brought in a bucket of water and three small tin pans. The large room, chosen for the dressing-room, was devoid of furniture, but some benches dragged in from an adjoining one were easily transformed into a table, on which we arranged our equipment. All this was done in feverish haste, Alexander Mikhaylovich having impressed upon us the fact that we might have to leave at any minute, and therefore, could not afford to waste a single moment.

Before we had had time to put on our white *khalati* [overalls], the
wounded were in the room—all stretcher cases, all in a terrible state of
suffering and exhaustion. To enquire as to when and how the wounds
had been inflicted was impossible; in the midst of that great wave
of suffering, the acuteness of which was plainly visible and audible,
we could but set our teeth and work . . . and work. The orderlies
would carry them in on improvised stretchers, would lift them on to
the floor and return for others. Where they found them, God only
knows—but there was no dearth of them—and they carried them in,
one after another until our room and the adjoining ones were full
of them; and the stench of the wounds and the unsanitary conditions
of many of the sufferers filled the place with a heavy, oppressive atmosphere. By this time, several ambulance vans of our Transport,
together with some half-dozen from the divisional vehicle-column,
had arrived and, with the help of a few divisional orderlies, we packed
many of the wounded into them and sent them off to the Base. Now
and then there was a shrapnel scare, but it caused little or no confusion. As the day drew on, however, the bombardment became more
severe and, after 9 in the evening, heavy shells began to fall.

In the next two hours we worked blindly and feverishly, knowing
that many lives depended on the swiftness and accuracy of our handi-
work. 'Water,' gasped parched lips, but we dared not break away
until the bandaging of the wound was complete. Hearing, yet as with
deafness, we listened to the entreaties of those agonised souls. 'Give
me something to ease my pain; for the love of God, give me something, *Sestritsa* [Sister].' With cheering words we strove to comfort
them, but pain is a hard master; and the wounds were such as to set
one's heart beating with wonder that a man could be so mutilated
in body and yet live, speak and understand.

The priest gave us what little help he could: supplying us with fresh
water, carrying off receptacles of blood-stained clothes and bandages.
In and out among the wounded he walked; placing more straw under
one man's head, raising a leg into a more comfortable position, holding, now and then, a cup of water to thirsty lips. His lips were com-
pressed, his face drawn, but only once did I notice that he was affected
by the sights around him. A soldier was lying in a corner, breathing

heavily, but otherwise quiet. It was his turn now; I went and knelt
down on the straw at his side. His left leg and side were saturated with
blood. I began to rip up the trouser-leg, clotted blood and filth flow-
ing over my gloved hands. He turned dull, uncomprehending eyes
towards me and I went on ripping the cloth up to the waist. I pushed
the clothes back and saw a pulp, a mere mass of smashed body from
the ribs downwards; the stomach and abdomen were completely
crushed and and his left leg was hanging to the pulped body by only a
few shreds of flesh. I heard a stifled groan at my side and, glancing
round, I saw the priest with his hand across his eyes turn and walk
heavily across the room towards the door. The soldier's dull eyes were
still looking at me and his lips moved, but no words came. What it
cost me to turn away without aiding him, I cannot describe, but we
could not waste time and material on hopeless cases, and there were so
many others . . . waiting . . . waiting. . . .

From one room to the other we went always bandaging and, when
darkness fell, bandaging by the flickering light of candles. Those
whose wounds were dressed were carried off immediately to the
Transport vans or cars awaiting them, and orders were given to the
drivers to make their way as quickly as possible to the Divisional Base
lazarets [hospitals], and to send back any other vans or cars available
without delay. Shrapnel was falling thickly now, but the monastery
did not alarm us overmuch. If only the wounded could be sent away
to a place of safety in time, that was the problem which worried us.

I think that, by now, some curious change had come over both
Anna and me. Anna's face was stony, quite expressionless, and while
she worked, the same words came from her lips every few moments.
'Nichevo! nichevo! golubchik. Skoro, skoro!'[3] Suddenly, with a shock I
realise that I, too, have been repeating similar words, repeating them
at intervals when the groans and cries of my patient have been too
heart-rending. I caught a glimpse of my white overall, covered with
blood-stains and dirt, but this was no place to probe my feelings,
or to ask myself what were my impressions, my sympathies. It was as
though I had become blunt to the fact that this was *war*, that these
were *wounded*. Mechanically my fingers worked: ripping, cleaning,
dressing, binding. Now this one was finished, another one begun; my

heart seemed empty of emotion, my mind dull, and all the time my lips comforted: '*Skoro, golubchik, skoro!*'

I was bandaging a young soldier, shot through the lung, when the first heavy shell fell. He was sitting up sideways against the wall, a wound the size of a small coin on his right breast and a wound big enough to put my hand into in his back. His right lung had been cruelly rent and his breath was coming out of the large back-wound in gurgling, bubbling sobs. The wounds had been quickly cleaned; the larger one filled with long swabs, a pad tightly bound over it, when an angry hiss was heard, grew louder and louder and then the explosion! The roar was deafening, the room shook and there were frightening noises of splintering, slicing masonry and of glass breaking and falling. A great silence followed, but the room continued to shake and tremble; or was it, perhaps, our own limbs? The soldier in front of me was shaking as with ague. '*Chemo-dan!* [heavy shell]' he whispered hoarsely. I turned towards the table for a new roll of bandage. When I returned my patient had disappeared. In his half-bandaged condition he had run off, not caring for aught else and possessed with the one wild desire to escape to a safer place. Strangely enough, the rooms had emptied themselves of several of their wounded occupants; many of those whom we had thought too weak to move had, under this violent shock, been imbued with supernatural strength, as it were, had arisen and crawled away out into the night.

After this, the work seemed to slacken. The remaining wounded were in a terrible, nervous state; the new ones brought in begged only to be sent on: no need for bandaging now, they urged. Almost every five minutes the explosion would be repeated, sometimes more distant, sometimes very near, so near as to seem on our very roof-top.

The divisional surgeon had taken his leave and had retired with his men. Alexander Mikhaylovich told us to prepare to leave in about a quarter of an hour; one of our light cars had been detained for us. The last vans had left; all the wounded had been safely despatched, with the exception of those who were nearing death's door. Our stained overalls off and folded up, we stood by the door, waiting for orders. Outside the night was dark.

The priest came round the corner of the house. 'There are three craters in the back garden,' he said in a muffled voice, 'and the out-houses have been destroyed.' 'Shall you stay here?' I enquired. 'Made-moiselle,' he answered slowly, 'I am in charge of the monastery. I cannot leave my post. And why should I leave when my flock re-mains?' 'Are there many people here?' 'There are many,' he replied, 'old men and many women and children.' He was silent and, in the half light, I saw that his eyes wandered towards the monastery win-dows, as if hoping to see some signs of life. I realised then that the house was a refuge for numberless poor people sheltering from the violent storms outside; and there might have been others in those 'outhouses' so lately destroyed. 'Pardon me,' the priest was saying, 'but Mademoiselle is not Russian?' 'No,' I answered, 'I am English.' 'Ah, English!' his voice took on a more animated tone. 'I knew that Mademoiselle was not Russian, for you have the look of the Western world. I, too, have been in France.' He broke off suddenly, the familiar hiss was in our ears and, once again, earth and air seemed convulsed with hideous noise in a world which swayed and rocked.

There were faint cries from within the monastery. I turned from the doorway and stepped inside over the littered floor and paused by that row of silent figures stretched out on their straw beds. Two were already dead, one with eyes wide open as though looking attentively at something—or someone; I closed them and laid his hands on his breast. To his left a man was lying; great convulsions ran every now and then down his long frame and a queer gurgling noise was audible in his throat; Death had taken his hand, too. And he—in the corner—was lying as before, with strangely contracted limb and eyes still dull and glazed, but his lips had ceased to move.

There were unaccountable noises outside—a sudden rush of sound, the buzz of many voices hushed and subdued, the tramp of many hurrying feet, and then Alexander Mikhaylovich's voice—loudly, per-emptorily. I turned to go, but, before I went, I moved towards the corner and laid my hand on the clammy forehead and seemed to hear once again his inarticulate entreaty. *'Skoro, golubchik, skoro,'* I whis-pered.

'Florence! Florence!' Anna called. I stumbled down the steps into the garden and followed her hurrying figure. There was tumult in the

air and tumult in my heart. 'I will do what I can for them,' I heard
the priest's voice say and then, to me: 'Adieu! Mademoiselle.' Shrapnel
was crackling the air every now and again with a fierce, metallic
menace. We huddled together, Anna and I, in the car.

Outside the gate, we found our own car and two large Red Cross
lorries. The lorries were packed with wounded. The drivers and
Alexander Mikhaylovich were doing their best to send off those soldiers who, at the last moment, sought to climb on to them: 'Nelzya!
Nelzya! [Keep off!] The men, desperate to get away, began tugging
at the lorries, shouting and climbing over each other to obtain a firmer
grip. Then another shell boomed out its savage warning from behind
the monastery. It helped us in that critical moment more than anything else could have done. In the hush that followed the explosion,
one heard only the clatter of feet hurrying and stumbling away; running figures were faintly seen in the distance, 'Sestritsa! Take us with
you; we can't walk.' But the authoritative voice of Alexander Mikhaylovich came to our ears: 'To your car at once!'

The driver was in a dreadful state of excitement; but he drove well,
though at a higher speed than usual. We huddled close to each other
in the car and Anna whispered in my ear: 'They say that the Germans
are entering Biyech at the other end.' The roadsides were strewn with
wounded and exhausted men; they called to us as we rocked past,
but we could not heed them. We could not have saved them *all;* there
was other important work waiting for us to do. We drove on, but
my heart seemed turned to stone and the weight of it was almost unbearable. Alexander Mikhaylovich had pulled his military cap far
down over his eyes; Anna's face was hidden by her veil; and still we
drove on. For all of us the evening's work had ended with nightmare-
like horror. The remembrance of those dreadful curses thrown at us
by desperate, pain-racked men could never be obliterated or forgotten.

· · · · ·

22nd June   From Lushchov we journeyed to Treschany and encamped
on a plain by a river. All night long rain fell and a thick mist rose
from the river and enveloped us in its icy embrace. We were sleeping
in the open-air and shivered continually, for the damp stood out on

our blankets like beads of perspiration. Next morning, two of our
Sisters had developed high temperatures; a third, the eldest of our
party, a quiet woman with soft grey hair, had reached such a pitch of
nervous tension owing to the lack of sleep and incessant buffeting
of the last weeks that she felt her health was giving way. She conferred
with our doctors, who regretfully accepted her resignation and she
left for Moscow on the following day.

Because of the incessant rain and mist, we transferred our camp to
an apple-orchard standing on higher ground, and our dressing-tent
was set up exactly opposite us on the other side of the road. After we
had settled in there, the weather changed and we found our tent-
home delightfully cool during the sultry noonday hours. Outside the
orchard a large corn-patch was gradually turning golden; poppies
and cornflowers grew abundantly among its waving, slender stems; a
little farther away a field of poppies all colours, from pink to dark
mauve, made a lovely splash of brightness.

Scarcely a day passed that did not bring some of our Divisional
doctors or officers from the surrounding villages. They had many tales
to tell and one and all were loud in their praise of the 3rd Caucasian
Cavalry Corps, who, they affirmed, fought like 'devils and not men'.
Our own 62nd Division was not far behind; at Yaroslav, as everybody
knew, it had more than distinguished itself. With a scanty supply of
ammunition, it had been ordered to hold the enemy at bay for 36
hours; it had resisted for three days, the soldiers using the butts of
their rifles as clubs when the cartridges gave out.

The first sign that the Germans had succeeded in bringing up their
heavy artillery on to our Front was received by us during one moonlit
night when, quite suddenly, shells came sweeping over our heads to
explode with much violence at a distance of about two miles eastwards. Next morning we were told that the house in which the divisional staff was stationed had been destroyed, some of the men and
officers had been wounded and many horses killed. The commotion
caused by this unexpected event was, naturally, very great. In the first
place, no one had realised that heavy artillery could have been brought
up on to our Front because of the treacherous roads; then, too, the
extraordinary accuracy of the German aim was ascribed to the treach-

ery of the village and town inhabitants, some of whom, it was discovered, had been in touch with the enemy and had supplied him with
the vital information. During the day one or two of us were given the
opportunity to view the ruined mansion. It was certainly a neat piece
of work: ten shells had been expended in all—three or four of them
falling directly on to the house and smashing in both roof and walls;
the remainder exploding in the garden, where large *voronki* [craters],
broken trees and about fifty dead horses bore silent witness to the
devastating power of the missiles which had descended upon them in
the night. This episode and several other instances of treachery in
the surrounding districts probably helped the Military Authorities to
come to their harsh decision which demanded the expulsion of the
peasantry from all those villages which had to be evacuated by our
retreating soldiers.

How we felt for them—these homeless wanderers. We heard their
muffled voices early in the morning hours, long before the birds began
to stir and twitter, and we heard their footsteps in the late hours
when darkness had fallen and only the cannonade broke the peace of
evening. Sometimes they came to us for bread, begging us to exchange a few loaves for poultry or a small pig. Once a distraught
peasant came lumbering from a neighboring wood to beg food for his
two children. His wife had died the previous day giving birth to a
baby. In barely coherent language, he told us how he had buried her
there among the trees—the living baby on her breast, for he could
not feed the infant, and he dared not watch it die. And when we told
him that we had but little to give him—how far would a couple of
loaves go with hungry children?—he turned without a word, and
with bowed head went back into the wood. His speechless grief communicated itself to us, for our hearts were heavy for many days, and
in quiet moments my thoughts would often turn towards the mother
and baby, the dead and the living who had found a grave together. . . .

The day before we left Treschany held both glad and sad hours for
us. We knew that we must leave very soon, our armies were retreating
and we could find no rest because of the raging of the rifles and guns.
Lately, ammunition had been sent in large quantities to our Front,

but little of it had been of any use. Out of one consignment of 30,000 shells, fewer than 200 were found to be serviceable. Cartridges were sent in their hundreds of thousands and distributed amongst the men in the trenches, but they were of a foreign cast and would not fit the Russian rifle. Large stores of Japanese rifles had been despatched to neighbouring divisions, but the Russian cartridge failed to fit them. Later, we learnt that Japanese cartridges had been supplied to our Armies on other Fronts, with the same disastrous results. So once again our Russian soldiers raised the butt of their rifles against the advancing enemy, many of them hewed themselves clubs from the forest.

So we knew quite well that today or tomorrow we had to go. In the morning I had been collecting letters from the soldiers stationed in our village to send to Moscow with a member of our *Letuchka* [flying column] who was leaving that same evening. One soldier presented me with a handkerchief, bearing the flags of the Allies in colours. It had been given to him, while in hospital in St. Petersburg, by the Empress Alexandra, but, he declared, it had always proved a source of discomfort and worry, as he was in constant fear of soiling or losing it. 'It will bring you luck, *Sestritsa,*' he added, 'and I shall be content knowing that it is in safe hands'.

And, indeed, joy and luck were to attend my footsteps that day! Alexander Ivanovich, our Plenipotentiary, arrived an hour or two later, bringing with him a batch of long-awaited letters for me, which he had collected from my 'Russian family' in Moscow. There were fifteen letters in all—twelve from England! Those from my Mother—which were instantly recognisable because of her beautiful writing—I put on one side, they were to be read after the others; a literary 'bonne bouche' [final tidbit] as it were, for they were the choicest and most precious letters of them all.

That day, some of our members were presented with the little silver medal of St. George, the 4th degree, and a modest banquet was arranged to celebrate the occasion. The award was for the faithful carrying out of arduous duties in the face of great danger on the Russian Front and was awarded to the Surgical Personnel of the 1st *Letuchka* of the 10th Red Cross Detachment of the *Zemstvo,* etc., etc., in recogni-

tion of their services during the incessant bombardment of the months
April to July, etc., etc. When we were alone together in our tent,
Anna and I looked with pride at the medals, with their black and gold
striped ribbon.

Shrapnel was falling thickly in and around Treschany as we hur-
riedly made our exit during the evening of the following day. The
road was scarcely distinguishable in the darkness, but we followed the
preceding vehicle and moved slowly over the invisible track. Rain
began to fall, at first slowly and then in large, angry drops. I was
aware that my black veil was soaked through and that something cold
was trickling down my neck under the leather collar.

Notes

❧

*From *Nurse at the Russian Front: A Diary, 1914–18* (London: Constable, 1974), p. 29. All diary selections here come from this edition. The quotation later in this introductory paragraph comes from p. 360.

1   Written from the southwest front, East Galicia.

2   One verst equals 3,500 feet, or slightly more than a kilometer.

3   It's nothing! It's nothing! my dear. Quickly, Quickly!

Nella Last

(1890–1966)

NELLA LAST (née Lord) was the country-bred daughter of an ac-
countant for the Furness Railway. During the diary period she lived in
the shipbuilding town of Barrow-in-Furness, Lancashire, her home
since her marriage at twenty-one to a man she refers to only as "my
husband," never by name. He was a joiner and shipfitter and, before
retiring, a self-employed builder. Though not wealthy, the Lasts led a
comfortable life, including even the luxury of some paid domestic
help, and Nella took great pride in her housekeeping skills and nur-
turance of her family. She loved to cook and to sew and had worked
as a dressmaker to make money at some time in the past. Arthur,
her elder son, born before the Great War, no longer lived at home,
but Cliff, the younger, did until he left for military service, and after
being wounded in Italy in 1944, returned to convalesce near Barrow.
An indefatigable volunteer, Last worked throughout the war on Tues-
days and Thursdays at the W.V.S. (Women's Voluntary Service) Centre,
formed in 1939 to provide welfare services to hospitals, evacuees, and
civilian casualties; later it also supplied the armed services and the
merchant navy. When a W.V.S. canteen opened in 1941, Last worked
there too on Friday afternoons; then she assisted with a Red Cross
shop begun in 1942. The diary she kept for Mass Observation from
1938 until just before her death in 1966 both confesses and demon-
strates her love of creativity; the published diary is an edited version
reduced from over two million words. She wrote copiously every
month, usually in pencil, sewing each monthly installment together
with cotton, and later wool thread, and creating one of the more
detailed diaries in the archive. Like her war work, her diary provided
an outlet for her apparently considerable skills; it probably also contributed to her sense of enfranchisement from her prewar domestic
self reflected in these excerpts from 1939 to 1945.*

From Nella Last's Diary

Sunday, 3 September 1939 Well, we know the worst. Whether it was a
kind of incredulous stubbornness or a faith in my old astrological
friend who was right in the last crisis when he said 'No war', I *never*
thought it would come. Looking back I think it was akin to a belief in
a fairy's wand which was going to be waved.

I'm a self-reliant kind of person, but today I've longed for a close
woman friend—for the first time in my life. When I heard Mr.
Chamberlain's voice, so slow and solemn, I seemed to see Southsea
Prom[enade] the July before the last crisis. The Fleet came into Ports-
mouth from Weymouth and there were hundreds of extra ratings
walking up and down. There was a sameness about them that was not
due to their clothes alone, and it puzzled me. It was the look on their
faces—a slighly brooding, faraway look. They all had it—even the
jolly-looking boys—and I felt I wanted to rush up and ask them what
they could see that I could not. And now I know.

The wind got up and brought rain, but on the Walney shore men
and boys worked filling sand-bags. I could tell by the dazed look
on many faces that I had not been alone in my belief that 'something'
would turn up to prevent war. The boys brought a friend in and insisted on me joining in a game, but I could not keep it up. I've tried
deep breathing, relaxing, knitting and more aspirins than I can remember, but all I can see are those boys with their look of 'beyond'.

My younger boy will go in just over a week. His friend who has no
mother and is like another son will go soon—he is twenty-six. My
elder boy works in Manchester. As a tax inspector he is at present in a
'reserved occupation'.

Monday, 4 September Today has been an effort to get round, for my
head is so bad. A cap of pain has settled down firmly and defies
aspirin. I managed to tidy up and wash some oddments and then, as
the neatness did not matter, made two cot blankets out of tailor's
pieces. I've nearly finished a knitted one. I have a plan to make good,
warm cot blankets out of old socks cut open and trimmed. It breaks
my heart to think about the little babies and the tiny children being
evacuated—and the feelings of their poor mothers. I've got lots of

plans made to spare time so as to work with the W.V.S.—including having my hair cut short at the back. I cannot bear the pins in now, and unless curls *are* curls they are just horrid. My husband laughs at me for what he terms 'raving', but he was glad to hear of a plan I made last crisis and have since polished up. It's to keep hens on half the lawn. The other half of the lawn will grow potatoes, and cabbage will grow under the apple trees and among the currant bushes. I'll try and buy this year's pullets and only get six, but when spring comes I'll get two sittings and have about twenty extra hens in the summer to kill. I know a little about keeping hens and I'll read up. My husband just said, 'Go ahead.'

Tuesday, 5 September   I went to the W.V.S. Centre today and was amazed at the huge crowd. We have moved into a big room in the middle of town now, but big as it is, every table was crowded uncomfortably with eager workers. Afterwards, huge stacks of wool to be knitted into bedcovers, and dozens of books of tailor's patterns to be machined together, were taken. They average about seventy-seven yards of machining to join each piece with a double row of stitching and a double-stitched hem. I'm on my third big one and have made about a dozen cot quilts. As my husband says, it would have been quicker to walk the distance than machine it. I'm lucky, for my machine is electric and so does not tire me. Everyone seemed to be so kind—no clever remarks made aside.

Tonight I had my first glimpse of a blackout, and the strangeness appalled me. A tag I'd heard somewhere, 'The City of Dreadful Night',[1] came into my mind and I wondered however the bus and lorry drivers would manage. I don't think there is much need for the wireless to advise people to stay indoors—I'd need a dog to lead me.

· · · · ·

Sunday, 8 October   I feel as if I have been on holiday these two days, I have felt so gay. Sorry, though, when I heard Arthur say he has given up the idea of finishing the book he was writing. I tried to persuade him to go on, if only a few lines at a time.

Next to being a mother I'd have loved to write books—that is, if I'd brains and time. I love to 'create', but turned to my home and cooking and find a lot of pleasure in making cakes etc. I wish, though, that Arthur would go on with his writing, for there's such fun in building up things. I've written enough letters to fill a few books—in words—and the boys tell me I've given them more pleasure than if I'd written best-sellers! Cliff's letter yesterday was a bit incoherent—a tirade against my cutting my back curls off. I see myself having to practise walking backwards when Cliff comes home, for you cannot see any difference from the front view. He seems to have got the idea I'll go into pants! Funny how my menfolk hate women in pants. I do myself, but if necessary for work or service, would wear them.

• • • • •

Tuesday, 19 December   There was very little bacon in town today and women were anxiously asking each other if they knew of a shop which had any in. We eat so little bacon and cheese, but I'll get my ration and start using it in place of other things—meat and fish—in my cooking. Fish is very dear and, in my budget, not worth the price for the nourishment. I've always been used to making 'hotel' meals, as the boys call them—soup, a savoury and a sweet. If one is a good cook and manager, it's the cheapest way in the long run—cheaper than getting a big roast and chops and steaks for frying. In the last war, we were living tolerably well when many were complaining of dullness and shortness of food. Now, when I'm out two days and have to come in and make a hot lunch, my soup-casserole / omelet lunch is a real boon, for I can prepare it beforehand and it's no trouble to serve—a few minutes to set on the table. . . .

• • • • •

Thursday, 14 March 1940   I reflected tonight on the changes the war had brought. I always used to worry and flutter round when I saw my husband working up for a mood; but now I just say calmly, 'Really dear, you *should* try and act as if you were a grown man and not a child of ten, and if you want to be awkward, I shall go out—ALONE!' I told him he had better take his lunch on Thursday, and several times I've not had tea quite ready when he has come in, on a Tuesday or Thursday, and I've felt quite unconcerned. He told me rather wistfully I was 'not so sweet' since I've been down at the Centre, and I said, 'Well! Who wants a woman of fifty to be sweet, anyway? And besides, I suit *me a lot* better!'

Arthur said last time he was here that I had altered, and when I
asked how, he said, 'You are like your photo taken a year last Christmas. It was quite a good photo except for the look in the eyes, which
looked sad'—I've always had 'laughing eyes'. I notice the same rather
subdued look in a lot of women's eyes. And yet we laugh a lot at
the Centre, and I know I laugh and clown more than I've done since I
was a girl. Perhaps the 'quiet look' is a hangover from nights when
we lie quiet and still, and all the worries and unhappy thoughts we
have put away in the day come and bring all their friends and relations!

• • • • •

Tuesday, 14 May   I think I'm the tiredest and happiest woman in
Barrow tonight! I've unpicked the mattress I was given, washed the
cover and half a dozen sugar sacks, and made four 6 ft. by 2 ½ ft.
mattresses out of them. Aunt Eliza teased me enough for one mattress
and she saw I was not going to have enough flocks for four. I'd set
my mind on four, for the sick-bay at the Sailors' Home, so I cut all
my scraps of winceyette and flannel into small pieces, sorted out all the
small scraps of silk out of the bit-bags, cut up silk stockings, too,
and I'll mix them well up with flocks. With the mattresses being well
shaken each day, they will be soft to lie on.

• • • • •

Sunday, 19 May   I'm shameless in bringing raffle books out to sell 3d.
tickets, and I don't wonder at my husband being surprised—when I
contrast the rather retiring woman who had such headaches, and used
to lie down so many afternoons with the woman of today who can
keep on and *will not think,* who coaxes pennies where once she would
have *died* rather than ask favours, who uses too bright lipstick and
on dim days makes the corners turn up when lips will not keep smil-
ing. Mrs. Waite[2] used to be *horrified* at my 'painted mouth', till one
day she said thoughtfully, 'It would not be a bad idea if we all bought
a lipstick and got little Last to show us how to paint a smile.' Since
then she has never made 'sick-making' noises when she has seen me
with my lipstick.

It was such a lovely May night tonight. I never remember a sweeter
sundown—or is it that I notice all the little beauties of life I had
grown so used to? The Port Missionary said a funny thing when I was

down the other night. He was thanking me for the mattresses, and he said earnestly, 'I try so hard to make them' (sailors, trawler-men etc.) 'comfortable for, who knows, it might be their last night on earth.' It's not a bad thought, either, for if we only had one night more to live we would all try and make it worthwhile. Perhaps it's the feeling that so much is passing and dying, but my lovely dark wine lilac tree never looked so gorgeous in her heavy crown of purple as this year; the blackbird's song at dawn seems more wonderful when I hear it, and last week when I heard a cuckoo in the early hours I could not have felt more thrilled if it had been the first I'd ever heard.

· · · · · ·

Monday, 17 June   My husband said, 'I quite thought at seven o'clock when I turned on the wireless that I'd hear France had ceased fire.' and to hear the words I had thought spoken by another made me cold. He went before one o'clock, and I was alone when I heard the announcement. As the announcer spoke, I suddenly thought of the B.E.F. [British Expeditionary Forces] and their plight—WHAT will happen to our men? Will they be prisoners or will Hitler in his power-drunk passion kill them? Or leave them without food. There will be no Dunkirk this time. There were so many went out only this week, thousands of them rushed out. My head felt as if it was full of broken glass instead of thoughts, and I felt if I could only cry—or better still scream and scream—it would have taken the sharp pain away. I felt so cold inside me that, when I dragged myself to the window to get the sun, it burned me without warmth.

My faith, my philosophy, my courage left me as I sat staring out at the trellis covered with cream overblown roses. Never have I felt so naked, never so alone. I've often said we were only 'grains of sand on the sands of time', but today I knew what the words meant, and for the first time in my life I was unable to 'ask' for courage and strength with the certainty I would receive it. When my legs would carry me into the kitchenette, I went to the cupboard and got some sal volatile. I slipped my overall off and splashed water on my neck and shoulders and let my hands steep in cold water. Suddenly the thought of thirsty men who needed water to drink, which I was lavish with, made me cry, and I cried like a child. With my tears went the feeling of tension, and the sun on my arms made me feel there *was* still good, and good was God, and I did not feel so lonely any more. . . .

Monday, 1 July   At times when I see such silly waste in shop windows, I think it's a pity there are no women in the War Cabinet. It's taken the powers that be all this time to see the shocking waste of sugar in confectioners' shops, and to realise it would be better to let people have sugar for jam. I'd like to have some of them to come and stay for a weekend. I'd show them a few things, and tell them what women thought—real everyday commonplace women like myself, who had to budget on a fixed income, and saw ordinary things wasted and no shortage of unnecessary things. It's getting easy to recognise the haves and have-nots now—womenfolk I mean—by the wearing of silk stockings and the frequent trips to the hairdresser's. I think silk stockings and lovely soft leather gloves are the only two things I envy women for. I can dodge and contrive dresses and, as I'm light on my feet, my shoes last a long time with care, but there is such an *uplift* about seeing one's feet and legs so sleek and silky, or in peeling off a pair of lovely leather-smelling gloves. My hands are small squarish paws, with knotting fingers, but my feet and legs are my one beauty and, when I have the choice of a birthday or Christmas present, I like to choose silk stockings—or if it will run to it, new shoes.

• • • • •

Thursday, 8 August   Arthur's birthday—his twenty-seventh. How the years fly! Today has seemed a kaleidoscope of brightly coloured bits of memory—things I never think of in ordinary life. I asked him last night what he would like best for a birthday tea. He thought very carefully and then said 'Orange whip and Viennese bread.' Such a simple wish, and such a boyish one. As oranges with full flavour are difficult to get, and 4d. each, I decided to use a Rowntree's orange jelly. I used to use the juice of four Jaffas in the old 1d. orange days, and 1d. worth of gelatine which now costs about 4d., for the same quantity. I made the jelly with slightly less water than usual, whipped it when cold but not set, and added three stiffly beaten whites of eggs that I had saved from baking. They did not know it was not made from fresh oranges, and I did not say anything when they said it was the 'best ever'! My Viennese rolls were a delight and I felt so

happy about them, for it's some time since I made them as my husband does not like either new or crusty bread. They turned out a
lovely golden shell of sweet crust that melted in the mouth, and I put
honey on the table to eat with them. I put my fine lace and linen
cloth on the table, and a big bowl of deep orange marigolds. There
was the birthday cake I made before Easter when butter was more
plentiful, and for effect I put a boat-shaped glass dish with goldeny-
green lettuce hearts piled in—which were eaten to the last bit. I felt as
gay as a bird when I saw my two darling faces, so bright and happy.
While no doubt a bit of their gaiety was a show for a birthday tea,
I knew they, like me, had memories of many happy birthdays. . . .

Saturday, 17 August   It's just a year ago tonight since we were starting
our holiday in Scarborough, and perhaps it's that, and also a remark
Arthur passed, which set me thinking and seeing how much both my
husband and I had changed. He talks things over quite a lot and does
not sit silently nearly as much. Perhaps it's because I get so cross,
for if he does not answer when I speak, I feel a hot flame of *rage* sweep
over me. I could slap him really hard, and say, 'Now if you are going
to be like that, I shall go out ALONE—my nerves are not as good as
they used to be, and I'm not as patient as I was.' I realise sadly how we
make mistakes, for if I had had the idea—the courage—of taking a
firm line instead of always thinking, 'Perhaps he is tired—I'll sit quiet
and not bother," it would have been better for us both. He even talks
pleasantly to people who drop in with socks etc.

· · · · ·

Saturday, 5 October   There was a ring at the bell at 9.30—a most unusual time for callers in the blackout. It was the church-warden of
a nearby church. They had sent out leaflets and an envelope asking for
'a hearty response to the the appeal'. It was for the vicar—a young
man of thirty to thirty-three, to obtain 'a curate as the parish has
grown so much these last few years'. I just burnt it—I considered it
the wrong time for an appeal like that. . . . I would not change my
mind—I'd not have given them a penny if I'd had a crock of gold. I
pointed out firmly to the church-warden—whom I knew well—that
we were all working overtime, many without extra pay and at a

personal sacrifice, and that with so many pressing demands I considered the request for a curate to be out of season.

When we sat down again, I saw my husband looking at me and I said, 'What do you look at me like that for?' He said, 'Well, I often feel you are a stranger. At one time you would given them something to get rid of them. Nowadays you seem to argue and lay the law down.' I considered for a while and then said, 'I believe I feel different. I seem to realise what a 'peace at any price' policy I've had in the past, and how I've given in so much to people and their whims. Perhaps it's nerves, perhaps a realisation of how little things matter, but I don't bother any more. Dr. Millar started me off when I was so ill three years ago, and I find his words truer every day—that 'repression is deadly'. So I give my honest opinion if asked.' And, I reflected as I looked at him, often unasked.

Friday, 22 November I fear I've had my last perm—or at least, almost the last one!—it's gone up to 25s. I always have a genuine Eugene. I've had them for over ten years, and need two a year as my hair grows so quickly. Sets and shampoo have gone up to 3s., too, and the hairdresser says the purchase tax will hit every beauty aid. Ah well! It's only a matter of thinking, and girls were just as pretty when I was young, although we washed our hair with soft soap once a week, rinsed it with a dash of vinegar in the last rinse if we were dark—or an infusion of a tenth of a pennyworth of camomile flowers if fair— and rubbed the shine off our noses with a scrap of chamois leather when we went dancing!

My husband said, 'You look lovely tonight.' and I got up and had a good look in the mirror. My crisp set waves certainly *were* lovely, but my face was no different, and I said, 'Would you always like me to look like a doll with a wig on?' He said '*Yes,* if you mean looking like you do tonight, and I would like you to never have to work, or worry over *anything,* to see you in the glowing silks and velvets I know you always admire in the shops, and fur, jewellery, perfume, lace—everything I've ever known you admire.' I said, 'I suppose you would only think I was putting a brave face on if I told you I'd sooner *die* than step into the frame you make for me. Do you know, my

dear, that I've never known the content—at times, real happiness—
that I've known since the war started? Because you always thought
like that and were so afraid of 'doing things', you have at times been
very *cruel*. Now my restless spirit is free, and I feel strength and
endurance comes stronger with every effort. I'm *not,* as you always
fear, wearing myself out—and even so, it's better to wear out than
rust out.' Gosh, but I hope he never comes into money. It would be
really terrible to be made to 'sit on a cushion and sew a fine seam'!

· · · · ·

Friday, 28 March 1941   I picked up a paper Ruth[3] brings, to take to a
cousin in the country—called 'Woman'—and was deeply interested in
an article. Not altogether in what was written, but in the line of
thought it started. It was a very outspoken article about the ethics of a
girl 'giving herself without marriage' to her soldier sweetheart when
he was on leave. It was outspoken, but in its simple straight-thinking
modesty was so far removed from what I can remember of the last
war.

I seem to remember a line of thought in which every unmarried
woman 'claimed the privilege of motherhood' without a wedding
ring, and know of two in our town who proudly wheeled prams out
and proclaimed that soon every woman would have to share her
husband with those who could never have one! My Mother was living, and I chuckle as I remember her quiet reply. She looked at the
sickly, scowling mite and said, 'Perhaps you are right, my dear, but
stud husbands will be carefully chosen, as they are in animals—a pity
you had not waited a while.' Another woman of about thirty, a member of a busy catering family, told her people she intended to have
a war baby as her *duty*—and had it too! Granted we have come a long
way since those days, and birth control has become general, but
among women I know, it's a firm idea that to bring a child into the
world now is a grave sin, that there is no place for a wee baby or sick
mother now, and to have one before things settle would be not folly
alone but criminal, unthinking cruelty. I always listen to them, but
won't take sides at all. I see both sides: one day I'll think one side
is right, and that it *is* the wrong time for a baby to be born, and the
next time there is an argument I'll think, 'Well, babies have been born

and cared for in pestilence and famine as well as war, and have
struggled through and been stronger for the struggle.'

· · · · ·

Good Friday, 11 April   So shut in by clouds, and everything so dark
and depressing, today might have been modelled on the first Good
Friday. My husband said, as it looked so unpromising, he would like
to do a bit of gardening, and I rested and read until lunch. It was
easily prepared, for I made the vegetable soup yesterday, and opened a
wee tin of pilchards, heated them and served them on hot toast. They
were only 5 ½ d., and yet were a better meal than two cod cutlets
costing at least 2s. I feel it would be better value if, instead of bulky,
flabby cod and other white fish from America, the Government
brought in only dried and tinned fish. So much can be made up from
a 1s. tin of salmon or tuna, and so little from the same value of white
wet fish. Besides, there's the 'keeping' value too.

   I packed up tea, greengage jam in a little pot, brown bread and
butter, a little cheese and a piece of cake each, and we set off after
lunch. I have been longing and yet dreading to cut into this particular
cake for some time now. I made it about last June, when butter was
more plentiful. It was one of two: and one was for Christmas, and
one to be shared between Cliff and my husband for their birthdays on
11 and 13 December. I cut only the one, made it do over Christmas
and thought I'd cut the other at New Year. With my 'squirrel's love' of
a little in reserve, I made do and kept putting it off until it got to
Easter! It's a 'perfect cake in perfect condition', as my husband said. I
wrapped it in grease-proof paper—four separate wrappings—and
then tied it and put it in an air-tight tin. I expect it's the last good cake
we will ever have—at least for years—and I do so love baking cakes
and watching people enjoy them (I myself prefer bread and butter
on the whole).

Easter Monday, 14 April   Last night, a noise like the crack of Doom
sounded, and brought us from our beds to rush downstairs, and my
husband said crossly, 'It's only an explosion somewhere. If it had been
a bomb, there would have been the sound of a plane—or the alert.
I'm going back to bed!' Just then the alert sounded, and a plane flying

so low that we feared for our housetop. Our gun fired one volley, then stopped; there was a frightful bang—crack—bang, the rattle of machine-guns and the sound of chaser planes. The noise was terrifying—all so near and low down.

Nothing more happened after the sound died away, as if the enemy was chased far out to sea, and after the all-clear we went to bed. . . .

I could not have believed so few bombs could do so much damage. It made me sick to think what *two* airplanes and about four bombs could do to our town.. . . Bulging walls, gaping windows, hundreds of broken panes of glass, crazily leaning chimneys, flying ambulances, dirty tired H[ome] G[uard] wardens, ordinary citizens in demolition gangs working like men possessed, with their shovels and picks going like clockwork as if to the sound of a hidden shanty, dazed-looking men who were piling mattresses on hand-carts where people had been ordered to evacuate, crowds of quiet white-faced spectators who needed no 'Pass along' from the guarding police and H.G.—they wanted to see, but not to linger over the sight of destruction.

My husband came in tired and saddened by all the mess and destruction and we went for a short drive to the Coast Road, to fill the remainder of the sandbags I had made. I will go on making them from any strong bits of material I can piece together; they would do for others if we did not want them. My husband said, 'I think we will order an indoor shelter after all.'

We have ordered one by tonight's post and will put it up in the lounge. I'll keep the rubber camp beds blown up ready in the shelter, and have rugs and blankets easy to get at. We have talked about it long enough—my husband doesn't like to make decisions of any kind, and if I make the pace too much, he takes the other road. It makes him stubborn, so I've to be very tactful. Today has shown him how quickly a house or building can be a heap of rubbish.

•　•　•　•　•

Sunday, 4 May　A night of terror, and there are few windows left in the district!—or roof tiles! Land mines, incendiaries and explosives were dropped, and we cowered thankfully under our indoor shelter. I've been so dreadfully sick all day, and I'm sure it's sheer fright, for last night I really thought our end had come. By the time the boys

come, I'll be able to laugh about it. Now I've a sick shadow over
me as I look at my loved little house that will never be the same
again. . . . I'll never forget my odd sensations, one a calm acceptance
of 'the end', the other a feeling of regret that I'd not opened a tin of
fruit salad for tea—and now it was too late!

I'm so very frugal nowadays, and I look at a tin of fruit longingly
sometimes, now that fruit is scarce—but I put it back on the shelf, for
I think we may need it more later. . . .

I've worked and worked, clearing glass and plaster and broken
china—all my loved old china plates from the oak panelling in the
hall. With no sleep at all last night, and little on Friday night, I've no
tiredness at all, no dread of the night, no regrets, just a feeling of
numbness. All the day, the tinkle of glass being swept up and dumped
in ash-bins has sounded like wind bells in a temple, together with
the knock-knock as anything handy was tacked in place over gaping
windows. We have brought the good spring-bed down into the
dining-room, both for comfort and safety. My chicks are safe, and
my cat, who fled terrified as a splintered door crashed, has come
home. The sun shines brightly, although it's after tea and there is no
sign of kindly clouds to hide the rising moon. . . .

The birds sang so sweetly at dawning today—just as the all-clear
sounded and people timidly went round looking at the damage. I
wonder if they will sing as sweetly in the morning—and if we will
hear them. Little sparrows had died as they crouched—from blast
possibly. It looked as if they had bent their little heads in prayer, and
had died as they did so. I held one in my hand: 'He counteth the
sparrow and not one falleth that He does not see'—Poles, Czechs,
Greeks, all sparrows. . . .

I've opened the tin of fruit salad, and put my best embroidered
cloth on, and made an egg-whip instead of cream. My husband will
be so tired. I'll not take my clothes off tonight, and I'll give the animals an aspirin. My face is clean and I've combed my hair and put
powder and lipstick on. I'm too tired and spent to have a bath and then
put my clothes on again. I could not settle at all if I'd to undress: we
may have to fight incendiaries—a lot more were dropped in other
parts of town. I thought Ruth and her aunt might be bombed out and
be coming, and I got all cleaned up in case they did. . . .

. . . . .

Tuesday, 13 May   A busy morning, and a rush to get washed before lunch and ready to go out and down to the Centre for two o'clock.

My sister-in-law [Beat] was so eager to start collecting her War Savings Certificates that she was there before I got to the Centre. We sat and looked at each other, wondering if anyone would come. We did not expect a lot, since I'd put the advert in so late in the day that it was only in the stop-press—too late for classification and not very noticeable. But we were surprised at the number who called, and Beat collected £38. A good few called who had 'heard in town' that the Centre was open, and who said they would come in on Thursday with extra contributions, with it being War Weapons Week.

I was quite busy, sorting wool and booking it carefully as I gave it out, and feeling pleased at the pile of returned work, when Mrs. Lord[4] swept in like an act of God! She was *furious* at my 'interference' and would *not* listen to anything I'd to say at all. That got my back up and I went 'all mischievous'—the best way I've found to deal with some people! I went 'big-eyed', and put my finger on my lips and said, 'Sh, sh, sh, *shush*—NOT in front of the children, dear,' and all the 'children' howled—women of fifty to sixty who had come in and sat down for a chat. Mrs. Wilkins looked ghastly, but she laughed till she cried, and then said, 'That's settled it—we will get a couple of tables up on Thursday and start. It's the only place crazy enough nowadays to get a laugh—pictures seem a waste of time and the wireless bores me.' Mrs. Lord said grandly, 'So *little* amuses us these hysterical times,' and her pursed mouth and prim look of disapproval set us off again like a pack of silly kids.

Tonight I was a bit tired perhaps, but I got *really* cross with my husband and told him a few things for the good of his soul. Each week since the war, I've always steadily saved a tin or two of meat, fish or soup and jam, syrup etc. I was so dreadfully short in the last war—not only money but food—when I lived in the New Forest near Southampton. A little while back, my husband said, 'How splendid of you!', 'How you must have planned and contrived!', 'What a sacrifice it must have been!', and so on and so on. Now, when there is more than a chance we will be bombed out, he *whines*, 'If you had only had *sense,* and saved the money instead of getting a dozen tins of meat'—forgetting that he has never given me a sliding-scale of housekeeping, and I've had to stretch and *stretch* it always. I find I'm 'short-sighted' and a 'silly hoarder', and that I may never use what I've saved, and so on. On reflection, I think I was more than a bit *bitchy,* to say the least of it. I did a bit of resurrecting of old history and a bit of 'yes and *anyway';* and I can remember clearly saying that I was tired of always having to do all the thinking and planning for the house, and that it was time he grew up. So undignified and tiresome to be so tired and edgy as to lose control of a temper schooled for thirty years.

This war seems to have no end—it's like a stone dropped in a lake where waves and surges are felt as unknown or unsuspected edges and shores.

. . . . .

Sunday, 15 June   As I sat so quiet and still, a question in a Mass Observation questionnaire that I'd done this morning came back into my mind—about the war's effect on 'sex'. Speaking personally, I could only say that, at fifty-one, sex questions answered themselves, war or no war; but I began to think back to when I was a girl—and after all, that's not such a very great while since. I remembered an incident that a parish nurse once told me.

Before Health Insurance, most churches had a nurse to look after the sick poor of the parish, and this one was so good and kind, she did that little bit more always. She was attending a woman who was far on her journey with T.B., and who had at times to stay in bed. Hearing she was not so well, the nurse went round early to get the children washed and ready for school. Not expecting the nurse so early, the woman called wearily over the stair-rail, thinking it was her husband off night-shift, 'Is that you, John? Do you want me before I get dressed?' The husband came in just then and, not quite catching what was said, shouted, 'What's that?' On the question being repeated, he said 'Aye' simply. That seemed the whole key-note of married life—to a greater or lesser degree. A woman was expected—and brought up—to obey, and we had not got far from the days of Victorian repression: men expected to be master in matters widely to do with sex. No woman was ever expected to be out, for instance, when her husband came in for a meal. Gosh, how I've nearly broken my neck to race home in time to brew the tea and pour it—even though the rest of the meal was laid ready. No woman was let go on a holiday alone—that is, in Barrow. I think perhaps Barrow was extra-provincial through its geographical position—shut off, as it were, on an island.

The last war was the start of a difference in sex life in a general way, with men having to go to France. Women did not always behave too well—there were some gay goings-on, and one heard whispers of 'women in the know' who, the munitions girls and women said, got one out of trouble and kept one out of trouble. I had been married four—nearly five—years before I knew of such a thing as birth control being a decent thing, and not a 'horrible French practice'. I went down to live in Southampton when my husband went into the R.N.V.R. [Royal Naval Volunteer Reserve]. He was a C3 man, and got a shore billet, which meant he could get home at weekends; and I went and lived in the New Forest, to make a home nearby. I remember the crowds of disreputable and diseased-looking girls and women who infested camps on the roads where soldiers went—and the way that the soldiers used to shout after you if you went out alone, and the bold glances you were always conscious of. I worked in a canteen after my Cliff was born—just at odd times, for I was always ailing. Girls were either unwilling or not allowed by their mothers to work there, for the soldiers were regarded as 'wild beasts, seeking whom they may devour' kind of thing! Now I sense a different spirit. One never sees the pub doors disgorge groups of fuddled soldiers, with harpies hanging on to their arms or waiting outside. Everything in respect of sex is altering—when I think of naughty old men I knew, engaging front seats at a music-hall we had then, because they could see the girls' knees when they danced! And when I think of what they could see of the 'female form divine' on a country walk—well, I chuckle.

As to actual intercourse, what sweeping changes *must* have taken place with everyone being parted—civilians through evacuation, as well as soldiers. At one time, it was taken as a forgone conclusion that, if a man left his wife alone or vice versa, they had 'asked for all they got' if the one behind 'went off the rails'! Yet here in Barrow

I've not noticed anything much different as a result of people being separated. When I tried once to explain my views to Cliff, he said about the Army, 'Ah, they *dope* the army lads—give 'em bromide or something.' I laughed and said, 'I see, you all line up and take it like good boys—like Mrs. Squeers and her brimstone and treacle.' He said, 'No, they put it in our tea,' which seems a bit tough on the two- and three-cup men!

.   .   .   .   .

Thursday, 28 August   I settled down to a real 'untidy' evening, so as to get the dollies' clothes sorted and machined, and then have all tidy for tomorrow when I've cleaned up. To my horror, there was a ring and Mrs. Thompson, our canteen head, was at the door. She had come to tell me that we will have the two new American mobile canteens any time now, as well as our own Jolly Roger, and also a 'first grade' canteen for the soldiers. She wants me to give an afternoon and / or evening as advisory cook. She says I'll not have to work really hard, only overlook and give advice on economical and tasty oddments. Mrs. Diss, who has taken over as head of W.V.S., had sent her. It's what I've always wanted to do—I am realising more each day what a knack of dodging and cooking and managing I possess, and my careful economies are things to pass on, not hide as I used to! She stressed the point that I would not have hard work to do, and I said, 'I'll do my share like the others.' But she said, 'Mrs. Diss said you do more than your share at Hospital Supply, and it's too bad to ask you to do more.'

When she had gone out, my husband said, 'You know, you amaze me really, when I think of the wretched health you had just before the war, and how long it took you to recover from that nervous breakdown.' I said, 'Well, I'm in rhythm now, instead of always fighting against things'—but stopped when I saw the hurt, surprised look on his face. He never realises—and never could—that the years when I had to sit quiet and always do everything he liked, and *never* the things he did not, were slavery years of mind and body.

Tuesday, 2 September   Down at the Centre, someone started a queer line of talk today—a kind of 'turn the clock back, if but for an hour'.

It started about peace again, and led on to whether we would like
the world to step back to old days and ways. I said, 'Speaking personally, I'd not live a year of my life over again, or go back to anything.
I'd rather 'march on' to better days, than go back to any I've lived.'
Mrs. Waite said, 'You would rather have the shadow than the bone, I
can see.' That started a discussion as to whether the old days *were*
the delight that the sentimentalists would have us believe—with beer
so cheap that Saturday night was a horror, and wages and standards of
life so low that children went barefoot. Mrs. Woods, who was a
teacher, recalled the swollen faces of poor kiddies with bad teeth,
which ached with every cold wind—and faces that were scabbed and
raw with impetigo. One woman talked of heavy woollen stockings
and underwear, boned bodices, dresses that were so sweetly feminine
and trailed in the dust! Then off we went along another track—men's
attitudes to their wives, and vice versa. There were two women in
the discussion whose husbands have always, to my knowledge, had
big salaries, but their lips had a bitter twist as they spoke of having to
account 'for every damned penny'! We wondered if this dreadful
mess of war would release people from taboos and inhibition, as the
last war undoubtedly had done.

· · · · ·

Monday, 19 October 1942 I'm not well perhaps—nervy probably, or
it's the time of year—but the longing to talk and listen to intelligent
conversation sometimes *chokes* me. There's the wireless, but I don't
always agree—or understand—and would like to answer back. I tell
myself sternly that I should count my blessings, think of the problems
and the heartbreaks of others, and not grizzle. I talk myself into a
decent frame of mind, as my fingers fly over my endless sewing, and
then look up and see my husband's vacant expression when I pass a
remark about something that is being broadcast. He has not been
listening. I say, 'Are you tired?' and he says, 'Yes'—or 'No'. I say, 'Are
you worried?' and he says, 'No'. He told a friend that his main thought
and chief delight was his food, that he *liked* eating and, as soon as he
had one meal, started looking forward to the next! He added piously
that he was always thankful I was such a marvellous cook and manager! Sometimes I could YELL. I feel I'd like to peel off the layers of

'patience', 'tact', 'cheerfulness', 'sweetness' that smother me like layers
of unwanted clothes. What would I find under all the trappings I'm
credited with? I might be surprised! I know how people feel who
'disappear'. They get up one morning and look out of the window—
maybe just up a long road, maybe the sun is shining, or there's a
bright poster on a wall, or a ship's siren is hoo-hooing its way out to
sea—and they go and go and GO.

· · · · ·

Sunday, 1 August 1943   I suddenly thought tonight, 'I know why a lot
of women have gone into pants—it's a sign that they are asserting
themselves in some way.' I feel pants are more of a sign of the times
than I realised. A growing contempt for man in general creeps over
me. For a craftsman, whether a sweep or Prime Minister—'hats off'
But why this 'Lords of Creation' attitude on men's part? I'm beginning to see I'm really a clever woman in my own line, and not the
'odd' or 'uneducated' woman that I've had dinned into me. Not that
in-laws have bothered me for some time now. I got on my top note,
and swept all clean, after one sticky bit of interference and bother.
I feel that, in the world of tomorrow, marriage will be—will *have* to
be—more of a partnership, less of this '*I* have spoken' attitude. They
will talk things over—talking *does* do good, if only to clear the air. I
run my house like a business: I have had to, to get all done properly,
everything fitted in. Why, then, should women not be looked on as
partners, as 'business women'? I feel thoroughly out of tune. I'm not
as patient as I used to be, and when one gets to fifty-three, and after
thirty-two years of married life, there are few illusions to cloud issues.

· · · · ·

17 May 1945   . . . I'm tired out tonight. I feel as if the week's events
are only just getting through to my real mind. When I read the letter
from Regional H.Q. and thought, 'Umph, we will soon all be out
of a job,' it was not with any sense of exultation. It's been a long and
often trying road, but I found comradeship, and it brought peace
of mind when otherwise I'd have broken. The knowledge that I was
'keeping things moving in the right direction', in however small a
degree, steadied me, helped my tired head to rest peacefully at night,
and have the strength to begin again when morning came. I wonder

if it's the same feeling some of the lads have when they think of being demobilised!

I love my home dearly, but *as* a home rather than a house. The latter can make a prison and a penance, if a woman makes too much of a fetish of cleaning and polishing. But I will not, *cannot,* go back to the narrowness of my husband's '*I* don't want anyone else's company but yours—why do *you* want anyone else?' I looked at his placid, blank face and marvelled at the way he had managed so to dominate me for all our married life, at how, to avoid hurting him, I had tried to keep him in a good mood, when a smacked head would have been the best treatment. His petulant moods only receive indifference now. I *know* I speak sharply at times, I *know* I'm 'not the sweet woman I used to be'—but then I never was! Rather was I a frayed, battered thing, with nerves kept in control by effort that at times became too much, and 'nervous breakdowns' were the result. No one would ever give me one again, *no* one. . . .

·   ·   ·   ·   ·

Wednesday, 25 July   I felt tired but ironed my washing, as I'm going out to the Centre in the morning. My husband is very sulky about it. He said, 'When the war got over, I thought you would always be in at lunch-time.' I said, 'Well, you always have a good lunch left—much better than many men whose wives are always at home.' He said, 'Well, I like you there always.' No thought as to either my feelings or to any service I could be doing. I thought of the false sentiment my generation had been reared with, the possessiveness which stood as the hallmark of love, with no regard to differences in temperament, inclination or ideals—when the 'head of the house' *was* a head, a little dictator in his own right; when a person of limited vision, or just plain fear of life, could crib and confine more restless spirits. I looked at my husband's petulant face and thought that if I'd never done anything else for my lads, at least I'd left them alone and had never given advice at pistol-point, shrinking from imposing my will in any way. A little chill fell on me—not from the dusk which was creeping on the garden, either. Rather did it blow from the past, when to go anywhere without my husband was a heinous crime—and he went practically nowhere! I had a pang as I wondered what I would do when all my little war activities stopped, when he *could* say plaintively, '*Must* you go?' or 'I don't feel like . . .'—and I wondered if my weak streak would crop up as strong as ever, and I'd give in for peace and to that unspoken, but *very* plain, Victorian–Edwardian accusation, 'I feed and clothe you, don't I? I've a right to say what you do.' It's not 'love', as the sloppy Vic-Eds. sang, it's sheer poverty of mind and fear of life. If you love a person in the real sense, you want them to be happy, not take them like butter and spread them thinly over your own bread, to make it more palatable for yourself.

Notes

*All selections are taken from *Nella Last's War: A Mother's Diary, 1939–45,* ed. Richard Broad and Suzie Fleming (London: Sphere Books, 1983). On Mass Observation, see the Introduction to this anthology, p. 8.

1   Actually, the title of a poem by James Thomson, first published in 1874.

2   Head of Hospital Supply at the W.V.S. Centre.

3   Nella Last's home help.

4   An organizer at the W.V.S. Centre.

Myrtle Wright

(b. 1903)

MYRTLE ALDREN WRIGHT, daughter of Rose and John Aldren Wright, studied at the Quaker college, Woodbrooke, at Selly Oak and took a science degree at Cambridge. She had just returned from India in 1939 when the Second World War began and was seeking some way in which she might constructively challenge the "curse of Nazism" (her words)* when she found the direction that would become the basis for the diary whose pages for 1942 are partly excerpted here. In 1940 the Friends Service Council of the Society of Friends in Great Britain sent her to Copenhagen to assist a group of Danish Quakers endeavoring to bring Jews out of Germany. En route, she intended a short visit in Norway. But because of bad weather that disrupted travel arrangements, coupled with the Nazi invasion, her short visit became a stay of four eventful years instead. Arrived in Oslo three days before the German attack, Wright increasingly participated in the Norwegian underground railway that smuggled Jews (and others) over the border into unoccupied Sweden. In 1942, as the resistance movement in Occupied Norway intensified, she decided to keep a discreet, partly coded, diary of events, hiding its pages beneath chickens' nesting boxes. Later, through the assistance of the chief librarian of the university library, the diary was hidden among some Tibetan manuscripts, until the Germans raided the library looking for radios, when its pages were smuggled out lying flat on a librarian's stomach and sent into the countryside for safekeeping. Smuggled out again in 1944, the pages accompanied Wright to England. In 1951 she married Philip Radley, headmaster of Ackworth School, a Quaker institution. The Radleys subsequently spent 1958–61 in South Africa as representatives of the Friends' Meeting for Sufferings, and in 1963–64 participated in the Quaker United Nations team in New York. Besides her diary, Wright has also published essays on Gandhi, occupied Norway, and Quakerism.

From Myrtle Wright's Diary

23 October 1942, Friday   Letter from Greta Stendhal (*in Stockholm*)[1]—
Rose (*my mother*) cannot make her hens lay, can we? Sends a recipe
for an eggless cake!

A day of sad news—the afternoon paper has big headlines of a
policeman shot in the train while checking passes on the way to Fred-
rikstad. The "murderer" jumped through the window and later two
of them—Jews—were arrested. Other Jews on the train were arrested.
This comes exactly at the moment when such an event could be used
as an excuse for strong measures. It must be either provocation or
an exceptionally unfortunately timed incident. Naturally we hear from
various sides of anxiety among Jews. It is such a helpless feeling—
what can one do?

There has also been trouble at Grini—some of the young ones,
working outside the prison, found taking in food, and some of them
and seven of the German guards put into solitary confinement. Fortunately Bernti[2] has not been outside recently as far as we know.

25 October, Sunday   Sigrid went to visit two small girls (*Czech Jewish
children*), one of whom has a birthday.

She hears rumours that American citizens have been taken into
internment at Grini. They can have parcels, visits, books. Said to be
reprisal for an action of the American government. . . .

Quiet morning; played some English hymn tunes, especially Whit-
tier's "Words are less than deeds"—"the shadow of thy Cross is better
than the sun"—"the wrong of man to man on thee inflicts a deeper
wrong". These words came all too true in the evening when rumour
reached us that Jews were to be arrested early tomorrow morning—
this has been current for some days.

But we had many guests—all the Müllers, Gulim, Marie and
George stayed the night.

(*This, for obvious reasons, is the only reference to the night of the arrest of
all male Jews.[3] The news was brought to the door by a strange man. Sigrid
Lund was out until the early hours of the morning warning all she knew.
Several were brought to spend the night. I stayed at home and received them.*)

26 October, Monday   All too true—telephone message that there had been a "big party"⁴ last night. Went down with Sigrid to Odd Nansen's office, then to Ruth Rønneberg and Bertha Erichsen's.

(All male Jews who could be found had been arrested and taken to Berg prison, Tønsberg. The visits referred to were all in connection with the hiding of Jews in families.)

The Norwegian theatre has lost one of its leading men in Lasse Segelcke, well-known actor, executed on October 24th. . . .

27 October, Tuesday   Sigrid was down at Nansenhjelp office⁵ all day— many wives came for advice *(of arrested Jews).*

I went on a shopping tour—"cotton wool" is made of paper, sugar is not only saccharine but a substitute for that! Darning wool is goodness knows what kind of cellular product, tooth-brushes have ceased to exist. Hoarded a little toilet paper.

Sigrid very tired when she came home—an exhausting day.

28 October, Wednesday   At last I have been to Grini! Sigrid and I took a taxi out with two parcels of clothes for Bernti; drove to the outer gate and walked up to the Guards' House. The buildings lie well hidden in woods, long, newly-built red brick with both swastika and S.S. flag flying. New barracks of good quality material built in front with stone pillars and verandah. Tall, square watch-towers in various places. Otherwise not much to suggest a prison. The guards were in a private looking house by the gate inside a second fence. A young boy in prison uniform was sweeping the steps. The guard opened the door and took the parcels inside. "Only clothes", said Sigrid. "No tobacco?" asked the guard rather officially. Sigrid innocently replied, "Oh, but *that* isn't allowed, is it?" and it sounded quite genuine, and the guards melted and both of them were very willing to converse. Sigrid asked if they knew Bernti "with red hair". "Ach, ja er is immer fröhlich" (*Oh, yes, he is always cheerful*), they replied, and they would give greetings from his mother. As we went out we passed the young boy; Sigrid looked straight ahead but said "Hils Bernti" (*greet Bernti*) and I saw that he nodded. It was sunny and beautiful as we walked through the woods and then over the open farm land to Roa station. We called at a farm where Bernti had worked, and Sigrid went to a home for 14 small Jewish children from Vienna. Will they start sending children from here as they have done from France?

After dinner went down to call on Ruth Erichsen; Ruth is nice and kind. Came home by 10, having found the evening profitable. . . .

(Ruth Erichsen and her sister had given hiding to Jews—no doubt the "profitable evening" had included some arrangements for them.)

30 October, Friday Now things are really pleasant! Death penalty for having secret papers in the house and not reporting them to the police; also for helping people over to Sweden, if you want a more difficult way of ending your life!

Since Monday's arrests and the news of the treatment of those arrested the sense of indignation and the wrongness of the whole thing has grown. Most people are filled with a sense of helplessness, but it was suggested that, if the feelings of the Norwegian people are expressed loudly enough, it might prevent the same fate coming to the women and children.

Engineer Viig had had a visit from a Jew and had not given him a bed and was very repentant. He was a man Diderich knew and neither of them liked. . . .

• • • • •

10 November, Tuesday It is so fine to have the Danish parcels; Sigrid took a piece of bacon to "Daddy"[6] and I sausages to Bertha Erichsen.

It has been a day of continuous telephone calls and visitors—among them fru Petlitz, from next door, whose husband is Jewish, Signe Hirsch to dinner, and "Uncle Fritz".[7] Signy Arctander's brother (a solicitor in Bergen) is arrested, but Kaare Schonning and several of the young men from Grini have come out. . . .

11 November, Wednesday . . . Per Backe came up after dinner as we cannot have the party we planned this evening. (*Reference to Jews' transport over frontier.*)

12 November, Thursday I have a visit from Hanna Lund—tells that 37 girls from "Storbrand" Insurance Company have been ordered to the North "til hygge" (*for the comfort*) of the troops on an airfield. The girls say that they would rather go to prison. Others have been commanded for other work, to salt herrings, for example. . . .

13 November, Friday . . . Church bells in England, which have been silent since September, 1939, and were only to be used in case of invasion, are to be rung on Sunday—all fear of invasion over. If only we in the occupied countries were so safe. Yet the security of England is founded on her physical might, by sea, air and land. Our security here is an inner security—the certainty that a free people are uncrushable.

. . . . .

19 November, Thursday The newspapers announce a law by which all Jews must register. This covers full Jews, half and quarter Jews. Information is given on what constitutes a "full" Jew and other classes. The former includes all with four grand-parents of full Jewish birth, and those who have at any time been members of a Mosaic society—that is all who have been born or brought up as practising Jews in the religious sense, without respect to the racial origin of all four grandparents. In case of doubt as to the degree of Jewishness the Minister President—Quisling—and the Department may decide! . . .

20 November, Friday Our party still does not come off—Sigrid is anxious. We have a visit from a lady who says Little Diderich has gone away, so he cannot be in it. But Diderich has a party of his own including Little Diderich and a friend of Signe's. (*Groups leaving for Sweden.*)

21 November, Saturday I found this quotation from von Hügel:—

> "No baseness or cruelty so deep or so tragic shall enter our human world but that loyal love shall be able in due time to oppose to just that deed of treason its fitting deed of atonement. . . . You say first, 'This deed was made possible by that treason', and secondly, 'The world as transformed by this creative deed is better than it would have been had all else remained the same, but had that deed of treason not been done at all'."

Here is the root of the matter in this Jewish question; the cruelty and baseness of the deed can only be matched by some act of loyal and understanding love, the risk taken, the price paid must be great indeed before it can be too high to atone for so great a crime against human personality.

In the latter part of the quotation is also a useful thought in connection with the problem of the fine and noble things that have been brought out by the war and its horrors. Do we need such terrible happenings in order to bring out so much that is good? Must we say that the courage and devotion and energy and "greatness" of personality which we see is *due* to the war? The quotation gives us the reply—the world is transformed by these deeds and is better for them, but would have been even better if the "treason" had never been done at all. . . .

The 400 prisoners from the North are today back at Grini; those who are teachers have gone home. . . . Odd Nansen looks well, says his sister-in-law. She also says her friend has had so many guests— seven at a time (*Jews in hiding*).

But from Grini Jews and some other Norwegians have been sent to Germany—said also to be a punishment for a recent escape from Grini. These Jews were under German control at Grini, while the main body of Jews arrested recently are at Tønsberg under N.S.[8] guard.

· · · · ·

November 25, Wednesday   Daddy rang up to say that his journey would probably be in order for today or tomorrow instead of Saturday, as he said to Sigrid this morning. That would be splendid for the earlier the better.

(*Message from "Daddy", Aage Biering, our contact with the transport, referred to a party to leave for Sweden—certainly mainly Jews.*)

Trunk-call while we ate dinner; Nora Lustig and the boys have left Trondheim for Oslo today. The whole family are coming.

Hoped to have a quiet evening with Sigrid while Diderich was at his Club. Signe (*Hirsch*) rang to ask us to invite Fransi and fru S. to Bridge. As we were about to do this Ingebjørg (*Sletten*) rang that she was visiting them this evening. Then fru Edwin rang and came.

Ingebjørg came. We went down to town; Sigrid to the children, I to Henrik, Per and Ruth. We got home at 2.30 a.m. Diderich was still awake—a mother and daughter had come. So we had company after all.

(This was the evening we received messages that all Jewish women and children were to be arrested early the following morning. The trainload of Jews from Trondheim was intended to arrive in time to be put on the same boat with those arrested in Oslo. It arrived only on the evening of the next day, November 26.)

26 November, Thursday   Busy day—so many guests. Worked with the wood, the only fuel we have for central heating, in the cellar, got out all the stockings for mending and cooked while Sigrid was out meeting Daddy.

Trunk call from Lillehammer Red Cross; they had met Nora (*Lustig*) and the boys.[9] Could we meet the train in Oslo with food and clothing for their further journey?

Marie Mohr came but had to leave as she had two guests for the night. Leiken (*Vogt*) had left her mother with two guests also.

Marie with Sigrid and Diderich and Ingebjørg went down to meet the train; they saw Nora and the boys and came home after 1 a.m. . . . [10]

27 November, Friday   One of those days which go "i et kjør" (*without a pause*). Kept Sigrid in bed for breakfast after two late nights, but the phone got her up.

Sigrid was in touch with the Statspoliti (*Norwegian N.S. police*) and got permission to see the children's clothing at Bredtvedt prison this morning. I went down town to see the guests at Ruth Erichsen's; found all ours gone when I got home and only Uncle Fritz there.

There are so many problems, especially how to deal with the children with whom Sigrid has been working for years (*the 19 Czech Jewish children*).[11]

28 November, Saturday   Sigrid goes out to Bredtvedt with blankets and sweets. . . .

29 November, Sunday   Tried to fix up the little (*Czech*) boy, and that is done—he will get to his sister and brother after all (*in Sweden*). There were also relations of one of those taken to Bredtvedt prison. Daddy was out for a trip.

One of our friends visited five Jewish families in Oslo; in all cases the flats were empty or the police had taken control.

(The main activity on this day was telephoning and asking for clothes for the Jews at Bredtvedt.)

All parcels are to be sent to Meltzersgate 1 (*the flat of Sigrid's brother, Henrik Helliesen*) and it will be exciting to see tomorrow how much has come.

30 November, Monday   Went down to Meltzersgate first thing and found a room already well filled with parcels. Went and ordered paper etc. for packing. When I got back Sigrid had returned from the police; we could go on collecting but no permission to send yet. She had met the Chief and he was surprised that she was not already arrested! Wasn't Nansenhjelp closed? Yes, but open again, she said. Anyway he would see that she was "taken" (*arrested*)! We went on with the packing as well as we could in spite of the mass of people who came and chattered. We packed a parcel for each prisoner.

Ate dinner with the Helliesens and went on until 8 o'clock. Rumours pour in that so many Jøssings [loyal Norwegians] are to be arrested tomorrow, as well as part-Jews. Go to bed wondering if the night will be disturbed!

1 December, Tuesday   We wake in our own beds at 8 o'clock. Fine— another day won! Again down at Meltzersgate by 9.45. Began on the women's packets and by 4 o'clock had them all done and some order made in the masses of things left over—chiefly women's and children's clothes.

Sigrid spent the morning with Daddy and other matters. Reimers from Nansenshjelp called, as the police have now given orders for the office to close.

2 December, Wednesday   Sigrid rang Bredtvedt early to enquire about sending spectacles for one of the prisoners. Then we waited and at last heard that the police would allow the parcels to be sent, but they would not say when. Meanwhile Marie Mohr went to Bredtvedt, taking the spectacles and one or two personal parcels. . . .

3 December, Thursday   Went down town with Sigrid at 11. She had been in touch with the Swedish Consul about those Jews who were Swedish subjects, the Danes about theirs and Advokat Nansen about the English.

In the course of the morning we had a message from Bredtvedt and checked the lists we had; spent the whole day up to 5 o'clock making up parcels. One helper is the daughter of a Jew who was born six years before her parents were married. They have now found her a new father!

Greetings from Bernti, also letter giving notice of what he can have in his Christmas parcel.

They say the "Donau"—the boat with the Jews aboard[12]—is in Porsgrunn.

At 2.30 Sigrid heard that all could be taken to the police; she went there and got permission to go further and took a taxi out to Bredtvedt. The driver told her he had orders to be at Kirkeveien 23 at 5 a.m. on Thursday morning last week—November 26th. He was horrified to find this address was the police and that there were other motors there. He had not the courage to refuse or go away. Two police went in his car and they called at eleven places. In only two of them did they find anyone at home—to the satisfaction of both himself and the police. At one place a mother and daughter were given two hours to arrange their things.

4 *December, Friday*   Went down early to Meltzersgate in the hope of getting all packed and off. They phoned from Bredtvedt at 11.30 with corrections of the lists and we were able to find practically everything asked for. . . .

Ingebjørg Sletton sent for wool underclothing, a thermos (which we luckily had) and rugs for her visitors.

At 2 o'clock we piled some of the parcels into a taxi and Sigrid sailed off to the police. All went well and she got her permit. She got back at 6.30, tired and cold but satisfied. Everything had been accepted by the guards except one small *red* gnome cap! Those who had already got clothes were in many cases wearing them. It was tiring living in such close quarters; Sjoa Eitinger was specially tired but all was well. Sigrid was sad to say goodbye to these folk. Will they be sent? The Swedish bishops have protested. . . .

6 *December, Sunday*   . . . My friend at the Electricity office is involved in questions relating to the payment of bills for Jewish families who

have been arrested. Her chief, who is N.S., is a decent sort of man and, when the non-payment of a family with the bread-winner in prison is concerned, is prepared to be helpful. But if it is a Jewish family he is without exception hard and unkind.

Fru Stensdrud was so glad that one of her Jewish pupils and his father and uncle had not been taken but, unfortunately, the wife and her sister were found at home—a beautiful house—and were ordered to be ready in four hours, with no luggage but food for four days. They had fur coats and these were torn from them as they went on board the "Donau". They are a well-known and well-liked family in the district.

8 December, Tuesday   Spent the day in answering the phone which rang continuously. Sigrid out on many errands. Discussed the possibility of going to approach the Nazi Bishop Frøyland if Skancke, Minister for Church Affairs, had not been to Bredtvedt, as he had been asked to see the condition of the Jewish prisoners.

9 December, Wednesday   Sigrid off to Bredtvedt at 10; but just before that she got a telephone message that she must report to the frontier police. That gave us an anxious day, for she did not finish at Bredtvedt until 1 o'clock and did not get to the police until 3. It was quite ridiculous—a young couple had come to Sigrid with some clothing for a relative who was among those in Bredtvedt. She had mentioned to them that there were rumours that half and quarter Jews might be arrested. They had gone off and made an attempt to cross the frontier, been taken, and given Sigrid's name as the one who had told them the rumour! Sigrid was finished with the police after 20 minutes and the policemen said it would not be a very serious story for her, or for the young couple either.

She had been two hours at Bredtvedt. Many of the prisoners had got clothes from home but did not want to give up their "personal" present from Nansenhjelp. She found that Skancke had been there on Saturday and spoke with Aaron Mendelssohn, seen his damaged arm and M. had told him all that had happened to him. On Sunday the Head of the Police had turned up. We hope this may help. Those married to Ayrans [*sic*] are to be moved tomorrow at 10.30. Signe rang up to say that the clothing from Falstad prison, near Trondheim, had arrived—at least the packing—the clothes had been taken.

Ingebjørg (*Sletton*) rang—the engine at last got going today (*the transport for her party of Jews was in order*).

Four hundred Norwegians are in prison in Germany and, with those in concentration camps, 1,500 altogether. There are distressingly many deaths from tuberculosis, especially among the younger prisoners. . . .

· · · · ·

16 December, Wednesday   Sigrid taken up with getting Israel's Mission to ask for permission to send parcels to Jews at Bredtvedt and Tønsberg (where Jews married to Ayrans [*sic*] still are). The Swedish consul is still working, not only to get into Sweden those who have connection with that country, but every one of them, including refugees from Germany and Czechoslovakia. This is a fine gesture from Sweden, if only it can be managed from the Norwegian N.S. side. The negotiations are with the Norwegians, and cannot include the Jews who are at Grini under German control.

(*The following is entirely to do with arrangements for Jews.*)

Arthur (*Rondan*) rings up as he has a message for Sigrid; I go down to see him as Sigrid is already in town. He told me that two boys would be arriving tonight; I assured him that Ingebjørg would meet them. (*Later: they were met and have gone on a transport to Sweden.*) Also news of two children from Bergen who come tomorrow evening to stay with friends in town. Sigrid is asked to meet them at the station and take them from the lady and gentleman with whom they are travelling. Arthur has five coming out of hospital and one already out. These are the ones Ingebjørg already knows about. Went with the message to Ingebjørg.

18 December, Friday   Telephone from Bredtvedt. They want ten Bibles. Old Testaments especially. The prisoners cannot have Christmas parcels, only sweets and biscuits for the children. They will not give us a complete list of the prisoners.

Sigrid went to Bredtvedt to investigate the question of the Christmas parcels. The Governor will telephone to the State Police (*Norwegian Nazi*) and will certainly get a refusal. She also went to the Swedish Embassy; the man is not very hopeful, what they have worked on has been refused. She comes back very tired. . . .

Bernti has not come out of Grini where, we hear, a transport to Germany is being prepared.

20 December, Sunday Visit of friend of Sigrid's who knows Prof. Skancke (*Minister of Church Affairs in Quisling Government*) and has been to see him. Skancke had not been impressed by his visit to the Jews at Bredtvedt—he thought they were unpleasant to look at and they were revengeful also.

. . . . .

27 December, Sunday Many callers; fru Edwin still has the blankets on loan as it is not so easy to move her guest. Also Einar (*Sverre Enevold*) and two of Bernti's friends.

The chickens have laid their second egg—wonderful! Cleaned out the chicken-house in celebration of the event.

Later Sigrid had a visit from H.: it had been a close shave, nearly an accident. (*Hans Holm, a German refugee for whom the Germans were looking, had eluded them on the stairs when they came to arrest him. . . .*)

29 December, Tuesday Uncle Fritz in this morning—very anxious about the accident and would break the news to Signe Hirsch. She decided to go away for two weeksy.(*Some Jews she had helped had been arrested and there was danger that the police might look for her in this connection.*)

Sigrid wants to go up to Bredtvedt and, while she was trying to find an excuse, they ring up and "invite" her to do so. She gets a car, taking packets of cakes and sweets for the children. . . .

31 December, Thursday Sigrid up to Bredtvedt again. One of the Jewish women, who had come originally from Poland, had crocheted a little pocket handkerchief for Sigrid. With it she had written a little message on a torn page from a pocket diary, thanking Sigrid for her help and interest in them. Where she could have got the material is a wonder.

Made arrangements for Ilse and Tommy (*two Czech children awaiting transport*). Marie Mohr has gone to Lesjaskog and will visit Vera and

Tibur and bring them to Oslo, following correspondence with Pastor Kragset.

(Vera and Tibur Tagelicht—two more Czech Jewish children who had their foster-home with Pastor Kragset at Nesjestranda, in Romsdalsfjord where the Lustig group had been. We were anxious to get them to Oslo in order that they might be sent to Sweden.)

The news is good; Russians going towards Rostov and have taken the railway junction.

And so 1942 slipped out.

Notes

❦

*Taken from *Norwegian Diary, 1940–45* (London: Friends Peace and International Relations Committee, 1974), p. i. All selections here come from this edition.

1   All italicized parenthetical information in these selections was added by Wright when the diary was published because Wright could refer to events of this period only in very circumspect fashion in her original pages.

2   The son of Sigrid Helliesen Lund; Wright lived with her and her husband Diderich and their children in the Oslo suburb of Vinderen. The Lunds were deeply committed to relief work. Bernti Lund, not quite eighteen, had been arrested along with many other students and sent to Grini, a concentration camp. He was later sent to Germany but survived the war and was returned to Norway.

3   On the night of 25–26 October 1942, a general arrest of Jewish men occurred, followed on 25–26 November by a general arrest of women and children.

4   References to "a party" mean assemblages of several Jews traveling together via the secret railroad to Sweden. "Guests" are those waiting to join a party.

5   Nansenhjelp was the relief organization founded in 1937 to assist refugees from Central Europe. The Germans closed it down in autumn 1942.

6   "Daddy" refers to Aage Biering, who was in charge of transport groups and forging passes for Jews and Norwegians sent to Sweden.

7   "Uncle Fritz" refers to Fritz Lund, another dedicated helper, who was particularly active in working to smuggle Czech-Jewish children out of Norway.

8   The National Socialist Party in Norway (Nasjonal Samling), equivalent to "Nazi."

9   A Czech-Jewish refugee and her seventeen-year-old twin sons. She had spent time in prison before coming to Norway on account of her work to help Jews escape. She later died in Auschwitz.

10   Wright next quotes passages from a letter of 13 December 1942 smuggled out to her mother, in which she described the events of the night, including
this:

> Fortunately warning of coming mass arrests or house-searchings come
> from the police in time to help. This was especially so in the case of
> the arrest of Jewish women and children. There were *two* air-raid alarms
> about midnight as families were being brought to other homes where
> they might escape arrest. The boat to take them was in the harbour, so it
> was a race against time. A taxi driver told S. that he had driven the
> police for eight hours round the town and they had found nobody. Yet
> the boat left with more than 500 on board, men, women and children.
> Ruth (*Erichsen*) had a mother and two children that night. Previously she
> had had an elderly Czech Jew, who inherited her father's arm-chair,
> hassock and some of the same care which she had given to her father
> until he died a year ago. The Jew was fetched there one evening about 8
> and was over the frontier round about midnight. This story could be
> repeated scores of times.

11   In 1939 Sigrid Lund had fetched a group of thirty-seven Jewish children from
Czechoslovakia, the plan being that their parents were later to join them. When the
occupation of Norway precluded this, half the children were sent back through relief
groups, on the premise that families should be kept intact (and later perished in
concentration camps). The remaining nineteen were gradually smuggled into Sweden,
especially during 1943.

12   Jews from the Oslo district had been sent off on this boat, under German
control, on 26 November 1942.

Bibliography

Bibliography

≈

Diary Sources for the Anthology

Asquith, Cynthia. *Lady Cynthia Asquith: Diaries, 1915–1918*. [Edited by E. M. Horsley.] London: Hutchinson, 1968.

[Boscawen, Fanny]. *Admiral's Wife: Being the Life and Letters of the Hon. Mrs. Edward Boscawen from 1719 to 1761*. By Cecil Aspinall-Oglander. London: Longmans, Green, 1940.

Brittain, Vera. *Chronicle of Friendship: Diary of the Thirties, 1932–1939*. Edited by Alan Bishop. London: Gollancz, 1986.

Bury, Charlotte. *The Diary of a Lady-in Waiting*. Edited by A. Frances Steuart. 2 vols. London and New York: John Lane, 1908. Vol. 2.

Carlyle, Jane Welsh. *Letters and Memorials of Jane Welsh Carlyle*. Edited by J. A. Froude. 2 vols. New York and London: Harper and Bros., 1883. Vol. 2.

Clifford, Anne. *The Diary of the Lady Anne Clifford*. Edited by Victoria Sackville-West. London: William Heinemann, 1924.

Cowper, Mary. *Diary of Mary, Countess Cowper, Lady of the Bedchamber to the Princess of Wales*. Edited by C. S. Cowper. London: John Murray, 1864.

Cullwick, Hannah. *The Diaries of Hannah Cullwick, Victorian Maidservant*, Edited by Liz Stanley. London: Virago, 1984.

Farmborough, Florence. *Nurse at the Russian Front: A Diary, 1914–18*. London: Constable, 1974. (Also published as *With the Armies of the Tsar: A Nurse at the Russian Front: A Diary, 1914–18*. New York: Stein and Day, 1974.)

Freke, Elizabeth. *Mrs. Elizabeth Freke, Her Diary: 1671 to1714*. Edited by Mary Carbery. Cork: Guy, 1913.

Gaskell, Elizabeth Cleghorn. *"My Diary": The Early Years of My Daughter Marianne*. London: privately printed by Clement Shorter, 1923.

George, Elizabeth. "The Journal of Elizabeth George, 1840–47. Kept at the farmhouse of the Duke of Buckingham's 'good old Tenant' at Stowe." *Cornhill*, no. 180 (Summer 1974): 283–311.

Hardy, Mary. *Mary Hardy's Diary*. Edited by B. Gozens-Hardy. Norfolk Record Society Publications, 37. Norfolk, Eng.: Norfolk Record Society, 1968.

Hoby, Margaret. *Diary of Lady Margaret Hoby*. Edited by Dorothy M. Meads. London: Routledge and Sons, 1930.

Hurnscot, Loran [pseud. for Gay Stuart Taylor]. *A Prison, a Paradise*. New York: Viking, 1959.

Jacquier, Ivy. *The Diary of Ivy Jacquier: 1907–1926*. London: Gollancz, 1960.

King, Mrs. Robert Moss (Emily Augusta). *The Diary of a Civilian's Wife in India, 1877–1882*. 2 vols. London: Richard Bentley and Son, 1884.

Last, Nella. *Nella Last's War: A Mother's Diary, 1939–45*. Edited by Richard Broad and Suzie Fleming. London: Sphere Books, 1983.

Macnaughtan, Sarah Broom. *A Woman's Diary of the War*. London: Thomas Nelson and Sons, 1915.

Pepys, Emily. *The Journal of Emily Pepys*. Edited by Gillian Avery. London: Prospect Books, 1984.

Raper, Elizabeth. *The Receipt-Book of Elizabeth Raper*. Edited by Bartle Grant. London: Nonesuch Press, 1924.

Shore, Emily. *Journal of Emily Shore*. [Editor not identified.] London: Kegan Paul, Trench, Trübner, 1898.

Stevenson, Frances Louise. *Lloyd George: A Diary by Frances Stevenson*. Edited by A. J. P. Taylor. London: Hutchinson, 1971.

Thrale, Hester Lynch Salusbury. *Thraliana: The Diary of Mrs. Hester Lynch Thrale*. Edited by Katharine C. Balderston. 2d ed. 2 vols. Oxford: Clarendon Press, 1951. Vol. 1: 1776–1809.

Trant, Clarissa Sandford. *The Journal of Clarissa Trant: 1800–1832*. Edited by C. G. Luard. London: John Lane, 1925.

Webb, Beatrice Potter. *The Diary of Beatrice Webb*. Edited by Norman and Jeanne MacKenzie. 4 vols. Cambridge, Mass.: Harvard University Press, 1982–85. Vol. 1: *1873–1892, "Glitter Around and Darkness Within."*

Weeton, Ellen. *Miss Weeton: Journal of a Governess, 1807–1825*. Edited by Edward Hall. 2 vols. London: Oxford University Press / Humphrey Milford, 1936–39. Vol. 2: 1811–1825. (Rpt. as *Miss Weeton's Journal of a Governess*. Newton Abbot, Eng.: David and Charles, 1969.)

Woodforde, Nancy (Anna Maria). *Woodforde Papers and Diaries*. Edited by Dorothy Heighes Woodforde. London: Peter Davies, 1932.

Woolf, Virginia. *The Diary of Virginia Woolf*. Edited by Anne Olivier Bell; assisted by Andrew McNeillie for vols. 2–5. 5 vols. New York: Harcourt Brace Jovanovich, 1977–84. Vol. 2: 1919–1924.

Wright, Myrtle. *Norwegian Diary, 1940–45*. London: Friends Peace and International Relations Committee, 1974.

Other Sources

Blodgett, Harriet. *Centuries of Female Days: Englishwomen's Private Diaries*. New Brunswick, N.J.: Rutgers University Press, 1988; Gloucester: Alan Sutton, 1989.

Carlyle, Jane Welsh. *New Letters and Memorials of Jane Welsh Carlyle*. Edited by Alexander Carlyle. London: John Lane, 1903. Vol. 2.

Fountaine, Margaret. *Love Among the Butterflies: The Travels and Adventures of a Victorian Lady*. Edited by W. F. Cater. Boston: Little, Brown, 1980.

Hamilton, Mary. *Mary Hamilton: Afterwards Mrs. John Dickenson: At Court and at Home*. Edited by Elizabeth and Florence Anson. London: John Murray, 1925.

Huff, Cynthia. *British Women's Diaries: A Descriptive Bibliography of Selected Nineteenth-Century Women's Manuscript Diaries*. New York: AMS Press, 1985.

Macnaughtan, Sarah. *My War Experiences in Two Continents*. Edited by Mrs. Lionel Salmon. London: John Murray, 1919.

Mansfield, Katherine. *Journal of Katherine Mansfield*. Edited by J. Middleton Murry. London: Constable, 1954.

Northumberland, Elizabeth, Duchess of. *The Diaries of a Duchess*. Edited by James Greig. New York: Doran, 1927.

Speak for Yourself: A Mass-Observation Anthology, 1937–49. Edited by Angus Calder and Dorothy Sheridan. London: Jonathan Cape, 1984.

Spender, Dale. *Man Made Language*. London: Routledge and Kegan Paul, 1980.

Twysden, Isabella. "The Diary of Isabella, Wife of Sir Roger Twysden, Baronet of Royden Hall, East Peckham, 1645–1651." Edited by F. W. Bennitt. In *Archaeologia Cantiana* 51 (1939): 117.

Webb, Beatrice. *Beatrice Webb's Diaries*. Edited by Margaret I. Cole. 2 vols. London: Longmans, Green, 1952–56. Vol. 1.

Woodforde, James. *The Diary of a Country Parson*. Edited by John Beresford. 5 vols. Oxford and New York: Oxford University Press, 1981.

Woolf, Virginia. "Elizabeth Lady Holland." In *Books and Portraits: Some Further Selections from the Literary and Biographical Writings of Virginia Woolf*. Edited by Mary Lyon. New York: Harcourt Brace Jovanovich, 1977.

Selected Bibliographies
Including Englishwomen's Published Diaries

Barrow, Margaret. *Women 1870–1928: A Select Guide to Printed and Archival Sources in the United Kingdom*. New York: Garland, 1981.

Begos, Jane Du Pree. *Annotated Bibliography of Published Women's Diaries*. Pound Ridge, N.Y.: Begos, 1977; Supplement 1, 1984.

Blodgett, Harriet. *Centuries of Female Days: Englishwomen's Private Diaries*. New Brunswick, N.J.: Rutgers University Press, 1988; Gloucester: Alan Sutton, 1989.

Cline, Cheryl. *Women's Diaries, Journals, and Letters: An Annotated Bibliography*. New York and London: Garland, 1989.

Havlice, Patricia. *And So to Bed: A Bibliography of Diaries Published in English*. Metuchen, N.J.: Scarecrow Press, 1987.

Kanner, Barbara. *Women in English Social History 1800–1914: A Guide to Research*. Vol. 3: *Autobiographical Writings*. New York and London: Garland, 1987.

Matthews, William. *British Diaries: An Annotated Bibliography of British Diaries Written between 1442 and 1942*. Berkeley and Los Angeles: University of California Press, 1950.

Ponsonby, Sir Arthur. *English Diaries: A Review of English Diaries from the Sixteenth to the Twentieth Centuries*. London: Methuen, 1923.

———. *More English Diaries: Further Reviews of English Diaries from the Sixteenth to the Twentieth Centuries*. London: Methuen, 1927.